Readings in Science Education
for the Elementary School

Readings in Science Education for the Elementary School

THIRD EDITION

EDWARD VICTOR

Professor of Science Education, Northwestern University

MARJORIE S. LERNER

Principal, Donoghue Elementary School, Chicago

Macmillan Publishing Co., Inc.

NEW YORK

Collier Macmillan Publishers

LONDON

Macmillan Publishing Co., Inc.
866 Third Avenue, New York, New York 10022

Collier-Macmillan Canada, Ltd.

Library of Congress Cataloging in Publication Data

Victor, Edward, (   )   ed.
    Readings in science education for the elementary school.

    Includes bibliographical references.
    1. Science—Study and teaching (Elementary)—
Addresses, essays, lectures. I. Lerner, Marjorie S.,
joint ed. II. Title.
LB1585.V45   1975   372.3'5   73–22626
ISBN 0–02–422810–9

Printing: 1 2 3 4 5 6 7 8   Year: 5 6 7 8 9 0

Preface

This third edition continues to be concerned not only with current thinking, practices, and research in elementary science but with innovations and changes as well. Consequently, approximately one third of the articles in the second edition have been replaced with articles that are more timely or have greater significance. Thus the book maintains a balance between the older key articles and the newer articles that describe both present and future patterns of thinking in elementary science.

The book is again designed to serve two purposes. First, the current widespread activity in elementary science is rapidly producing new developments in several directions. So much is being written today about issues, problems, practices, current thinking, innovations, and trends in elementary science that it is difficult to read all the literature, digest it, and separate the wheat from the chaff. A book of selected readings makes it possible to include under one cover the key articles that will give a clear picture of what is happening in elementary science today.

Second, instructors of methods courses and of graduate seminars in elementary science often distribute reading lists and require outside reading. With today's large enrollments in our colleges and universities, the assignment of articles to be read places a heavy burden on the students and on the already overtaxed library facilities. The demand for periodicals that contain these articles becomes great, and the students must wait their turn to obtain them. A book of readings eliminates this problem and makes the articles readily accessible to each student.

A book of readings in elementary science has several worthwhile features:

1. It can familiarize the student with the professional journals that are concerned with education and the teaching of science.
2. It can introduce the student to a comprehensive sample of the best thinking in elementary science today.
3. It can acquaint the student with points of view of other persons besides the instructor and the author of the textbook used in the course.

4. It can present a number of different positions that have been taken on controversial topics.
5. It can be used either as a basic text or as a supplementary text.
6. It can be especially helpful in late afternoon, evening, Saturday, extension, or summer courses, where the in-service teachers who take the course are hard pressed to find enough time to locate the articles in the campus library and to read them.

The book continues to be organized into eight sections. However, in order to keep up with the new developments and current thinking in elementary science, changes have been made in the titles, content, and sequence of the sections.

Section 1 deals with the role of science in the elementary school. Section 2 describes the theories of Piaget, Bruner, and Gagné regarding learning and intellectual development in children. Section 3 discusses the major objectives of elementary science: the learning of content and process. Section 4 takes up the prerequisites of an effective science program and also describes the current status of the large-scale elementary science curriculum projects.

Sections 5, 6, and 7 deal, respectively, with the strategies and innovations in teaching elementary science, the evaluation of both science learning and the science program, and the need for adequate materials and facilities for elementary science. Finally, Section 8 takes up the preservice and in-service science training of elementary teachers, describes the need for science supervision, and lists the qualifications and functions of the science supervisor.

We wish to express our appreciation and thanks to the authors, publishers, organizations, and institutions who gave us permission to reprint the material that appears in this book.

E. V.
M. S. L.

Contents

SECTION 7
Materials and Facilities for Elementary Science 341

SECTION 8
Improving the Quality of Elementary Science Teaching 375

The Role of Science in the Elementary School

INTRODUCTION

Science is a comparative newcomer to the elementary school curriculum, although its roots can be traced back a hundred years or more. In the latter part of the nineteenth century, children were introduced to object study, where both animate and inanimate objects were observed and described. In the early part of the twentieth century, nature study became very popular in many elementary schools.

However, there is general agreement that elementary science really began around 1930 with the growth of a movement to reach all areas of science in the elementary school and to make science a dynamic and integral part of the elementary school curriculum. This movement grew rather slowly, but steadily, gaining support throughout the country.

In the past twenty years two phenomena have taken place which have given the movement tremendous impetus and rapid growth. First, the vast and almost explosive scientific and technological revolution in our midst has produced a fantastic growth of scientific knowledge in all areas of science, and this wealth of knowledge is now exerting an effect on all of science education. Second, the impact of the satellite Sputnik succeeded in arousing the concern of scientists, science educators, teachers, administrators, the public in general, and the government in the kind and amount of science being taught and learned in our schools. As a result, there is widespread interest and activity in elementary (as well as secondary) science today. There is also unanimous agreement on a strong K-12 science sequence in our schools, and on a well-developed science program in the elementary school as part of this sequence.

An effective science program can play an important role in the elementary school. The goal of all science education is to develop scientifically literate citizens who can think and act rationally. The science program should lay the foundations for achieving this goal. The program can help the child understand his environment and the problems of controlling the environment. It can make the child aware of the impact, as well as the social and economic aspects and values, of science and technology on

1

society. It can give the child an insight into the structure of science, enabling the child to learn key concepts, conceptual schemes, and their relationships to each other. It can help the child live successfully in a changing world by showing that our universe is based upon change. Learning about change in science, and how to cope with change, will help the child react more intelligently to the changes he may expect in his future.

Elementary science can play an important role in helping the child learn the nature of scientific inquiry and the key operations, or processes, of science and of the scientist. A program based on inquiry and process will encourage real learning to take place, not the memorization of facts. The child will learn to solve problems by thinking critically and creatively, and will develop scientific attitudes and skills.

The very nature of an effective science program makes it possible to offer a wide variety of learning activities and experiences which can provide for the individual differences in ability, interest, and need that all children have. The science program lends itself very well to individual learning, making it possible for each child to develop to the limit of his capacity.

Finally, the science program can be correlated very effectively with other programs in the elementary school curriculum. Learning is always more effective when all phases of the curriculum are integrated. There are many opportunities in the elementary school to correlate science with mathematics, language arts, social studies, and the creative arts.

Historical Background of Elementary Science*

HERBERT A. SMITH

The following is a portion of an article by Herbert A. Smith entitled "Educational Research Related to Science Instruction for the Elementary and Junior High School: A Review and Commentary." Dr. Smith traces the history of elementary science education, beginning with its roots in Britain and Germany. He describes the influence of object teaching, the National Education Association Committee of Ten, the nature study movement, and the works of Harris, Hall, Strait, Jackman, Parker, Pierce, James, and Dewey. Two historical landmarks are discussed—the published thesis of Gerald S. Craig in 1927, and the Thirty-first Yearbook of the National Society for the Study of Education in 1932.

The roots of the modern American elementary school science program can be traced through their development of more than 100 years. Two definite influences can be identified as early as the decade of the 1850's. One of these was the didactic literature brought into this country largely from Britain and adapted and then reprinted by American publishers. This instructional literature reflected its origins in an aristocratic conception of education and was designed for use by private tutors or by parents teaching the children at home. It was within the financial reach of only the upper classes. Most of this material was directed to children's observation and to study of natural phenomena. Underhill has traced the didactic literature to the influence of such men as Francis Bacon, John Locke, and other writers who at that time were stimulating democratic thought in Europe as well as in America.[1] When the National Education Association was organized in 1857, it helped to stimulate the task of adapting some of this literature for use in school classrooms.

The second influential factor during the late 1850's rose from the "Pestalozzian object teaching" movement. This method of teaching was very widespread and was an international educational development. The applications made of the method varied greatly from one country to another. In Germany it developed into *Heimatkunde*,[2] or "community study." In England and in the United States object teaching evolved into, and was later supplanted by, nature study. However, the American and

*REPRINTED FROM *Journal of Research in Science Teaching*, Vol. 1, Issue 3, 1963, pp. 200–205, 223, by permission of the author and the editor. Dr. Smith is Professor of Education at Colorado State University, Fort Collins.

English versions of nature study varied greatly in spite of their common origin in object teaching.

The best known American adaption of the Pestalozzian method was developed at Oswego, New York. Due to the influence of the National Education Association which supported it, the "Oswego method" [3] was given nearly universal acceptance in this country. The new method aroused interest in the revision of content and in the method of study in the rapidly growing elementary schools.

The methodology of object teaching had a highly formal structure which tended to obscure the legitimate purposes of science instruction; it did not contribute effectively to a sense of sequence and direction. Men like Franklin and Jefferson had encouraged the development of science in elementary education hoping for and working for programs that had merit due to their continuity and practicality. Object teaching destroyed whatever gains had been made in this direction because the emphasis tended to shift to mere description of animate and inanimate objects and to neglect the interpretation and understanding of events and phenomena. The content was further fragmented by the organization of information concerning the particular object of study into formal separate sciences, thus imposing a mature scientist's view on children. Profound meanings tended to be neglected in favor of mere obvious descriptions.

The old method of object teaching tended to be supported by the principles of faculty psychology. [4] The emphasis on observation and memorization for very young children was based on the assumption of the sequential development of capacities. It was falsely assumed that young children were able only to observe and identify objects but were unable to reason or to interpret phenomena. In addition, the specialized methodology of object teaching, together with the exclusion of the use of books, made heavy demands upon the ability and knowledge of the teacher. It appeared to be particularly ill-suited to the purposes and needs of teachers and pupils in a rapidly developing industrial society.

Some insight into the nature of the ideas underlying the "object study" movement may be gained from the following selected excerpts. The method was:

to place objects before them [children] in which they are interested, and which tend to cultivate their perceptive faculties; and, at the same time, lead them to name the object, to describe its parts, and to state the relation of these parts. Thus, language also is cultivated; and, from the observation of a single object, the pupil is led to compare it with others, and the first steps in classification are taken.

. . . These lessons are designed specially to cultivate the perceptive faculty; and hence, in any true system of education, they must be considered as fundamental—not only in their relation to the faculties, but as giving the first ideas, or laying the foundation of all branches of knowledge. Object Lessons in form lead directly to Drawing, Writing, and Geometry; in sound and form, to Language, including Reading, Speaking, and Spelling; in place, to Geography; and in animals, plants, minerals, etc., to Natural History . . .

This method commences with an examination of objects and facts, then institutes comparisons by which resemblances, differences, and relations are observed; and with the results so obtained, repeats the process until the remotest relations are known and the highest generalizations reached. This process may, with propriety, be called the Objective Method or Objective Teaching.

Objective Teaching, in this enlarged sense, includes object lessons, and a great deal more. It comprehends the unfolding of the faculties in the order of their growth and use, and the presentation of the several branches of instruction in their natural order. Its great aims are mental growth and the acquisition of knowledge.[5]

The decade of 1870 witnessed the culmination of a number of developing trends. The writings of such men as Herbert Spencer [6] in his essay, "What Knowledge Is of Most Worth," and the rising importance of science and technology had forced the consideration of science as a field of study upon the public. It was during this decade that colleges and universities first came to accept science subjects as satisfactory prerequisites for admission to colleges.

The depression of 1873 spurred a critical examination of the program of the public schools; and the elementary schools, particularly, were the object of a veritable storm of abusive criticism. Tax-conscious citizens were demanding clarification of the aims and purposes of education. Most of the educational journals joined the hue and cry for more science in the public school programs. There were accompanying changes in the social and economic patterns of the time. Old patterns of teaching and learning were seen to be ill-adapted to the changing times and not fully in accord with characteristics of the learning process.

Near the end of the 19th century, the National Education Association sponsored an extensive study at the secondary school level that was to influence the entire educational system. This was the work of the National Education Association Committee of Ten. The results of this Committee's study tended to stabilize science offerings and led to the discontinuance of a large number of short-term specialized science courses taught in the secondary school. The report put emphasis on laboratory and other direct experiences and on the need for special training for science teachers. Its influence was effective primarily on textbooks, syllabi and other instructional material. These changes at the secondary level were reflected rather quickly in the elementary schools. It was only after the report of the Committee of Ten that materials for pupil use and teacher planning appeared in any appreciable volume.

A number of men rose to prominence in the field of elementary school science around the turn of the century. Of these, William F. Harris[4] first translated philosophy and educational theory into a specific and extensively detailed elementary science curriculum which provided help to teachers in the field. G. Stanley Hall[7] and Colonel Francis W. Parker[8] contributed general philosophies of education supporting nature study. These philosophies opened the way for others to experiment and to work out detailed elementary programs, especially in elementary science. Much of this work was done by Henry H. Strait and Wilbur S. Jackman at the Practice School of the Cook County Normal School, later the Chicago Institute, and now the School of Education at the University of Chicago.[1] Parker strongly supported the work of Strait and Jackman in Chicago, influencing the use of science as a unifying principle in elementary school curricula. Jackman's writings represent a connecting link between early writers of children's literature and modern elementary science. His positive, dynamic view of children and science is in close accord with modern ideas. Jackman's contributions to elementary science were obscured for a time by the extended development of a nature study movement.

Liberty Hyde Bailey and associates at Cornell University were prime movers of the nature study movement. They were motivated by the need to improve agriculture and to halt the increasing migration of young people from farms to cities where they would add to already swollen city relief rolls.[9] One of the important publications to come out of Cornell was the *Handbook of Nature Study* by Mrs. Anna Botsford Comstock which ran through many editions after 1911. This book, along with the Cornell rural school leaflets was, and still is, widely distributed to schools. These and other publications by the Cornell group rank among the most comprehensive efforts in teacher education ever undertaken in the field of science education. Like object study, nature study was based on the principles of faculty psychology and on the alleged serial development of traits. The child was considered in terms of his limitations rather than in terms of his capabilities. Nature study had been developed by specialists in science who lacked the perception and understanding of men like Jackman who were specialists in science as well as experienced teachers of children.

By the 1920's the enthusiasm for nature study was beginning to wane. The influence of the new designs in curricula for science was beginning to be felt. In addition, new thinking in other fields was again beginning to make an impact on all of education and was particularly relevant to science instruction. Men of the stature of Charles Sanders Peirce,[10] William James,[11] and John Dewey[12] were having tremendous influence on education. William James and Charles Sanders Peirce had contributed a theory of pragmatism which meant in essence that the meaning of a conception is to be found in the working out of its implications. The link between concept and experience was seen as fundamental. Peirce's thinking was basic to the development of the operational theory of meaning which was closely associated with the development of pragmatism. Dewey's contributions were numerous; but, perhaps, the most significant for the developing field of elementary science was his contention that the methodology of science is at least of equal—or perhaps of greater—significance than the actual knowledge accumulated. The present emphasis on "science as inquiry" would seem to be a reaffirmation of a position which Dewey took nearly half a century ago. It was apparent by the middle of the 1920's that nature study was no longer a satisfactory vehicle for a modern science program. Its whole rationale was no longer consistent with the psychology, philosophy and methodology of the time. It was inconsistent with the existing social and economic realities. With the benefit of historical perspective it is patently obvious that a substantial change in the science program for the elementary school was in order.

It is probably no exaggeration to say that Columbia University was, at that time, the colossus of American education as a training institution for public school administration and for other general leadership positions in the educational field. In 1927 a thesis was written at Columbia which came at a time when the situation was ripe for change. It represented the then most prestigious institution in professional education and was to have, perhaps, the most far-reaching influence on the development of elementary science of any single event in the history of the field. The study was entitled *Certain Techniques Used in Developing a Course of Study in Science for the Horace Mann Elementary School.*[13] It represented the culmination of three years of work by Gerald S. Craig at the famous laboratory school and profoundly affected subsequent developments in elementary school science. Craig turned his back resolutely on the nature study movement and, in so doing, took note of the great chaos of educational goals to which lip service was then being paid. These goals included various esthetic, ethical, spiritual, intellectual, and civil-training goals without adequate indication as to how such aims were to be achieved. Parenthetically, it is perhaps worth noting at this point that the question of purposes is one which is still not fully resolved, although it is certain that there is far more unanimity as to the purposes and ends to be served today than there was at the time that Craig was doing his original study. Some of the present arguments and debates in the profession represent confusion among the disputing parties as to the real purposes to be served by the elementary science program. Craig saw the function of science in the elementary school to be significant in terms of general education, pointing out that the laws, generalizations, and principles of science have vital meanings to individuals regarding numerous questions which confront them. He also saw the utilitarian aspect as it is related to health, safety, and the economy. He was aware, moreover, of more than the cognitive aspects of science instruction and emphasized also the affective dimensions: attitudes, appreciations, and interests. Clearly, Craig's thesis has been one of the landmarks in elementary science and is basic to much of the later writings in the field including his own.

Another important step forward was taken when the Thirty-first Yearbook[14] of the National Society for the Study of Education was published in 1923. This Yearbook presented a plan for an integrated program of science teaching. This marked the beginning of a trend which has continued to be more and more emphasized down to the present time. Problems involving sequence and articulation of science instruction between the various grades and school units have continued as vexing difficulties. The National Science Teachers Association has had a committee at work for several years on the K–12 science program. Others are equally concerned with problems of articulation between high schools and colleges. The design of an appropriate sequential series of science experiences which shall extend from elementary school through college is a problem which has occupied the thinking of many persons. This problem has stimulated study of such diverse questions as content and placement, when track programs should be instituted, when non-science and non-college bound students should terminate their study of science, when advanced placement programs should be used, and how elementary teachers should be educated. These questions are obviously inter-twined with conceptions of the ultimate purposes and goals of education and no universal agreement has been attained as to what these should be. Perhaps no such agreement is possible or even desirable; but an understanding of the problems and their complexities would at least reduce the confusion.

The Thirty-first Yearbook also placed an emphasis on the major generalizations of science as objectives of instruction. This emphasis had profound effects on course syllabi and textbooks, and a generation of these documents tended to emphasize the understandings and applications of the principles of science. One other obvious example of the Yearbook's influence was the great amount of research devoted to identifying the major principles of science which were of significance to general education. In fact, a great body of the research that was subsequently done in science education was a reflection of the influence of this famous Yearbook. The Yearbook was clear and definite in its support of elementary science rather than nature study and, as a result, it contributed to the rapid advancement of science at the elementary school level. The report advocated basing the selection of science content on personal and social criteria; thus, probably, both conforming to and augmenting the educational thinking that was then developing in this direction.

The Society also devoted its Forty-sixth Yearbook, published in 1947, to problems of science education. The increasing impact which science was obviously having upon the social, cultural, and economic affairs of men continued to be very much in evidence in the thinking revealed in this Yearbook. The following quotation is illustrative of this fact.

Instruction in science must take cognizance of the social impact of developments produced by science. It is not enough that they be understood in a technical or scientific sense; it is most important that their effects on attitudes and relationships of people be studied and understood. Science instruction has not only a great potential contribution to make but also a responsibility to help develop in our youth the qualities of mind and the attitudes that will be of greatest usefulness to them in meeting the pressing social and economic problems that face the world.[15]

There is a marked sensitivity to some of the "affective" objectives of science instruction in this Yearbook. There is also a more obvious reflection of sensitivity to the responsibility which educators have to prescribe the precise way in which statements of intangible and illusive objectives can be translated into practical programs and to determine how the effectiveness of instruction can be measured.

The most recent document prepared by the National Society for the Study of Education of primary concern to science education was the Fifty-ninth Yearbook which was published in 1960. This Yearbook takes cognizance of the increasing dependence of society on science. The implications for the scientific training of citizens of such a society are clearly considered to be of fundamental importance. The Yearbook goes further than preceding reports of the society in stressing that characteristic of science which is known as "process" or "inquiry." It is perhaps significant to quote the Yearbook with respect to this latter observation.

One function of the elementary school has always been to help children learn a part of what they need to know from the world's storehouse of knowledge. In recent years this function has embraced more and more science. Scientific methods of investigation, by which knowledge may be acquired and tested, are now very much a part of our culture. The elementary school should help children become acquainted with these methods.[16]

One may summarize the historical overview by pointing out that the past century has been a century of unprecedented social, economic, scientific, and technological change. The elementary schools are to a very large degree a mirror of the ambient culture, and they are probably more sensitive to social change than any other educational level. They are always, to a degree, consonant with the prevailing philosophies and state of knowledge in existence at any particular time. Fundamental changes in philosophy, in theories of child rearing and educability, in the need for universal and extended educational training for all children and adolescents of our society with capacity to learn, have been accepted within this century. Science, itself, has progressed from the dilettantism of the leisured intellectual to a basic and fundamental activity of a substantial percentage of mankind. No human being of any civilized nation can remain untouched by these multifarious developments. In such a milieu it is not surprising that elementary science instruction has been beset by numerous perplexing problems.

References

1. Underhill, Orra E., *The Origin and Development of Elementary School Science*, Scott, Foresman and Company, Chicago, 1941.
2. Shoemaker, Lois Meier, *Natural Science Education in the German Elementary Schools*, Bureau of Publications, Teachers College, Columbia University, Contributions to Education, No. 445, New York, 1930.
3. Lammers, Theresa J., "The Thirty-first Yearbook and 20 Years of Elementary Science," *Science Education*, **39**, 39-40 (February, 1955).
4. Craig, Gerald S., "Elementary School Science in the Past Century," *Science Teacher*, **24**, 4, 11-14 (February, 1957).
5. Krusi, Hermann, *Pestalozzi: His Life, Work and Influence*, Wilson, Hinkle and Co., Cincinnati, 1875, pp. 162-164.
6. Spencer, Herbert, "What Knowledge Is of Most Worth?" in *Education*, Appleton, New York, 1926 (Reprinted from 1860 edition).
7. Hall, G. Stanley, *Aspects of Child Life and Education*, Appleton, New York, 1921.
8. Parker, Francis W., *Talks on Pedagogics*, Kellogg, New York, 1894.
9. Comstock, Anna Botsford, *The Comstocks of Cornell: John Henry and Anna Botsford Comstock, An Autobiography by Anna Botsford Comstock*, Comstock Publishing Associates, New York, 1953.
10. Peirce, Charles Sanders, *Philosophical Writings of Peirce*, Dover, New York, 1955.
11. James, William, *The Principles of Psychology*, Holt, New York, 1890.
12. Dewey, John, *Democracy and Education*, Macmillan, New York, 1916.
13. Craig, Gerald S., *Certain Techniques Used in Developing a Course of Study in Science for the Horace Mann Elementary School*, Bureau of Publications, Teachers College, Columbia University, Contributions to Education, No. 276, New York, 1927.
14. National Society for the Study of Education, *A Program for Teaching Science*, Thirty-first Yearbook, Part I, Public School Publishing Company, Bloomington, Illinois, 1932.
15. National Society for the Study of Education, *Science Education in American Schools*, Forty-sixth Yearbook, Part I, The University of Chicago Press, Chicago, Illinois, 1947, pp. 1, 145-147.
16. National Society for the Study of Education, *Rethinking Science Education*, Fifty-ninth Yearbook, Part I, The University of Chicago Press, Chicago, Illinois, 1960, pp. 112-113.

Education and the Spirit of Science*

EDUCATIONAL POLICIES COMMISSION

The following article is an excerpt of a larger report of the Educational Policies Commission of the National Education Association and the American Association of School Administrators. The Commission believes that the following seven basic values underlie science: (1) longing to know and to understand, (2) questioning of all things, (3) search for data and their meaning, (4) demand for verification, (5) respect for logic, (6) consideration of premises, and (7) consideration of consequences. The Commission states that to communicate the Spirit of Science and to develop people's capacity to use its values should be among the principal goals of education.

The schools should help to realize the great opportunities which the development of science has made apparent in the world. They can do this by promoting understanding of the values on which science is everywhere based. Although no particular scientist may fully exemplify all these values, they characterize the enterprise of science as a whole. We believe that the following values underlie science:

1. Longing to know and to understand.
2. Questioning of all things.
3. Search for data and their meaning.
4. Demand for verification.
5. Respect for logic.
6. Consideration of premises.
7. Consideration of consequences.

These values are not stated the way more traditional values are stated. They do not contain some of the traditional value words, such as *love, honesty, beauty,* or *patriotism.* But neither are they necessarily in conflict with traditional values. Like all values, they are guidelines for belief and hence, for action. Some of them merely define traditional values; for example, the demand for verification is nothing other than an approach to, and a profound respect for, honesty. Some of them undergird, and almost make inevitable, values which are often expressed as self-evident truths;

*REPRINTED FROM *Education and the Spirit of Science,* 1966, Section 4, pp. 15–27. Educational Policies Commission, National Education Association, Washington, D.C. Copyright, 1966, by the National Education Association, Washington, D.C. Reprinted by permission of the publisher.

for example, an awareness of consequences makes love of one's children and responsibility to one's neighbors essential. And, like other sets of values, they have the defect that neither individually nor jointly do they provide a fully adequate guide to action; in many concrete human situations, various values, all cherished, are involved, and the choice of action involves an ethical compromise. The values of the spirit of science express the belief that the compromise is likely to be better if based on thoughtful choice; in this respect they differ from those value systems which hesitate to submit all problems to reason. Perhaps they differ from some other sets of values in the degree of reliance they place on the individual. Instead of insisting on his acceptance of certain values favored by men or groups allegedly wiser than he, the spirit of science insists that he make up his own mind. In this, the values of science are the most complete expression of one of the deepest of humane values—the belief in human dignity.

By their very nature, these values cannot be acquired through indoctrination. For the spirit of certainty upon which indoctrination rests is contradictory to each of them. Dictatorships do not make progress in knowledge and capability in those areas in which they insist that the truth is already known. Consequently these values, unlike indoctrinated values, are part and parcel of any true education. These are characteristic not only of what is commonly called science but, more basically, of rational thought—and that applies not only in science, but in every area of life. What is being advocated here is not the production of more physicists, biologists, or mathematicians, but rather the development of persons whose approach to life as a whole is that of a person who thinks—a rational person. The characteristics of this mode of thought merit consideration in greater detail.

1. LONGING TO KNOW AND TO UNDERSTAND

The spirit of science is, at bottom, a longing to understand. It seeks to understand because it accepts knowledge as desirable in itself. It expresses its curiosity endlessly, recognizing that questions are infinite, answers finite. The events which surround an inquiring person pose for him the fundamental problems of why and how. He deems it a worthy investment of himself and of mankind to become mobilized in the search for answers.

2. QUESTIONING OF ALL THINGS

There is no perfect knowledge and no perfect knower. Certainty, as a concept, is replaced by probability. All conclusions and decisions are more or less suspect; science rides on a preference for the less over the more.

If certainty is illusory, it is partly because men cannot be fully objective. Some tinge of the observer must color any observation. If men cannot eliminate this influence, they can at least take it into account. The pursuit of the highest probability of accuracy in conclusions calls on an observer to be aware of the full range of experiences within which he operates, including his own subjective, intuitive, aesthetic, and nonrational responses. These responses have their own uses and compose also part of the reality to which the spirit of science extends. They could not be eliminated even if that were desirable. A scientific thinker does not attempt to snuff them out; he tries rather to be aware of them and to understand which of them are helpful and which are harmful, which are harmless, and which irrelevant.

Here is a prime source of that attitude of modesty and humility which characterizes the general posture of the seeker after knowledge. Conscious of the uncertainties with which he deals, he must nevertheless reach some sorts of operating conclusions. He must, from time to time, act or decide, always with incomplete evidence, by incomplete intellectual devices, with even incomplete means of reading results. Incompleteness rules science, producing a universal spirit of tentativeness and inhibiting the development of that ferocious intolerance so often revealed when supposedly definitive beliefs are challenged.

Since scientific knowledge is tentative, all propositions are subject to being revised or discarded. Reluctance to discard beliefs is one of the most difficult problems of rational thought for two reasons: (1) A thinker himself treasures certain concepts, values, or "self-evident" truths which have served him in his own life; these he challenges only with difficulty. (2) A thinker usually depends on support from the larger community in which he works, and that community may be unwilling to examine certain values—for example, those of religious or national traditions—which his work may call into question. He may thus be confronted with a conflict between loyalty to the basic values of the scientific spirit and the practical steps necessary to advance it.

In spite of these difficulties, a thinker feels compelled to insist that the range of his curiosity cannot accept limits imposed by external authority. He examines external authority as well. There is no sanctuary for ideas.

3. SEARCH FOR DATA AND THEIR MEANING

The longing to know is the motivation for learning; data and generalizations are the forms which knowledge takes. Generalizations are induced from discrete bits of information gathered through observation conducted as accurately as the circumstances permit.

Much of science consists of the acquisition and ordering of data. But data taken by themselves normally have little meaning. The principal contribution of scholarship to an understanding of the world is found, not in such data, but in theories which explain phenomena. Scientists often refer to these theories or insights which interrelate data and give them meaning as *conceptual schemes*. The evolution of these conceptual schemes is an intuitive, highly creative process. It involves seeing connections and meanings others have not seen. Here is the place for intuition and creativity in science and in all other modes of thinking which seek the same values. The process of creating new integrations implies flexibility, originality, breadth and fluency of mind, and freedom to skip from one frame of reference to another sensing new relationships and hidden meanings.

4. DEMAND FOR VERIFICATION

Implicit in the concept of the tentativeness of knowledge and of conceptual schemes is the concept of test. Knowledge is, at best, hypothetical, and the statement of a hypothesis suggests that it is subject to test. A thinker, therefore, consciously seeks to find ways to expose the results of his thinkings to test or experiment and to the play of as many other minds as possible.

Conceptual schemes may be arrived at both inductively and deductively. Unless they can be confronted with the results of empirical test, however, they are little likely to gain widespread support. The scientific spirit is therefore predisposed to the search for such test as the basis for favorable evaluation.

The search for a testing situation is itself a highly creative act. A scientist does not merely permit the evaluation of his conceptual schemes; he actively seeks it. He values the positive and imaginative creation of situations which test hypotheses, suggest new ones, promote exploration, and give expression to the spirit of excitement and adventure which suffuses the scientific enterprise. Furthermore, the creation of new means of verification may itself be a significant scientific advance.

5. RESPECT FOR LOGIC

Logic is the science of valid inference. Logical systems constitute agreed bases by which the validity of inferences may be judged. There are a number of such logical systems, and new ones are in constant process of growth. But all of them agree on the meaning of such basic concepts as consistency and contradiction.

Logic is used in connecting a thinker's concepts in a manner open to evaluation by other persons. A thinker judges the validity of inferences and deductions in terms of logic. But he recognizes also that no amount of logical consistency will make valid any inferences or deductions which proceed from inadequate or faulty premises. Mere logical consistency does not constitute an adequate appraisal of a concept, proposition, or idea. It is also necessary to ask whether the data being reviewed are relevant and necessary in the situation and whether the premises are both relevant and sufficient.

6. CONSIDERATION OF PREMISES

A thinker is at the center of any situation involving knowledge. As he seeks knowledge or understanding in any situation, he recognizes that he must keep in mind not only the external questions which confront him, but also internal predispositions that shape his thoughts. As he applies and develops the values of science, he does so consciously, and tries to be sensitive to his own inadequacies in that effort.

There is a limit to fruitful inquiry into one's premises and assumptions. In this effort, too, certainty is unobtainable. But, in choosing to act or conclude, a thinker does not rest assured that he has reached the firm bedrock of faith. Rather, he recognizes that he has reached the present limitations of his abilities. Humility is required, and fanaticism excluded, by the spirit of science.

7. CONSIDERATION OF CONSEQUENCES

To hold to a value or to decide upon an action without awareness of its implications or its consequences is to believe or act in partial ignorance. Awareness of implications can, like the rest of knowledge, at best be incomplete. But a rational person does not accept a value or decide upon an action without trying to be aware of its implications. He recognizes that he is, after all, part of the human race and that his decisions will have bearing on other persons and will be judged by other persons. He cannot, therefore, think of his single localized decision only, but must recognize that each conclusion or decision will reach a wider circle of influence. He must, then, think about implications and consequences, take them into consideration, and avoid actions whose backwash will be harmful. A sense of responsibility is inherent in honest thought.

This does not mean that the search for knowledge must lead only to happy results. But neither does any other value. The search for knowledge made the atomic bomb possible, but it led to that result only in the service of other values—love of country and hatred of tyranny. One would be hard put to name a value whose results, in the light of all other cherished values, have always been exclusively good.

If a single word summarizes the various characteristics of the scientific spirit, it is *awareness*—awareness of the uncertainty of man's knowledge, awareness of the extent to which the self influences one's perceptions, awareness of the consequences of one's values and actions, awareness of the painstaking modes of thought which have enabled man gradually to develop his knowledge of the world. This awareness is the basic stuff of freedom; only insofar as a man is aware of the influences upon him can he filter them and become himself, and only insofar as he is aware of the problems and modes of knowing can he help himself and others to understand the world.

Here, then, is a group of values which schools can promote without doing violence to the dignity of the individual. Here are values which are not intended to be accepted on the basis of external authority. On the contrary, they are themselves frankly intended to be challenged. The school here envisioned would have failed in the case of any student who has never questioned the desirability of these values. It would have failed in the case of any student who has never compared the various bases which different men deem sufficient for knowing or for acting. The view of teaching as the indoctrination of superior knowledge and wisdom here gives way to a concept of teaching as promotion of the development of the learner from within.

In this way, schools can be profoundly concerned with values and ethics in a manner fully consistent with the democratic belief in the dignity of the individual and with the scientific belief that no one—the school included—knows the final answers.

What is advocated here is not a separation of science from other aspects of life but rather the understanding that the spirit of science applies to other facets of man's existence. It fuses with many kinds of thinking that men traditionally consider distinct from it.

The view that there is a necessary conflict between the scientific and the humanistic approaches to life is not valid. When science is isolated from the moral and spiritual aspects of life it can produce the monstrosities so often feared, just as the acceptance of values on the basis of emotion and without rigorous examination of their likely consequences has often produced abominations.

The values of which the spirit of science consists should permeate the educative process, serving as objectives of learning in every field, including the humanities and practical studies. These values can be learned in connection with any kind of intellectual activity. Indeed, all parts of the educational program should reflect the unity of life. For example, any subject can be so taught as to contribute to the student's tendency both to examine all concepts and to inquire into the social implications of the questioning spirit. The thorough compartmentalization of subjects in a school is in conflict with human experience and the best interests of human development. The schools must continue to sensitize students to the aesthetic and ethical experience of civilization and should try to unify all these considerations.

It cannot be assumed that the addition of science courses to a curriculum would necessarily contribute to the achievement of these goals. Indeed, science can be so taught as to be irrelevant or even opposed to their achievement. Efforts to discourage challenges to traditional beliefs and attempts to indoctrinate are probably widespread in every school system, however advanced the content of science courses. What is needed is an education which turns the child's curiosity into a lifelong drive and which leads students to consider seriously the various possibilities of satisfying that curiosity and the many limitations on those possibilities.

Just as the values of the spirit of science can serve as educational goals in American schools, they can also serve to help orient the foreign operations of the United States government. It should be a direct aim of American foreign aid and technical assistance programs to help other nations to foster these values. This may not be an appropriate immediate objective for many countries, but without it as a long-range goal, a nation's intellectual, and hence other, resources cannot be satisfactorily developed. Two objections immediately arise. The first is related to the propriety of setting goals for other peoples. Certainly, to set goals for foreign peoples is not only contrary to the American sense of justice, it is also impossible to carry out, for the United States does not rule the countries which it aids. But in most cases the problem is not likely to arise in any more acute form than it does in economic development. All countries, however poorly endowed in mineral resources, have a vast and largely untapped potential in mental resources. Increasingly they are recognizing that their progress—as they define it—hinges on their success in developing the minds of their people. In particular, as noted earlier, all countries wish to foster their scientific development. They themselves realize that if they lack people who master the spirit of science, they will be dependent on the creative science of other countries. To countries that wish to foster individual freedom, the relationship between the values of the spirit of science and individual freedom is evident.

The second objection that arises is that little is known about how to promote learning of these seven values. The objection is valid, but inadequate. Little is known, too, about fostering the economic development of nations; but that has not kept nations from trying—or from succeeding to some extent. That goal has been deemed important enough to justify doing the best one can with inadequate knowledge. The goal here proposed is, in our opinion, also important enough to justify trying. Indeed, we think that economic development itself calls for the achievement of this goal. Furthermore, educators traditionally have sought goals which they have known only imperfectly how to achieve. Among them are social responsibility, creativity, honesty, and patriotism. For these reasons, we do not regard the scantiness of knowledge of how to foster rationality as a sufficient argument against making the attempt. It is rather a challenge to do the best that can be done with present knowledge and to undertake the sorts of research that will enable mankind to do the job better.

Furthermore, these seven values of the scientific spirit are all quite specific educational goals. There is no reason to doubt that they can be sought and gradually promoted. Certainly the rewards for doing so might be immense.

Not only would solid progress in the direction of these educational goals yield immediate benefits such as improved standards of living and health, but also there might be found in these developments gains in ethical dimensions which have long eluded man. Although these values are those of science, and although science is often said to be neutral on questions of value, there are many ethical implications which flow from these scientific beliefs. The longing to know and the demand for verification imply honesty, reliability, and responsibility; every practitioner of science depends on the honesty of other scientists. Each realizes that this requirement also rests on him. The pursuit of truth is impeded by a lack of mutual trust and faith.

Implicit also in these values is a modesty or humility which contrasts with the boastful self-assurance of arbitrary authority. A man of science is suspicious of certainty. He insists that no concept, proposition, or belief is immune to examination and possible rejection. He is willing to challenge even the scientific approach as he understands it. Most of all, he is willing to see his own conclusions challenged. He recognizes his own failings and those of others. He knows that no observer, thinker, communicator, corroborator, or other human link in the scientific process is perfect.

It is often said that science is amoral. One may legitimately ask, however, whether the spirit of science does not have truly humane implications. What are the ethical implications of recognizing that all that is known is known by minds; or recognizing that there is no science—or art— except that which is carried by human beings; or recognizing that every human being has at least the potential of contributing to that which is known? Those who are conscious of the power of the human mind and of the vastness, if not infinity, of the fields for minds to conquer, can hardly avoid a profound longing for all minds to be developed.

Moreover, as noted above, a reluctance to accept ignorance as a basis for belief or action implies a responsibility to understand the premises and consequences of one's beliefs and actions. But to say that a sense of responsibility is inherent in the scientific spirit is not to say that all scientific thinkers will inevitably come to conclusions acceptable to most other people. Thus, there may be some dangers in a commitment to individual freedom and in a true acceptance of the belief that no one knows the final answers. But there have been great dangers also in other commitments. The traditional morality has, after all, included such items as devotion to nation and the supposed unquestionability of certain knowledge; and acceptance of each has repeatedly occasioned misery to the world. Perhaps it would be no less safe to entrust the future to people who constantly ask "why," to people whose acceptance of the need for certain social rules derives from understanding rather than obedience, to people who doubt the finality of their own wisdom and of the wisdom of others, to people who try hard to understand the premises and implications of their values and decisions.

I cannot be guaranteed that a society which seeks the scientific spirit will avoid repetition of the inhumane acts with which history is replete. Religious wars have repeatedly been fought by men who professed belief in faiths devoted to peace. Science might be similarly distorted by scientists, but such distortion is neither required nor justified by scientific traditions. It arises, not from devotion to the spirit of science, but from failure to be guided by it.

The spread of science and technology may indeed carry seeds of a most hopeful future for man. Perhaps the most visible phenomena of international relations are nationalism, hatred, and violence. They account for the headlines, and their genuine significance cannot be denied. But there may be a deeper tide in world affairs, a tide too quiet to produce headlines but of overwhelming importance to the future of mankind. That tide is the development of a common commitment to a set of values which, in the hands of a very few persons in a very few countries over a very short period of years, has given man unprecedented powers to perceive, to understand, to predict, to control, and to act.

The profound changes men have wrought in the world by their uses of science and technology have been for better and for worse. But the spirit underlying science is a highly desirable spirit. It can enable entire peoples to use their minds with breadth and dignity and with striking benefit to their health and standard of living. It promotes individuality. It can strengthen man's efforts in behalf of world community, peace, and brotherhood. It develops a sense of one's power tempered by an awareness of the minute and tenuous nature of one's contributions. Insofar as an individual learns to live by the spirit of science, he shares in the liberation of mankind's intelligence and achieves an invigorating sense of participation in the spirit of the modern world. To communicate the spirit of science and to develop people's capacity to use its values should therefore be among the principal goals of education in our own and every other country.

Toward a Theory of Science Education Consistent with Modern Science*

PAUL DeH. HURD

This statement of issues and suggestions by Paul DeH. Hurd provides for the formulation of acceptable purposes in science education and gives some needed insight into the basis for curriculum development. Seven challenging issues of science teaching are presented, together with seven equally challenging viewpoints which offer suggestions for the advancement of science teaching as related to these issues. A logical plan is presented for science teaching that is consistent with the structure of science.

*REPRINTED FROM *Theory into Action . . . in Science Curriculum Development*, National Science Teachers Association Document, Stock No. 471–14282, 1964, pp. 5–15. Copyright, 1964, by the National Science Teachers Association, Washington, D.C. Reprinted by permission of the author and the publisher. Dr. Hurd is Professor of Education Emeritus at Stanford University.

Introduction

The purpose of this paper is twofold—to describe issues and to make suggestions for the advancement of science teaching. It provides a basis for discussion and debate; it does not pretend to supply answers to all questions that may be raised.

Science curriculum developments are influenced both by changes in society as well as by new developments in science. This means that the curriculum specialist in science needs to examine the writings and research in a wide range of fields: economics, sociology, public policy and manpower, as well as the current status of science. Each of these areas has relevance for the teaching of science.

The development of a literate citizenry in science does not result from the teaching in a single grade nor is it the product of any one course. It can be achieved with a carefully planned kindergarten through grade 12 (K–12) program in which there is a vertical as well as a grade-level coherence within the science curriculum. Curriculum improvement in science then, should be viewed from kindergarten through grade 12 and perhaps through the undergraduate years of college.

To begin a curriculum reform without first establishing at least a tentative basis for decisions is wasteful of time and effort and seldom produces significant improvements. A major problem in science education in American schools has been the lack of a viable theory of science teaching which could serve as a base for decision making. Consequently the schools can make no answer to their critics. The value of theory in education is that it frees the teacher and the researcher from the constraints of tradition and makes the development of new ideas more likely. It gives perspective to curriculum and instructional issues and provides a basis for making decisions.

Local action groups can make the best use of this document by first comparing it, issue by issue, with their own views on science teaching, noting what they can or cannot accept. Second, they should prepare a clear-cut formulation of acceptable purposes for an education in science, using this as a basis to assess the need and directions in curriculum reform. It should be expected that working groups will wish to change their viewpoints as progress is made in curriculum design and communication between members of the curriculum committee becomes clearer.

In formulating this statement, advantage has been taken of the ideas expressed in the modern science curriculum studies developed over the past decade. At the secondary school level, the works of the Biological Sciences Curriculum Study, the Chemical Bond Approach Project, the Chemical Education Material Study, the Earth Science Curriculum Project, the Junior High School Science Project (Princeton University), and the Physical Sciences Study Committee have been particularly enlightening. At the elementary school level, curriculum studies developed by the American Association for the Advancement of Science, the Educational Services Incorporated, the University of California, the University of Illinois, the Minne Math Science Project, the School Mathematics Study Group, and the United States Office of Education have provided new insights into science teaching.

Science Teaching and Cultural Change

A rapidly changing society stimulated by advances in science demands an educational program designed to meet the challenge of change.

Schools exist to help young people know about and participate in the life of their time. In the past when cultural change and progress in science were slow, instruction in science could lag fifty years or more with little ill consequence for the individual or the nation. At the turn of the century, however, America began to move from an agrarian society to a scientific-technological society. Adjustments made in the science curricula reflected new technological developments but generally failed to reflect the advent of modern science. The impact of science on man's thinking, on social conditions, on economic development and on political action escaped widespread attention, even among highly educated nonscientists. In many ways the influence of science in shaping modern America is the unwritten history of the Twentieth Century.

By the close of World War II it was evident to nearly everyone that America had changed from an agrarian to a scientific-technological society, from rural to metropolitan communities, and that in a thousand related ways our pattern of life and philosophic values had changed. The demand for men and women trained for scientific and technological vocations more than doubled in a decade. But the science curriculum remained static, largely oriented to a culture that no longer existed, and taught from a content that had lost its scientific significance.

POINT OF VIEW

To escape the threat of obsolescence, education in the sciences must be based upon the kind of information that has survival value and upon strategies of inquiry that facilitate the adaptation of knowledge to new demands.

American schools need a science curriculum suited to recent advances in science and to a changing society. They require courses to prepare young people for change and progress and to help them meet the problems they will face during their lifetimes. A rapidly changing society stimulated by advances in science demands an educational program designed to meet the challenge of change.

Because our culture is characterized by change and progress, the greatest threat to either the individual or national security is obsolescence. This means that an education in the sciences must be based upon the kind of information that has survival value and upon strategies of inquiry that facilitate the adaptation of knowledge to new demands. This education must go beyond the immediate and include the future. What is more important, it should provide young people with the background and intellectual talents for shaping the future in a manner that assures the welfare of human beings and sustains progress. Progress is found not so much in tools and material resources as in the extension of intellectual capabilities of people and the viability of their knowledge. This suggests an education in the sciences that is oriented to lifelong learning, rational and independent thinking, and the acquisition of productive knowledge. A curriculum is needed that is oriented toward a period not yet lived, influenced by discoveries not yet made and beset with social problems not yet predicted. The need is for an education designed to meet change, to appreciate the processes of change, and to influence the direction of change.

The influence of science on national policy, on the thought of our times, on economics, social and political problems, and on the life of each person means that everyone needs an understanding of science. Men and women who do not have this background will be excluded from the intellectual life of the times and blindly buffeted by the forces that give direction and meaning to modern living. Without a grasp of science they will not be prepared to partake fully of the culture in which they are living.

Goals of Science Teaching

Science teaching must result in scientifically literate citizens.

Goals of education tend to be an expression of American values. They describe what the ideal American citizen should be like. As such they remain fairly stable over long periods of time. Our conception of the ideal does not change very rapidly. What changes are our ideas of how to achieve the ideals expressed through the goals. Unfortunately the connection between goals and the methods employed to reach them seldom is clear. We encounter very diverse kinds of curricula, all directed toward essentially the same ends. But we possess no satisfactory method for connecting the curriculum to abstract goals.

POINT OF VIEW

To state the goals of science education is to describe the cognitive skills expected in the student rather than the knowledge assumed essential to attaining these skills.

Goals generally are stated in terms which are much too abstract to be useful as a guide in building a curriculum. It would be more to the point to break general goals down into smaller component steps that could be attained one after the other. Thus, for example, the general goal of producing independent inquirers might be achieved by first discovering what support skills should be learned and which ones should be learned first. Thus, the operative goals for a course would consist of precise statements of specific cognitive skills to be attained each year in science.

Talking about goals is a little like talking about building a bridge. We may know the concept of "bridge" just as we know the concept of "inquiry" but that, by itself, will not suffice to build a satisfactory bridge. We need to know where and for what purpose the bridge will be constructed. Similarly we need to examine the goal of "inquiry" to find out what kind of inquiry and the purposes for which we intend to use the inquiry skills. Once these general questions are answered, criteria or standards for curriculum design, teaching methods, and evaluative procedures may be established.

A statement of goals should describe what we mean by a scientifically literate person living in the last half of the twentieth century. A person literate in science knows something of the role of science in society and appreciates the cultural conditions under which science thrives. He also understands its conceptual inventions and its investigative procedures.

Learning Science

The strategies of learning must be related to the conditions that will lead to an understanding of the conceptual structures of science and of the modes of scientific inquiry.

It is difficult at any time to formulate a satisfactory definition of learning, and it is particularly difficult if we wish to apply this definition specifically to the learning of science. Learning is sometimes defined as the relatively permanent behavior changes which result from experience. The goals of science teaching describe the desired behaviors. We can assume that some teaching procedures and learning materials are better than others for motivating inquiry and for developing an understanding of science concepts.

POINT OF VIEW
The educational setting and the choice of instructional materials are closely related to achieving the goals of science teaching.

We must assume that the educational setting for attaining the goals of science teaching can be facilitated and that some instructional materials are more efficient than others for achieving goals. In the paragraphs that follow, a few learning principles relevant to science teaching will be identified and their significance for curriculum development and instruction will be illustrated.

One of the first tasks in teaching science is to teach the inquiry processes of science. Inquiry skills provide the learner with tools for independent learning. By means of extensive experience in inquiry the student learns to place objects and events in categories or classes. He discovers the utility of coding systems and becomes aware that systems of classification are not inherent in nature but are man-made. He establishes a conceptual framework. This conceptual framework, in turn, focuses his attention on other phenomena and helps him build new categories which are more comprehensive or more abstract. The conceptual structure ties past experience to the present and serves as a guide for the comprehension and assimilation of new facts and concepts. It serves as a basis for prediction of what will happen in a new problem or situation.

While the significant facts in science change at a bewildering rate, the conceptual structure are more stable. However, we need to recognize that conceptual frameworks also change. The problem is to produce learners with the concepts and modes of inquiry that will permit them to understand these changes.

The ability to form science concepts depends upon the learner's own background and the conditions under which he is taught. To insure in some measure the likelihood that a concept will be acquired, it must be presented and used in different contexts. In a well-organized course of study, concepts formed early in the year are used to develop new concepts that occur later. Concepts are most easily acquired when familiar and concrete perceptual materials are used. To enlarge the understanding of a concept requires that it be taught many times at different levels of abstraction.

Words facilitate the development of concepts only when the ideas they represent are understood. Verbalization without understanding is likely to hinder the learning of concepts. This is the danger of attempting to teach science concepts through definitions and names. The ability to verbalize a concept is not a guarantee that the learner can apply or relate the concept. Nevertheless, there is an interdependence of concept and language. It is difficult to form a concept without a language rich enough to express it.

How shall we teach the investigatory process that characterizes a researcher and marks the skilled learner? Research provides some suggestions. It is wasteful to teach facts divorced from a meaningful concept. When facts, which have meanings for the learner, are tied into a logically related conceptual pattern, retention is improved and insight is more likely to occur. After learning one pattern, a student tends to respond more systematically to the alternatives in a new situation. An understanding of conceptual structure and training in inquiry help him select what is pertinent in a new situation. The test of learning is the extent to which a student is able to use a conceptual pattern and associated inquiry skills in new contexts.

In any given situation, more than one explanation may seem to apply.

There may be no good basis for choosing among alternatives until rather late in the decision-making or problem-solving process. Uncertainties exist during the interval in which the learner actively seeks and processes more data, examines other possible solutions, and finally makes a choice. Children have to be taught to consider alternatives and to recognize that answers must be sought in the environment of the problem, not primarily in the activities of the teacher. That is, they need to learn a pattern of delaying responses and of tolerating uncertainty until sufficient data are collected and alternative hypotheses are evaluated.

These procedures imply that the concepts which form the core of a course must be something more than questions for which students seek answers. Problem-solving is only one small part of scientific inquiry. We are seeking to develop a range of inquiry skills within the structure of a discipline which permits the student to increase his own efficiency in knowing.

The investigative strategies in science and the organization of scientific knowledge suggest valid and desirable principles of teaching. Stressing these procedures has the effect of minimizing authoritarian teaching and encouraging independent learning.

Selecting the Content of the Curriculum

Because science and the cultural scene are in a continuous process of change, the content of science courses must be constantly re-evaluated and, if necessary, revised to reflect major shifts in thinking and new interpretations of phenomena.

Science is a systematic and connected arrangement of knowledge within a logical structure of theory. Science is also a *process* of forming such a structure. Much of the effort in science is directed toward seeking new knowledge. There is also a certain lack of durability in this knowledge and scientists are dedicated to keeping this so. The significance of facts and concepts is constantly shifting within the scientific discipline. New ideas and theories cause the meaning of present knowledge to change. Correction and refinement are always operating to modify scientific information. And in science there is always more to be discovered and new relationships to be described.

Although the information phase of science is tenuous and overwhelming in amount, there are a small number of theories, laws, principles, and inquiry processes which provide the basis for interpreting a great variety of phenomena.

POINT OF VIEW
To develop a comprehensive science program that will achieve the goals of science teaching, the curriculum-maker must extract the essence of sci-

entific knowledge and define the significant concepts in terms of their usefulness for understanding the structure of science.

Criteria for the selection of curriculum materials should be consistent with the purposes of science teaching and consistent with the structure of science. The task of the curriculum-maker is to extract the essence of scientific knowledge and define the significant concepts in terms of their usefulness for understanding the structure of science. This is a process that begins with the "big picture" of science, not with bits of information, bodies of facts, or concepts in isolation. Thus it is the conceptual schemes and the inquiry processes that provide the framework for curriculum design and for developing courses at each grade level. By this approach we can reasonably expect to develop a comprehensive science program that presents a valid image of a science and will achieve the goals of science teaching.

Criteria for the selection of curriculum materials should be consistent with the purposes of teaching science and consistent with the structure of science.

1. The knowledge must be familiar to the scholar in the discipline and useful in advancing the learner's understanding of science. 2. The content should serve the future as well as the present; therefore the selection of content should focus on the conceptual aspects of knowledge. 3. Every field of science has a basis in experimental and investigative processes. To know science is to know its methods of inquiry. 4. There are connections between the sciences themselves and between the sciences and other subjects. The content for courses needs to be selected to take full advantage of these relationships and to provide wherever possible a logical integration of knowledge. Transdisciplinary skills, intra- and interdisciplinary understanding should rank high as instructional aims. 5. Only a small fraction of the basic knowledge of science can be selected for teaching in a K–12 program; consequently special attention should be given to including those concepts that are most likely to promote the welfare of mankind as well as the advancement of science. This must also include the knowledge that will enable individuals to participate in the intellectual and cultural life of a scientific age.

Organizing the Science Curriculum for Learning

Organization of the science curriculum demands a dominant cognitive pattern.

A science curriculum is a systematic organization of instructional materials designed to achieve the purposes of science teaching with maximum efficiency. The science curriculum developer begins his task by considering the nature of the knowledge he is to work with and what is involved in learning this field of knowledge. Because we are interested in how the pupil gains knowledge and understanding, the implication of cognitive processes for curriculum development must be considered. There are other aspects to curriculum planning, but these are the major considerations.

POINT OF VIEW

To assure that at every point there will be a readiness for more advanced learning, the curriculum continuum needs to be planned to provide for increasingly complex inquiry skills as well as for growth in the meaning of the conceptual schemes.

The patterning and integrating of information is essential for developing knowledge, suggesting that the logical schematization peculiar to the nature of science should be used in organizing the science curriculum. The materials chosen to form the curriculum should be organized in a manner that requires the learner continually to reorganize, synthesize, and use his knowledge.

A comprehensive curriculum should have unity resulting from a coherent structure and continuity. This suggests that learning should take place in a context which relates to previous knowledge and supplies a foundation for what is to come. The curriculum continuum needs to be planned to provide for increasingly complex inquiry skills as well as for growth in the meaning of significant concepts. This helps to assure that at every point there will be a readiness for more advanced learning. Good curriculum organization establishes its own continuity by making the next steps in learning seem reasonable.

Construction of a science curriculum should not be done in isolation from other parts of the school curriculum. In addition to modes of thought which can be useful in other subjects, there are transcurricular skills such as measuring, coding, observing, and inferring. These skills, rather than information, are the most fertile connections between subjects.

The organizational basis for designing a science curriculum is derived from the nature of science and from the intellectual development of the learner. Conceptual schemes and inquiry processes provide the integrative basis which serves to give both coherence and continuity to the curriculum. Within this framework it is then possible to select information that represents the current status of the discipline and will be most likely to move the learner toward the goals of science teaching.

The Teaching of Science

A newly conceived curriculum prescribes a style of teaching consistent with the goals of instruction and with the nature of the discipline.

The success of a new curriculum greatly depends upon how it will be taught. A curriculum reform is as much a matter of improving instruction as it is a re-evaluation of course content. A newly conceived curriculum prescribes a style of teaching consistent with the goals of instruction and the nature of the discipline.

POINT OF VIEW

To encourage independent learning in science, teaching practices should be related to the inquiry aspects of science, to its investigative strategies, and to the structure of scientific knowledge.

A theory of instruction that is particularly suited to the teaching of science is crucial to modern curriculum development. This theory needs to have a broad base and should include the following aspects of instruction: 1. *The nature of science*: its structure, its processes of inquiry and its conceptual schemes. 2. *The nature of the learner*: his motives, cognitive style, emotional background, and intellectual potential. 3. *The nature of the teacher*: his cognitive style, ability to communicate, control pattern, educational philosophy, and understanding of science. 4. *The nature of learning*: its processes, contexts, conditions, and purposes. 5. *The nature of the curriculum*: its organization, its sequence, and its substantive, attitudinal, and procedural dimensions. 6. *The nature of the social structure*: social and cultural forces with their demands and incentives.

Instruction links curriculum with teaching goals. While we have recognized instruction as the role of the teacher, we have not fully recognized it as a function of the student. What the pupil does, determines in some measures what the teacher does, for both pupil and teacher are influenced by the texture of the teaching and learning environment. There is also an interplay between instructional activities and the materials of instruction and both of these in turn are influenced by the discipline.

Laboratory Work in Science Teaching

Laboratory and field work are central to the teaching of science.

Learning from work in the laboratory and field is central to the teaching of science. It is here that the student relates concepts, theories, experiments, and observations as a means of exploring ideas. While technical skill and precision are important outcomes of the laboratory, it is the meaning they have for the interpretation of data that is more significant.

POINT OF VIEW

To achieve its greatest educational value, work in the laboratory must provide opportunities for the student to interpret observations and data.

The laboratory is a place to explore ideas, test theories, and raise questions. Here, meaning is given to observations and data. The data from an experiment remain inert facts until rational thinking makes something more of them. It is at this point that work in the laboratory has its greatest educational value.

Experiments, at whatever grade level, should have a dimension in the investigative aspects of science and provide a variety of experiences with scientific inquiry. Experiments solely for the purpose of gathering data, even though the data are carefully described and summarized, represent merely a preliminary step for understanding science. To collect experimental data is not enough. The student must learn to formulate statements against theory. The conclusion to an experiment is found in the interpretation of data, and it is this interpretation that generates new questions, stimulates further inquiry, helps to solve problems, and leads to the refinement of theories.

A few of the elements of scientific inquiry that need to be systematically introduced throughout science laboratory work are: 1. The variety, characteristics, and limitations of experimental designs. 2. The relationship between experimental options and the nature of the data obtained. 3. The relationships between observed data, experimental results, and the inferences based on the data and results. 4. The tools of measurement and their influence on experimental accuracy. 5. The use of data in generating hypotheses and defining questions and, conversely, the use of hypotheses to guide data collection. 6. The use of theories and models in interpreting data and in making predictions. 7. The analyzing, ordering, and displaying of data in precise and valid ways.

Laboratory work should be seen as a means of relating science concepts, inquiry processes, observation, and experimentation. The child's first experiences with science, even in the primary school, should involve aspects of experimental inquiry. He should learn how to observe with all of his senses, how to measure, classify, use numbers, communicate, and practice similar subdisciplinary skills. As he progresses through school he should have opportunities to use these knowledge skills to further his understanding of science concepts.

Laboratory experiences need to be planned in both horizontal and vertical sequences, thus providing for progressive learning within as well as across problems. A good laboratory program at any grade level is not a series of "one shot" activities. Some laboratory experiences form substructures for others. The proper sequencing of experiments makes it possible for the pupil to use earlier learning to attack increasingly complex problems.

There are other factors associated with making the best use of laboratory procedures in schools. These include communicating the results of experiments, pacing inquiry skills in science with those in mathematics, and providing for a wider use of mental experiments. We need to recognize that the value of an experiment lies more in the means it presents for exploring the unknown than in the verification of the known.

Concluding Remarks

It would be rash to suggest that a new curriculum in science has been developed, but it is clear that new viewpoints have emerged. The purpose of this section of "Theory Into Action" has been to present a logical plan for science teaching that is consistent with the structure of science and a modern view of science education.

Not all phases of science teaching have been discussed. There is need for more research and experimentation on some of the proposals. For others, the answers must emerge from one's own rational analysis of the problems. The need for a new approach to science teaching is no longer a matter for debate; it is the nature of the new curriculum that is not clear. The issues and viewpoints presented here are intended to focus discussion and provide a pivot for local action.

Scientific Enlightenment for an Age of Science*

PAUL DeH. HURD

Paul Hurd believes that our major educational problem is how to prepare young people to cope with an intellectual and cultural environment characterized by rapid change. As science becomes broadly integrated into all phases of our culture, its significance as a part of general education becomes more important. Thus, the broad goal of science teaching should be to foster the emergence of an enlightened citizenry, capable of using the intellectual resources of science to create a favorable environment that will promote the development of man as a humane being. Dr. Hurd lists twelve knowledges and attitudes that the scientifically enlightened should understand operationally.

We live in an era most accurately described by its scientific and technological progress. It is a period in history not like any we have known before. Today's condition in our culture is not the result of a simple transition from an agrarian society. The scientific and technological revolutions

*REPRINTED FROM The Science Teacher, Vol. 37, No. 1, January 1970, pp. 13–15. Copyright, 1970, by the National Science Teachers Association, Washington, D.C. Reprinted by permission of the author and the publisher. Dr. Hurd is Professor of Education Emeritus at Stanford University.

over the past quarter of a century more closely resemble a cultural mutation. However, the influence of science upon our economy, upon international politics, and upon other fields of inquiry is not obvious to most people. Furthermore, the educational demands for an age of science are without precedents; the gulf between today's and yesterday's world surpasses any that schools have previously had to deal with.

The major educational problem is how to prepare young people to cope with an intellectual and cultural environment characterized by rapid change. For centuries, the science curriculum has been designed with the idea in mind that tomorrow would not be much different from yesterday. Conventionally, young people have been educated for the present; this, in a modern, science-oriented society, is education for a world that never exists for the student. To educate for change is to focus on the future. Therefore, the teacher has to teach more than he knows and for times he has not yet experienced. For young people, this means knowing more than they have been taught. As we look to the future we can be certain only that the tempo of change will increase, because the scientific operation is aimed specifically at change. Herein lies our problem: The consequences of modern science have made myths of traditional educational goals in science and rendered obsolete large amounts of subject matter in our courses.

A serious credibility gap, greater than we have dared to admit, has developed between the school science curricula and the present character of our society. As science becomes broadly integrated into all phases of our culture, its significance as a part of general education becomes more important. However, a majority of adults are unaware of or are misinformed about the meaning of science and its influences on the material, social, and intellectual life of our time. As a result, they have little insight into the meaning of problems which plague mankind today—environmental pollution, poverty, disease, overpopulation, and the management of leisure. The scientist has confined his interests to exploring and interpreting the natural world, he has not had a primary interest in managing it for the common good. The science curriculum designer has also shied away from any direct consideration of the connections between science, technology, society, and the individual. This has undoubtedly contributed to the current antiscience feeling among students and the notion that science has spawned an unmanageable technology which seems to swamp human individuality.

As the role of science in man's affairs accelerates and as its potential for human betterment becomes more realizable, the subject matter of school science courses has been increasingly restricted to conveying a notion of the structure and research techniques of specific disciplines. The curriculum has not considered in any direct way the relation of science to the affairs of man, the actualities of life, and the human condition. The scientific enterprise as a part of general education has meaning only in a cultural and social context.

The broad goal of science teaching ought to foster the emergence of an enlightened citizenry, capable of using the intellectual resources of science to create a favorable environment that will promote the development of man as a humane being. To attain this goal will require, among other things, that the science curriculum be recast within a personal and societal context. The work of the laboratory could very well deal with significant problems of personal and community life. This does not mean, in any way, a neglect of the basic concepts, laws, theories, and methods of science, nor a violation of their meaning. It does mean choosing subject matter for science courses that transcends the classroom and has relevance for the individual and vitality for deeper insights into scientific-societal problems. The significance of a science concept for general education is more its meaning for problems of human living than its importance for basic research. It should be vital for the advancement of the individual rather than for the promotion of science. The curriculum we seek, then, is one which interprets the scientific enterprise within the broader perspectives of society.

The scientific-technological revolution has brought us intellectual and material wealth, but at the same time has complicated immensely the human environment. The resulting imbalances are evident everywhere. In part, this condition has resulted from the persistence of organized society to move in traditional ways and for schools to prepare young people for a yesteryear without regard for the great scientific achievement and social upheavals of the twentieth century and their possible consequences in the twenty-first. Although new science curricula have recently been developed, for the most part they have not provided the educational means to fit a modern society or an individual safely into the new habitat which science is producing for man. We are only beginning to identify the components of a scientific literacy and those of a humane literacy to provide a wholeness to the study of science in schools. This is the relevancy the younger generation so urgently seeks.

The phrase *scientific enlightenment* represents a point of view about the purposes for teaching science. Statements defining its meaning represent the goals for a general education in the sciences. These descriptions in turn provide criteria for selecting new subject matter and suggest its organization. Because the goals differ, a curriculum designed to foster scientific enlightenment is not a mirror image of a science discipline. The discipline-centered focus of current science curriculum reform is intended to update and validate the subject matter in the school sciences, a sorely needed effort. There is little consideration, however, of the growing impact of science and technology on individuals or on our social structure, although modern science has greatly increased man's command over nature and enlarged his understanding of himself. What is now needed is a curriculum designed to bring about an understanding of the scientific and technological enterprises and the ramifications of social integration of both. Science and technology have come close to providing us the world mankind has been seeking for thousands of years; however, we have not been successful in teaching man how to live successfully in this new world.

The age of science has generated a sizeable number of educational problems, critical because their seriousness is underestimated and their causes are misjudged. Some of these problems are: How can we develop ways to learn and manage larger amounts of new knowledge? How can we take advantage of the power of theoretical knowledge and, at the same time, provide information on the practical problems of the "real world"? How should we prepare young people for a life of radical change in which the pace and depth of change are accelerating?" How do we develop people who are attuned to change, and who have qualities of versatility and adaptability? Essentially, these problems involve educating for instability.

This will require curricula formed from basic principles originating from diverse fields of inquiry. Insofar as possible, it is desirable to select concepts which are not bound within the context of a single discipline; for example, such ideas as interaction, energy, evolution, and cyclic systems. Topics selected from these areas, along with corresponding analogies, should be those which relate to the concerns of students and the social encounters they are likely to have. We also need to include in the instructional materials a wide range of methodologies, logical processes, and inquiry procedures selected from both the natural and behavioral sciences. The educative function is one of preparing young people to learn and think on their own and to be motivated to do so. Furthermore, we need to consider in a more direct way than in the past the development, by students, of sustaining attitudes and values. These dimensions for the teaching of the sciences and the kind of learning they imply suggest a new and more unorthodox educational program than we now have. Traditional science courses in which the emphasis is upon a specific discipline and limited to the basic laws and theories which describe its structure, leave youth strangely unable to cope with either the demands or problems of a science-oriented society.

This leads us to suggest new purposes for science instruction which are more vital and relevant to the conditions which are determining our present and potential mode of living. With a focus upon the broader perspective of scientific enlightenment embedded in a social context, we have the potential of moving school science courses from their present isolation into the "real world" of the student. To be more specific, a scientifically enlightened person has an operational understanding of the following knowledges and attitudes:

- The scientifically enlightened person understands the purposes of the scientific endeavor to be the establishment of general laws and the conceptualization of knowledge about the natural envoironment. At the same time, he is aware that the laws of nature are man-bounded, and, therefore, that explanations represent the insights of the persons who make them.

- He recognizes that scientific knowledge grows, possibly without limit, where each new step depends upon and engulfs all that was known before. Knowledge in science is not simply an endless array of new facts and concepts; it has an organic quality, which allows concepts and theories to grow and change in meaning as they are nourished by new data and insights. Although new facts become intellectually useful as they are harbored in theory, their status remains forever tentative and their completeness doubtful.

- He knows in a functional way some of the major concepts, hypotheses, laws, and theories of several different sciences. He recognizes these forms of scientific knowledge as more intellectually powerful than the discrete observations of which they are composed. The essence of scientific knowledge is found in its conceptual framework, and understanding is derived from the ordering man is able to impose on facts and concepts.

- He appreciates the worthiness of systematic investigation in the sciences and the necessity of checking observations, laws, and theories experimentally. Data in science are sought in many different ways, but the idea of a specific "scientific method" is an illusion. There is no one method, no single logic, no uniform canon of validity which represents science as a whole. There is, however, more to science than common sense judgments; the basis for validation lies within experimental inquiry, and explanation is embodied in theories. There is a difference between scientific argument and the dialectic process, between science and nonscience.

- He recognizes the interdependency of inquiry processes and the derived concepts, laws, or theories. The results of a scientific endeavor are not fully understood outside the context of the investigative procedures giving rise to the findings—to know only the processes of science *or* the findings is only to half understand either.

- He appreciates science for the intellectual stimulus it provides, the intimacy with nature it gives, the beauty and simplicity of its explanations, the unknowns it identifies, and the excitement it generates from discovery.

- He sees the need to view the scientific enterprise within the broad perspectives of culture, society, and history. Advances in science challenge man to revise his social outlook and value assumptions as new knowledge and technology extend the range of what hc can do.

- He appreciates the cultural conditions within which science thrives. The setting of democracy in America has been particularly favorable to the growth of the sciences. The dependence of our society upon new knowledge is leading to the institutionalization of scientific research and making it a matter of public policy.

- He expects that social and economic innovations may be necessary to keep pace with and to enhance scientific and technological developments with regard to both solving contemporary social problems and making it possible to use research knowledge for improving the condition of man. Scientists and technologists must interact with an enlightened citizenry to create a favorable environment for the survival of each.

- He views science and technology as interrelated and dependent upon each other; however, he is also aware that they are not synonymous and that their goals are different. Modern societies depend upon innovative technology supported by scientific knowledge for their progress and, perhaps, survival. While, in the long run, it is likely to be science that will determine the future course of civilization, it is technology which more quickly disturbs the cultural, social, economic, political, and physical aspects of human existence.

- He appreciates the universality of scientific endeavors, their lack of national, cultural, or ethnic boundaries, and their potential for developing bonds of understanding between countries that can lead to worldwide cooperation in research. Science, by its nature and character, by its history, is international. The pursuit, production, and application of scientific knowledge has become a significant economic resource for countries throughout the world.

- He has some awareness of the need to generate a system of concepts within which science, society, and the humanities can fit.

Over the past two decades, it has become increasingly apparent that a new approach to science teaching is needed, due to radically changing conditions in science, society, and schools. The recent science curriculum reform movement has dealt with many aspects of these changes. New purposes, new content, and new procedures for science teaching have been devised. The educational rationale underlying these curriculum projects is essentially that of an apprentice's orientation to science—"being like a scientist." One does *not* find in the curricular reform evidence of any serious effort to place the scientific enterprise in a social or cultural setting or to consider it in the broad perspective of the humanities. The work of the laboratory is confined to the bench; significant and relevant problems within the community are not investigated. As a result, young people acquire the impression that science is divorced from modern life and has no meaning but for the professional scientist.

A general education in the sciences should make it possible for people to appreciate the worthiness of the scientific enterprise and to use its achievements for attacking contemporary problems, as well as for designing the future we seek. This means that the present science curriculum will need to be changed to provide a wider picture of science; it does *not* mean that the virtues, processes, and concepts of science will be taught with lesser meaning. It will require reordering the subject matter of science, placing it within a cultural context, and demonstrating more concern for human betterment. The implementation of this program should be phase two of the current curriculum reform.

NSTA Position Statement on School Science Education for the 70's*

NSTA COMMITTEE on CURRICULUM STUDIES: K-12

Since NSTA issued its first position paper on curriculum development in 1962, many changes have occurred. In view of these changes, and believing that curriculum development should be a continuing process, the NSTA Committee on Curriculum Studies: K–12 has re-examined the 1962 views on the science curriculum and produced this revised position statement. Members of the Committee included Glenn D. Berkheimer (Chairman), Patricia E. Blosser, Arthur A. Carin, Wilmer W. Cooksey, Paul B. Hounshell, Clyde E. Parrish, Victor M. Showalter, Lucy L. Smith, Richard J. Merrill, and Robert H. Carleton.

General Goals of Science Education

The major goal of science education is to develop scientifically literate and personally concerned individuals with a high competence for rational thought and action. This choice of goals is based on the belief that achieving scientific literacy involves the development of attitudes, process skills, and concepts, necessary to meet the more general goals of all education, such as:

- Learning how to learn, how to attack new problems, how to acquire new knowledge.
- Using rational processes.
- Building competence in basic skills.
- Developing intellectual and vocational competence.
- Exploring values in new experiences.
- Understanding concepts and generalizations.
- Learning to live harmoniously within the biosphere.

*REPRINTED FROM *The Science Teacher,* Vol. 38, No. 8, November 1971, pp. 46–51. Copyright, 1971, by the National Science Teachers Association, Washington, D.C. Reprinted by permission of the publisher.

Above all, the school must develop in the individual an ability to learn under his own initiative and an abiding interest in doing so. [1]

The goal of science education should be to develop scientifically literate citizens with the necessary intellectual resources, values, attitudes, and inquiry skills to promote the development of man as a rational human being.

THE SCIENTIFICALLY LITERATE PERSON

Many traits may be typical of a scientifically literate person. Each of these characteristics should be thought of as describing a continuum along which the individual may progress.

Likewise, the combined characteristics may be viewed as a larger continuum. Progress in an individual's science education should be equated with progress along this continuum.

The scientifically literate person

- Uses science concepts, process skills, and values in making everyday decisions as he interacts with other people and with his environment.
- Understands that the generation of scientific knowledge depends upon the inquiry process and upon conceptual theories.
- Distinguishes between scientific evidence and personal opinion.
- Identifies the relationship between facts and theory.
- Recognizes the limitations as well as the usefulness of science and technology in advancing human welfare.
- Understands the interrelationships between science, technology, and other facets of society, including social and economic development.
- Recognizes the human origin of science and understands that scientific knowledge is tentative, subject to change as evidence accumulates.
- Has sufficient knowledge and experience so that he can appreciate the scientific work being carried out by others.
- Has a richer and more exciting view of the world as a result of his science education.
- Has adopted values similar to those that underlie science so that he can use and enjoy science for its intellectual stimulation, its elegance of explanation, and its excitement of inquiry.
- Continues to inquire and increase his scientific knowledge throughout his life.

To promote scientific literacy, science curricula must contain a balanced consideration among conceptual schemes, science concepts, and science processes including rational thought processes, the social aspects of science and technology, and values deriving from science. Scientifically literate persons will use the achievements of science and technology for the benefit of mankind. These goals must be achievable, at least in part, during the immediate school experience.

Science, because it is a human undertaking, cannot be value-free. Emphases on values and on the social aspects of science and technology must be integral parts of any science curriculum.

The following values underlie science:

• Longing to know and understand.
• Questioning of all things.
• Search for data and their meaning.
• Demand for verification.
• Respect for logic.
• Consideration of premises.
• Consideration of consequences [2].

The major educational challenge of the next decade is to develop learning environments to prepare young people to cope with a society characterized by rapid change. To cope with and attempt to solve problems in a rapidly changing society, young people will need to develop science process skills and associated values to a greater extent than have similar groups in the past. All teachers, and especially science teachers, are challenged to educate young people to expect, to promote, and to direct societal change.

Awareness of the social aspects of science includes

• Perception of the cultural conditions within which science thrives.
• Recognition of the need to view the scientific enterprise within broad perspectives of culture, society, and history.
• Expectation that social and economic innovations may be necessary to improve man's condition.
• Appreciation of the universality of scientific endeavors [3].

Curriculum Development, Revision, and Implementation

Although the development of scientifically literate individuals is considered to be the central purpose of science education, a single or "best way" of pursuing this goal cannot be specified. The diverse nature of schools, students, and teachers necessitates a variety of programs and approaches.

To develop a scientifically literate citizenry, the NSTA Committee on Curriculum Studies: K–12 recommends that:

• Every individual have an opportunity for many science experiences, every year.
• Every science teacher be supplied with adequate science facilities, equipment, and supplies, and time to utilize these [4].

- Science be taught as a unified discipline, integrated and/or coordinated with other disciplines, such as mathematics, social science, economics, political science, and others.
- Increasing emphasis be placed on science processes, conceptual schemes, and values; and less emphasis on factual information.
- Direct experiences with the natural world or in the laboratory should comprise the major portion of the science program.
- Textbooks should facilitate inquiry, rather than being written to replace laboratory experiences. The use of recorded material (other media as well as printed material) should be integral parts of and dependent upon laboratory experiences.
- Science education programs include environmental education that inter-relates natural phenomena, environmental influences, science, technology, social implications of science and technology, and economic considerations.
- Opportunities for the professional growth of teachers be considered an integral part of science education programs so that teachers' own deeper insights can be brought to bear on the science programs designed for scientific literacy [5].

The achievement of scientific literacy should be the basis for setting objectives; for selecting content, learning experiences, and methodology; and for developing a system of evaluation.

The following groups of questions may be used in guiding the development or revision of a science curriculum and in assessing a science program designed to promote the development of scientific literacy. In posing these particular questions, the Association is taking the position that these questions emphasize important areas of concern for the development, revision, or implementation of curriculum.

Appropriateness of Objectives

To verify the appropriateness and validity of objectives, in their original selection and in periodic assessment later, questions such as the following should be asked:

- Is the objective consistent with the nature of science?
- Is the objective consistent with the nature of the learner?
- In what respects does the objective have relevance for students?
- Will what is proposed for learning contribute to a student's progress toward the achievement of scientific literacy?
- Have the proposed objectives been examined for authenticity and importance by scholars in science and in science education?
  for suitability as educational tasks by school personnel?

for desirability and potential usefulness by thoughtful lay citizens?
for potential interest by students?

Content, Learning Experiences, and Methodology

Selection of content, learning experiences, and methodology used in the science program should be made by the individual involved in each school system. The following questions are posed as guides to help school personnel develop science programs and/or modify available materials and programs to meet local needs.

- Does the program contribute to the development of a student's concept of himself as an adequate person?
- Does the program foster student liking for science in general and for independent investigation in particular?
- Is the total science program student-centered?
  sequential, K–12?
  structured to enable students to pursue topics of their choice in depth?
  structured to enable students to explore a great variety of topics?
- Is there a sound rationale for the organization of content and learning experiences?
  Does the organization provide for flexibility consistent with the nature of the students for whom it is intended?
  Is the organization consistent with the structure of science?
- Does the program foster student perceptions and relationships among the sciences and other school subjects, such as social studies and mathematics?
- Do the media chosen enable students to pursue science in various ways? (Media should not be chosen as ends in themselves.)
- Does the individual have an opportunity for investigative activities involving open inquiry?
  first-hand experience with physical and living things?
  a variety of settings (laboratory, field work, library, etc.)?
- Does the program provide opportunities for students to work both on an individual basis and as members of various-size groups?
- Does the program contain provisions for students to explore individual interests?
- Does the program *not* overwhelm the students with masses of knowledge?

Evaluation

The Association reaffirms its belief that evaluation should be closely tied to the stated objectives of a given curriculum. Objectives should be stated independently of the problem of evaluation, and methods should then be sought to test the attainment of these objectives. Where the evaluation of valid, clearly stated objectives turns out to be difficult, this should be interpreted as a weakness in our techniques of evaluation, not necessarily as a weakness in the objectives. This may be especially true in the affective domain, in the development of an individual's self-image, and in the determination of his values.

Questions such as the following are important when evaluation activities and instruments are being designed or selected.

Does the evaluation system

- Reflect the same relative emphasis among conceptual schemes, process skills, social aspects of science, and values as do the stated objectives?
- Contain an ongoing program of student self-evaluation based on criterion performances and providing feedback to the students?
- Go beyond paper-and-pencil tests so that a variety of means are used for collecting data about student achievement?
- Provide a basis for judging the effectiveness of instruction, in revising programs, and in improving feedback to the students?
- Include instruments and techniques that measure what they purport to measure?
- Acknowledge the concept of student and teacher progress along a continuum toward the goal of scientific literacy and provide a means for each to assess his position on the continuum?
- Does the evaluation system attempt to measure the higher thought processes and the affective domain, as well as recall, association, and other common areas?

Science education for the 70's, therefore, has as its goal a deepening and expanding concept of man in the universe, with a parallel development of attitudes and values that, together with similar literacy in other areas of experience, will determine the way individuals and communities of individuals make use of knowledge, perceive consequences of their actions, and balance freedom and responsibility within their own lives and in the structure of society.

The Role of NSTA in Curriculum Development

RECOMMENDED ACTION

The National Science Teachers Association considers the development of a science program for a school system to be the responsibility of the science personnel of that system. However, the Association also recognizes a responsibility to assist the practitioner of science education in translating the ideas contained in the NSTA Position Statement on School Science Education for the 70's into viable science programs. Therefore, the NSTA

Committee on Curriculum Studies: K–12 recommends that the Association involve itself in curriculum development and makes the following specific recommendations to the Association and its sections and affiliated groups for action in regard to curriculum development.

INTERPRETATION AND DISSEMINATION

The ideas set forth in the Position Statement must be translated into a form that has utility for curriculum specialists and for classroom teachers. Therefore, NSTA should undertake actions such as the following:

- A publication on science curriculum development that illustrates how broad goals can be translated into instructional programs.
- Development of curriculum modules, on a sample or pilot basis, that exemplify the approaches suggested above for content and process and that demonstrate techniques to *facilitate flexibility* and *individualization* in program organization.
- Inclusion of workshops on curriculum development and teaching style at meetings of the Association.
- Further identification of criteria for making curriculum decisions that are based on the goals previously described.
- Continuing review of curricula and curriculum development processes.
- Action as a clearinghouse, through its various journals, for ideas on science curriculum development, design, and production.

SUPPORTIVE ACTION

NSTA should catalyze and support the efforts of local, state, and national groups through activities, such as:

- Establishment of a consultant bureau of NSTA members especially knowledgeable in the area of science curriculum as a clearinghouse for requests for curriculum assistance.
- Assistance to groups that wish to experiment with differing patterns of organization, such as unified science, integrated science-humanities courses, problem-centered courses, and efforts to individualize instruction.
- Encouragement of programs and courses for teachers that implement the recommendations of this Position Statement.

DATA COLLECTION

NSTA should collect data concerning science instruction in our schools and colleges and disseminate this information. This might include:

- Research, done by the Association or by cooperating groups, to determine how various kinds of curricula function in differing educational environments.

- Publications and meetings to serve as forums for the discussion of all elements of curriculum development and implementation.
- Forums at national and regional meetings of the profession.
- Centers for curriculum materials and instructional demonstrations, at meetings of the Association.
- Articles in appropriate professional journals that reach all science teachers.

References

1. The statements are adapted from *Schools of the 60's*, a product of the NEA Project for Instruction. Although it was produced ten years ago it is still a valid, viable statement of goals.
2. The Educational Policies Commission. *Education and the Spirit of Science*. National Education Association, Washington, D.C. 1966.
3. Hurd, Paul DeHart. "Scientific Enlightenment for an Age of Science." *The Science Teacher* 37: 13-15; January 1970.
4. See also *Conditions for Good Science Teaching*. Recommendations of the Commission on Professional Standards and Practices of the National Science Teachers Association. The Association, Washington, D.C. 1970.
5. See also *Annual Self-Inventory for Science Teachers in Secondary Schools*. Commission on Professional Standards and Practices. National Science Teachers Association, Washington, D.C. 1970.

To Action in Science Education*

WILLARD J. JACOBSON

Willard Jacobson maintains that many of our young people are rejecting science because it is often blamed for many of society's ills. He suggests five actions we might take to improve science and science education in our schools: (1) enlarge our present narrow view of the nature of science, (2) deal with the educational dimensions when solving problems in science, (3) recognize the importance of how we teach science, (4) learn how to be more effective in the political area by recognizing who our allies are and joining forces with them, and (5) gain a perspective on the problems and issues of our times.

*REPRINTED FROM *The Science Teacher*, Vol. 38, No. 5, May 1971, pp. 24–26. Copyright, 1971, by the National Science Teachers Association, Washington, D.C. Reprinted by permission of the author and the publisher. Dr. Jacobson is Chairman of the Department of Science Education at Teachers College, Columbia University.

All is not well with science and science education. After years of uncritical trust, science and scientists are suspect and sometimes blamed for many of our society's ills. Many of our young people are rejecting science, and this bodes ill for the future. But, science and technology are essential in our society; we probably cannot survive without them. Therefore, it is important that we make a critical examination of the past, take a hard look at the present, and an imaginative view of the future. The following are some of the actions we might take to improve science and science education.

A broader view of science. We are paying a bitter price for our narrow view of the nature of science—to a certain extent we are paying the price of rejection by the public.[1]

Science is more than "what scientists do." It is more than white-coated researchers working in sterile laboratories or brilliant men and women pondering the mysteries of the universe. *Science is one of mankind's attempts to gain a better understanding and clearer interpretation of ourselves and the universe in which we exist.* Science is more than the quest of any individual; it is the struggle of mankind for better understanding. We wonder about the meaning of that remarkable rock brought back by Apollo 12 that is older than any rock found on earth and probably almost as old as the solar system. But, science is also the quest of those children who wonder how a tree could have grown so crooked or how come people have different colored skins. These are not adjuncts to science but integral parts of mankind's quest for better understanding.

In the future, it may be more useful to view science as being one of the ways we struggle for understanding. When we search, when we try to find out, and when we struggle to know we are engaged in science. Those of us who teach science have the privilege of participating with children and young people as they begin their quest.

Education is an integral part of science. Education is an integral part of most, if not all, sciences. Many of the problems with which we deal in the sciences have an educational dimension, and the problems cannot be resolved unless we deal with the educational dimension.

Consider the "population problem." Garrett Hardin[2] has suggested that we do know a great deal about human reproduction and that we have developed a technology, namely the contraceptive pill, that has ". . . an intrinsic failure rate of only 0.1 pregnancy per hundred woman-years of exposure to the risk of pregnancy." Obviously, there are only limited opportunities for improvement in these directions. In what directions can we work? Now, the problem is primarily an educational one.

To deal with the "population problem," young people throughout the world will have to gain a better understanding of the problem. They will have to understand it as it affects *Homo sapiens* and as it affects them as individuals. Certainly, young people will have to understand the process of human reproduction and how reproduction can be controlled. It would also be desirable to have them consider the possibilities and broader consequences of the choices that they make. All of these actions are within the realm of education, and with this problem, as well as with many others "This is where the action is."

If we are really concerned with problem solving in science, then education is an integral part of most sciences. In the science of ecology, the problems are not solved until actions are taken in our environment that are consistent with ecological principles. In nutrition, the tasks are not completed as long as millions of children are undernourished and millions of adults are malnourished, both, in part, because of ignorance. In the nuclear sciences, the tasks are not completed as long as the nuclear sword of Damocles hangs over our heads, and our communities have not learned how best to make use of this most important source of energy. In the future it will be more useful to think of education as being part of science rather than as a peripheral activity.

The importance of how we teach. How long is it going to take us to recognize the central importance of the teacher of science? The most important elements of science can be communicated only by a living, breathing model—the teacher of science. We want to stimulate the curiosity of children and nourish the desire to find out; what better way to do this than to have them study and work with a teacher who is curious and eager to find out? We want students to learn how to investigate and design experiments so that we can learn from our experiences; in the beginning, at least, this probably requires a teacher who can ask the critical questions, demonstrate alternatives, and help when the obstacles seem insurmountable. Certainly, science involves a willingness to consider questions and observations even though they may be inconvenient and upsetting; it is difficult to see how this attitude of open-mindedness can be communicated other than through a teacher model who demonstrates this approach to students.

Every teacher needs to develop a unique style. At the recent convention of the National Science Teachers Association we heard some of the best teachers in the nation describe how they teach. Some work in a very informal way with students as they work on their individual projects; others cooperate with teachers in other areas as they study the history, ecology, geology, and land use practices in an area. Some described how they make imaginative use of new technology; others take a highly personalized, idiosyncratic approach to teaching. All of these styles have much to commend them. It is a fortunate student who has an opportunity to come into contact with a rich variety of teaching styles.

In science, how we teach is of special importance because it is in the way we teach that we convey some of the most important dimensions of science. If this is so, then more opportunities should be provided for us to improve the ways we teach. If we ask ourselves, "What factors would most help me to become a better teacher?", some of us might want to try to understand and deal with such problems as the following:

1. "How can I, in my class, reach certain youngsters who seem almost unreachable?"
2. "How can I help deal with some of the intractable problems, such as drug use and sex education, that many communities insist must be dealt with in the schools?"
3. "How can I best teach those who have great difficulty in reading, communicating, and studying, and yet are very mature and whose basic concerns are those of adults?"

Summer institutes and inservice workshops that would help us to deal with such problems might be of greatest usefulness.

Political decision-making in science education. John Goodlad has suggested that the 70s will be a decade of political decision-making.[3] If this is so, then perhaps we had better learn how to be more effective in the political arena. Many of us believe that education is a society's most critical undertaking; while adaption leads to survival of a species, education may lead to survival and further development of a culture. As Goodlad has said, "To be true to one's calling is to argue for it in the marketplace."[4]

An important step is to recognize who our allies are and in many cases to join forces with them.

1. *The students.* Our students have the greatest stake in education and in the future. Some of them seem to be flaying out in many directions. While they sense that there is something wrong and are impatient to do something, they often seem not to know what to do or how to do it. We, on the other hand, too often bicker over the inconsequential and are so concerned over "doing the right thing" that we yield the field to others who are much surer of the rightness of their cause.

Why can't we work with our clientele—the students—for certainly they have the most to gain or lose. Long time members of the Council on Elementary Science International have often said, "Children are our best lobbyists for science. Give a child a taste of the excitement of science, and he usually wants more." Why shouldn't we give students a better peek at exciting science and good education? My guess is they will want more and insist that they get it.

Once in a while we see students and teachers working together in the marketplace of ideas and in the political arena. They are a very powerful force—so powerful that one almost hesitates to suggest it, but we shall probably have to marshall powerful forces in the support of education in the '70s.

2. *Parents.* While there is great criticism of the schools and the colleges are under fire, parents still want the best possible education for their children and often are willing to make great sacrifices to acquire it.

The parents' criticisms and frustrations are often due to a sensing that all is not right with the schools and the frustration caused by the apparent difficulty of doing anything about it. But, hopefully, working together we can build schools in which the children will not be forgotten. To do this, we need the ideas and support of the parents who want the best for their children.

3. *Colleges and universities.* Our colleges and universities can be powerful forces working for better education, but we have discovered what fragile institutions they are. While they undoubtedly can survive a long time if they retreat into a cocoon-like dormancy, we need them as centers for probing and action to move into a better world.

Some say that there is a lot of fat in the universities that needs to be excised, and this is undoubtedly true, but the trouble is that our society has not found a reliable muscle-fat test, and at many institutions it is the hardest working, who have gone unsung, teaching large classes or supervising student teachers, who are being excised. Can we afford to do this? Fortunately, there are some signs that both students and faculties are beginning to recognize the stake they have in the college or university.

These are among our allies. We probably have more to gain by working together than by bickering among each other.

Gaining a perspective on our problems. One of the great difficulties facing citizens in this and other nations is that of gaining a perspective on the problems and issues of our times. We are assaulted with a cacophony of stimuli, a superfluity of information, and are inundated by opinion. But what does it all mean? What ideas are of the greatest worth?

A recent cartoon showed emanations from a cocktail party wafting into a turgid cloud over the assembled multitude. "I hear Chicago is rapidly deteriorating!" "They say Lake Michigan has become a mass of garbage!" "Have you heard how awful the schools are?" "I have heard that all of the teachers are on LSD." Certainly, there are many things wrong and there is much that needs to be done, but, if we are to attain the perspective needed to deal effectively with our problems, we and our friends need to see other elements in our situation. Perhaps, we need to encourage critics to go see what is going on in the schools and to "see where they have only spoken before."

A visitor to the recent NSTA Convention would have heard descriptions of:

• A work with paraprofessionals which makes possible new approaches to teaching in the classroom and opens up possibilities for service for many who thought life was only a succession of frustrations.

- how the great scientific and educational institutions in a large city can be utilized to enrich and enliven the education of children.
- how elementary school children in a large urban school can study ecology within the big city.
- new approaches to science experiences for the visually handicapped.
- student film production as an approach to environmental studies.
- of field biology being taught as a part of a more comprehensive study of the history, culture, and geology of a region.

To gain a perspective on our problems we should also recognize the efforts of "those who are trying to do something." It may be that at least as much effort should be devoted to supporting those who are trying to do something about our problems as is expended on decrying the situation in which we exist.

It has been two minutes to midnight for 25 years.[5] We have lived with prophets of doom and purveyors of gloom. I suggest that we do, somewhat as we will in a few days, unilaterally declare a "universe saving time." It is no longer two minutes to midnight; it is two minutes to one. We have at least 23 hours and 2 minutes to savor our science, to cherish our work with children, and to work to save our world.

I would suggest that we go onto "universe saving time" so that when the bell strikes it tolls for thee and me, but it strikes not the hour of midnight—the end—but strikes the hour of one and heralds the dawning—the beginning of an era not the end.

References

1. Francis Finigan, "The Need for Change in the Teaching of Science." Paper delivered at the NSSA-AETS Annual Luncheon, Washington, D.C., March 26, 1971.
2. Garrett Hardin, "Education in an Overpopulated World." Paper delivered at the 19th Annual Convention of the National Science Teachers Association, Washington, D. C., March 28, 1971.
3. John I. Goodlad, "What Educational Decisions by Whom?" Paper delivered at the 19th Annual Convention of the National Science Teachers Association, Washington, D. C., March 27, 1971.
4. John I. Goodlad, Ibid.
5. This reference is to the clock depicted in Science and Public Affairs: Bulletin of Atomic Scientists which has often shown the time to be "two minutes to midnight."

Theories of Intellectual Development and Learning in Children

INTRODUCTION

An understanding of how children develop intellectually, and also how children learn, is essential to teaching science effectively in the classroom. For guidance in this aspect, science educators have turned to the research and theories of developmental psychologists. Improvements and innovations in elementary science education often follow new discoveries or theories in the field of child development.

The theories of three psychologists, Piaget, Bruner, and Gagné, have had a major impact on elementary science. The theories have broad implications for what should be taught in elementary science, how it should be taught, and also the sequence in which it should be taught. As a result, their theories have exerted an influence in the development of the new large-scale elementary science curriculum projects, the revision or development of local elementary science programs, the content and approach of elementary science textbook series, and the teaching strategies recommended in methods books on the teaching of elementary science.

Piaget has developed a theory of intellectual development in children. According to Piaget, children develop intellectually in a sequence of stages by age from infancy to post-adolescence. Each stage of learning is necessary for the development of the stages that follow. A child cannot skip a stage because each stage not only utilizes and integrates the preceding stage but paves the way for the one that follows. Although the sequence of stages is the same for all children, the rate at which particular children pass through these stages will depend upon both the children's heredity and their socioeconomic environment. There are four major stages in Piaget's theory: the sensori-motor, the preoperational, the concrete operations, and the formal operations stage.

According to Bruner, any subject can be taught effectively in some form to any child at any stage of development. When a child learns science concepts, he can only learn them within the framework of whichever of Piaget's stage of intellectual development the child is in at the time. When teaching science to children, it is essential that the child be helped to pass

49

progressively from one stage of intellectual development to the next. This can be done by providing challenging but usable opportunities and problems for the child which tempt him to forge ahead into the next stages of development. As a result, the child acquires a deeper understanding of science concepts and conceptual schemes.

Bruner states that, since a major objective of learning is to introduce the child at an early age to the ideas and styles that will make him a scientifically literate citizen, the science program should be built around the major conceptual schemes, skills, and values that society considers to be of vital importance. These conceptual schemes, skills, and values should be taught as early as possible in a manner that is consistent with the child's stages of development and forms of thought. Finally, Bruner recommends that the child in the elementary school be encouraged to learn through discovery.

Gagné is concerned with the successful teaching and learning of inquiry as a vital objective of science education. Giving the child practice in inquiry involves opportunities to carry out inductive thinking, to make hypotheses, and to test these hypotheses in a large variety of situations in the laboratory, in the classroom, and in individual study.

Gagné believes that, as the child progresses from kindergarten through college, the child should go through four levels of science instruction. The first level should be conducted in the elementary school. At this level the child should be given instruction in certain kinds of skills or competencies that will stay with him for the rest of his life. These would include number computation, spatial and manipulative skills, and the skills of observing, describing, classifying, measuring, inferring, and model conceptualizing. While developing these skills, the child will acquire some knowledge of scientific principles.

Piaget and Elementary Science*

EDWARD A. CHITTENDEN

Research in child development by psychologist Jean Piaget is reflected in current changes in elementary science curriculum designs and methods of science teaching. This article offers a capsulized discussion of Piaget's research as it relates directly to pupil learning in elementary science. It describes the major stages of intellectual development proposed by Piaget, and discusses their implications for science education. The author notes that the most important aspect of Piaget's work is his portrayal of how children go about learning.

There has been a substantial revival of interest in this country in the research and theory of Jean Piaget, the Swiss child psychologist. This interest probably stems to some extent from the general current concern with questions regarding cognition and the development of intellectual abilities. But it also must stem from a growing awareness that his work represents a major contribution to our understanding of the development of human thought. During 50 years of studies he and his co-workers in Geneva have observed and examined thousands of subjects, ranging in age from the newborn to the adolescent. Some 30 volumes and countless articles on the subject of infant and child thought have been published. As it stands today, Piaget's theory of intelligence is unique in its complexity and comprehensiveness.

Piaget's Methods

In his studies of children's thinking, Piaget has never been especially interested in depicting, in a normative way, the various responses that may occur at particular ages, and one finds few statistical descriptions of children's responses in his books. Instead he has attempted to discover the underlying structures which give rise to children's responses. When he poses, to a five-year-old child, the task of putting into serial order a set of ten graded sticks, he wants to find out how the child will go about handling the task. He is interested in the kinds of errors the child may

*REPRINTED FROM Science and Children, Vol. 8, No. 4, December 1970, pp. 9–15. Copyright, 1970, by the National Science Teachers Association, Washington, D.C. Reprinted by permission of the author and the publisher. Dr. Chittenden is Research Psychologist at the Educational Testing Service.

make and in the kinds of groupings he may attempt, rather than only the final result or the final arrangement made by the child. It is not surprising, then, that he dismisses the traditional intelligence tests as mere catalogues of behavior, useful for certain purposes, but not very enlightening if we want to know something about the nature of child thought. These points should be stressed because Piaget's early books (4, 5)* as well as his later books have sometimes been misinterpreted by people who were looking for normative description. In essence, his books offer theoretical analysis of thought processes, and the data, in the form of children's answers, serve primarily to illustrate and verify his theory.

Piaget's concern with theory can also be seen in his interviewing methods. He has described his method as a "clinical method" (5)—very similar to the procedures of psychiatric examination. The interview with the child must be flexible. The investigator, drawing upon theory, must be ready to vary the form of his questions and tasks depending upon the response of the subject. The good interviewer, says Piaget, must combine two seemingly incompatible qualities. On the one hand, "he must know how to observe, that is to say, to let the child talk freely, without ever checking or side-tracking his utterance." And, on the other hand, the interviewer "must constantly be alert for something definitive, at every moment he must have some working hypothesis, some theory, true or false, which he is seeking to check." (5) He notes the child's verbal reaction to the problem and the child's justification of his solution.

A final point to make about Piaget's methods concerns the distinction between typical and maximal performance. Cronbach (2) suggests that in the usual procedures for testing intelligence we are interested in obtaining evidence of maximal performance—we want to find out whether the child can or cannot handle a particular problem. In personality assessment, on the other hand, we are concerned with typical performance —whether the child does or does not behave in certain ways. The intent of Piaget's interviews seems much closer to personality assessment. The interest is in typical or natural behavior. To illustrate, I once observed a five-year-old boy was methodically breaking up his cracker into small pieces. I asked him why he was doing this and he answered, with hesitation, "there's more to eat." I quizzed him further, as adults do, trying to get him to admit that breaking the cracker really did not affect quantity. He put up a pretty good argument; "If it's broken up, it takes longer to eat." Finally, after further prodding, he did seem to admit that quantity really would remain unchanged. But in the course of this conversation it became obvious to me that my idea of quantity was not typical of him (at least in the setting of eating). Moreover, he seemed to find this adult concept of quantity to be somewhat puzzling and not terribly useful.

*See References.

Piaget admits that it is sometimes possible to push children to the point where they express an advanced idea, but such maximal responses tell us a lot less about the nature of thought than do the typical responses. It therefore seems misleading to interpret Piaget as saying that children can or cannot think in certain ways; a more accurate interpretation would be that Piaget tells us how children *typically do or do not think*.

Piaget's theory has been more concerned with understanding, rather than controlling behavior. Intelligence is viewed as a process of organization and adaptation. When a child encounters an object, he will attempt to organize the object into his present schema or structure. When schema are present, assimilation will occur. If the assimilation does not take place, the child is at disequilibrium until present schemas are altered or new ones developed. A group of schema that occur more or less at the same time make up a "stage" in Piaget's model of child development. The clinical methods used by Piaget could be utilized much more frequently in this country. In our research on children's thinking, some of us rely too much on data from rather rigid standardized interviews— others rely too much on the casual observation and anecdote. Piaget's method falls somewhere between and it could serve to correct the distortions inherent in these other approaches.

There are three major periods in Piaget's account of the development of thought. The sensori motor period, extending from birth to one-and-a-half or two years; secondly, the period in which concrete logical operations emerge, encompassing the years from two to eleven or twelve; and finally, the period of formal logical operations, from eleven or twelve into adolescence. The second period is divided into two major stages: the stage of preoperational thought, from two to around seven years, and the stage of concrete logical operations, from seven to eleven or twelve. (See also the chart to the right.)

Sensori-Motor

The sensori-motor period marks the development from reflexive behavior of the newborn to development of symbolic behavior at one-and-a-half years. At the beginning of this period, the world is undifferentiated from self; at the conclusion of the period, events and objects in the world have some identity of their own. For the young infant, objects seem to have no independent existence. The infant acts as though he "believed that an object is alternately made and unmade." (7) Thus, the six-months-old baby reaches for a bottle held in front of him, but if the bottle is then moved behind an arm of the adult, out of the visual field, the reaching activity ceases. Later in the first year, active search for vanished objects does begin, but with noticeable restrictions. If an object is hidden under a pillow, the ten-months-old baby may reach for and attain it. However, if next, before his eyes, the object is placed under a second pillow, the baby makes his initial search under the first pillow. Such behavior indicates that successive displacements of objects are still not easily handled. Later, around one year, such a problem is solved as long as the displacements of the object are perceptible. Finally, at one-and-a-half, the child can cope with unseen as well as seen displacements. By this time Piaget believes there is evidence of a mature object concept. The object now has its own existence, apart from the child, and its own movement through space.

Toward the end of the sensori-motor period, symbolic behavior appears. Nevertheless, even at its highest level, sensori-motor intelligence is not reflective. Sensori-motor intelligence, Piaget says, "acts like a slow-motion film, in which all the pictures are seen in succession but without fusion, and so without the continuous vision necessary for understanding the whole." Sensori-motor thought is "an intelligence in action and in no way reflective." (6)

Preoperational Thinking

The preoperational stage can be divided into two substages: that of preconceptual thought, from two to four years, and intuitive thought from four to around seven. In general, the characteristics of this stage are more exaggerated or pronounced in the earlier years. Of all the age groups, the intuitive stage has received the most extensive study by Piaget. John Flavell's excellent book on Piaget (3) summarizes some of this vast research.

One general characteristic of preoperational thought is egocentrism. In its more exaggerated form, egocentrism is seen in children's ideas about various natural phenomena. In examples given by Piaget (5) the child claims that the sun moves when he moves. ". . . when one walks, it follows. When one turns round it turns round too. Doesn't it ever follow you too?" the child asks the interviewer. The question of whether the sun really moves or only appears to move is not understood by the child and, according to Piaget, it does not occur to him to think of this question.

Another example of egocentrism comes from the experiments reported in the *Child's Conception of Space* (8). The subject is shown a display of model mountains. He is then shown photographs that represent these mountains from different viewpoints. The child is seated in one position and a doll in another and the child asked to indicate what the doll will see in various positions. The preoperational subject has great difficulty, on this task, in imagining the succession of perspectives viewed from positions other than his own.

Egocentric orientation is also revealed in children's conversations of this stage. Piaget describes (4) the results of a simple experiment in which one child explains something to another. The explaining child, says Piaget, gives one "the impression of talking to himself, without bothering about the other child. Very rarely did he succeed in placing himself at the latter's point of view." Piaget believes that children fail to communicate for egocentric reasons, "because they think that they do understand one another. The explainer believes from the start that the listener will grasp everything, will almost know beforehand all that should be known, and will interpret every subtlety." When the listener seems puzzled, the explainer may try to clarify simply by repeating what he has said; sometimes he repeats in louder tones as if addressing someone who is hard of hearing. This egocentric conviction that others know what you know is encouraged by the fact that adults in the child's world often do understand what the child is going to say.

Toward the end of the stage egocentrism in communication may not be as pronounced, but it is evident in another form in children's explanations. Recently, as part of a research project (1), we asked children some questions about flotation. Various objects were placed on a table (a small stone, toothpick, block of wood, etc.), A large container of water was set nearby and children were asked to select those objects they thought would float, and those that would sink. They were also asked to explain their predictions. The predictions of the younger kindergarten subjects and the older, second-grade subjects did not differ in accuracy. Instead, the differences between the kindergarten and older children came in their explanations of their predictions. The younger child would say, "the little stone will sink because it's little," and then, when asked about a big stone, would say, "It will sink because it's big." In other words, two contrasting attributes, big and little, are offered in explanation for the identical action of the objects. Similarly, a toothpick would float because "it's light" and the block of wood would float because "it's heavy." The younger subjects did not seem to be bothered by apparent contradictions. Older children often tried to avoid inconsistent explanations. The toothpick would float "because it's light," and the block of wood "because it's not very heavy." Sometimes the kindergarten children would offer a single explanation for contrasting actions of the objects, asserting that the toothpick would float, because it's light and the nail would sink because it's light. Older children tried to use weight and size terms in a more consistent way even though they could not formulate a weight-per-volume statement about density. This attempt of older children to be more systematic very likely led them to errors in prediction that the younger subjects did not make. Thus, there was a steady decline in accuracy of prediction for the block of wood. Younger children simply asserted that it would float because "it's wood" or because it was big, or heavy, or whatever. Older ones, following a more logical pattern, seemed to conclude wrongly that since it was big or heavy, it should sink.

The young child's reasoning is often more a logic of convenience than a logic of conviction. When asked why an object will float, any convenient

Intellectual Development Stages—Interpreted from Writings of Jean Piaget*

DEVELOPMENTAL STAGE	GENERAL AGE RANGE	CHARACTERISTICS OF STAGE PERTAINING TO PROBLEM-SOLVING ACTIVITIES; COMMENTS AND EXAMPLES
Sensori-motor	Birth to approximately 18 months	Stage is preverbal An object "exists" only when in the perceptual field of the child Hidden objects are located through random physical searching Practical basic knowledge is developed which forms the substructure of later representational knowledge
Preoperational or "representational"	18 months to 7–8 years	Stage marks the beginning of organized language and symbolic function, and, as a result, thought and representation develop The child is perceptually oriented, does not use logical thinking, and therefore cannot reason by implication The child is simple-goal directed; activity includes crude trial-and-error corrections The child lacks the ability to coordinate variables, has difficulty in realizing that an object has several properties, and is commonly satisfied with multiple and contradictory formulations Since the concept of conservation is not yet developed, the child lacks operational reversibility in thought and action
Concrete operations	7–8 years to 11–12 years	Thinking is concrete rather than abstract, but the child can now perform elementary logical operations and make elementary groupings of classes and relations (e.g., serial ordering) The concepts of conservation develop (first of number, then of substance, of length, of area, of weight and finally of volume) The concept of reversibility develops The child is unable to isolate variables, and proceeds from step to step in thinking without relating each link to all others
	11–12 years to 14–15 years	Stage of formal (abstract) thought marked by the appearance of hypothetical-deductive reasoning based upon the logic of all possible combinations; the develop-

Developmental Stage	General Age Range	Characteristics of Stage Pertaining to Problem-Solving Activities; Comments and Examples
Propositional or "formal operations"	14–15 years and onwards	ment of a combinatorial system and unification of operations into a structured whole The development of the ability to perform controlled experimentation, setting all factors "equal" but one variable (at 11–12 years to 14–15 years, the child's formal logic is superior to his experimental capacity). Individuals discover that a particular factor can be eliminated to analyze its role, or the roles of associated factors Reversal of direction between reality and possibility (variables are hypothesized before experimentation). Individuals discover that factors can be separated by neutralization as well as by exclusion The individual can use interpropositional operations, combining propositions by conjunction, disjunction, negation, and implication (all arise in the course of experimental implications).

*Dyrli, Odvard Egil. "Intellectual Development Stages," from *Developing Chilren's Thinking Through Science* by Anderson, DeVito, Dyrli, Kellogg, Kochendorfer, and Weigand. Prentice-Hall, Inc., Englewood Cliffs, New Jersey. 1970. p. 121. Reprinted with permission.

attribute is used; any handy characteristic, big, small, fat, light, etc., is referred to. It does not occur to the child of the preoperational stage to look for contradictions in his explanations. This is in line with Piaget's belief that the preoperational child does not examine his own thought processes nor does he feel it necessary to justify his thinking to others. He thinks, but he does not think about his thinking.

Another general characteristic of preoperational thought is the tendency for the child to "center" upon one prominent feature of an object or array of objects, excluding simultaneous consideration of other features. Piaget's conservation experiments can be used here for illustration. In one version the child is shown two identical balls of clay, and he agrees that they are equivalent in amount. In full view of the child, the experimenter then stretches one of the balls of clay into a sausage shape, and asks the child whether the sausage contains as much clay as the remaining ball. "Do they still have the same amount of clay?" Prior to the age of seven, Piaget reports that children are apt to answer "No, the sausage has more clay because it is longer," or, "It has less clay because it is thinner."

Either way, the preoperational child is "centering" attention on some particular feature to the neglect of others. He may focus on length and assert that there is more clay because the sausage is longer, or he may center on width and conclude there is less because the sausage is thinner. Unlike the older child, he does not "decenter," or "reverse," and consider the two attributes simultaneously.

Piaget reports that one often finds children moving toward decentration toward the end of the stage. Thus, in the clay experiment, they may at first center on length, but if the clay is stretched even further, they recenter on width, noting the obvious thinness, and conclude that the sausage contains less. Such successive recenterings sometimes lead the child into flagrant contradictions, but they herald the beginnings of logical operations in which coordination of attributes will replace alternating centrations.

The clay experiment shows that the preoperational child does not view quantity as a constant—a constant unaffected by changes in shape and appearance. In Piaget's terms, he does not "conserve" such quantities as mass, weight, or number. If a child counts 14 cubes in a row, and then the experimenter bunches the cubes together, the child may not be sure there are still 14. He may want to count them again. Changes in appearance influence his thinking about number; 14 cubes in a row look quite different from 14 cubes clustered together. Because of this general tendency to center on prominent features, the stage is sometimes described as a stage of perceptual thought.

Centering also takes the form of attending to the beginning or end states of an object rather than to the process of transformation. In the clay experiment, preoperational attention centers on resulting configurations of the clay rather than on the transformation from one state to another. In a different experiment, two model cars are placed in parallel starting positions. They are both moved forward, starting and stopping at the same time. However, one car has been moved faster than the other and its stopping point is further from the start position. The preoperational child, focusing on the unequal stopping positions, is quite certain that one car has taken longer than the other. Similarly, he finds it very difficult to reconstruct a possible series of positions through which a bar passes when it falls from a vertical to a horizontal state. In all these examples, the focus is on states and not upon transformation from one state to another.

Piaget has also emphasized that thinking of the preoperational stage is ". . . a kind of action carried out in thought." (7) Thought takes the form of imagined representations of concrete events. Reasoning takes the form of a "mental experiment," that is, "an internal imitation of actions and their results." Such thinking is laborious and prone to error and confusion. For example, in a problem involving transitive relations, if A is found shorter than B, and B shorter than C, the preoperational child does not necessarily conclude that A is shorter than C. One reason for the difficulty may be that in reconstructing these events, he must explicitly represent them in thought; A is imagined with B, B with C, etc. Unlike the case of the older child, the observations "shorter than" are not represented as general symbolic statements; rather, they may take the form of imagined replication.

Such thinking moves in one direction only and is irreversible, because the premises with which the child starts cannot remain unaltered through a reasoning sequence.

The child's unstable system of thought leads him into contradiction and conflict. Denied reversible systems, he is buffeted about by appearances of reality. Piaget states that preoperational thought "provides a map of reality, . . . but it is still imaginal, with many blank spaces and without sufficient coordinations to pass from one point to another." (7) Nevertheless, in Piaget's theory, it is this very state of disequilibrium which eventually leads to the resolution of the stage and to the reversible systems of concrete logical operations.

Concrete and Formal Logical Operations

With the emergence of concrete operations, at age seven or so, Piaget reports that a profound reorientation in thinking becomes evident. This is best illustrated in conservation. The seven- or eight-year-old is sure that amount of clay remains constant. He is surprised that you should even ask such a question. "Of course, they're the same," he says, "you've only changed the shape." Appearances are explicitly denied. On a seriation task, the approach is different from that of a younger child. In putting ten sticks into serial order, the method of the eight-year-old reflects a logical system and a recognition of order. The older child approaches many other problems in a new way; ". . . thought is no longer tied to particular states of the object, but (can) follow successive changes with all their possible detours and reversals; and (thought) no longer issues from a particular viewpoint of the subject, but co-ordinates all the different viewpoints in a system of objective reciprocities." (7) In short, concrete operations represent a much more flexible and comprehensive system.

It should be emphasized that although the transition from preoperational thinking to concrete operations is relatively rapid, this does not mean that the child goes to bed one night, an unsettled preoperational being, and wakes up the next morning with the world put into logical order. Instead, from seven on, operational thought appears in certain areas of experience and only gradually extends to other areas. The logic of the concrete stage is closely tied to the content of the problem. Unlike formal operations of adolescence, it does not constitute a hypothetical system in which the form of the logic can be independent of the particular content of the problem at hand. To illustrate, consider the riddle, "Which is heavier—a pound of feathers or a pound of lead?" In the concrete stage, reason may dictate that a pound is a pound, but it is still a stage in which feathers and lead can very easily interfere with reasoning. For that matter, neither the child nor the adult ever entirely abandons earlier ways of thinking. Rather, the earlier ways appear less frequently for problems where they would be inappropriate.

In the concrete operational stage, the child is able to observe, judge, and evaluate in less egocentric terms and formulate more objective explanations than in the preoperational stage, but even now he cannot verbally express hypotheses following a long series of related ideas, or if concrete referents are not available.

In the formal operational stage the child is emancipated from dependence on direct perception of objects as a mediator of thought. Mental experiences can be carried out as well as actual ones, and probability is well understood.

Implications for Education

There are interesting implications for educators in Piaget's work on preoperational thought, particularly for science educators. For example, consider an experiment conducted by Jan Smedslund (9). The subjects, five- to seven-year-old children, were given a pretest of conservation of weight. Two balls of clay were placed on a platform balance and their equivalence in weight demonstrated. The child was then asked if they would still weigh the same when one of the balls was changed (shaped into a sausage). This pretest identified two groups of subjects; one which conserved and one which did not. Next, training sessions were given to the non-conserving group. Constancy of weight was demonstrated in various ways. After training, these children readily asserted that weight would indeed remain constant. After an interval, a post-test was given to all subjects, those originally conserving and those trained to conserve. The post-test was exactly the same as the pre-test; two equivalent balls of clay were placed on the balance and subjects asked to predict what would happen when one of the balls was changed in some way. All subjects now believed that the pieces would continue to weigh the same. However, and this is the crux of the experiment, the interviewer cheated the subjects; he surreptitiously removed some clay from the changed piece so that when placed on the scale, the pieces actually did not balance. When asked to explain this unexpected event, all the trained subjects quickly reverted back to their original preoperational answers ("it's skinnier, so doesn't weigh as much," etc.), while the majority of the children who had acquired conservation on their own resisted this type of explanation. They generally remarked that something was "fishy," that some clay must have been removed, that something was wrong with the balance, etc.

The findings in this experiment illustrate Piaget's belief that formal instruction cannot accelerate acquisition of operational systems. One cannot speed up this process very much through a formal program of demonstrations.

More generally, if we consider the characteristics of preoperational thought, we might conclude that any instruction which attempts to prove some principle through appeals to logic or scientific experiments would be wasted on children of this stage. Piaget has remarked, for example, that children do not learn conservation of quantity through being shown that quantity is constant. In fact, in the Piagetian model this is a theoretical impossibility because if the child possessed the capacity to understand the implications of such a proof—of such a demonstration—then most likely he would already understand the principle. The conviction in conservation of older children is really a symptom of the development of logical structures and one cannot bring about these structures through teaching the symptom. On the other hand, it does appear that educational experiences for young children aimed at giving them the opportunity to observe and describe on the level of perception would be fruitful. The preoperational child's capacities for observation, for discriminating between fine and gross details, are comparable to abilities of older children. It is when we ask him to put these observations into some logical system that the purpose may escape him. When we ask him to attend, not to the perceived data, but to a system which relates the data, he is puzzled. The characteristics of egocentrism, centration, and unconcern with thought do not readily permit such a shift in cognitive orientation.

What then does account for cognitive growth? for the beginnings of logical operations at age seven? for later extensions of operations? In answering this question, Piaget has pointed to three realms of experience.

First, and possibly the least important, there is social experience. This is the experience of confronting the views and ideas of other children and adults. It serves as an important force in overcoming egocentrism by stimulating the child to consider and adapt to other viewpoints.

Secondly, there is physical experience. This consists of activities aimed at exploring the properties of objects. It is an "acting upon objects in order to find something from the objects themselves." (1) It includes explorations of their color, weight, form, movement in space.

Third, there is what Piaget calls "logico-mathematical experience." "In this case, while the actions are once again carried out on objects, knowledge is derived from the actions which transform the objects, and not from the objects themselves." (1) Thus, if a child counts three groups of two objects and two groups of three, obtaining the same sum, he is learning that sum and the order of counting are independent. He is learning something from the actions themselves, rather than from the particular objects involved in the actions. Activities of bringing together, taking apart, grouping, ordering, counting, are of this type.

No matter what type of experience, it is evident from Piaget's work that cognitive change, in any stage, depends on a long history of trans-action with the object world. The infant who demonstrates a persisting fascination with peek-a-boo games, who wants to repeat the game over and over, also demonstrates that the idea of the permanent object does not arise out of a few experiences with disappearing and reappearing objects. The Piagetian child is an active, exploring creature, not a passive receiver of external stimuli. But he is also thorough, and from the adult point of view, somewhat repetitious. Actions performed on objects and activities performed with objects are carried out on all fronts—piling up pots and pans in the kitchen, building with blocks, making colors, squeez-ing mud, comparing lengths. No one of these explorations, in itself, brings about marked changes in thought. Instead, eventually the actions performed in one setting combine with actions in others, leading to more general systems of ordering, comparing, etc.

Piaget has stated that in school, children should be "allowed a *maximum* of activity of their own, directed by means of materials which permit their activities to be cognitively useful. In the area of logico-mathematical structures, children have real understanding only of that which they invent themselves, and each time that we try to teach them something too quickly, we keep them from reinventing it themselves." (1) He points out that the time which seems to be wasted in children's personal ex-plorations is really gained in the construction of methods. The important aspect of the discovery or invention process lies in the actions involved, in the methods, and not in the end product of a concept or fact.

By way of conclusion, a cautionary observation should be made: The most valuable aspect of Piaget's work is not his delineation of the various stages and substages (provocative as it may be) but rather his portrayal of how children go about learning. There is a real danger in focusing only upon the stages for it too readily leads to attempts to cate-gorize children (*late preoperational* or *early concrete*) rather than to observe them for what they are really up to. This focus on stages also leads to unwarranted attempts to speed up the progression to the next stage and to view earlier stages as "bad" ways of thinking, processes that must be gotten over like the measles. Each stage should be viewed as legitimate in its own right, for the ways of learning of each stage make necessary contributions to capabilities at later ages.

References

1. Almy, M., Chittenden, E. A., and Miller, P. *Young Children's Thinking: Studies of Some Aspects of Piaget's Theory.* Teachers College Press, New York City. 1966.

2. Cronbach, L. J. *Essentials of Pyschological Testing.* Second Edition. Harper & Row, New York City. 1960.
3. Flavell, J. H. *The Developmental Psychology of Jean Piaget.* D. Van Nostrand, Princeton, New Jersey. 1963.
4. Piaget, J. *The Language and Thought of the Child.* Harcourt, Brace & Company, New York City. 1926.
5. Piaget, J. *The Child's Conception of the World.* Harcourt, Brace & Company, New York City. 1929.
6. Piaget, J. *The Psychology of Intelligence.* Routledge & Kegan Paul, Ltd., London, England. 1950.
7. Piaget, J. *The Construction of Reality in the Child.* Basic Books, New York City. 1954.
8. Piaget, J., and Inhelder, B. *The Child's Conception of Space.* Routledge & Kegan Paul, Ltd., London, England, 1956.
9. Smedslund, J. "The Acquisition of Conservation of Substance and Weight in Children, III: Extinction of Conservation of Weight Acquired 'Normally' and by Means of Empirical Controls on a Balance Scale." *Scandinavian Journal of Psychology* 2: 85-87. 1961.

Piaget and Science Education *

DAVID ELKIND

David Elkind discusses the implications of Piaget's work and theory for (1) the sequencing of science activities, (2) the methods of science instruction, and (3) the contents of science teaching in the elementary school. The author cautions the reader not to ignore the theories and contributions of other educational psychologists. He states that one should consider Piaget's work as adding to, but not supplanting, the insights of other workers in the field of child development.

The publication of Jean Jacques Rousseau's *Emile* in 1762 introduced a revolutionary idea into educational philosophy, namely, that sound pedagogy should be based upon a knowledge of child development. This idea has now become a fundamental principle of educational practice and pedagogical styles often follow new discoveries or theories in the field of child development. A case in point is the influence which Freudian psychology had upon progressive education in the 1920's, '30's, and '40's. While educational styles are probably dictated by many other sociocultural

*REPRINTED FROM *Science and Children*, Vol. 10, No. 3, November 1972, pp. 9–12. Copyright, 1972, by the National Science Teachers Association, Washington, D.C. Reprinted by permission of the author and the publisher. Dr. Elkind is professor of Psychology at the University of Rochester.

factors, such styles clearly owe a good deal to contemporary innovations in the psychology of the child.

It is in the context of this historical relationship between pedagogy and child development, that the current interest in the work of Jean Piaget must be seen and evaluated. No one doubts any longer that Piaget is to developmental psychology what Freud is to psychiatry, namely *the* giant in the field. Indeed, it will take decades for us to assimilate and apply the vast body of information he and his colleagues have gathered in close to fifty years of studying the development of children's thinking. And here lies the danger and the reason I began my remarks with an historical allusion. Piaget's work adds to but does not supplant the insights of other child development workers. In trying to adapt educational practice according to the contributions provided by Piaget, we must not forget the lessons that innovators such as Montessori, Dewey, and Freud had to teach. Our zeal to be modern should not blind us to all that is valuable from the past.

With these few historical and cautionary remarks out of the way we can turn to the issue at hand; namely, some implications of Piaget's work and theory for science education. As I said, it will take decades to digest all of Piaget's contribution, so that all I can do here is illustrate some of the new paths along which Piaget's work will take us. These new paths lead in the direction of: a) the sequencing of science activities, b) the methods of science instruction, and c) the contents of science teaching. Let us now take up each of these problems in turn with the reservation that I am suggesting directions only and that we have only begun to tap the wealth that lies in Piaget's books and articles.

Sequencing Science Activities

One of the dominant themes of Piaget's developmental psychology of intelligence is that the mind develops in a sequence of stages that is related to age. While the sequence remains the same for all children, the rate at which particular children pass through the stages will depend upon genetic endowment as well as socio-cultural circumstances. Piaget has described four major stages each of which, for heuristic purposes, can be described with regard to the major cognitive task it poses for the child.

The first, or sensori-motor stage, lasts from birth to about the age of two. During this period the infant's principal task is to construct a world of permanent objects so as to arrive at a conception of things which continue to exist even when they are not present to his senses. This stage might be described as dominated by a "search for conservation." At the next (preoperational) stage, usually ages 2 to 6 or 7, the child's major task is to master the symbolic or representational function. It is during this period that the child acquires language, discovers symbolic play, and experiences his first dreams. At this stage the child might be said to be involved in "a search for representation."

At about the age of 6 or 7, the child enters the concrete operational stage, which lasts until about the age of 11 or 12. During this period the young person has to master the interrelationship of classes, relations, and members, and he does this with respect to things and with the aid of syllogistic reasoning. The concrete operational stage is, therefore, one in which the young person is engaged in "a search for relations." During the last or final operational stage (usually ages 12 to 15) the young adolescent's major task is to conquer thought. Formal operational structures enable him to take his own thinking as an object and think about thought, about contrary fact conditions, and about ideal situations. In a word it makes possible theoretical and philosophical speculations and might be called the stage in which the young person is engaged in "a search for comprehension."

What have these stages to teach us about the sequencing of science activities for children? A great deal, it seems to me. First of all, these stages nicely parallel the stages that characterize the development of any science, namely: observation (sensori-motor period or the search for conservation); naming and labeling (preoperational period or the search for representation); formal classification and quantification (concrete operational period or the search for relations) and controlled experimentation and theory building (formal operational period or the search for comprehension). While it is not necessarily true that children will learn science best if it is taught on the model of the growth of thought and of science, it is at least a possibility worth exploring.

It seems to me that Piaget's work implies that science education ought to begin with teaching children the fine art of observation. Actually children are often far better at this than we are because our concepts blind us to concrete realities. Or repeated experience has for adults taken much of the interest and curiosity out of many of nature's mysteries. It is not enough, however, simply to have animals in the room, or to have children look at leaves and squirrels on nature walks. What children need to be taught is how to focus their observation, how to look for similarities and differences among natural elements, among leaves, animals, grasses, sounds, and smells. Instruction in observation cannot be hurried and a year or two of science teaching ought to be devoted to instruction in observation.

Thereafter children might proceed to collect specimens that they can sort, label, and classify. The nature of physical and biological classifications might well be described and discussed. My impression is that we often take the child's ability to classify for granted and do not spend enough time talking about the criteria of classification, multiple classification of a single specimen, and so on. Quantification can be introduced at the same time as children weigh, measure, and sort the specimens that they work with. In general the wider the range of materials children have to work with, the more interested they will be, and the more solid will be their grounding in the rudiments of science.

From the standpoint of mental development, instruction in controlled experimentation probably should generally not be introduced until adolescence when young people can deal with multiple simultaneous variations. By and large the concrete operations of children are not sufficient to grasp the intricacies of multiple variable experiments. Obviously this is not a hard and fast rule; bright children may be able to appreciate experimental procedures by the age of ten. For the average child, however, experimental science might well be delayed until adolescence when the young person's mental abilities are sufficiently mature to cope with holding some factors constant while others are systematically varied.

Perhaps it is unnecessary to stress to science teachers the importance of training children in observation and classification before they are introduced to experimentation. At the college level, however, I am impressed at how few students are trained to be good observers before they are trained to be good experimenters. Experimentation is a precision tool, but its effectiveness depends upon the skill, experience, and openness of the experimenter. If a youngster is so set on the experimental variables that he misses some of the novel and significant side effects of his experiment, then he is not a good experimenter in the best and most general sense of the term.

Methods of Science Instruction

I have probably stepped on some people's toes by now and I am probably about to step on some more. That is inevitable, I suppose, when one presumes to discuss subjects outside his own field of expertise. What I have to say about methods of science instruction may therefore sound quite naïve! My only defense is that sometimes naïveté can be refreshing and strike at a problem that the experts have been bypassing as too touchy and sensitive. Let me plunge in again.

What impresses me about American education, at all levels, is its extreme verbalism. Enter any classroom above the kindergarten level and most of what you see are books and more books. Our national preoccupation with reading, currently embodied in the Office of Education's right to read program, practically amounts to an obsession. So preoccupied are we with reading that any youngster who has a reading problem soon develops an emotional problem about it which ends up being far worse than the reading handicap itself.

Now while I do not wish to downplay the importance of language arts in grade school, I do want to say that I believe language has been given exaggerated importance in the elementary school curriculum. Young people who are successful in our schools are remarkably adept at the verbal level and become increasingly so as they move through high school and college. The problem is that their language facility is often divorced from reality and experience, and often amounts to empty verbalism. I would not be surprised if at least some of our problems with young people today derive from the discrepancy between their language sophistication and their experiential naïveté.

In this connection Piaget's work suggests that language and thought are different systems that develop at different rates. The linguistic system appears to be relatively complete by the age of seven or eight when all the major elements of generative grammar are present. Growth in language thereafter appears largely in vocabulary and proficiency in such skills as reading, writing, and spelling. Thought, on the other hand, is much more gradual in its development, as I described earlier, and the mental systems for thinking are not complete until the middle of adolescence when mental ability at last catches up with verbal facility.

From an educational standpoint it seems to me that these considerations support Dewey's contention that there should be more emphasis on doing and less on talking during the elementary school years, particularly in the teaching of science. I hope I don't offend anyone if I say that teachers, including college professors like myself, simply talk too much. If we spent less time talking and more time showing children how to observe, classify, measure, then young people would get more out of it. We also put too much reliance on books and published materials and too little faith on our own resources and in our own ingenuity. Science can be taught with such a wide variety of readily available materials that we really don't need prepackaged programs in order to teach science well. Science is first and foremost an attitude of curiosity and that is what the use of everyday materials promotes. Packaged materials lead children to believe that science always comes Christmas-wrapped.

Please understand, I am not pooh-poohing all prepackaged science programs. I am, for example, particularly impressed with the work of Robert Karplus at Berkeley* who is trying to get away from the empty verbalism that is present in so much of our teaching. Many of the Karplus programs are first rate. The problem with packaged programs, as I see it, is that they often make for rigidity and hamper the teacher's initiative. On the other hand, if teachers are given the freedom to use the materials in their own way, then packaged programs can be useful. They are even more useful if supplanted with everyday living materials.

Now I suppose I should say something about the so-called discovery method. To the extent that the discovery method suggests that children should be active in learning, then certainly one can endorse it. If it means that a child must discover by himself that which others have discovered

*The Science Curriculum Improvement Study.

for him, it may be a futile and unrewarding enterprise. The whole point of discoveries is that once they are made everyone can share in them without having to repeat the process of discovery. Life is too short for each child to rediscover all of science. Likewise, to argue that children should be active does not mean that they should be active *all the time*. Some science facts have to be learned by rote and without complete understanding. Learning things that we are not inclined to learn is an important part of education as it is an important part of life. Unfortunately, not everything we need to learn is especially interesting and children and teachers must accept that fact.

Educational Content

One of the domains in which Piaget's work is likely to have its greatest impact is in the domain of the content of science and mathematics teaching. This is true because Piaget's work often reveals a previously unknown and complex substructure to concepts that were previously taught simply or even taken completely for granted. To illustrate the implications of some of Piaget's findings for teaching particular concepts I have selected Piaget's work on number and upon identity. The work on identity should be of particular interest to those concerned with teaching in the biological sciences.

First, with respect to number, Piaget undertook his investigations in order to resolve a long-standing controversy between mathematicians and logicians. As you know, the mathematicians, following Peano, argued that mathematics was built upon several simple postulates which were relational in character. The whole number system could, in Peano's view, be derived from the notions of a number and its successor $(n + 1)$. Logicians, following Russell and Whitehead, argued that number was not derived from a relation but rather that it constituted a class, namely, the class of all classes. The number six, for example, is the class of all classes of things taken six at a time.

Piaget sought to resolve this controversy by determining how number concepts are arrived at by children. He undertook a series of novel investigations into children's ideas about number, classes, and relations. What he discovered was the child's understanding of classes, of relations, and of numbers all appear at the same time. Indeed, Piaget found that it was the child's ability to coordinate the idea of classes with the idea of relations that led to a true conception of number.

To make Piaget's discovery concrete let me describe two of the studies concerned with classification and with seriation. In the classification study, Piaget presented children (aged 4 to 7) with a box in which there were 20 white and 7 brown wooden beads. He asked the child whether there were more white than brown beads and then whether there were more white than wooden beads. It was not until the age of six or seven that most children could solve the latter problem and could recognize that there were more wooden beads because only some of the beads were white while all of the beads were wooden.

In the domain of relations, Piaget presented 4- to 7-year-old children with a set of size-graded sticks. The child's task was to arrange the set to form a sort of staircase with the shortest to the longest stick arranged in a regular order. Piaget found that many five-year-old children could construct such a series. When, however, he presented the children with a second set of sticks, intermediary in size to the first, and asked the children to insert this new set into the staircase formed with the other set, children of five years for the most part could not solve the problem. It was only at the age of 6-7 that children could place the second set correctly within the readymade series; i.e., place an element b' between A which was smaller and B which was bigger than b'.

In both the class and the relation studies, the crucial task for the child was the discovery that one and the same element could be in two classes or in two relations at once. In the class concept study the children had to discover that a particular bead could be both white *and* wooden at the same time. Likewise in the seriation task, the solution rested upon the child's discovery that a particular element could, at one and the same time, be both longer *and* shorter than the elements on either side of it. In both instances the child resolved the problems by moving to a new level of abstraction wherein one and the same element could be doubly represented without conflict.

In Piaget's view, this is just what is required to attain the adult or true conception of number. The true conception of number is founded upon the concept of a unit. Now the unit concept is one which presupposes that the unit is both like every other unit and different from every other unit in its order of enumeration. Every penny in a row of six is like every other as they are interchangeable. Their difference lies in the order in which they are counted or enumerated. In short, for the child, the concept of a unit or a number presupposes the same mental ability as that required to nest classes or to seriate relationships, namely, the ability to grasp that one and the same element can be represented in two different ways at the same time.

From an educational perspective this finding has important implications. It means that the understanding of number develops hand-in-hand with the understanding of classification and seriation. Accordingly, practice in classification and in seriation might play a more dominant role than heretofore in children's preparation for instruction in mathematics. This is already being done in some nursery schools and kindergartens but much more could be done if the materials for classification and seriation were available in greater quantity and in greater variety.

A second example of how Piaget's work might influence educational content comes from Piaget's work on identity. Actually, some of Piaget's earliest studies dealt with this issue, to which he has recently returned after some forty years of concern with other matters. In the original studies Piaget had children arrange a series of pictures (which resemble a set of frames from a comic strip) into the right order so that they would tell a story. Piaget found that young children had great difficulty with this task. One of the reasons was that they did not seem to recognize that it was the same character in each successive frame. The child's failure to understand the continuity of a sequence thus seemed to reflect his inability to detect the identity of the characters who participated in the sequence.

In more recent years Piaget has pursued this issue with materials related to growth and aging. He and his colleagues (notably Gilbert Voyat) presented children with photographs of a plant at various stages of growth. Although the children could recognize that adjacent photos were of the same plant they had trouble believing that the early photos in the series were of the same plant as that depicted in the last photos in the series. Again, the child's concept of growth was affected by his difficulty in grasping the notion of the plant's identity across transformations. Clearly this finding has implications for biology teaching and suggests that, as a bare minimum, we know whether or not children understand the identity of plants or organisms across various transformations before we proceed to more complex topics.

These are but two fairly simple examples of the significance of Piaget's research for the content science teaching. Many more could be easily cited. As in the case of sequencing and methods discussed earlier, these are merely examples of the treasures Piaget has uncovered for us. Much of the treasure remains to be mined.

Conclusion

In concluding this brief discussion of Piaget and science education, I want to reiterate the caution with which I began. The value of Piaget's work should not blind us to the value of the work of his predecessors. Too great an emphasis on cognitive development, stimulated by the heady richness of Piaget's work, will lead to an inevitable counter reaction that could prevent us from fully assimilating and benefiting from Piaget's work. In looking at children's minds through the new lenses Piaget has ground for us, we must not forget that children still have physical needs and are social beings. Lasting educational advances will be made only when our concern for the growth of the child's intellect is tempered with consideration for his body and concern for his sense of self-esteem.

Readiness for Learning*

JEROME S. BRUNER

The following article consists of key excerpts from Chapter III of Jerome S. Bruner's book The Process of Education. Dr. Bruner proposes his widely quoted hypothesis that "any subject can be taught effectively in some intellectually honest form to any child at any stage of development." To clarify the implications of this hypothesis, he examines three general ideas: (1) the process of intellectual development in children, (2) the act of learning, and (3) the notion of the "spiral curriculum." All three ideas have broad significance for curriculum development.

We begin with the hypothesis that any subject can be taught effectively in some intellectually honest form to any child at any stage of development. It is a bold hypothesis and an essential one in thinking about the nature of a curriculum. No evidence exists to contradict it; considerable evidence is being amassed that supports it.

To make clear what is implied, let us examine three general ideas. The first has to do with the process of intellectual development in children, the second with the act of learning, and the third with the notion of the "spiral curriculum" introduced earlier.

INTELLECTUAL DEVELOPMENT. Research on the intellectual development of the child highlights the fact that at each stage of development the child has a characteristic way of viewing the world and explaining it to himself. The task of teaching a subject to a child at any particular age is one of representing the structure of that subject in terms of the child's way of viewing things. The task can be thought of as one of translation. The general hypothesis that has just been stated is premised on the considered judgment that any idea can be represented honestly and usefully in the thought forms of children of school age, and that these first representations can later be made more powerful and precise the more easily by virtue of this early planning. To illustrate and support this view, we present here a somewhat detailed picture of the course of intellectual development, along with some suggestions about teaching at different stages of it.

*REPRINTED by permission of the publishers from Jerome Bruner, The Process of Education. Cambridge, Mass.: Harvard University Press. Copyright, 1960, by the President and Fellows of Harvard College. Dr. Bruner is Professor of Psychology and Director of the Center for Cognitive Studies at Harvard University, and at present is Watts Professor of Psychology at Oxford, England.

The work of Piaget and others suggests that, roughly speaking, one may distinguish three stages in the intellectual development of the child. The first stage need not concern us in detail, for it is characteristic principally of the pre-school child. In this stage, which ends (at least for Swiss school children) around the fifth or sixth year, the child's mental work consists principally in establishing relationships between experience and action; his concern is with manipulating the world through action. This stage corresponds roughly to the period from the first development of language to the point at which the child learns to manipulate symbols. In this so-called preoperational stage, the principal symbolic achievement is that the child learns how to represent the external world through symbols established by simple generalization; things are represented as equivalent in terms of sharing some common property. But the child's symbolic world does not make a clear separation between internal motives and feelings on the one hand and external reality on the other. The sun moves because God pushes it, and the stars, like himself, have to go to bed. The child is little able to separate his own goals from the means for achieving them, and when he has to make corrections in his activity after unsuccessful attempts at manipulating reality, he does so by what are called intuitive regulations rather than by symbolic operations, the former being of a crude trial-and-error nature rather than the result of taking thought.

What is principally lacking at this stage of development is what the Geneva school has called the concept of reversibility. When the shape of an object is changed, as when one changes the shape of a ball of plasticene, the preoperational child cannot grasp the idea that it can be brought back readily to its original state. Because of this fundamental lack the child cannot understand certain fundamental ideas that lie at the basis of mathematics and physics—the mathematical idea that one conserves quantity even when one partitions a set of things into subgroups, or the physical idea that one conserves mass and weight even though one transforms the shape of an object. It goes without saying that teachers are severely limited in transmitting concepts to a child at this stage, even in a highly intuitive manner.

The second stage of development—and now the child is in school—is called the stage of concrete operations. This stage is operational in contrast to the preceding stage, which is merely active. An operation is a type of action: it can be carried out rather directly by the manipulation of objects, or internally, as when one manipulates the symbols that represent things and relations in one's mind. Roughly, an operation is a means of getting data about the real world into the mind and there transforming them so that they can be organized and used selectively in the solution of problems. Assume a child is presented with a pinball machine which bounces a ball off a wall at an angle. Let us find out what he appreciates about the relation between the angle of incidence and the angle of reflection. The young child sees no problem: for him, the ball travels in an arc, touching the wall on the way. The somewhat older child, say age ten, sees the two angles as roughly related—as one changes so does the other. The still older child begins to grasp that there is a fixed relation between the two, and usually says it is a right angle. Finally, the thirteen- or fourteen-year-old, often by pointing the ejector directly at the wall and seeing the ball come back at the ejector, gets the idea that the two angles are equal. Each way of looking at the phenomenon represents the result of an operation in this sense, and the child's thinking is constrained by his way of pulling his observations together.

An operation differs from simple action or goal-directed behavior in that it is internalized and reversible. "Internalized" means that the child does not have to go about his problem-solving any longer by overt trial and error, but can actually carry out trial and error in his head. Reversibility is present because operations are seen as characterized where appropriate by what is called "complete compensation"; that is to say, an operation can be compensated for by an inverse operation. If marbles, for example, are divided into subgroups, the child can grasp intuitively that the original collection of marbles can be restored by being added back together again. The child tips a balance scale too far with a weight and then searches systematically for a lighter weight or for something with which to get the scale rebalanced. He may carry the reversibility too far by assuming that a piece of paper, once burned, can also be restored.

With the advent of concrete operations, the child develops an internalized structure with which to operate. In the example of the balance scale the structure is a serial order of weights that the child has in his mind. Such internal structures are of the essence. They are the internalized symbolic systems by which the child represents the world, as in the example of the pinball machine and the angles of incidence and reflection. It is into the language of these internal structures that one must translate ideas if the child is to grasp them.

But concrete operations, though they are guided by the logic of classes and the logic of relations, are means for structuring only immediately present reality. The child is able to give structure to the things he encounters, but he is not yet readily able to deal with possibilities not directly before him or not already experienced. This is not to say that children operating concretely are not able to anticipate things that are not present. Rather, it is that they do not command the operations for conjuring up systematically the full range of alternative possibilities that could exist at any given time. They cannot go systematically beyond the information given them to a description of what else might occur. Somewhere between ten and fourteen years of age the child passes into a third stage, which is called the stage of "formal operations" by the Geneva school.

Now the child's intellectual activity seems to be based upon an ability to operate on hypothetical propositions rather than being constrained to what he has experienced or what is before him. The child can now think of possible variables and even reduce potential relationships that can later be verified by experiment or observation. Intellectual operations now appear to be predicated upon the same kinds of logical operations that are the stock in trade of the logician, the scientist, or the abstract thinker. It is at this point that the child is able to give formal or axiomatic expression to the concrete ideas that before guided his problem-solving but could not be described or formally understood.

Earlier, while the child is in the stage of concrete operations, he is capable of grasping intuitively and concretely a great many of the basic ideas of mathematics, the sciences, the humanities, and the social sciences. But he can do so only in terms of concrete operations. It can be demonstrated that fifth-grade children can play mathematical games with rules modeled on highly advanced mathematics; indeed, they can arrive at these rules inductively, and learn how to work with them. They will flounder, however, if one attempts to force upon them a formal mathematical description of what they have been doing, though they are perfectly capable of guiding their behavior by these rules. At the Woods Hole Conference we were privileged to see a demonstration of teaching in which fifth-grade children very rapidly grasped central ideas from the theory of functions, although had the teacher attempted to explain to them what the theory of functions was, he would have drawn a blank. Later, at the appropriate stage of development and given a certain amount of practice in concrete operations, the time would be ripe for introducing them to the necessary formalism.

What is most important for teaching basic concepts is that the child be helped to pass progressively from concrete thinking to the utilization of more conceptually adequate modes of thought. But it is futile to attempt this by presenting formal explanations based on a logic that is distant from the child's manner of thinking and sterile in its implications for him. Much teaching in mathematics is of this sort. The child learns not to understand mathematical order but rather to apply certain devices or recipes without understanding their significance and connectedness. They are not translated into his way of thinking. Given this inappropriate start, he is easily led to believe that the important thing is for him to be "accurate"—though accuracy has less to do with mathematics than with computation. Perhaps the most striking example of this type of thing is to be found in the manner in which the high school student meets Euclidian geometry for the first time, as a set of axioms and theorems, without having had some experience with simple geometric configurations and the intuitive means whereby one deals with them. If the child were earlier given the concepts and strategies in the form of intuitive geometry at a level that he could easily follow, he might be far better able to grasp deeply the meaning of the theorems and axioms to which he is exposed later.

But the intellectual development of the child is no clockwork sequence of events; it also responds to influences from the environment, notably the school environment. Thus, instruction in scientific ideas, even at the elementary level, need not follow slavishly the natural course of cognitive development in the child. It can also lead intellectual development by providing challenging but usable opportunities for the child to forge ahead in his development. Experience has shown that it is worth the effort to provide the growing child with problems that tempt him into next stages of development. As David Page, one of the most experienced teachers of elementary mathematics, has commented: "In teaching from kindergarten to graduate school, I have been amazed at the intellectual similarity of human beings at all ages, although children are perhaps more spontaneous, creative, and energetic than adults. As far as I am concerned young children learn almost anything faster than adults do if it can be given to them in terms they understand. Giving the material to them in terms they understand, interestingly enough, turns out to involve knowing the mathematics oneself, and the better one knows it, the better it can be taught. It is appropriate that we warn ourselves to be careful of assigning an absolute level of difficulty to any particular topic. When I tell mathematicians that fourth-grade students can go a long way into 'set theory' a few of them reply: 'Of course.' Most of them are startled. The latter ones are completely wrong in assuming that 'set theory' is intrinsically difficult. Of course it may be that nothing is intrinsically difficult. We just have to wait until the proper point of view and corresponding language for presenting it are revealed. Given particular subject matter or a particular concept, it is easy to ask trivial questions, or to lead the child to ask trivial questions. It is also easy to ask impossibly difficult questions. The trick is to find the medium questions that can be answered and that take you somewhere. This is the big job of teachers and textbooks." One leads the child by the well-wrought "medium questions" to move more rapidly through the stages of intellectual development, to a deeper understanding of mathematical, physical, and historical principles. We must know far more about the ways in which this can be done.

THE ACT OF LEARNING. Learning a subject seems to involve three almost simultaneous processes. First there is *acquisition* of new information—often information that runs counter to or is a replacement for what the person has previously known implicitly or explicitly. At the very least it is a refinement of previous knowledge. Thus one teaches a student Newton's laws of motion, which violate the testimony of the senses. Or in teaching a student about wave mechanics, one violates the student's belief in mechanical impact as the sole source of real energy transfer. Or one bucks the language and its built-in way of thinking in terms of "wasting energy" by introducing the student to the conservation theorem in physics which asserts that no energy is lost. More often the situation is less drastic, as when one teaches the details of the circulatory system to a student who already knows vaguely or intuitively that blood circulates.

A second aspect of learning may be called *transformation*—the process of manipulating knowledge to make it fit new tasks. We learn to "unmask" or analyze information, to order it in a way that permits extrapolation of interpolation or conversion into another form. Transformation comprises the ways we deal with information in order to go beyond it.

A third aspect of learning is *evaluation*: checking whether the way we have manipulated information is adequate to the task. Is the generalization fitting, have we extrapolated appropriately, are we operating properly? Often a teacher is crucial in helping with evaluation, but much of it takes place by judgments of plausibility without our actually being able to check rigorously whether we are correct in our efforts.

In the learning of any subject matter, there is usually a series of episodes, each episode involving the three processes. Photosynthesis might reasonably comprise material for a learning episode in biology, fitted into a more comprehensive learning experience such as learning about the conversion of energy generally. At its best a learning episode reflects what has gone before it and permits one to generalize beyond it.

A learning episode can be brief or long, contain many ideas or a few. How sustained an episode a learner is willing to undergo depends upon what the person expects to get from his efforts, in the sense of such external things as grades but also in the sense of a gain in understanding.

We usually tailor material to the capacities and needs of students by manipulating learning episodes in several ways: by shortening or lengthening the episode, by piling on extrinsic rewards in the form of praise and gold stars, or by dramatizing the shock of recognition of what the material means when fully understood. The unit in a curriculum is meant to be a recognition of the importance of learning episodes, though many units drag on with no climax in understanding. There is a surprising lack of research on how one most wisely devises adequate learning episodes for children at different ages and in different subject matters.

THE "SPIRAL CURRICULUM." If one respects the ways of thought of the growing child, if one is courteous enough to translate material into his logical forms and challenging enough to tempt him to advance, then it is possible to introduce him at an early age to the ideas and styles that in later life make an educated man. We might ask, as a criterion for any subject taught in primary school, whether, when fully developed, it is worth an adult's knowing, and whether having known it as a child makes a person a better adult. If the answer to both questions is negative or ambiguous, then the material is cluttering the curriculum.

If the hypothesis with which this section was introduced is true—that any subject can be taught to any child in some honest form—then it should follow that a curriculum ought to be built around the great issues, principles, and values that a society deems worthy of the continual concern of its members.

If the understanding of number, measure, and probability is judged crucial in the pursuit of science, then instruction in these subjects should begin as intellectually honestly and as early as possible in a manner consistent with the child's forms of thought. Let the topics be developed and redeveloped in later grades. Thus, if most children are to take a tenth-grade unit in biology, need they approach the subject cold? Is it not possible, with a minimum of formal laboratory work if necessary, to introduce them to some of the major biological ideas earlier, in a spirit perhaps less exact and more intuitive?

Many curricula are originally planned with a guiding idea much like the one set forth here. But as curricula are actually executed, as they grow and change, they often lose their original form and suffer a relapse into a certain shapelessness. It is not amiss to urge that actual curricula be reexamined with an eye to the issues of continuity and development referred to in the preceding pages. One cannot predict the exact forms that revision might take; indeed, it is plain that there is now available too little research to provide adequate answers. One can only propose that appropriate research be undertaken with the greatest vigor and as soon as possible.

The Act of Discovery[*]

JEROME S. BRUNER

Jerome S. Bruner believes that it is only through the exercise of problem-solving and the effort of discovery that one learns the working heuristics of discovery; and the more one has practice, the more likely is one to generalize what one has learned into a style of inquiry that serves for any kind of task. Dr. Bruner discusses what the act of discovery entails. He also describes four major benefits derived by children when they learn how to investigate and discover for themselves: (1) an increase in intellectual potency, (2) a shift from extrinsic to intrinsic rewards, (3) learning the heuristics of discovery, and (4) aid in memory processing.

[*]REPRINTED FROM *Harvard Educational Review*, Vol. 31, No. 1, 1961, pp. 21–32, by permission of the author and the publisher. Dr. Bruner is Professor of Psychology and Director of the Center for Cognitive Studies at Harvard University, and at present is Watts Professor of Psychology at Oxford, England.

Maimonides, in his *Guide for the Perplexed*,[1] speaks of four forms of perfection that men might seek. The first and lowest form is perfection in the acquisition of wordly goods. The great philosopher dismisses such perfection on the ground that the possessions one acquires bear no meaningful relation to the possessor: "A great king may one morning find that there is no difference between him and the lowest person." A second perfection is of the body, its conformation and skills. Its failing is that it does not reflect on what is uniquely human about man: "he could (in any case) not be as strong as a mule." Moral perfection is the third, "the highest degree of excellency in man's character." Of this perfection Maimonides says: "Imagine a person being alone, and having no connection whatever with any other person; all his good moral principles are at rest, they are not required and give man no perfection whatever. These principles are only necessary and useful when man comes in contact with others." The fourth kind of perfection is "the true perfection of man; the possession of the highest intellectual faculties . . ." In justification of his assertion, this extraordinary Spanish-Judaic philosopher urges: "Examine the first three kinds of perfection; you will find that if you possess them, they are not your property, but the property of others. . . . But the last kind of perfection is exclusively yours; no one else owns any part of it."

It is a conjecture much like that of Maimonides that leads me to examine the act of discovery in man's intellectual life. For if man's intellectual excellence is the most his own among other perfections, it is also the case that the most uniquely personal of all that he knows is that which he has discovered for himself. What difference does it make, then, that we encourage discovery in the learning of the young? Does it, as Maimonides would say, create a special and unique relation between knowledge possessed and the possessor? And what may such a unique relation do for a man—or for a child, if you will, for our concern is with the education of the young?

The immediate occasion for my concern with discovery—and I do not restrict discovery to the act of finding out something that before was unknown to mankind, but rather include all forms of obtaining knowledge for oneself by the use of one's own mind— the immediate occasion is the work of the various new curriculum projects that have grown up in America during the last six or seven years. For whether one speaks to mathematicians or physicists or historians, one encounters repeatedly an expression of faith in the powerful effects that come from permitting the student to put things together for himself, to be his own discoverer.

First, let it be clear what the act of discovery entails. It is rarely, on the frontier of knowledge or elsewhere, that new facts are "discovered" in the sense of being encountered as Newton suggested in the form of islands of

[1] Maimonides, *Guide for the Perplexed* (New York: Dover Publications, 1956).

truth in an uncharted sea of ignorance. Or if they appear to be discovered in this way, it is almost always thanks to some happy hypotheses about where to navigate. Discovery, like surprise, favors the well prepared mind. In playing bridge, one is surprised by a hand with no honors in it at all and also by hands that are all in one suit. Yet all hands in bridge are equiprobable: one must know to be surprised. So, too, in discovery. The history of science is studded with examples of men "finding out" something and not knowing it. I shall operate on the assumption that discovery, whether by a schoolboy going it on his own or by a scientist cultivating the growing edge of his field, is in its essence a matter of rearranging or transforming evidence in such a way that one is enabled to go beyond the evidence so reassembled to additional new insights. It may well be that an additional fact or shred of evidence makes this larger transformation of evidence possible. But it is often not even dependent on new information.

It goes without saying that, left to himself, the child will go about discovering things for himself within limits. It also goes without saying that there are certain forms of child rearing, certain home atmospheres that lead some children to be their own discoverers more than other children. There are both topics of great interest, but I shall not be discussing them. Rather, I should like to confine myself to the consideration of discovery and "finding-out-for-oneself" within an educational setting—especially the school. Our aim as teachers is to give our student as firm a grasp of a subject as we can, and to make him as autonomous and self-propelled a thinker as we can—one who will go along on his own after formal schooling has ended. I shall return in the end to the question of the kind of classroom and the style of teaching that encourage an attitude of wanting to discover. For purposes of orienting the discussion, however, I would like to make an overly simplified distinction between teaching that takes place in the *expository mode* and teaching that utilizes the *hypothetical mode*. In the former, the decisions concerning the mode and pace and style of exposition are principally determined by the teacher as expositor; the student is the listener. If I can put the matter in terms of structural linguistics, the speaker has a quite different set of decisions to make than the listener: the former has a wide choice of alternatives for structuring, he is anticipating paragraph content while the listener is still intent on the words, he is manipulating the content of the material by various transformations while the listener is quite unaware of these internal manipulations. In the hypothetical mode, the teacher and the student are in a more cooperative position with respect to what in linguistics would be called "speaker's decisions." The student is not a bench-bound listener, but is taking a part in the formulation and at times may play the principal role in it. He will be aware of alternatives and may even have an "as if" attitude toward these, and as he receives information he may evaluate it as it comes. One cannot describe the process in either mode with great precision as to detail, but I think the foregoing may serve to illustrate what is meant.

Consider now what benefit might be derived from the experience of learning through discoveries that one makes for oneself. I should like to discuss these under four headings: (1) The increase in intellectual potency, (2) the shift from extrinsic to intrinsic rewards, (3) learning the heuristics of discovery, and (4) the aid to memory processing.

1. INTELLECTUAL POTENCY. If you will permit me, I would like to consider the difference between subjects in a highly constrained psychological experiment involving a two-choice apparatus. In order to win chips, they must depress a key either on the right or the left side of the machine. A pattern of payoff is designed such that, say, they will be paid off on the right side 70 per cent of the time, on the left 30 per cent, although this detail is not important. What is important is that the payoff sequence is arranged at random, and there is no pattern. I should like to contrast the behavior of subjects who think that there *is* some pattern to be found in the sequence—who think that regularities are discoverable—in contrast to subjects who think that things are happening quite by *chance*. The former group adopts what is called an "event-matching" strategy in which the number of responses given to each side is roughly equal to the proportion of times it pays off: in the present case R70:L30. The group that believes there is no pattern very soon reverts to a much more primitive strategy wherein *all* responses are allocated to the side that has the greater payoff. A little arithmetic will show you that the lazy all-and-none strategy pays off more if indeed the environment is random: namely, they win seventy per cent of the time. The event-matching subjects win about 70 per cent on the 70 per cent payoff side (or 49 per cent of the time there) and 30 per cent of the time on the side that pays off 30 per cent of the time (another 9 per cent for a total take-home wage of 58 per cent of the time (another 9 per cent for a total take-home is not always or not even frequently random, and if one analyzes carefully what the event-matchers are doing, it turns out that they are trying out hypotheses one after the other, all of them containing a term such that they distribute bets on the two sides with a frequency to match the actual occurrence of events. If it should turn out that there is a pattern to be discovered, their payoff would become 100 per cent. The other group would go on at the middling rate of 70 per cent.

What has this to do with the subject at hand? For the person to search out and find regularities and relationships in his environment, he must be armed with an expectancy that there will be something to find and, once aroused by expectancy, he must devise ways of search and finding. One of the chief enemies of such expectancy is the assumption that there is nothing one can find in the environment by way of regularity or relationship. In the experiment just cited, subjects often fall into a habitual attitude that there is either nothing to be found or that they can find a pattern by looking. There is an important sequel in behavior to the two attitudes, and to this I should like to turn now.

We have been conducting a series of experimental studies on a group of some seventy school children over the last four years. The studies have led us to distinguish an interesting dimension of cognitive activity that can be described as ranging from *episodic empiricism* at one end to *cumulative constructionism* at the other. The two attitudes in the choice experiments just cited are illustrative of the extremes of the dimension. I might mention some other illustrations. One of the experiments employs the game of Twenty Questions. A child—in this case he is between 10 and 12—is told that a car has gone off the road and hit a tree. He is to ask questions that can be answered by "yes" or "no" to discover the cause of the accident. After completing the problem, the same task is given him again, though he is told that the accident had a different cause this time. In all, the procedure is repeated four times. Children enjoy playing the game. They also differ quite markedly in the approach or strategy they bring to the task. There are various elements in the strategies employed. In the first place, one may distinguish clearly between two types of questions asked: the one is designed for locating constraints in the problem, constraints that will eventually give shape to an hypothesis; the other is the hypothesis as question. It is the difference between, "Was there anything wrong with the driver?" and "Was the driver rushing to the doctor's office for an appointment and the car got out of control?" There are children who precede hypotheses with efforts to locate constraint and there are those who, to use our local slang, are "pot-shotters," who string out hypotheses non-cumulatively one after the other. A second element of strategy is its connectivity of information gathering: the extent to which questions asked utilize or ignore or violate information previously obtained. The questions asked by children tend to be organized in cycles, each cycle of questions usually being given over to the pursuit of some particular notion. Both within cycles and between cycles one can discern a marked difference on the connectivity of the child's performance. Needless to say, children who employ constraint location as a technique preliminary to the formulation of hypotheses tend to be far more connected in their harvesting of information. Persistence is another feature of strategy, a characteristic compounded on what appear to be two components: a sheer doggedness component, and a persistence that stems from the sequential organization that a child brings to the task. Doggedness is probably just animal spirits or the need for achievement— what has come to be called *n-ach*. Organized persistence is a maneuver for protecting our fragile cognitive apparatus from overload. The child who has flooded himself with disorganized information from unconnected hypotheses will become discouraged and confused sooner than the child who has shown a certain cunning in his strategy of getting information—a cunning whose principal component is the recognition that the value of information is not simply in getting it but in being able to carry it. The persistence of the organized child stems from his knowledge of how to organize questions in cycles, how to summarize things to himself, and the like.

Episodic empiricism is illustrated by information gathering that is unbound by prior constraints, that lacks connectivity, and that is deficient in organizational persistence. The opposite extreme is illustrated by an approach that is characterized by constraint sensitivity, by connective maneuvers, and by organized persistence. Brute persistence seems to be one of those gifts from the gods that make people more exaggeratedly what they are.[2]

Before returning to the issue of discovery and its role in the development of thinking, let me say a word more about the ways in which information may get transformed when the problem solved has actively processed it. There is first of all a pragmatic question: what does it take to get information processed into a form best designed to fit some future use? Take an experiment by Zajonc[3] as a case in point. He gives groups of subjects information of a controlled kind, some groups being told that their task is to transmit the information to others, others that it is merely to be kept in mind. In general, he finds more differentiation and organization of the information received with the intention of being transmitted than there is for information received passively. An active set leads to a transformation related to a task to be performed. The risk, to be sure, is in possible overspecialization of information processing that may lead to such a high degree of specific organization that information is lost for general use.

I would urge now in the spirit of an hypothesis that emphasis upon discovery in learning has precisely the effect upon the learner of leading him to be a constructionist, to organize what he is encountering in a manner not only designed to discover regularity and relatedness, but also to avoid the kind of information drift that fails to keep account of the uses to which information might have to be put. It is, if you will, a necessary condition for learning the variety of techniques of problem solving, of transforming information for better use, indeed for learning how to go about the very task of learning. Practice in discovering for oneself teaches one to acquire information in a way that makes that information more readily viable in problem-solving. So goes the hypothesis. It is still in need of testing. But it is an hypothesis of such important human implications that we cannot afford not to test it—and testing will have to be in the schools.

---

[2] I should also remark in passing that the two extremes also characterize concept attainment strategies as reported in A Study of Thinking by J. S. Bruner et al. (New York: J. Wiley, 1956). Successive scanning illustrates well what is meant here by episodic empiricism; conservative focusing is an example of cumulative constructionism.

[3] R. B. Zajonc (Personal communication, 1957).

The Act of Discovery 83

2. Intrinsic and Extrinsic Motives. Much of the problem in leading a child to effective cognitive activity is to free him from the immediate control of environmental rewards and punishments. That is to say, learning that starts in response to the rewards of parental or teacher approval or the avoidance of failure can too readily develop a pattern in which the child is seeking cues as to how to conform to what is expected of him. We know from studies of children who tend to be early over-achievers in school that they are likely to be seekers after the "right way to do it" and that their capacity for transforming their learning into viable thought structures tends to be lower than children merely achieving at levels predicted by intelligence tests. Our tests on such children show them to be lower in analytic ability than those who are not conspicuous in overachievement.[4] As we shall see later, they develop rote abilities and depend upon being able to "give back" what is expected rather than to make it into something that relates to the rest of their cognitive life. As Maimonides would say, their learning is not their own.

The hypothesis that I would propose here is that to the degree that one is able to approach learning as a task of discovering something rather than "learning about" it, to that degree will there be a tendency for the child to carry out his learning activities with the autonomy of self-reward or more properly by reward that is discovery itself.

To those of you familiar with the battles of the last half-century in the field of motivation, the above hypothesis will be recognized as controversial. For the classic view of motivation in learning has been, until very recently, couched in terms of a theory of drives and reinforcement: that learning occurred by virtue of the fact that a response produced by a stimulus was followed by the reduction in a primary drive state. The doctrine is greatly extended by the idea of secondary reinforcement: any state associated even remotely with the reduction of a primary drive could also have the effect of producing learning. There has recently appeared a most searching and important criticism of this position, written by Professor Robert White,[5] reviewing the evidence of recently published animal studies, of work in the field of psychoanalysis, and of research on the development of cognitive processes in children. Professor White comes to the conclusion, quite rightly I think, that the drive-reduction model of learning runs counter to too many important phenomena of learning and development to be either regarded as general in its applicability or even correct in its general approach. Let me summarize some of his principal conclusions and explore their applicability to the hypothesis stated above.

I now propose that we gather the various kinds of behavior just mentioned, all of which have to do with effective interaction with the environment, under

---

[4] J. S. Bruner and A. J. Caron, "Cognition, Anxiety, and Achievement in the Pre-adolescent," *Journal of Educational Psychology* (in press).

[5] R. W. White, "Motivation Reconsidered: The Concept of Competence," *Psychological Review*, LXVI (1959), pp. 297–333.

the general heading of competence. According to Webster, competence means fitness or ability, and the suggested synonyms include capability, capacity efficiency, proficiency, and skill. It is, therefore, a suitable word to describe such things as grasping and exploring, crawling and walking, attention and perception, language and thinking, manipulating and changing the surroundings, all of which promote an effective—a competent—interaction with the environment. It is true, of course, that maturation plays a part in all these developments, but this part is heavily overshadowed by learning in all the more complex accomplishments like speech or skilled manipulation. I shall argue that it is necessary to make competence a motivational concept; there is *competence motivation* as well as competence in its more familiar sense of achieved capacity. The behavior that leads to the building up of effective grasping, handling, and letting go of objects, to take one example, is not random behavior that is produced by an overflow of energy. It is directed, selective, and persistent, and it continues not because it serves primary drives, which indeed it cannot serve until it is almost perfected, but because it satisfies an intrinsic need to deal with the environment.[6]

I am suggesting that there are forms of activity that serve to enlist and develop the competence motive, that serve to make it the driving force behind behavior. I should like to add to White's general premise that the *exercise* of competence motives has the effect of strengthening the degree to which they gain control over behavior and thereby reduce the effects of extrinsic rewards or drive gratification.

The brilliant Russian psychologist Vigotsky[7] characterizes the growth of thought processes as starting with a dialogue of speech and gesture between child and parent; autonomous thinking begins at the stage when the child is first able to internalize these conversations and "run them off" himself. This is a typical sequence in the development of competence. So, too, in instruction. The narrative of teaching is of the order of the conversation. The next move in the development of competence is the internalization of the narrative and its "rules of generation" so that the child is now capable of running off the narrative on his own. The hypothetical mode in teaching by encouraging the child to participate in "speaker's decisions" speeds this process along. Once internalization has occurred, the child is in a vastly improved position from several obvious points of view—notably that he is able to go beyond the information he has been given to generate additional ideas that can either be checked immediately from experience or can, at least, be used as a basis for formulating reasonable hypotheses. But over and beyond that, the child is now in a position to experience success and failure not as reward and punishment, but as information. For when the task is his own rather than a matter of matching environmental demands, he becomes his own paymaster in a certain measure. Seeking to gain control over his

[6] *Ibid.*, pp. 317–318.
[7] L. S. Vigotsky, *Thinking and Speech* (Moscow, 1934).

environment, he can now treat success as indicating that he is on the right track, failure as indicating he is on the wrong one.

In the end, this development has the effect of freeing learning from immediate stimulus control. When learning in the short run leads only to pellets of this or that rather than to mastery in the long run, then behavior can be readily "shaped" by extrinsic rewards. When behavior becomes more long-range and competence-oriented, it comes under the control of more complex cognitive structures, plans and the like, and operates more from the inside out. It is interesting that even Pavlov—whose early account of the learning process was based entirely on a notion of stimulus control of behavior through the conditioning mechanism in which, through contiguity, a new conditioned stimulus was substituted for an old unconditioned stimulus by the mechanism of stimulus substitution—that even Pavlov recognized his account as insufficient to deal with higher forms of learning. To supplement the account, he introduced the idea of the "second signalling system," with central importance placed on symbolic systems such as language in mediating and giving shape to mental life. Or as Luria[8] has put it, "the first signal system [is] concerned with directly perceived stimuli, the second with systems of verbal elaboration." Luria commenting on the importance of the transition from first to second signal system says: "It would be mistaken to suppose that verbal intercourse with adults merely changes the contents of the child's conscious activity without changing its form. ... The word has a basic function not only because it indicates a corresponding object in the external world, but also because it abstracts, isolates the necessary signal, generalizes perceived signals and relates them to certain categories; it is this systematization of direct experience that makes the role of the word in the formation of mental processes so exceptionally important." [9,10]

It is interesting that the final rejection of the universality of the doctrine of reinforcement in direct conditioning came from some of Pavlov's own students. Ivanov-Smolensky[11] and Krasnogorsky[12] published papers showing the manner in which symbolized linguistic messages could take over the place of the unconditioned stimulus and of the unconditioned response (gratification of hunger) in children. In all instances, they speak of these as *replacements* of lower, first-system mental or neural processes by higher order or second-system controls. A strange irony, then, that

[8] A. L. Luria, "The Directive Function of Speech in Development and Dissolution," *Word*, XV (1959), pp. 341–464.

[9] *Ibid.*, p. 12.

[10] For an elaboration of the view expressed by Luria, the reader is referred to the forthcoming translation of L. S. Vigotsky's 1934 book being published by John Wiley and Sons and the Technology Press.

[11] A. G. Ivanov-Smolensky, "Concerning the Study of the Joint Activity of the First and Second Signal Systems," *Journal of Higher Nervous Activity*, 1, (1951), p. 1.

[12] N. D. Krasnogorsky, *Studies of Higher Nervous Activity in Animals and in Man*, Vol. 1 (Moscow, 1954).

Russian psychology that gave us the notion of the conditioned response and the assumption that higher order activities are built up out of colligations or structurings of such primitive units, rejected this notion while much of American learning psychology has stayed until quite recently within the early Pavlovian fold (see, for example, a recent article by Spence[13] in the *Harvard Educational Review*, or Skinner's treatment of language[14] and the attacks that have been made upon it by linguists such as Chomsky[15] who has become concerned with the relation of language and cognitive activity). What is the more interesting is that Russian pedagogical theory has become deeply influenced by this new trend and is now placing much stress upon the importance of building up a more active symbolical approach to problem-solving among children.

To sum up the matter of the control of learning, then, I am proposing that the degree to which competence or mastery motives comes to control behavior, to that degree the role of reinforcement or "extrinsic pleasure" wanes in shaping behavior. The child comes to manipulate his environment more actively and achieves his gratification from coping with problems. Symbolic modes of representing and transforming the environment arise and the importance of stimulus-response-reward sequences declines. To use the metaphor that David Riesman developed in a quite different context, mental life moves from a state of outer-directedness in which the fortuity of stimuli and reinforcement are crucial to a state of inner-directedness in which the growth and maintenance of mastery become central and dominant.

3. LEARNING THE HEURISTICS OF DISCOVERY. Lincoln Steffens,[16] reflecting in his *Autobiography* on his undergraduate education at Berkeley, comments that his schooling was overly specialized on learning about the known and that too little attention was given to the task of finding out about what was not known. But how does one train a student in the techniques of discovery? Again I would like to offer some hypotheses. There are many ways of coming to the arts of inquiry. One of them is by careful study of its formalization in logic, statistics, mathematics, and the like. If a person is going to pursue inquiry as a way of life, particularly in the sciences, certainly such study is essential. Yet, whoever has taught kindergarten and the early primary grades or has had graduate students working with him on their theses—I choose the two extremes for they are both periods of intense inquiry—knows that an understanding of the formal aspect of inquiry is not sufficient. There appear to be, rather, a series of activities and attitudes, some directly related to a particular

---

[13] K. W. Spence, "The Relation of Learning Theory to the Technique of Education," *Harvard Educational Review,* XXIX (1959), pp. 84–95.

[14] B. F. Skinner, *Verbal Behavior* (New York: Appleton-Century-Crofts, 1957).

[15] N. Chomsky, *Syntactic Structure* (The Hague, The Netherlands: Mouton & Co., 1957).

[16] L. Steffens, *Autobiography of Lincoln Steffens* (New York: Harcourt Brace, 1931).

subject and some of them fairly generalized, that go with inquiry and research. These have to do with the *process* of trying to find out something, and while they provide no guarantee that the *product* will be any *great* discovery, their absence is likely to lead to awkwardness or aridity or confusion. How difficult it is to describe these matters—the heuristics of inquiry. There is one set of attitudes or ways of doing that has to do with sensing the relevance of variables—how to avoid getting stuck with edge effects and getting instead to the big sources of variance. Partly this gift comes from intuitive familiarity with a range of phenomena, sheer "knowing the stuff." But it also comes out of a sense of what things among an ensemble of things "smell right" in the sense of being of the right order of magnitude or scope or severity.

The English philosopher, Weldon, describes problem-solving in an interesting and picturesque way. He distinguishes between difficulties, puzzles, and problems. We solve a problem or make a discovery when we impose a puzzle form on to a difficulty that converts it into a problem that can be solved in such a way that it gets us where we want to be. That is to say, we recast the difficulty into a form that we know how to work with, then work it. Much of what we speak of as discovery consists of knowing how to impose what kind of form on various kinds of difficulties. A small part but a crucial part of discovery of the highest order is to invent and develop models of "puzzle forms" that can be imposed on difficulties with good effect. It is in this area that the truly powerful mind shines. But it is interesting to what degree perfectly ordinary people can, given the benefit of instruction, construct quite interesting and what, a century ago, would have been considered greatly original models.

Now to the hypothesis. It is my hunch that it is only through the exercise of problem-solving and the effort of discovery that one learns the working heuristics of discovery, and the more one has practice, the more likely is one to generalize what one has learned into a style of problem solving or inquiry that serves for any kind of task one may encounter—or almost any kind of task. I think the matter is self-evident, but what is unclear is what kinds of training and teaching produce the best effects. How do we teach a child to, say, cut his losses but at the same time be persistent in trying out an idea; to risk forming an early hunch without at the same time formulating the one *so* early and with so little evidence as to be stuck with it waiting for appropriate evidence to materialize; to pose good testable guesses that are neither too brittle nor too sinuously incorrigible. Practice in inquiry, in trying to figure out things for oneself, is indeed what is needed, but in what form? Of only one thing I am convinced. I have never seen anybody improve in the art and technique of inquiry by any means other than engaging in inquiry.

4. CONSERVATION OF MEMORY. I should like to take what some psychologists might consider a rather drastic view of the memory process.

It is a view that in large measure derives from the work of my colleague, Professor George Miller.[17] Its first premise is that the principal problem of human memory is not storage, but retrieval. In spite of the biological unlikeliness of it, we seem to be able to store a huge quantity of information—perhaps not a full tape recording, though at times it seems we even do that, but a great sufficiency of impressions. We may infer this from the fact that recognition (i.e., recall with the aid of maximum prompts) is so extraordinarily good in human beings—particularly in comparison with spontaneous recall where, so to speak, we must get out stored information without external aids or prompts. The key to retrieval is organization or, in even simpler terms, knowing where to find information and how to get there.

Let me illustrate the point with a simple experiment. We present pairs of words to twelve-year-old children. One group is simply told to remember the pairs, that they will be asked to repeat them later. Another is told to remember them by producing a word or idea that will tie the pair together in a way that will make sense to them. A third group is given the mediators used by the second group when presented with the pairs to aid them in tying the pairs into working units. The word pairs include such juxtapositions as "chair-forest," "sidewalk-square," and the like. One can distinguish three styles of mediators and children can be scaled in terms of their relative preference for each: *generic mediation* in which a pair is tied together by a superordinate idea: "chair and forest are both made of wood"; *thematic mediation* in which the two terms are imbedded in a theme or little story: "the lost child sat on a chair in the middle of the forest"; and *part-whole mediation* where "chairs are made from trees in the forest" is typical. Now, the chief result, as you would all predict, is that children who provide their own mediators do best—indeed, one time through a set of thirty pairs, they recover up to 95 per cent of the second words when presented with the first ones of the pairs, whereas the uninstructed children reach a maximum of less than 50 per cent recovered. Interestingly enough, children do best in recovering materials tied together by the form of mediator they most often use.

One can cite a myriad of findings to indicate that any organization of information that reduces the aggregate complexity of material by imbedding it into a cognitive structure a person has constructed will make that material more accessible for retrieval. In short, we may say that the process of memory, looked at from the retrieval side, is also a process of problem-solving: how can material be "placed" in memory so that it can be got on demand?

We can take as a point of departure the example of the children who developed their own technique for relating the members of each word

[17] G. A. Miller, "The Magical Number Seven, Plus or Minus Two," *Psychological Review*, LXIII (1956), pp. 81–97.

pair. You will recall that they did better than the children who were given by exposition the mediators they had developed. Let me suggest that in general, material that is organized in terms of a person's own interests and cognitive structures is material that has the best chance of being accessible in memory. That is to say, it is more likely to be placed along routes that are connected to one's own ways of intellectual travel.

In sum, the very attitudes and activities that characterize "figuring out" or "discovering" things for oneself also seem to have the effect of making material more readily accessible in memory.

The Learning Requirements for Enquiry*

ROBERT M. GAGNÉ

Robert M. Gagné agrees with other authors that enquiry is a necessary and vital objective of science instruction. He maintains, however, that if the practice of enquiry is to be carried out successfully, there are two major prerequisites: (1) a suitable background of broad generalized knowledge, which can be used in solving problems to make the inductive leap that characterizes enquiry; and (2) the possession of incisive knowledge, which makes it possible to discriminate between a good idea and a bad one. Dr. Gagné believes that, as the child progresses from kindergarten through college, there should be four levels of instruction which would enable the child to become progressively a competent performer, a student of knowledge, a scientific enquirer, and an independent investigator. There is constant overlap in the competencies and capabilities that are acquired at each level of instruction.

One of the most interesting and important ideas which has been given emphasis in recent discussions of science education is the idea of enquiry. It has been stated to be perhaps the most critical kind of activity that the scientist engages in, and for that reason to represent one of the most essential objectives of science instruction. Accordingly, there appears to be a very widespread agreement that enquiry is a worthwhile objective— something that our various educational efforts should deliberately try to

* REPRINTED FROM *Journal of Research in Science Teaching*, Vol. 1, Issue 2, 1963, pp 144–153, by permission of the author and the editor. Dr. Gagné is Professor of Psychology at the University of California, Berkeley.

achieve. And there is a widespread consensus that an instructional program for the student of science most clearly achieves this rightful goal when it enables such a student to adopt the procedures of scientific enquiry in response to any new unsolved problem he encounters.

Along with this emphasis on the importance of the method of enquiry there has been an accompanying realization that many traditional courses in science, at all levels of education, exhibit serious deficiencies insofar as they fail to get across to students the elements of this method. Many such courses seem to be neglecting the student in the most important sense that they do not encourage him to acquire the attitudes of enquiry, the methods of enquiry, the understanding of enquiry. They may provide him with a great many facts, with knowledge of important principles, even with the capability of using previously discovered principles in situations novel to him. But they omit this essential part of his education as a scientist, or even as an informed citizen, by not establishing within him the disposition which makes him able to employ enquiry in the manner so well-known to scientists.

Perhaps no writer has described this deficiency in science education so cogently and so thoroughly as has Schwab. It is worthwhile to quote here a short passage from his Inglis Lecture: [1]

It is the almost total absence of this portrayal of science which marks the greatest disparity between science as it is and science as seen through most textbooks of science. We are shown conclusions of enquiry as if they were certain or nearly certain facts. Further, we rarely see these conclusions as other than isolated, independent "facts." Their coherence and organization—the defining marks of *scientific* knowledge—are underemphasized or omitted. And we catch hardly a glimpse of the other constituents of scientific enquiry: organizing principles, data, and the interpretation of data.

The problem, then, seems pretty well-defined and agreed upon. It is, "How can one go about introducing, or perhaps restoring, to the process of instruction the necesary conditions which will make it more probable that the student learns about science as enquiry?" Obviously this is not as simple a matter as is "adding material" on neutrinos in atomic structure, or even as is "revising material" such as that on the reactivity of inert chemical elements. It is more complicated than either of these, because it is more difficult to identify and specify what it is that the student must learn. Yet this is the task that must be faced, complicated or not, if the desired change is to be brought about.

Let us assume, then, that there is general agreement about the problem and about the objective to be sought in its solution. Now, what, if anything, can the methods and results of research on the learning process contribute to this problem? This is the interest of the student of learning theory. Obviously, dealing with science as enquiry must be something that is learned. What do we know about learning that is relevant in establishing such a capability in the student?

Analysis of the Problem

As is the case with other users of scientific methods, the investigator of human learning customarily begins by defining or specifying what the problem is in terms which have served this function in the past. These terms serve to separate the general aspects of the problem situation from the specific and therefore incidental ones, and thus enable him to think about it in a rigorous fashion.

When this basic method is applied to the problem, the first distinction which becomes apparent is this: First, there is something we may call a *terminal capability*, something that the student is able to do after he has learned. That is to say, if we have been successful in establishing the correct conditions for learning, we will be able to infer that the student is or is not capable of employing the methods of scientific enquiry. To make this inference possible, of course, we must observe some kinds of behavior, which may also be specified, and we might refer to these observed events as *terminal behaviors*.

Second, the other major category of events with which we must deal in this problem is a set of conditions which are used to bring about a *change* in the student's capability. These we may call the *instructional conditions*. Potentially, these conditions include everything that is done to or by the student from some initial point in time (when he does not possess the desired capability) to some other point in time (when he does). But more specifically, they are all the aspects of the instructional situation which can be shown to affect this change, including the events that take place in classrooms, laboratories, libraries, at his desk, or elsewhere.

Perhaps this distinction seems obvious to you—the terminal capability, on the one hand, and the instructional conditions which accomplish the change between initial and terminal capability, on the other. But this distinction has not always been carefully maintained in thinking about this problem, even by people who think profoundly about it. It is nonetheless an essential distinction, and one which will be referred to again later.

The Terminal Capability

In order to understand and specify the problem further, we need to ask again, what is the nature of this desired capability of using the approach of enquiry towards the solution of problems? Having read the authors who have written on this subject, one concludes that they have spent many more words describing what it is *not* than in describing what it *is*.

What it is not, all agree, is an activity which deals with scientific concepts as things rather than abstractions, or with scientific hypotheses and theories as fixed facts rather than as convenient models subject to empirical test. I judge them to mean, that what it *is* is a set of activities characterized by a problem-solving approach, in which each newly encountered phenomenon becomes a challenge for thinking. Such thinking begins with a careful set of systematic observations, proceeds to design the measurements required, clearly distinguishes between what is observed and what is inferred, invents interpretations which are under ideal circumstances brilliant leaps, but always testable, and draws reasonable conclusions. In other words, it is the kind of activity that might be called the essence of scientific research (neglecting for the moment such clearly relevant components as obtaining research funds and writing good scientific reports, among others).

Can such inferred capabilities as these be observed as behavior? It does not seem unreasonable that this is possible, provided we accept the fact that the sample of behavior we may be able to observe is somewhat limited and therefore somewhat unreliable. This appears to be the kind of behavior the university science faculty tries to observe in its graduate students. It uses various methods of doing this, such as requiring the execution of an initial problem before the dissertation, or requiring the completion of a series of partial problems, or by asking the student to "think through" how he would approach an already reported investigation, or in some other manner. In many instances, more and better observation of this sort could actually be done, if some greater thought were given to it.

Observation of such behavior is also done with increasing frequency at the undergraduate college level. Here we find programs of independent study, honors programs, and other devices which require students to take an independent approach of enquiry towards a scientific problem. Again, the frequency and representativeness of this kind of observation of "enquiry behavior" can be improved. A number of authors suggest, for example, that the laboratory be made the setting for the practice of this approach, by designing and using the kinds of laboratory problems which are invitations to careful thought, rather than "standard exercises."

Can this kind of activity of scientific enquiry be extended downward to the secondary school and even into the primary grades? Of course it can, in some sense, since we know that even elementary students are quite capable of some pretty good thinking. But whether it should or not may involve some other considerations which we have not yet touched upon.

Conditions of Instruction

We are now ready to look more closely at the other part of the problem—how do we effect a change such that a student who doesn't initially employ the approach of enquiry toward problems will employ this approach? What are the conditions of instruction which are likely to effect this change?

Practice in Enquiry

One of the conditions emphasized by several writers on this question is that of *practicing strategies* in proceeding from the known to the unknown. Bruner,[2] for example, calls this "learning the heuristics of discovery," and states that although the form that such learning should take is not known in detail, it seems reasonable that improvement in the technique of enquiry should depend upon practice in enquiry. Schwab [1] points out the ways that such practice can be conducted in the laboratory and in the classroom. The import of these writings for the design of instructional conditions is clear: the student should be provided with opportunities to carry out inductive thinking; to make hypotheses and to test them, in a great variety of situations, in the laboratory, in the classroom, and by his own individual efforts.

It is impossible not to agree with this prescription in a specific sense. The student who has been given practice merely in the recall of ideas, or in their application in particular situations, will not necessarily acquire these important techniques of enquiry. In physics, for example, the setting of problems like this one is a common practice in many textbooks: "A box slides down a 30° inclined plane with an acceleration of 10 ft./sec.^{2} What is the coefficient of friction between the box and the plane?" Now the student obviously is getting practice from performing such problems, but the question is, what kind of practice? Obviously not the same kind he would get if this kind of problem were stated: "A box slides down an inclined plane. Can this event be shown to be compatible with Newton's second law of motion?" In this second case, what is being required of the student is that he relate some observed events to a general principle (or "law"), and that he himself *think out* what these relationships are. First he must identify the forces at work, specify the mass and acceleration, and then induce how these specific variables may be related to the general equation $F = ma$. And in carrying out this enquiry, he is obtaining valuable practice which will doubtless be transferable to other problems, not necessarily within the field of physics alone. A similar technique, or thinking strategy, may be useful in quite a different situation—in thinking about the reactions of chemical solutions, or about the metabolism of a cell, or even about the relation of national income to productivity.

If there are any limitations to the value of *practice in enquiry*, they are probably to be found in this fact: such practice is *not the whole story*. Establishing conditions for practice in enquiry does not by any means exhaust the requirements for the instructional conditions needed for the achievement of the desired terminal capability. And there are real dangers in thinking that such practice does constitute the entire set of requirements for this purpose.

Some scholars have perceived this danger. In a recent interview recorded in the newspapers, the noted physicist Dr. C. N. Yang [3] states his concern about the increasingly common practice of starting students on basic research early in their college careers. Students who are educated in this way, he says, will not be able to stand away from their work and see it in perspective; they will think of research as a study of a single problem rather than as a broad attack on the entire frontier of the unknown. In dealing with new problems, such students will lack the deep understanding on which to draw for help.

Dr. Yang's concern is essentially the same as that just mentioned. There is nothing wrong with practicing enquiry, and surely enquiry is the kind of capability we want students of science to attain in some terminal sense. But practicing enquiry too soon, and without a suitable background of knowledge, can have a narrowing and cramping effect on the individual's development of independent thinking. And if this is true at the level of the college sophomore, surely this danger must be all the more severe if we consider the instuctional situation in the high school and the elementary school.

Is this a valid objection? If practice in enquiry can be given too soon, or too exclusively, what other parts are there to the instructional situation? What else is there to learn, if one does not practice the strategies of thinking?

Two Other Components of Instruction

There are two other major capabilities which are of importance as objectives of instruction. It is possible to think that they are at least as important as practice in enquiry, and it is possible to argue that they are even more *essential*, in the sense that they represent *prior requirements*, if the practice of enquiry is to be carried out successfully. These two other capabilities may be characterized as follows:

(1) the capability of *generalizing* the principles of knowledge to the variety of situations to which they are applicable (and have been shown to be applicable by earlier scholars).

(2) the capability of *discriminating* the probable and improbable applicability of hypotheses to new problem situations.

In general terms, the reasons why these kinds of capability need to be fostered by the instructional situation are easy to understand. If an individual is to try to solve new problems, he must have a knowledge of a great variety of principles which can be potentially applicable to these problems. The best guarantee that these principles are available will be to insure that he has acquired generalizable knowledge, in other words, that he has *broad knowledge*. And when he does make the inductive leap that characterizes enquiry, he should be able to know that he is doing something that has a probability of being right, rather than of just being silly. He must discriminate the good ideas from the bad, in accordance with their probable consequences. One might call this *critical or incisive knowledge*. But both of these are needed *before* practice in enquiry can have the positive effects that are expected of it.

GENERALIZABLE KNOWLEDGE

Consider again the student who is asked to use the sliding of a weight down an inclined plane as an instance compatible with Newton's second law. It is obvious, isn't it, that the student must have a rather sizeable amount of broad knowledge before he can be successful at this problem? Among other things, he must know (1) what Newton's second law is, in terms which make sense to him; (2) what acceleration is, and its relation to velocity, time, and distance; (3) what mass is, and how it is related to weight; (4) how the angles of an inclined plane can lead to a conceptualization of the magnitude and direction of the forces at work. Others could undoubtedly be mentioned. It is senseless to think that these principles of knowledge are trivial, or that the student can easily have "picked them up" incidentally to some other learning, including perhaps previous practice in enquiry. It is surely wrong to believe that the student can *think* without *knowing* these principles. This would be like asking him to play chess without even having learned what the rules are. And it is probably quite contrary to the interests of learning to ask the student to undertake "enquiry practice" without knowing these principles. As evidence for the latter statement I refer to some work of my own and my colleagues on learning in mathematics, which has shown clearly that learning to solve new problems is critically dependent upon the acquisition of previous knowledge.[4]

Broad, generalizable knowledge is a prerequisite for the successful practice of enquiry, whether as a part of the total instructional process or as a terminal capability. How does the student acquire this broad knowledge? Well, that is a question of great interest to a student of human learning. And some things are known about it, some things not yet. Here are some observations about this broad, generalizable knowledge that are relevant.

1. Such knowledge cannot all be attained by a student by the use of the method of enquiry itself. Were we to follow this suggestion, we should have to put the student back in the original situation that Newon found himself in, and ask the student to invent a solution, as Newton did. It would be difficult to achieve this situation, in the first place, and presumably not all students would achieve what Newton did, even then.

But the major difficulty with this suggestion is that it would be a most terrible waste of time. Are we going to have students rediscover the laws of motion, the periodic table, the structure of the atom, the circulation of the blood, and all the other achievements of science simply in order to ensure that instructional conditions are "pure," in the sense that they demand enquiry? Surely no one seriously proposes that this method should be followed.

2. The possession of broad and generalizable knowledge is an admirable capability, and not to be equated with "knowing facts." There is quite a difference between knowing a *fact*, such as "Newton invented the laws of motion," and a *principle*, such as might be exhibited if we asked a student to describe a situation which could be used to test Newton's second law of motion. One might call the ability to repeat verbally the statement, "If an unbalanced force acts upon a body, the body will accelerate in proportion to the magnitude, etc.," knowing a fact. But to know such a fact is not the same as knowing this law of motion as a principle, as the previous example has indicated. Knowledge of principles is generalizable; one expects a student who knows Newton's second law as a principle to be able to describe a wide variety of specific situations in which the validity of the law can be tested. Such knowledge is of tremendous value, not just in and of itself, but because it constitutes an essential basis for acquiring other knowledge. To an equal degree, it is an essential basis for the practice of the strategies of enquiry.

3. As to how knowledge is acquired, one should not assume that this has to be done, or is best accomplished by "routine drill." Repetition does indeed appear to be one desirable condition for instruction, but only one. At least equally important, if not more so, is the condition which fosters the use of *discovery* on the part of the student. In its simplest form, this means simply that it seems to be better for learning if one can get the student to respond to a situation in his own way, and in a way which is also correct, rather than having him "copy" or "echo" something that the teacher says or the book says.[2, 5] In other words, discovery appears to be a very fundamental principle of good instruction. It applies to *all* conceptual learning, the learning of principles and generalizations, and may even apply to the learning of a simpler sort such as the memorizing of names or facts. But discovery, as a very fundamental condition of most learning, should not be equated with enquiry, which is the exercise of all the various activities making up what we have identified as the terminal capability. The construction of a response by a learner, something that happens nearly every step of the way in the process of learning, is what usually has been called discovery. In contrast to this, enquiry is the terminal thinking process we want the student to be able to engage in, *after* he has taken all the necessary previous steps in learning.

In summary then, it appears that broad, generalizable knowledge is best conceived as knowledge of principles. As such, it may be attained in the context of instructional conditions which include "discovery" on the part of the learner. Knowledge of principles is not what is usually referred to in a deprecating manner as "knowledge of mere facts," nor is such knowledge best acquired under conditions of sheer repetition. But knowledge of principles is prerequisite to the successful practice of the techniques of enquiry.

INCISIVE KNOWLEDGE
The other kind of capability we have identified as prerequisite to successful enquiry is the possession of critical or incisive knowledge. In terms that the psychologist uses, this is the capability of *discriminating* between a good idea and a bad one, or between a probably successful course of action and a probably unsuccessful one.

Just for variety of illustration, let us take a new example. Suppose we set the student this problem in enquiry: "How does the picture of an object get 'into the head' in the sense of being experienced as a picture and retained from one occasion to another?" Suppose that the student has a certain amount of generalizable knowledge about the eye, and its function as a camera, so that he is able readily to recall the principles which get the picture onto the retina. But now, how does it get "into the head"? If he has no more knowledge than this, he may think of a variety of mechanisms, each of which may be brilliantly inventive, but some of which may be silly. Perhaps it is carried by a scanning mechanism similar to television. Perhaps the frequencies of various light waves are transmitted directly over nerves. Perhaps the pattern of neurones stimulated corresponds to the pattern of physical energy. Perhaps the stimulation is carried in some mechanical way. Perhaps there are differences in the strength of transmission. Perhaps the pattern of brightness is transmitted as a pattern of frequencies, different from those of the light waves themselves. And so on. Any fairly bright student can probably think of quite a large number of possibilities.

Is there an instructional value to encouraging students to make such guesses? Probably so, but *only when* the means are simultaneously provided for the student to estimate that an idea is probably good or probably bad. The wildness of the guesses, or perhaps even the frequency of wild guesses, is a most doubtful criterion. (People whose guesses are extremely wild are called schizophrenics.) It seems to me that if the student is encouraged to form hypotheses, even to follow hunches, as a part of practice in enquiry, that these hunches and guesses should be *disciplined* ones. This does not mean at all that hypotheses need to be restricted in scope or simple in content. On the contrary, they can be as elaborate as his abilities and his generalizable knowledge will permit. But he should be able to estimate their consequences. Any hypothesis is subject to the discipline of ultimate verification.

What kind of knowledge is it that makes possible the discrimination of good ideas from bad? Well, it is not very different in kind, although it is different in content, from the other kind of knowledge we have described. Generally speaking, it is knowledge of principles, sprinkled here and there, perhaps, with a few facts. In the case of our example of the picture in the head, the student needs to know at least the following principles: (1) the relation between intensity of stimulation and frequency of neural response; (2) the frequency and strength of neural responses; (3) the rapidity of the nervous impulse; (4) the relation between distribution of nerve endings and distribution of frequency of nervous impulses; and a number of others. Each of these principles and facts provides him with a means of checking the compatibility of the hypotheses he generates in terms of their probability or improbability.

Here again, then, in this capability for *self-criticism of ideas*, we come upon another essential need for knowledge, prior to the exercise of enquiry. From a base of knowledge of principles, enquiry takes off. Where it comes to rest is also dependent upon the possession of knowledge. Enquiry which cannot be checked against estimates that hypotheses are probably good or probably bad will be undisciplined enquiry, possibly as satisfying as the daydreams of Walter Mitty, but of no greater social importance. Likewise, the practice of enquiry which lacks the discipline of self-criticism may be expected to be of no positive value to the development of the individual, and could even be harmful. Which teacher of science has not encountered the student who is constantly willing to display a bubbling fountain of ideas, almost all of them worthless? Is this what we want to encourage?

The Instructional Basis of Enquiry

This analysis of the instructional conditions required to establish the capabilities for enquiry emphasizes that the major essential is the possession of a body of organized knowledge. On the whole, the more highly organized this knowledge is, the better; it will be better retained that way.

What are the implications of this line of reasoning for the science curriculum and for science instruction? It may be of greatest meaningfulness if the answer to this question is attempted by considering what science instruction might be like, not at some particular level of development, such as high school or college, but throughout the entire range of the educational sequence from kindergarten onwards. However, this might be better done "from the top down," because the interrelationships of problem-solving, knowledge, and fundamental skills are most clearly revealed by such an analysis. Accordingly, let us consider what seem to be approximately definable "levels" of science instruction. Of course these are not hard and fast distinctions, nor are they exclusive categories. Learning takes place during the entire course of an individual's lifetime, and it is only the relative priorities which can be indicated by such an analysis.

THE INDEPENDENT INVESTIGATOR

At the highest level of development we have the student who is beginning to take all of the responsibilities of an independent scientist. He has broad knowledge, not only within his specialized field, but of others as well. Furthermore, he understands and has practiced the methods of enquiry sufficiently so that he knows what he is doing, and understands his own limitations. He is able to begin a new line of investigation in a disciplined, responsible manner, with deliberate attention to what has gone before, but with a mind unhampered by tradition. Currently, we think of this capability as being possessed by the second- or third-year graduate student. If our educational system were reasonably effective, this level could perhaps be achieved by people of the age of present college juniors.

THE SCIENTIFIC ENQUIRER

At the next lower level, we find the student who has acquired enough broad subject-matter knowledge to be able to learn to speculate, to form and test hypotheses about scientific problems which are not trivial, and which he himself can subject to the discipline of self-criticism. In other words, the emphasis at this level of instruction might profitably be upon the method of enquiry. This should be practiced in the discussion class, in the laboratory, as well as in individual study. Again, making the assumption of a reasonably efficient educational system, the student should probably be able to begin this phase of instruction at the age of present 11th graders.

But in order to do this successfully, we have argued, he must have acquired a great deal of broad and incisive knowledge. The latter kinds of knowledge are not confined to the facts and principles of content, it should be noted. They also include knowledge about methods—of observing, classifying, describing, inferring, and conceptual invention.

THE STUDENT OF KNOWLEDGE

This level of instruction emphasizes the learning of broad and critical knowledge, particularly of what previous generations of scientists have found out about the world, as well as the most fundamental principles which have led to the formulation of modern scientific conceptions. At this stage, the student needs to begin to acquire large masses of previously formulated principles of knowledge. At the same time, he needs to learn to engage deliberately and systematically in the fundamental activities used by the scientist, in as wide a variety of contexts as possible. Such activities include controlled observation, classification, measurement, inference, the formulation of models. Accordingly, there is definite need for the "laboratory" at this level. But the activities resemble those of the "laboratory exercise" more than they do the "independent enquiry." If he is encouraged to do the latter, he will fail because he doesn't *know* enough to behave like a scientist. Accordingly, his activity will either be extremely narrow in scope or will tend to be ridiculous, neither of which outcomes will have salutary effects upon his learning.

Does this suggestion of an emphasis on acquiring broad knowledge carry the implication of "stifling curiosity"? Not at all. There are plenty of rewards for curiosity, in discovering new things about the world, in exploring previously unknown paths of knowledge, in trying one's hand at new kinds of classification, in finding out how indirect measurements can be made and verified, in seeing how one can best communicate scientific information, and in many other areas. Curiosity is not the special possession of the fully trained scientist. Neither is the method of discovery in learning, as has been pointed out previously.

This level of instruction could probably have its inception around the age level currently attending the 6th or 7th grade.

THE COMPETENT PERFORMER

Acquiring broad knowledge in the way that it should be acquired, and particularly knowledge of the methods of the scientist, is in turn based upon a stage of instruction which extends downward to the kindergarten (and informally, farther than that). For what is needed first of all in science instruction are certain kinds of performance capabilities. The word *skills* should carry no negative aura, but it seems to for some people, so let us avoid it and refer to *competencies*. At this level, the question is not so much "Does the student *know* something," but "Can he *do* something." We are used to thinking of these competencies as "reading, writing, and arithmetic," but what an inadequate description that is! When one considers the competencies needed for learning about science, it is quite probable, first of all, that this set of three leaves important ones out. Beyond this, they do not adequately convey what kinds of specific capabilities are really intended.

No one seems to have adequately faced up to the necessity for identifying and describing these fundamental competencies which underlie all of learning about science. A good list would include not only number computation, but also spatial and manipulative skills, and the capabilities of observing, classifying, measuring, describing, inferring, and model conceptualizing. In general, there should be good agreement that these competencies are important to science instruction. Shouldn't the high school student know how to *describe* an unfamiliar object seen for the first time? More than this, though, the suggestion made here is that the later acquisition of broad and incisive knowledge about science will be inadequate and unsuccessful unless the student has already acquired the capability of observing and describing what he sees. How can he acquire such knowledge unless he is able to distinguish clearly, and in terms of his own behavior, the description of an observed object or event from the description of a conceptual model?

As stated earlier, instruction in these fundamental capabilities so essential to the understanding of science carries no implication of the "routinizing of instruction" or the "deadening of curiosity." A child simply has to learn to read before he can understand printed texts. Similarly, an individual needs to know how to observe, to classify, to describe, to conceptualize, before he can understand science or the activities of scientists. All of these competencies can be acquired through his own efforts, motivated by his own curiosity, and by means of his own discoveries.

At the same time, it seems to be totally erroneous to look upon these early attainments as having anything but a specious resemblance to the activities of disciplined enquiry, or to contend that they can be acquired by "practice in enquiry." One doesn't learn to be a scientist, or to appreciate science, by pretending to be a scientist. What is the difference, in principle, between trying to "practice enquiry" in the second grade, and trying to practice "being a physician" at the same age level? Why should anyone be led, perhaps by wishful thinking, to give serious consideration to the former, while at the same time chuckling patronizingly at the latter? Engaging in enquiry of a successful, productive, and useful variety can be undertaken when the individual has acquired a store of broad and critical knowledge, and this in turn can be acquired when he has learned some prerequisite but very important fundamental capabilities. At the earliest stage of instruction, one needs to be most concerned with these latter competencies, which will remain with the student all his life.

Having described a sequence of acquired competencies from top to bottom which is based upon the best generalizations from studies of the learning process, one must be careful not to imply that there is no overlap among the kinds of capabilities to be acquired at each of these four "levels" of instruction. At the earliest stage, for example, the child is certainly acquiring some knowledge of principles, and even a little bit of the strategy of clear thinking, even though the major part of what he most needs to learn are the competencies (or skills) mentioned. And similar comments could be made about other stages. None of them is "pure." Even at the highest of these levels, as we know, the student may often have to "catch up" on some broad knowledge he somehow missed at a much earlier level. If he has missed some of the important competencies at the earliest level, the chances are very good that he has some time previously decided to major in some field other than science.

In summary then, let us consider what would happen in science instruction, this time beginning at the bottom, if it were seriously designed to establish the terminal capability of enquiry. This is not an attempt to describe what *does* happen, because we are far from that condition, but what *should* happen. At the earliest level of instruction, the individual needs to learn how to observe, how to figure, how to measure, how to orient things in space, how to describe, how to classify objects and events, how to infer, and how to make conceptual models. These capabilities he will use all of his life. If he becomes a student of science, they will make possible the acquiring of broad knowledge of principles, the incisive knowledge which makes possible the self-criticism of new ideas, and the disciplined exercise of the method of enquiry. If he chooses some other field as a career, they will provide a fundamental understanding of science which is quite independent of any particular scientific knowledge he may read about. At the next level, he needs to make a thoroughgoing start at acquiring broad knowledge and critical knowledge of the principles of science, throughout the various disciplines, and including knowledge of both content and method. This knowledge is essential if he is later going to practice making reasonable hypotheses and testing them; in other words, if he is later to practice enquiry. The practice of enquiry itself might begin at the next stage, along with a continuation of the learning of substantive knowledge, perhaps with a somewhat greater degree of specialization. This enquiry practice will, on the one hand, be soundly derived from suitably broad knowledge; and on the other, it will be carried out so as to make possible discriminations between "good" and "bad" ideas. But it will nevertheless be genuine enquiry, in which the student is encouraged to solve problems by means of unrestrained inductive thinking, and in which he is rewarded for his ingenuity. Having done all this, the student is then ready for the final stage, learning to assume the full responsibilities of the scientific investigator. At this stage, he must learn to depend upon himself, and to trust himself, to look upon problems objectively; to have new ideas; and to be able to judge them critically. In all of these activities he will be enormously aided by his previous practice in enquiry, as well as by his knowledge of scientific principles and methods, and by the fundamental capabilities he acquired early in his educational career.

It must be quite clear that "practice in enquiry" for the student of science has great value. But to be successful it must be based upon a great variety of prerequisite knowledge and competencies which themselves are learned, sometimes by "discovery," but inconceivably by what is called "enquiry."

References

1. Schwab, J. J., "The Teaching of Science as Enquiry," *The Teaching of Science*, Harvard University Press, Cambridge, 1962.
2. Bruner, J. S., "The Act of Discovery," *Harvard Educational Review*, **31**, 21-32 (1961).

3. Yang, C. N., quoted in article in *Pittsburgh Post-Gazette*, Friday, December 28, 1962.
4. Gagné, R. M., J. R. Mayor, H. L. Garstens, and N. E. Paradise, "Factors in Acquiring Knowledge of a Mathematical Task," *Psychol. Monographs*, **76**, No. 7 (Whole No. 526) (1962).
5. Gagné, R. M., "The Acquisition of Knowledge," *Psychol. Rev.*, **69**, 355-365 (1962).

The Objectives of Elementary Science

INTRODUCTION

The objectives of science education have changed very little in the past twenty-five years. The same objectives apply to both the secondary and the elementary school, the only difference being one of depth and degree of attainment. Although the literature lists a wide variety of objectives, they all fall into two categories: (1) those that pertain to the product of science and (2) those that pertain to the process of science.

The product of science refers to science content. An effective science program aims for the acquisition of concepts and principles. There is no rote memorization of facts or laws, but the learning through appropriate techniques of concepts which lead to an understanding of conceptual schemes.

The process of science is a comparatively recent term in science education. However, its frame of reference is not new. It refers to the key operations, or processes, of science and the scientist. In earlier years such terms as "ways of the scientist" and "desirable behaviors" have been used in the same context as process. They all refer to the methods of science that make it possible for children to learn science. These include all those abilities, skills, and attitudes that make critical thinking and problem-solving possible. In an effective science program great emphasis is placed upon process, because process is the means whereby real learning of the structure, or content, of science takes place in the classroom.

Science yearbooks, methods books, articles, and curriculum guides all have consistently urged for years that both objectives be given equal consideration when teaching science. Teachers have been encouraged to use the processes of science to achieve the learning of science content. However, all too often the major emphasis has been on content, and process has been ignored. This has resulted in memorization rather than thinking and in the learning of facts rather than concepts and principles. Furthermore, the children have been deprived of needed experiences with scientific inquiry and the process of science.

It is easily understandable, then, why today there is widespread preoccupation with revising existing science programs and developing new programs in such a way that the process approach to the learning of science is stressed. The following are some of the key processes, or operations, of science and the scientist that are being suggested for inclusion in the elementary science program: observation, analysis, classification, description, interpretation, inference, induction, deduction, hypothesis, prediction, planning, experimentation, designing of experiments, keeping of records, measurement, use of controls, and communication. Thus, concerted efforts are being made to bring the spirit as well as the substance of science into the classroom.

At first this enthusiasm about the process approach to learning science became so great that the pendulum began to swing the other way, and process began to be emphasized at the expense of content in some programs. This overemphasis upon process caused some concern among many scientists and science educators, but it did serve to bring strongly into focus the need for process as well as content in the teaching and learning of science.

However, the pendulum has already made its swing back, and a happy medium of both process and content in elementary science is being effected. Today, scientists and science educators agree that the dual objectives of content and process are of equal importance. Both objectives are not mutually exclusive, but instead are complementary and mutually interdependent. When we teach for content, the child should be learning process; and when we teach for process, the child should be learning content.

Science Education for Changing Times*

NATIONAL SOCIETY for the STUDY of EDUCATION

The following is an excerpt from Chapter 2 of the Fifty-ninth NSSE Year-book, Part 1, Rethinking Science Education. It shows how little the objectives of science education have changed since they were stated in the Society's Forty-sixth Yearbook. These objectives included the develop-ment of such learning outcomes as (1) functional information, concepts, and principles; (2) instrumental and problem-solving skills; (3) attitudes; (4) appreciations; and (5) interests. In the Fifty-ninth Yearbook, such terms as "critical thinking," "scientific process," and "inquiry" are intro-duced, and greater emphasis is placed upon those aspects of science that deal with these terms. Members of the committee who wrote Chapter Two include Paul DeH. Hurd, Vernon E. Anderson, J. W. Buchta, John H. Fisher, Eric M. Rogers, Guy Suits, and Ralph W. Tyler.

The objectives of science-teaching as they appear in educational litera-ture have changed little in the past twenty-five years. On the other hand, there have been changes in the nature of the science taught; for example, the sciences have become more unified and have gained an important position in world affairs. These factors suggest the need to re-think the purposes of teaching science in schools.

Recently there has been much criticism of science-teaching. Some scientists have been concerned that science was not being taught either as understanding or as enterprise. They have thought that science-teaching should reflect the nature of science, and it should harmonize with the scientific point of view. The lack of social orientation in science-teaching and the failure to teach modern science have concerned other groups.

The objectives of the teaching of science are essentially the same from the elementary through the high school. The degree of attainment and the level of competency vary according to the development, interest, and abilities of young people. We cannot expect that every objective will be achieved by all students, that the rate of achievement will be uniform, or that everyone will reach the same level of understanding. This suggests that the objectives of the student who is oriented to a science career and

---

*REPRINTED FROM Rethinking Science Education, Fifty-ninth Yearbook of the National Society for the Study of Education, Part I (Chicago: University of Chicago Press, 1960), pp. 33–37, by permission of the publisher.

those of the college-bound student will be different from those of other pupils.

Many criticisms directed toward the objectives of science-teaching are actually a censure of classroom procedures which fail to realize those objectives; for example, methods which demand too many facts, too little conceptualizing, too much memorizing, and too little thinking.

The following list of objectives provides a model by which the teacher may orient his thinking in developing his own purposes for teaching science.

Understanding Science

There are two major aspects of science-teaching: one is knowledge, and the other is enterprise. From science courses, pupils should acquire a useful command of science concepts and principles. Science is more than a collection of isolated and assorted facts; to be meaningful and valuable, they must be woven into generalized concepts. A student should learn something about the character of scientific knowledge, how it has been developed, and how it is used. He must see that knowledge has a certain dynamic quality and that it is quite likely to shift in meaning and status with time.

The pupil needs at each grade level to acquire a background of ordered knowledge, to develop an adequate vocabulary in science for effective communication, and to learn some facts because they are important in everyday living, such as knowledge that is useful in maintaining health, promoting safety, and interpreting the immediate environment.

Recent theories and new knowledge should have priority in science-teaching when they are significant and can be made understandable at a specified grade level. The generalized concepts selected for teaching should be those which tend to explain or involve many science facts.

Problem-Solving

Science is a process in which observations and their interpretations are used to develop new concepts, to extend our understanding of the world, to suggest new areas for exploration, and to provide some predictions about the future. It is focused upon inquiry and subsequent action.

Methods for solving problems in science are numerous. There is no one scientific method; in fact, there are almost as many methods as there are scientists and problems to be solved. Inevitably the details of scientific investigation are seldom the same for any two problems. What is done is highly flexible and quite personal. Incentive, intuition, the play of imagination, fertility of ideas, and creativeness in testing hypotheses are important parts of the process. The methods of science are something more than measurement, laboratory techniques, and data processing followed by logical deductions. Sometimes they are not very logical, but the search for truth is always present. Presenting problem-solving as a series of logically ordered steps is simply a technique to isolate the critical skills and abilities and to give them special attention in teaching.

A process of inquiry involves careful observing, seeking the most reliable data, and then using rational processes to give order to the data and to suggest possible conclusions or further research. At higher levels of achievement the student should be able to establish relationships from his findings, and in turn to make predictions about future observations.

The Social Aspects of Science

Young people need to understand the dependence of our society upon scientific and technological achievement and to realize that science is a basic part of modern living. The scientific process and the knowledge produced cannot be assumed to be ends in themselves except for the classical scientist. For him the pursuit of new knowledge is a professional effort, and any lack of social concern on his part may be accepted. But a liberal education has a wider orientation, particularly at precollege levels. A student should understand the relation of basic research to applied research, and the interplay of technological innovations and human affairs. More of technology than science will be involved in social decisions; both are important in public policy.

Appreciations

A student with a liberal education in science should be able to appreciate:

1. The importance of science for understanding the modern world.
2. The methods and procedures of science for their value in discovering new knowledge and extending the meaning of previously developed ideas.
3. The men who add to the storehouse of knowledge.
4. The intellectual satisfaction to be gained from the pursuit of science either as a scientist or as a layman.

Attitudes

The knowledge and methods of science are of little importance if there is no disposition to use them appropriately. Open-mindedness, a desire for accurate knowledge, confidence in the procedures for seeking knowledge and the expectation that the solution of problems will come through the use of verified knowledge, these are among the "scientific attitudes."

To understand the scientist is also to understand some of his attitudes, such as the desire to know and to discover, a curiosity about the world, the excitement of discovery, and the desire to be creative.

Careers

Science instruction should acquaint students with career possibilities in technical fields and in science-teaching. A continuous effort should be made to identify and motivate those who develop special interests. They should be given opportunities for some direct experience of a professional nature and a perspective of the fields of science.

Abilities

Science as a field of study is characterized by a moving frontier and an ever increasing amount of knowledge. Young people need to acquire those skills and abilities which will enable them to assume responsibility for expanding their own learning. Some of these skills and abilities are:

1. Reading and interpreting science writings.
2. Locating authoritative sources of science information.
3. Performing suitable experiments for testing ideas.
4. Using the tools and techniques of science.
5. Recognizing the pertinency and adequacy of data.
6. Making valid inferences and predictions from data.
7. Recognizing and evaluating assumptions underlying techniques and processes used in solving problems.
8. Expressing ideas qualitatively and quantitatively.
9. Using the knowledge of science for responsible social action.
10. Seeking new relationships and ideas from known facts and concepts.

Statement of Purposes and Objectives of Science Education in the Elementary School[*]

WILLIAM KESSEN

William Kessen defines science as a structured and directed way of asking and answering questions. He believes that science is best taught as a procedure of enquiry. Dr. Kessen believes that the objectives in science education should include an attitude of intelligent caution and such procedures of science as the ability to state a problem, use sources of reliable information, observe, compare, classify, measure, experiment, evaluate evidence, draw conclusions, invent a model or theory and communicate in science. Dr. Kessen also sketches an outline of the basic areas of scientific knowledge that a properly educated child should possess within the first ten years of school.

There is joy in the search for knowledge; there is excitement in seeing, however partially, into the workings of the physical and biological world; there is intellectual power to be gained in learning the scientist's approach to the solution of human problems. The first task and central purpose of science education is to awaken in the child, whether or not he will become a professional scientist, a sense of the joy, the excitement, and the intellectual power of science. Education in science, like education in letters and the arts, will enlarge the child's appreciation of his world; it will also lead him to a better understanding of the range and limits of man's control over nature.

Science As Inquiry

Science is best taught as a procedure of enquiry. Just as reading is a fundamental instrument for exploring whatever may be written, so science is a fundamental instrument for exploring whatever may be tested by observation and experiment. Science is more than a body of facts, a collection of principles, and a set of machines for measurement; it is a structured and directed way of asking and answering questions. It is no

*REPRINTED FROM *Journal of Research in Science Teaching*, Vol. 2, Issue 1, 1964, pp. 4–6, by permission of the author and the editor. Dr. Kessen is Professor of Psychology at Yale University.

mean pedagogical feat to teach a child the facts of science and technology; it is a pedagogical triumph to teach him these facts in their relation to the procedures of scientific enquiry. And the intellectual gain is far greater than the child's ability to conduct a chemical experiment or to discover some of the characteristics of static electricity. The procedures of scientific enquiry, learned not as a canon of rules but as ways of finding answers, can be applied without limit. The well-taught child will approach human behavior and social structure and the claims of authority with the same spirit of alert skepticism that he adopts toward scientific theories. It is here that the future citizen who will not become a scientist will learn that science is not memory or magic but rather a disciplined form of human curiosity.

The Scientific Attitude

The willingness to wait for a conclusive answer—the skepticism that requires intellectual restraint and the maintenance of doubt—is oftentimes difficult for adult and child alike. The discipline of scientific enquiry demands respect for the work of the past together with a willingness to question the claims of authority. The attitude of intelligent caution, the restraint of commitment, the belief that difficult problems are always susceptible to scientific analysis, and the courage to maintain doubt will be learned best by the child who is given an honest opportunity to try his hand at scientific enquiry. With his successes will come an optimistic appreciation of the strength of enquiry; with his failures will come an understanding of the variety and challenge of our ignorance. For the scientist, child and adult, novelty is permanent; scientific enquiry continually builds novelty into a coherent design, full of promise, always tentative, that tames our terror and satisfies for a while the human desire for simplicity.

The Procedures of Science

Scientific problems arise in the play of children just as they arise in the guided exploration of scientists. Astonishment in the presence of natural beauty, surprise—even frustration—at the failure of a prediction, and the demand for sense in the face of confusion are the beginnings of scientific enquiry. But how do we then proceed?

Among the most demanding of scientific tasks and certainly among the most difficult to teach is the *statement* of a problem. Is there a meaningful question to be asked? What techniques should be used to answer it? How does one go about making a prediction or developing a hypothesis? As he asks these questions, the student begins to learn how active enquiry can lead to testable questions and eventually to the solution of problems. He is introduced also to the pleasures and problems of inventive thought—of considering what might be as well as what is.

There are many ways to answer a provocative question in science and the child should come to recognize that he must adapt his method to the problem in hand. As he runs against different problems, the child will learn to use several *sources of reliable information*—observation, experiment, books, museums, and informed adults.

Whatever the problem, the child's *ability to observe* should be extended so that he understands the wide range of observations possible even when simple phenomena are under study. He must learn to order the evidence of all his senses.

Attention to the complex activity of *comparison of phenomena* will introduce the child to an essential task in science—the perception of differences and similarities among events.

The child will use his ability to observe and to compare in building *systems of classification* and in recognizing their usefulness and their limitations in science.

The child should learn to use the *instruments of science*. As he studies these instruments, the teacher is given an opportunity to instruct the child in *measurement*. He will learn the need for precision in measurement, the importance of agreement among observers, and the relations among different systems of measurement.

The use of laboratory techniques—especially *the experiment*—deserves special attention. The experiment is the sharpest tool of science and in devising an experiment, the child exercises his ability to pose a question, to consider possible answers, to select appropriate instruments, to make careful measurements, and to be aware of sources of error. It is unlikely that children in the first years of school will manage well all aspects of sound laboratory procedure but the best lessons of the experiment can be taught only to the child who is actively engaged with the equipment and procedures of the laboratory. The teacher must adapt his desire for precision to the child's excitement in the search; a premature demand for exactness in experimental manipulation may blunt the student's commitment and pleasure.

After the problem is posed, a hypothesis developed, and the data gathered, the science student must *evaluate evidence and draw conclusions*. Sometimes this is a simple step; sometimes it involves the review and modification of the entire plan with renewed attention to problem, to hypothesis, and to data-protocols. The goal is to make sense of the data and the pursuit of this goal will on occasion lead to the detection of an error or to the design of another study. It may also lead to the *invention of a model or theory* through which we can comprehend data.

Throughout the course of science education, the *need to communicate* is present. Describing a bird to his class, graphing a mathematical function, writing an experimental paper—experience with each mode of report is essential to the development of the science student.

The child's ability to communicate in science will both depend upon and contribute to the achievement of this most general goal of the curriculum—accurate and effective communication.

The procedures of science described here in the context of early science education are recognizably the procedures of science at all levels of sophistication. Scientific enquiry is a seamless fabric. The content will change, the demand for precision will vary, the generality of conclusion will be different, the interrelation of studies will be understood in different ways, but the procedures and attitudes of scientific study remain remarkably the same from the time the kindergarten child wonders about color to the time the graduate physicist wonders about particle emission.

Scientific Knowledge

The facts and principles of science change with each advance in our understanding of the world. For this reason, it is difficult to forecast with precision what scientific content the child should know. Nonetheless, it is possible to sketch in outline the scientific knowledge that the properly educated child will possess within the first ten years of school. A knowledge of the basic findings of centuries of scientific enquiry gives boundaries and direction to the child's active exploration of his world. Under the governing premise that the curriculum in science must be defined by the child's growing comprehension of nature's order and beauty more than by the conventional categories of scientific knowledge, the child should know as much as he can actively seize about:

1. *the universe*, its galaxies, our solar system, the earth, and his immediate environment; the range of measurements used to describe astronomical and geological phenomena;

2. *the structure and reactions of matter* from the smallest particles to their combination in minerals and rocks; elements, compounds and mixtures, large and small molecules, atoms, protons, neutrons, and electrons;

3. *the conservation and transformation of energy*; the electro-magnetic spectrum, energy of motion and potential energy, electrical energy and chemical energy; force and work, gravitational and magnetic fields;

4. *the interaction between living things and their environment*; animal and human behavior, the relation between biological structure and function, reproduction, development, genetics, evolution, and the biological units—cell, organism, and population.

Science cannot be divided easily into labeled categories without loss. An emphasis on *scientific principles* that bridge the conventional subject-matter divisions will improve and simplify the teaching of science, making it more easily understood and more productive of meaningful problems for the child's own enquiry.

Scientific enquiry, moreover, is partner and peer of the traditional divisions of study; decisions about education in science must always be made with consideration of the relation of science to the child's other studies. Levers and poems, energy exchange and historical analysis, genetics and geography—all present to the child an opportunity to extend his reach into the world and, in their different ways, all present to the child an opportunity to see beauty.

The Child and the Teacher

Rising above any statement of objectives for education is an irreducible fact. Teaching is an exchange between people. This simple human fact is both problem and promise for education in science as it is for all education. The child can understand only what he has been prepared to understand, the teacher can teach only what he knows, and the meeting of the prepared child with skillful teacher is an unforgettable encounter for them both. In the successful educational encounter, the child will become an active searcher for knowledge and the teacher will form attitudes toward enquiry as well as offer information about the world. The related and intricate problems of teacher training and the nature of learning are closely interwined with the goals of science education. Science, rooted in man's curiosity and love of order, is called to its full humanity by the child's desire to know.

Science Teaching in the Elementary School*

PAUL E. BLACKWOOD

Paul E. Blackwood presents his definition of science as "man's relentless search for verifiable patterns, concepts, descriptions, or explanations of phenomena in the universe." The recorded knowledge that results from this search, and about which people communicate, is an important part of science. Dr. Blackwood briefly discusses three basic things that scientists do: they make descriptions, explanations, and predictions. He uses a three-sided polygon to describe the necessary components of a good science education. Side 1 represents objects, forces, and phenomena that make up the universe. Side 2 represents methods of inquiry used to study the uni-

*REPRINTED FROM *Science and Children*, Vol. 2, No. 1, September 1964, pp. 21–25. Copyright, 1964, by the National Science Teachers Association, Washington, D.C. Reprinted by permission of the author and the publisher. Dr. Blackwood is Specialist for Elementary Science at the U.S. Office of Education.

verse. *Side 3 represents the knowledge (classified as concepts, principles, laws, facts, etc.) developed about the universe.*

What you see and hear in the corridor of an elementary school is often related to what goes on in classrooms. This visitor was lured into a fifth-grade classroom by a girl energetically bouncing a red rubber ball.

Inside the classroom other pupils were dropping rubber balls. They were investigating how high a ball would bounce when dropped freely from various heights. After a short period of activity, the children and teacher were confronted with 15 sets of data collected independently by 15 two-man teams. What one team recorded is shown in Chart 1.

Chart 1

HEIGHT OF DROP (INCHES)	TRIAL	REBOUND (INCHES)
24″ (2′)	1	11.00″
	2	11.50″
	3	11.75″
	Average	11.41″
48″ (4′)	1	22.50″
	2	22.75″
	3	23.25″
	Average	22.83″
72″ (6′)	1	33.00″
	2	33.75″
	3	34.00″
	Average	33.58″
96″ (8′)		?
120″ (10′)		?

How would these results look on a graph? The question by the teacher was sufficient motivation to cause the team to prepare a graph of the results similar to the one below.

Fig. 13

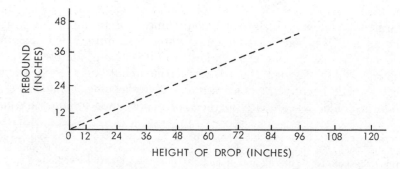

HEIGHT OF DROP (INCHES)

Additional questions began to emerge:

1. How far would the ball bounce if dropped from 8, 10, or 12 feet.
2. By using the graph, can one predict the height of rebound?
3. Is there a maximum height the ball will bounce, regardless of the distance it falls?
4. How does the bounce of different balls compare?
5. Do heavier balls bounce higher than lighter balls?

In another class, children were discussing the question, "How does the length of a stick's shadow change as the sun moves across the sky?" First, the children changed the question into a form which could be investigated more directly. They worded it this way: "What is the length of a stick's shadow at different times of the day?" An answer to this question could be obtained by direct measurement, and data collected to answer it would help answer the first question, so the class decided. It was not long before 15 pairs of pupils were busy in the schoolyard collecting information. Each pair was confronted with certain questions:

How long a pole shall we use?
Where shall we place it?
At what intervals during the day shall we measure the shadow?

Two children decided to measure the length of the shadow of an 88-inch pole every hour from 8 AM to 3 PM, just south of the school house. They measured it on June 7 and again on June 10 because the sun disappeared just after noon on the 7th. Their recorded data are illustrated in Chart 2.

Chart 2, Length of Pole: 88" (7'4") Position: South of School House

	LENGTH	
TIME	JUNE 7	JUNE 10
8 AM	122" (10'2")	
9 AM	81" (6'9")	
10 AM	54" (4'6")	
11 AM	37" (3'1")	
12 M	28" (2'4")	
1 PM	Cloudy	36" (3')
2 PM	Cloudy	53" (4'5")
3 PM	Cloudy	79" (6'7")

Based on these figures, the children were able to answer their questions about the changing length of shadows in relation to the position of the sun. But one youngster asked, "Does this experiment prove that the earth rotates or that the sun moves?"

The two learning experiences described above may well illustrate some characteristics of good science teaching. But a judgment can be made only in terms of what one accepts as a model of science education. Before evaluating these, or any science experiences, let us consider a model of science education which clearly recognizes two essential and perhaps interrelated features.

1. The nature of science.
2. The purposes and methods of teaching science.

Surely a growing understanding of each of these by teachers of elementary school science is essential.

1. THE NATURE OF SCIENCE

A working definition of science is helpful in giving clues as to what may properly be included in the study of science. The following tentative definition has the virtue of including enough ingredients to reflect the breadth and richness of science. *Science is man's relentless search for verifiable patterns, concepts, descriptions, or explanations of phenomena in the universe.*

In this definition, we see that man is in the picture. Science is an enterprise, an activity of people. Science is people searching. It is men, women, and children investigating, inquiring, and seeking verifiable knowledge. It is relentless, a continuous, never-ending attempt to find more accurate descriptions of things and events and to seek reasonable explanations of these events. The search leads to new discoveries, to new insights about unifying patterns, to concepts, to understandings, and to new knowledge. Many of these observations, descriptions, and explanations have been recorded by scientists and are available for use by other people as they attempt to extend their knowledge and understanding of the natural environment. This recorded knowledge, about which people can communicate, is an important part of science.

A definition of science like that discussed above has been eschewed by some scientists on the grounds that you can define science better in terms of what scientists do. It seems simple to say, "Science is what scientists do." But to understand this statement requires an analysis of what it is that men and women do when they are being scientists. Let us then, in our exploration of what science is, look briefly at three of the basic things that scientists do.

A. SCIENTISTS MAKE DESCRIPTIONS. What is in the universe? How many? How much? How long? How frequently? Where? When? Under what circumstances? Answers to such questions are descriptions.

Astronomers use telescopes, cameras, and instruments of other kinds. They use mathematics and their minds to try to get a picture of our universe and how the bodies in space are interrelated. Geologists study rock structures, formations of the earth, and changes in its surface. The study requires careful observation and accurate reporting. Physicists attempt to find out how energy flows from one material to another and what happens to the materials.

Thus, scientists attempt to describe what is, how things are, what things are like, how they change, and how they interrelate. Improved descriptions of things and events in our universe enable scientists to discover unity within vast diversity. Methods that have proven practical in discovering the elements of unity within diversity and in getting "check-up-able" knowledge we sometimes call scientific methods. As other people use these methods, they are able to verify what someone else has observed.

B. Scientists Make Explanations. In a sense, scientists attempt to tell "why" certain events and phenomena occur the way they do. This usually involves observing carefully how things interact with each other. What are the interrelationships? What precedes what? What follows what? Under what conditions do certain phenomena occur? Making explanations usually involves showing the connections between events or phenomena.

In a way, an explanation is a very careful description. For example, to explain why water evaporates from an open dish requires knowledge about the physical structure of water, about the nature of molecular action, about the capacity of air to hold water molecules, the behavior of water molecules when heat energy is increased, and the like. Scientists are detectives attempting to put descriptions together in ways that help us understand events. In this way, they make explanations.

C. Scientists Make Predictions. In order to make knowledge more widely applicable and to extend our confidence in its validity, it must be tested in many situations. Extending our knowledge to new situations involves prediction. We have observed that water will evaporate from a dish on a window sill. We predict that it will evaporate also if placed on a warm radiator. We test to see. If it does, then our prediction is correct.

Scientists are continually testing to see if principles that apply in one situation will apply in another. Making use of a concept of generalizations or law in a situation which has not yet been tested involves prediction. Scientists have not been on the moon. Yet numerous predictions of what it is like there have been made and may be proven true. Actually, the acceptance of certain predictions as fact enables planning for the moon launch to proceed with confidence. Making predictions is an important part of what scientists do.

In making descriptions, explanations, and predictions, scientists use their minds; they use ideas of their own and ideas of others as tools for testing and gaining knowledge. They use many resources to get valid answers to their questions or solutions to their problems. They may invent new tools with which to observe or to check phenomena more accurately. Thus, scientists do many things in relation to making valid descriptions, explanations, and predictions.

Now, having considered briefly the meaning of science and what scientists do, it is appropriate to ask whether good science teaching should make provisions for children to experience science in the sense discussed. Let us postpone consideration of this question while we examine the second feature of our science education model.

2. THE PURPOSES AND METHODS OF SCIENCE TEACHING

One way of representing a science education program is shown in the accompanying figures. It provides us with a way of describing a science education program and of questioning and constructively criticizing our efforts. In Figure 1, we see a three-sided polygon tapering off toward the bottom and flaring out at the top.[1] If this three-sided figure is opened to show its three faces, it would appear as in Figure 2.

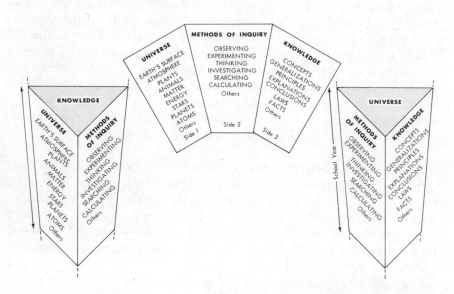

Side 1 represents our universe which is the subject matter of our study in the natural sciences. It includes objects and forces and phenomena. However, the universe and things in it are *not* science. They are simply objects and forces and phenomena. These things can be grouped and organized in various ways for purposes of study.

[1] Adapted from an unpublished working paper produced at the American Association for the Advancement of Science Conference on Science Programs for the Elementary and Junior High School, Cornell University, Ithaca, New York. 1962.

When we begin to study, to investigate, and to inquire into things in the universe, then science appears. Side 2 of the model represents some of the ways people go about investigating their world.

As a result of investigating the universe, people develop knowledge about it. Some of this is scientific knowledge which we may classify as concepts, principles, laws, and facts, for example. This knowledge is represented by Side 3 of the figure.

With this model before us for purposes of discussion (no model can *be* a science curriculum) we can visualize and think about the minimum requirements of a science program in the elementary school. Most important, the model suggests that our program must thoughtfully embrace a total concept of what science is. It is a study of the universe by methods that yield valid and reproducible knowledge. Reference to our model suggests a number of more specific considerations.

a. The universe is all around but how it is organized for study and what topics, questions, or areas are selected at a particular time is a matter of choice. Since everything cannot be studied at once, choices do have to be made. Though our model does not tell us this, it seems reasonable to believe that a variety of different choices may help children equally well to gain an adequate understanding of basic laws, principles, and concepts. For example, curriculums in some schools may focus on developing the concept of *variety* through study of "plants" and "rock forms" while another school system may organize such learning around "astronomical bodies" and "animals." To help children develop an understanding of the concept of *interaction*, some schools may organize learnings around "forms of energy" and "plant growth" while another may use "atmosphere" and "geologic changes" for this purpose.

Concept Development

b. The scientific knowledge which children learn may appear in different forms—as generalizations, principles, facts, conclusions, laws. Year by year children develop a more comprehensive set of concepts which they use as intellectual tools in interpreting and understanding new phenomena or problems. Keeping the focus on concept development enables curriculum planners and the teacher, in particular, to make judicious selection of the aspects of the environment to study so that there is not a compulsion to try to "cover" all aspects of our universe each year, or indeed year after year.

c. Helping children grow from less mature to more mature "practitioners" of the methods of inquiry is an inherent part of science teaching.

It is at this point that the temptation is great to insist that children should continuously have experiences doing the kinds of things scientists do.[2] If we recognize that children are not studying science primarily to become scientists and that science teachers may use a variety of methods and materials not necessarily used by scientists, then it seems safe to say that in good science teaching children should make inquiries and investigations, should make descriptions and explanations, and should make predictions. It might follow that teaching which denies children a variety of opportunities to "be like scientists" is neither science nor science teaching.

In this way of thinking about science teaching, the teacher has day-to-day responsibility for involving children in behaviors that are characteristic of scientists at work. Side 2 of Figure 2 shows some of the behaviors or activities of scientists. Lest the kinds of behaviors we refer to seem few, remote, and unidentifiable, we report here a longer list [3] of clue words that suggest how rich is the array of possibilities.

d. The science curriculum must enable children at every level to build on their present experience and knowledge of science, always deepening and broadening their skills of inquiry and their understanding of concepts. The experience of each child must grow and expand as he explores new areas of the environment and deepens knowledge in old ones.

Attitudes and Objectives

Let us return to our polygon again and view it from another side. (Figure 3.) Other implications for a good science program can be deduced from the model. Perhaps the reader will attempt to enumerate additional implications. Do you see a place for considering attitudes and predispositions about science? Do you see implications for statements of objectives and purposes for teaching science?

Does the model serve as a guide for evaluating specific science activities? Let us try it on the activities described earlier—the children bouncing the rubber ball and measuring shadows—and begin to make a judgment about their potential value. Answers to questions such as the following are pertinent:

1. Did the activity involve the children in describing or explaining some phenomenon?
2. Did the children collect original data from which to draw conclusions?

---

[2] An opposite point of view is developed by Derek de S. Price in an article, "Two Cultures—and One Historian of Science." *Teachers College Record*, Columbia University, April 1963, pp. 527–535.

[3] Based on an unpublished committee report of The American Association for the Advancement of Science Conference on Science for the Elementary and Junior High School, Cornell University, Ithaca, New York. 1962.

CLUE WORDS

Knowing

Observes	Describes	Accumulates	Looks
Identifies	Gathers	Counts	Sees

Manipulating

Measures	Selects	Computes	Weighs
Balances	instruments	Demonstrates	

Applying

Classifies	Distinguishes	Plans	Ponders
Assigns	Organizes	Compares	Groups
Defines	Estimates	Concludes	Decides
Associates	Equals	Experiments	
Arranges	Sorts	Controls	

Creating

Hypothesizes	Reflects	Incubates	Formulates
Induces	Proposes	Predicts	Interrelates
Deduces	Criticizes	Estimates	Generalizes
Speculates	Conceives	Explains	Forecasts
Analyzes	Invents	Appreciates	Extrapolates
Selects data	Guesses	Infers	Interpolates
Designs	Comprehends	Abstracts	
experiments	Doubts	Synthesizes	

Evaluating

Ponders	Pools data	Doubts	Transposes
Rejects	Recognizes	Verifies	Generalizes
Accepts	errors	Decides	Controls
Believes	Equates	Interprets	variables
Disbelieves	Distinguishes	Criticizes	
	Questions		

Communicating

Tabulates	Explains	Debates	Questions
Graphs	Teaches	Argues	Instructs
Writes	Informs	Describes	Plots
Speaks	Charts	Demonstrates	Draws
Reports	Reads	Compares	

3. Did the children organize and communicate about the data in useful ways?
4. Did the children have opportunities to speculate and predict?
5. Did the experience relate clearly to development of a major science concept?
6. Were some questions raised that provided stimulation for further study?

If the answer to most of these questions is yes, it is probable the science experiences in question are making a positive contribution to the science education of the children engaged in it.

This article has attempted to suggest that an understanding by teachers of what science is, particularly in terms of knowing what scientists do, is essential in developing the science curriculum or course of study. A rich science program involves children in activities that encompass the entire spectrum of ways of investigating the environment used by scientists. The effective science curriculum is planned so that children's learning activities are focused on gaining understandings of selected concepts as intellectual tools for dealing with new problems. At every level of school, children's insights and understanding of science concepts and methods should be deepened and broadened if the science program is to make its fullest contribution to the education of children.

Formulating Objectives for Elementary Science*

RONALD D. ANDERSON

Ronald D. Anderson recommends that, when formulating objectives, provision must be made for instruction in and evaluation of all the important outcomes of science instruction. All objectives can be classified into three domains: (1) cognitive, (2) affective, and (3) psychomotor. The objectives should be behavioral, and should be stated in terms of the specific behaviors which will be exhibited by the children. Also, the objectives should be dynamic, not static.

*REPRINTED FROM Science and Children, Vol. 5, No. 1, September 1967, pp. 20–23. Copyright, 1967, by the National Science Teachers Association, Washington, D.C. Reprinted by permission of the author and the publisher. Dr. Anderson is Associate Dean and Professor of Education at the University of Colorado.

The Key to Good Evaluation

The objectives of an instructional program and the program's evaluation are intimately related. Without well-stated objectives there is no basis for making any judgment as to whether or not the program has achieved the desired goals (objectives). Before examining evaluation practices and procedures, it is first necessary for us, as teachers, to be sure we have a set of objectives which is an adequate basis for our evaluation. In this first of a series of two articles on evaluation, attention will be centered on the formulation of such objectives.

Stated objectives for elementary school science, as well as other parts of the curriculum, are found in abundance in textbooks, curriculum guides, and courses of study. In most cases, however, they are so general and vague that they are of little help to the classroom teacher either in determining what he will do in teaching science to his children at 10:25 AM, Tuesday, or in evaluating the success of his efforts. For example, a frequently identified objective in science is that children should develop problem-solving skills. Although it is agreed that this is a worthwhile and important objective of science instruction, it is so general and vague that it is of little worth to a teacher in determining specifically what he will do with the children. Also this vagueness makes it almost impossible to determine at the end of a unit whether or not the objective has been achieved. In sharp contrast to the above-mentioned objective is this specific one concerning observation and classification: Each child will be able to separate a group of twelve different leaves into four groups according to their size and shape.

At this point some readers are probably asking, "Why be so specific?" The answer is simple. Unless an objective is stated precisely, it is not clear what steps should be taken to achieve the objective. Some teachers teach science only because it is part of the school program or because it has always been taught in their school. They have not stopped to consider carefully *why* science is taught. Whereas, the reasons why science is part of the curriculum determine what aspects of science will be emphasized, what approach will be used, and what objectives will be realized. Without clearly defined reasons, which in turn determine the objectives, teachers have no basis for deciding the questions of "what aspects" and "how." A broad objective such as "to develop problem-solving ability" may be a good starting point but it must be broken down into a more detailed description before decisions are made about "what aspects" and "how" for classroom use. In the grouping of leaves activity, the broad objective has not been rejected, only stated in much greater detail, i.e., classifying objects is part of solving some problems.

Basically, science is included in the curriculum because it is such a large and influential part of our culture. Of course, science is much more than a body of knowledge about the material universe. To understand science, one must understand the process of science (the means of investigation by which the body of knowledge is acquired) as well as the products of science (the body of knowledge that results from the investigations). Since a basic objective is for children to understand science, our specific objectives for each unit or day should reflect this basic and far-reaching objective. The precise objectives that are formulated for each class period should reflect the fact that a basic and overriding objective is that children will acquire an understanding of both the products and processes of the scientific enterprise.

Make Provisions for All Objectives

A basic consideration in preparing objectives is that provision must be made for instruction in and evaluation of all the important desired outcomes of science instruction. The stated objectives which serve as the basis for instruction and evaluation should reflect all of the desired outcomes. A brief look at a classification of educational objectives might be useful in determining if the objectives are limited and unimaginative. Such a classification is Bloom's *Taxonomy of Educational Objectives*.[1] In this scheme, all objectives have been classified into one of three "domains"— *cognitive, affective,* and *psychomotor*. The objectives which are generally given most attention by the teacher of elementary science fall within the cognitive domain which includes the recognition and recall of information and also the development of various intellectual abilities. Many of the objectives which are included in textbooks and curriculum guides, but to which teachers less often direct their teachings, are part of the affective domain. These pertain to the development of attitudes, values, interest, and appreciation. Physical, manipulative, and motor abilities are part of the psychomotor domain.

Since the cognitive domain receives most attention, it will be examined here in greater detail. A look at the various levels of this domain will give some insight into the level of sophistication of objectives.

The first and lowest level in the cognitive domain is the *knowledge* level. It includes the recall of specifics (e.g. ice is a form of water), structures (e.g. the skeletal structure of vertebrates), or scientific processes (e.g. a control is an important part of an experiment). The knowledge level emphasizes that which would be described as remembering. Of course, the examples given here could be understood at a deeper level. They are

[1] Bloom, Benjamin S., Editor. *Taxonomy of Educational Objectives, The Classification of Educational Goals, Handbook I: Cognitive Domain.* David McKay Company, Inc., New York City. 1956.

classified at this level if it is only a matter of being able to remember the information rather than a deeper understanding such as being able to apply it to a new situation or synthesizing several items of knowledge. These deeper understandings are dealt with in other levels of this classification system. The entire taxonomy is a hierarchy in which each lower level of understanding is necessary before understanding at the next higher level is possible.

The second level is *comprehension* which includes translation from one form to another. Examples would be drawing a graph of daily temperature changes from a list of temperatures recorded over a period of days or weeks, or explaining verbally what is meant by a statement which is expressed in mathematical symbols.

Application, which is the third level, requires the ability to apply abstract ideas in a concrete situation. Examples would be the ability to use a knowledge of the relationship between heat and the expansion and contraction of liquids to explain how a thermometer works, use a knowledge of classification to classify a group of seashells according to size, shape, or color, or use a knowledge of electric circuits to cause a light bulb to light a cell, bulb, and pieces of wire.

Analysis, the fourth level, involves breaking down an idea into its various parts and determining the relationship between the parts. Determining which statements about an experiment are facts and which are hypotheses, or determining which factors led to an unexpected conclusion of any experiment would be examples.

Synthesis, the fifth level, includes taking parts and putting them together to form a whole such as skill in expressing verbally or in writing the results of an experiment using an appropriate organization of ideas. Other examples would be formulating a hypothesis to explain why some animals are less active in the daytime than at night or why water poured on a fire will often put out the fire.

Evaluation, the highest of the six levels in the cognitive domain, includes making judgments. An example is the ability to state the fallacies in an analysis of an experiment. Another example is the ability to evaluate popular beliefs about health.

The reason for looking at this classification of objectives is to gain some insight into the sophistication of the objectives we actually are endeavoring to reach in our teaching. Is teaching aimed at the remembering of facts and ideas or are children expected to be able to apply these facts and ideas? Do some children arrive at junior high school without having been challenged to analyze, synthesize, or evaluate ideas? Do the children gain a greater interest in science or a better appreciation of its place in society? If this classification of objectives has caused the readers to think critically about the objectives of their science program, it has served the purpose for which it was included here.

Objectives Should Be Behavioral

So far, it has been pointed out that objectives should be specific, in keeping with the area of study at hand, and not be limited to the knowledge level. In addition, objectives should be stated in a manner that permits a judgment about the attainment of the objectives. To make this possible, objectives should be stated in terms of the behaviors which will be exhibited by the children. Objectives stated in this form are often spoken of as behavioral objectives or performance objectives. Behavioral objectives have been talked about for years, but recently they have received renewed and closer attention. For example, *Preparing Instructional Objectives*, a small book by Mager,[2] is devoted entirely to the "how" of writing good behavioral objectives. *Science—A Process Approach*,[3] the experimental elementary science program sponsored by the American Association for the Advancement of Science, has behavioral objectives set up for each lesson in the program. In addition to providing a basis for the teacher's efforts in aiding student learning, the behavioral objectives provide the basis for the extensive evaluation which is being conducted by the sponsors of the program.

In order to understand what is meant by a behavioral objective, let us look at some of the basic ideas presented by Mager. First of all, an appropriate objective is *not* a description of what the lesson is about, but is a statement of what the learner will be able to DO at the end of the learning activity. For example, "a study of the kinds of materials that are attracted by magnets" is a description of what is to be included in a certain science lesson. It is an objective. In contrast, although in some ways incomplete, the following is an objective: "At the conclusion of this lesson the children will be able to state what kinds of materials are attracted by magnets." It describes what the children will be able to do. Thus, the first step in formulating good behavioral objectives is deciding what the child should be DOING when the instruction has been successful.

A key to writing good objectives is the verb which describes what the child will be able to do. Some are vague and open to many interpretations. Others have clarity and convey a definite meaning. Consider carefully the chart of examples from Mager[4] on the opposite page:

There is nothing wrong with teaching children to "understand" and "enjoy," but clear communication of ideas requires that objectives be stated in terms of what they will be DOING that indicates they "understand" or "enjoy." How else will teachers know if children are "understanding" or "enjoying?"

[2] Mager, Robert F. *Preparing Instructional Objectives*. Fearon Publishers, Palo Alto, California. 1962.

[3] *Science—A Progress Approach*. American Association for the Advancement of Science, Washington, D.C. 1966.

[4] Mager, *op. cit.*, p. 11.

WORDS OPEN TO MANY INTERPRETATIONS	WORDS OPEN TO FEWER INTERPRETATIONS
to know	to write
to understand	to recite
to *really* understand	to identify
to appreciate	to differentiate
to fully appreciate	to solve
to grasp the significance of	to construct
to enjoy	to list
to believe	to compare
to have faith in	to contrast

After determining what behaviors are the object of instruction, a second major question can be considered: Under what conditions will these behaviors be observed? The answer to the question will progress one step further toward a precisely stated performance objective. Consider this objective: At the end of this lesson, the child should be able to identify constellations in the night sky. Does it state the conditions under which the objective is to be reached?

It does not indicate whether the child is expected to make the identification with or without the aid of a star chart or other reference. It does not state whether the student is given a list of the names and asked to assign these names to the appropriate constellation or whether the student is expected to produce the names from memory. Therefore, the objective should be restated.

A third major question that should be considered in formulating performance objectives is "How well is the child expected to perform?" or "What is the minimum acceptable level of performance?" Look again at the objective above on identifying constellations in the night sky. Is the objective stated in such a way that this kind of question is answered? It does not tell *how many* constellations the child is expected to identify. Also, in the case of some objectives, it may be desirable to indicate *how long* the child has to attain the objective.

Now the objective concerning identification of constellations can be restated in a more precise form: At the end of this lesson the child should be able to identify at least five constellations when given a star chart as a guide. This objective answers the three basic questions: What is the behavior? What are the conditions? and What is the minimum acceptable level of performance?

Can Objectives Be Made Behavioral?

Readers are no doubt asking "Can all of our objectives be stated in behavioral form with the conditions and minimum level of performance clearly indicated?" It may not always be easy. For example, a common objective of science education is the development of interest in science. It must be asked what behaviors on the part of the child will indicate that this interest is present. Would behaviors such as reading books on science, visiting a local science museum, or building a simple telescope for observing the stars and planets be indicators of this interest? Difficulties may be encountered in giving the *conditions* and *minimum level* of performance for such an objective, but the objectives can be framed in terms that will allow teachers to make judgments on the basis of student performance. A teacher's objective might be: the child will pursue his interest in astronomy by such means as, reading library books on astronomy, visiting the local museum, and making night-sky observations.

As another example, there is certainly a place in the elementary school science curriculum for free exploration on the part of children, such as "playing around" with magnets in an undirected fashion or observing mealworms for an extended period of time without definite directions concerning what they should observe. Such activities often lead to the posing of interesting questions and interesting hypotheses that might answer the questions as well as creating means of testing hypotheses. Objectives for such activities should reflect *why* the children are being encouraged in this direction. Objectives might be: by the end of the class the child will have posed two or more questions concerning magnets, or by the end of the class the child will have posed two or more hypotheses as possible answers to questions concerning the behavior of mealworms, or the child will design an experiment for testing a hypothesis concerning the behavior of mealworms. Here again, there may be some difficulties stating conditions and minimum levels, but the children's behavior can be used as the referent in determining if the activity was worthwhile. It must be granted that educators cannot always state their objectives as precisely as they would like, but they can certainly do better than they often have done in the past.

Objectives are dynamic not static. They are based on more than the structure of the subject and thus they change as a result of experience with children in the classroom. The teacher may find that an object is not realistic in view of the level of maturity of the children or classroom experience may suggest a different objective which is more profitable to pursue than the one originally stated. It is necessary to begin by carefully specifying objectives, but to be flexible enough to alter them as experience indicates. Careful stating of objectives provides an aid to the clear thinking and planning which must continue throughout the duration of the science instruction.

This article has been concerned with the formulation of objectives for the elementary school science curriculum. After they are formulated, the next step is to teach to attain these objectives. That is the job of the reader.

The Development of Scientific Attitudes *

RICHARD E. HANEY

Although considerable emphasis has been placed recently on the teaching of inquiry skills, manipulative skills, and science knowledge, Richard E. Haney sees the need to re-focus attention on the learning of scientific attitudes. He discusses the following attitudes which directly govern the intellectual behavior of scientists and science students: curiosity, rationality, suspended judgment, open-mindedness, critical-mindedness, objectivity, honesty, and humility. These attitudes must be planned for and not simply accepted as concomitants to cognitive outcomes. Eight steps are suggested that teachers can take to facilitate the learning of attitudes.

In the last few years considerable emphasis has been placed on the teaching of inquiry skills as well as on useful knowledge and manipulative skills. Some mention has been made of scientific attitudes, to be sure, but these still remain inconsistently defined in the literature and obscure in teaching plans. Daily lessons tend to center around some conceptual theme, a major principle, or some other form of cognitive learning outcome while affective learnings at best are considered peripheral to this central idea.

The habits of thought associated with scientific thinking deserve more careful consideration. Problem-solving skills are essentially amoral. Knowledge and intellectual prowess divorced from the controlling influence of desirable attitudes toward man and nature contribute to the phenomenon which Robert Cohen termed the "frustration of humane living inherent in science of the twentieth century." (2) Science supposedly molds the character of its practitioners. To be scientific means that one has such attitudes as curiosity, rationality, suspended judgment, open-mindedness, critical-mindedness, objectivity, honesty, and humility.

Science lessons present many opportunities for teachers to help pupils

*REPRINTED FROM *The Science Teacher*, Vol. 31, No. 8, December 1964, pp. 33–35. Copyright, 1964, by the National Science Teachers Association, Washington, D.C. Reprinted by permission of the author and the publisher. Dr. Haney is Associate Professor of Education at the University of Wisconsin, Milwaukee.

develop these attitudes, which also have value outside the classroom and in other areas of human experience. Let us then consider the nature of attitudes, examine these eight attitudes and the overt behavior governed by them, and suggest appropriate learning experiences.

One of the most frequently quoted definitions of attitudes is the statement by Allport in which an attitude is described as a "mental and neural state of readiness, organized through experience, exerting a directive or dynamic influence upon the individual's response to all objectives and situations with which it is related." (1) Sells and Trites point out that such mental and neural states cannot be observed directly in students. "An attitude is a psychological construct, or latent variable, inferred from observable responses to stimuli, which is assumed to mediate consistency and covariation among these responses." (6) Attitudes regulate behavior that is directed toward or away from some object or situation or group of objects or situations. Attitudes have emotional content and vary in intensity and generality according to the range of objects or situations over which they apply. For the most part, attitudes are learned and are difficult to distinguish from such affective attributes of personality as interests, appreciations, likes, dislikes, opinions, values, ideals, and character traits.

Guides to Scientific Behavior

A recent attempt to analyze the process through which attitudes are acquired appears in the *Taxonomy of Educational Objectives, Handbook II: Affective Domain*. Attitudes are said to emerge first at the level of "willingness to respond" and become increasingly internalized in the learner through the stages of "satisfaction in response," "acceptance of a value," "preference for a value," "commitment," and "conceptualization of a value." At this last stage the learner is able to "see how the value relates to those that he already holds or to new ones that he is coming to hold." (4)

The first attitude to be considered is *curiosity*. This is the desire for understanding on the part of the student when confronted by a novel situation which he cannot explain in terms of his existing knowledge. A curious person asks questions, reads to find information, and readily initiates and carries out investigations. Curiosity is a stimulus to inquiry, and it is a desirable outcome of instructon as well. Each discovery raises new questions and suggests new undertakings. Pupils should leave science courses with greater curiosity than they had at the outset. But, who are the most curious? Usually they are the younger children. Somehow our pupils manage to lose the spirit of inquiry with advancing age. Each teacher must ask himself how he can teach for heightened curiosity. Curiosity is learned. It can be learned or repressed in the classroom.

Problematic situations in which answers and explanations are not immediately available help to stimulate curiosity. The solutions of problems should raise new problems.

While curiosity stimulates inquiry, the attitude of *rationality* guides the scientist's behavior throughout his investigation. This is the habit of looking for natural causes for natural events. The rational person is not superstitious. The prescientific period in our history was marked by numerous examples of mythological explanations. This tradition still abounds in our folklore and in the everyday thinking of many persons. To help them develop the attitude of rationality, pupils can be confronted with situations in which careful reasoning proves superior to explanations of a superstitious nature.

Willingness to suspend judgment is another attribute of personality fundamental to scientific behavior. Persons with this attitude accumulate sufficient evidence before making judgments or drawing conclusions. They recognize the tentative nature of hypotheses and the revisionary character of our knowledge. To learn the attitude of suspended judgment, our students should be confronted with situations in which this behavior is rewarded or in some way leads to success while formation of conclusions without evidence leads to failure. Pupils should examine explicitly the consequences of jumping to conclusions.

Science teachers ought to examine closely the common practice of asking students to formulate a conclusion at the end of every five-minute demonstration or forty-minute experiment. These activities concern but a limited sample of all the phenomena governed by the principle under consideration. At the end of these experiences students should have the opportunity to choose among formulating a generalization with various qualifications, stating that they have only learned something about the particular operation at hand, or stating that they could make no sense of the data.

Acceptance of New Ideas

Open-mindedness is closely akin to suspended judgment. To comprehend science as the human enterprise that it is, our future citizens must learn from experience that our ideas of what is true may change. They must be able to revise their opinions or conclusions in the light of new evidence. Experiences that foster open-mindedness include those in which pupils are confronted with the need to revise a belief as the result of having acquired new information on the subject.

The willingness to consider novel hypotheses and explanations and to attempt unorthodox procedures is a form of open-mindedness toward creative ideas which amounts to the "no holds barred" attitude of the scientist. The scientific method is not simply the application of routine and predetermined procedures to new problems. The study of new areas of knowledge often requires the invention of new methods of inquiry. Popular conceptions and explanations may fail to fit new bits of evidence. The history of science contains the stories of men who broke with traditions and saw nature in a new light. To foster this creative spirit in the classroom, teachers can provide experiences in which pupils have the opportunity to design their own investigations and invent and evaluate their own explanations for natural phenomena.

New ideas are not accepted in science simply because they are new or different. To be scientific also means to be *critically minded*. A person with this attitude looks for evidence and arguments that support other persons' assertions. He challenges authority with the quesions "How do you know?" and "Why do we believe?" He is concerned about the sources of his knowledge. One of the greatest temptations confronting the science teacher is that of giving direct answers to children's questions and of offering glib explanations. Teachers need to be careful of answers that include the word "because." Most explanations are not as simple as they might possibly appear at first.

How must teachers behave if their students are to learn the attitude of critical-mindedness? How often do they encourage their students to ask in class "How do you know?" To foster the learning of this attitude, teachers should provide evidence to support the generalizations in the lessons. Pupils should be taught to look for arguments and evidence supporting important propositions, and they should be taught to provide these in their own communications. The reading of historical and biographical accounts of investigations are also valuable experiences from which pupils can learn of the sources of our current knowledge.

The scientist must also be *objective* in gathering and interpreting his data and intellectually *honest* in communicating his findings. To learn the attitude of objectivity, students may be confronted by situations in which the temptation to permit personal feelings to interfere with the recording of an observation or the interpretation of data must be successfully resisted in order to achieve a correct or accurate solution of a problem. Complete objectivity is difficult to achieve because an observer's perceptions are governed by his previous experiences and his expectations.

Intellectual honesty, on the other hand, is concerned with the conscious act of truthfully reporting observations. Teachers have to ask themselves how they reward honesty in their classrooms. In the laboratory, for instance, do the pupils know the *right* answers to report regardless of their actual sense data? The value of open-ended experiences for instructional purposes is that they are more like those of the scientist at the frontier of knowledge where the answers are not yet known. Science could not be the cumulative enterprise that it is if it were not for the objectivity and honesty of its practitioners.

Personal View of World

The foregoing attitudes directly govern the intellectual behavior of scientists and science students. To be "scientific" means to have these personality traits. In our classrooms, however, children learn more than the content and processes of science. They incorporate these bits of knowledge and skills along with those gained in other subjects and extracurricular experiences into their personal views of the world and their places in it. Each student gradually builds his own philosophy of life.

Humility is a desirable ingredient of the mature personality. It can be learned, at least in part, as a result of science instruction. Science can teach children to recognize their own limitations as well as the limitations of science itself. This is the attitude that underlies the conservation movement. It is the humble person who uses natural resources wisely, for the common good, even though he might have to forego immediate gains that could accrue from their exploitation.

Relationship to Nature

On the other hand, man's relationship to nature is more than a matter of "wise use." He shares this world with other beings whose "rights" deserve to be recognized. The history of science and also of religion is a story of man's struggle with his own egocentricism. The message that Rachel Carson gave us in *Silent Spring* relates a current episode in that story. Albert Schweitzer has expressed the attitude of humility in terms of "reverence for life" which identifies the moral principle that the good consists in the preservation, enhancement, and exaltation of life, and that destruction, injury, and retardation of life are evil. The world presents a spectacle of "will-to-live" contending against itself. One organism asserts itself at the expense of another. Man can only preserve his own life at the cost of taking lives. One who holds to the ethic of reverence for life injures or destroys only out of necessity. Never does such a person kill other beings from thoughtlessness. (5) There is a curious similarity in the messages of Rachel Carson, the scientist, and Albert Schweitzer, the theologian.

What sort of humility or reverence for life is taught in our biology classes? The trend, at present, is to increase the amount of experimentation with living materials in order to make the work of the student more like that of the scientist. But, perhaps, we have in "reverence for life" a limitation to the discovery method of teaching. What attitudes do the students learn if animals are dissected merely to show that the chart on the wall or the plastic model on the demonstration table is correct? What concern for other lives is taught if an anesthetized rat is cut open so that the students can experiment with the heart of a dying animal? Such activities are likely to reaffirm the attitude that all of creation belongs to man to be plucked, manipulated, harvested, or controlled at his will for purposes *he* considers essential. To teach the attitude of reverence for life, it may be that vicarious experiences will have to be employed to a great extent, even though to do so would be to compromise the principle of making learning experiences as much like those of the scientist as possible.

To Foster Attitude Building

The attitudes which have been explored are attributes of intellectually and emotionally mature individuals, persons who do not only behave outwardly in desirable ways but who understand why they act as they do. If these and other attitudes are to be fostered, they must be planned for and not simply accepted as concomitants to cognitive outcomes. Klaus-meier suggests eight steps that teachers can take to facilitate the learning of attitudes. (3) These may be interpreted in terms of the problems of science teaching in the following manner:

1. The attitude to be taught must be identified. Examples of attitudes related to science have been identified in this article.
2. The meanings of the vocabulary used to describe attitudes or the behaviors related to them must be clarified for the learner.
3. Informative experience about the attitude "object" should be provided. In the case of scientific attitudes these "objects" are usually the various situations that occur in the problem-solving process. Typical of these are (a) the sensing of the problem in a perplexing situation, (b) clarifying and defining the problem, (c) formulating of hypotheses, (d) reasoning out the consequences of the hypotheses and the designing of investigations, (e) gathering of data, (f) treating and interpreting of data, (g) generalizing or drawing conclusions, and (h) communicating the results of the investigation to others. Students need to be instructed in the performance of each of these steps and in their relationships to the various attitudes that characterize the scientifically minded person. It is hoped, of course, that pupils will exhibit these attitudes in appropriate situations outside the classroom. To help them generalize these attitudes, teachers can point out the general nature of the attitude object by showing similarities between scientific problem-solving procedures and the treatment of problematic situations in daily affairs.
4. Desirable identifying figures for the learner should be provided. These models, whether they be teachers, parents, peers, or historical figures, provide the learner with ready-made behaviors which he can use as his first attempts at the desired behavior.
5. Pleasant emotional experiences should accompany the learning of the

attitudes. Pupils need freedom to attempt their own patterns of exploration and sufficient time to pursue an investigation to the point where they experience the satisfaction that accompanies inquiry and discovery.

6. Appropriate contexts for practice and confirmation should be arranged. Learning experiences must be selected on the basis of knowledge, skills, and attitudes to be learned. At times the central theme of a lesson might have to be a particular attitude with other learnings playing secondary roles.

7. Group techniques should be used to facilitate understanding and acceptance. The varied activities possible in well-equipped science rooms permit students to learn as individuals on some occasions and as members of groups of varying sizes on others. Group decision making that occurs in the planning and carrying out of investigations and the evaluation of results permits a sharing of emotional commitment which can enhance the learning of an attitude.

8. Deliberate cultivation of the desired attitude should also be encouraged. Pupils need to be aware of the behaviors that accompany an attitude and to practice them. Sometimes this requires the difficult task of breaking old habits or of improving poorly learned ones. The teacher must be able to provide guidance for this learning.

There are implications in what has been said for the education of teachers as well as for the instruction of schoolchildren. It has often been said that "you can't teach something you don't know." A corollary to this generalization might be this: "Pupils cannot learn attitudes that their teachers don't have." It may very well be that the first step in meeting this challenge to science education will consist of an inward look upon our own knowledge and value systems. Science teachers have a responsibility. It is to them that the public turns for an understanding of science, not just the facts of science, or the skills, but also for a perspective that relates science to all other areas of human experience.

References

1. Gordon Allport. "Attitudes." Chapter 17 in *Handbook of Social Psychology*, C. Murchison, Editor. Clark University Press, 1935. p. 806. Quoted in *Children's Thinking* by David Russell. Ginn and Company, Boston, Massachusetts. 1956. p. 170.

2. Robert S. Cohen. "Individuality and Common Purpose: The Philosophy of Science." *The Science Teacher*, 31:27-33. May 1964, p. 31.

3. Herbert Klausmeier. *Learning and Human Abilities: Educational Psychology*. Harper & Row, Publishers, New York. 1961. p. 267.

4. David Krathwohl et al. *Taxonomy of Educational Objectives, Handbook II: Affective Domain*. David McKay Company, Inc., New York. 1964. p. 36.

5. Albert Schweitzer. *The Philosophy of Civilization*, translated by C. T. Campion. The Macmillan Company, New York. 1959. pp. 307-329.
6. Saul Sells and David Trites. "Attitudes" in *Encyclopedia of Educational Research*, Chester Harris, Editor. The Macmillan Company, New York. 1960. p. 103.

Behavioral Objectives in Curriculum Design: A Cautionary Note*

J. MYRON ATKIN

Dr. Atkin has several reservations about the use of behaviorally stated objectives for curriculum design. He sees the fundamental problem as being the easy assumption that we either know or can readily identify the educational objectives for which we strive and the educational outcomes that result. He believes that when any curriculum is used, there are important learning outcomes which cannot have been anticipated when the objectives were formulated. He also believes that certain types of innovation are hampered and frustrated by early demands for behavioral statements of objectives. Finally, Dr. Atkin discusses the question of priorities of objectives. He concludes that, although behavioral goals can be stated in a relatively easy fashion, they may or may not be worthwhile.

In certain influential circles, anyone who confesses to reservations about the use of behaviorally stated objectives for curriculum planning runs the risk of being labeled as the type of individual who would attack the virtues of motherhood. Bumper stickers have appeared at my own institution, and probably at yours, reading, STAMP OUT NON-BEHAVIORAL OBJECTIVES. I trust that the person who prepared the stickers had humor as his primary aim; nevertheless, the crusade for specificity of educational outcome has become intense and evangelical. The worthiness of this particular approach has come to be accepted as self-evident by ardent proponents, proponents who sometimes sound like the true believers who cluster about a new social or religious movement.

Behavioral objectives enthusiasts are warmly endorsed and embraced by the systems and operations analysis advocates, most educational technologists, the cost-benefit economists, the planning-programing budgeting

*REPRINTED FROM *The Science Teacher*, Vol. 35, No. 5, May 1968, pp. 27–30. Copyright, 1968, by the National Science Teachers Association, Washington, D.C. Reprinted by permission of the author and the publisher. Dr. Atkin is Dean of the College of Education and Professor of Education at the University of Illinois.

system stylists, and many others. In fact, the behavioral objectives people are now near the center of curriculum decision making. Make no mistake; they have replaced the academicians and the general curriculum theorists— especially in the new electronically based education industries and in governmental planning agencies. The engineering model for educational research and development represents a forceful tide today. Those who have a few doubts about the effects of the tide had better be prepared to be considered uninitiated and naive, if not slightly addlepated and antiquarian.

To utilize the techniques for long-term planning and rational decision making that have been developed with such apparent success in the Department of Defense, and that are now being applied to a range of domestic and civilian problems, it is essential that hard data be secured. Otherwise these modes for developmental work and planning are severely limited. Fuzzy and tentative statements of possible achievement and questions of conflict with respect to underlying values are not compatible with the new instructional systems management approaches—at least not with the present state of the art. In fact, delineating instructional objectives in terms of identifiable pupil behaviors or performances seems essential in 1968 for assessing the output of the educational system. Currently accepted wisdom does not seem to admit an alternative.

There are overwhelmingly useful purposes served by attempting to identify educational goals in non-ambiguous terms. To plan rationally for a growing educational system, and to continue to justify relatively high public expenditures for education, it seems that we do need a firmer basis for making assessments and decisions than now exists. Current attention to specification of curriculum objectives in terms of pupil performance represents an attempt to provide direction for collection of data that will result in more informed choice among competing alternatives.

Efforts to identify educational outcomes in behavioral terms also provide a fertile ground for coping with interesting research problems and challenging technical puzzles. A world of educational research opens to the investigator when he has reliable measures of educational output (even when their validity for educational purposes is low). Pressures from researchers are difficult to resist since they do carry influence in the educational community, particularly in academic settings and in educational development laboratories.

Hence I am not unmindful of some of the possible benefits to be derived from attempts to rationalize our decision-making processes through the use of behaviorally stated objectives. Schools need a basis for informed choice. And the care and feeding of educational researchers is a central part of my job at Illinois. However, many of the enthusiasts have given insufficient attention to underlying assumptions and broad questions of educational policy. I intend in this brief paper to highlight a few of these issues in the hope that the exercise might be productive of further and deeper discussion.

Several reservations about the use of behaviorally stated objectives for curriculum design will be catalogued here. But perhaps the fundamental problem, as I see it, lies in the easy assumption that we either know or can readily identify the educational objectives for which we strive, and thereafter the educational outcomes that result from our programs. One contention basic to my argument is that we presently are making progress toward thousands of goals in any existing educational program, progress of which we are perhaps dimly aware, can articulate only with great difficulty, and that contribute toward goals which are incompletely stated (or unrecognized), but which are often worthy.

For example, a child who is learning about mealworm behavior by blowing against the animal through a straw is probably learning much more than how this insect responds to a gentle stream of warm air. Let's assume for the moment that we can specify "behaviorally" all that he might learn about mealworm *behavior* (an arduous and never-ending task). In addition, in this "simple" activity, he is probably finding out something about interaction of objects, forces, humane treatment of animals, his own ability to manipulate the environment, structural characterisics of the larval form of certain insects, equilibrium, the results of doing an experiment at the suggestion of the teacher, the rewards of independent experimentation, the judgment of the curriculum developers in suggesting that children engage in such an exercise, possible uses of a plastic straw, and the length of time for which one individual might be engaged in a learning activity and still display a high degree of interest. I am sure there are many additional learnings, literally too numerous to mention in fewer than eight or ten pages. When any piece of curriculum is used with real people, there are important learning outcomes that cannot have been anticipated when the objectives were formulated. And of the relatively few outcomes that can be identified at all, a smaller number still are translatable readily in terms of student behavior. There is a possibility the cumulative side effects are at least as important as the intended main effects.

Multiply learning outcomes from the mealworm activity by all the various curriculum elements we attempt to build into a school day. Then multiply this by the number of days in a school year, and you have some indication of the oversimplification that *always* occurs when curriculum intents or outcomes are articulated in any form that is considered manageable.

If my argument has validity to this point, the possible implications are potentially dangerous. If identification of all worthwhile outcomes in behavioral terms comes to be commonly accepted and expected, then it is inevitable that, over time, the curriculum will tend to emphasize those elements which have been thus identified. Important outcomes which are detected only with great difficulty and which are translated only rarely into behavioral terms tend to atrophy. They disappear from the curriculum because we spend all the time allotted to us in teaching explicitly for the more readily specifiable learnings to which we have been directed.

We have a rough analogy in the use of tests. Prestigious examinations that are widely accepted and broadly used, such as the New York State Regents examinations, tend over time to determine the curriculum. Whether or not these examinations indeed measure all outcomes that are worth achieving, the curriculum regresses toward the objectives reflected by the test items. Delineation of lists of behavioral objectives, like broadly used testing programs, may admirably serve the educational researcher because it gives him indices of gross achievement as well as detail of particular achievement; it may also provide input for cost-benefit analysts and governmental planners at all levels because it gives them hard data with which to work; but the program in the schools may be affected detrimentally by the gradual disappearance of worthwhile learning activities for which we have not succeeded in establishing a one-to-one correspondence between curriculum elements and rather difficult-to-measure educational results.

Among the learning activities most readily lost are those that are long term and private in effect and those for which a single course provides only a small increment. If even that increment cannot be identified, it tends to lose out in the teacher's priority scheme, because it is competing with other objectives which have been elaborately stated and to which he has been alerted. But I will get to the question of priority of objectives a bit later.

The second point I would like to develop relates to the effect of demands for behavioral specification on innovation. My claim here is that certain types of innovation, highly desirable ones, are hampered and frustrated by early demands for behavioral statements of objectives.

Let's focus on the curriculum reform movement of the past 15 years, the movement initiated by Max Beberman in 1952 when he began to design a mathematics program in order that the high school curriculum would reflect concepts central to modern mathematics. We have now seen curriculum development efforts, with this basic flavor, in many science fields, the social sciences, English, esthetics, etc. When one talks with the initiators of such projects, particularly at the beginning of their efforts, one finds that they do not begin by talking about the manner in which they would like to change pupils' behavior. Rather they are dissatisfied with existing curricula in their respective subject fields, and they want to build something new. If pressed, they might indicate that existing programs stress concepts considered trivial by those who practice the discipline. They might also say that the curriculum poorly reflects styles of intellectual inquiry in the various fields. Press them further, and they might say that they want to build a new program that more accurately displays the "essence" of history, or physics, or economics, or whatever. Or a program that better transmits a comprehension of the elaborate and elegant interconnections among various concepts within the discipline.

If they are asked at an early stage just how they want pupils to behave differently, they are likely to look quite blank. Academicians in the various cognate fields do not speak the language of short-term or long-term behavioral change, as do many psychologists. In fact, if a hard-driving behaviorist attempts to force the issue and succeeds, one finds that the disciplinarians can come up with a list of behavioral goals that looks like a caricature of the subject field in question. (Witness the AAAS elementary-school science program directed toward teaching "process.")

Further, early articulation of behavioral objectives by the curriculum developer inevitably tends to limit the range of his exploration. He becomes committed to designing programs that achieve these goals. Thus if specific objectives in behavioral terms are identified early, there tends to be a limiting element built into the new curriculum. The innovator is less alert to potentially productive tangents.

The effective curriculum developer typically begins with *general* objectives. He then refines the program through a series of successive approximations. He doesn't start with a blueprint, and he isn't in much of a hurry to get his ideas represented by a blueprint.

A situation is created in the newer curriculum design procedures based on behaviorally stated objectives in which scholars who do not talk a behavioral-change language are expected to describe their goals at a time when the intricate intellectual subtleties of their work may not be clear, even in the disciplinary language with which they are familiar. At the other end, the educational evaluator, the behavioral specifier, typically has very little understanding of the curriculum that is being designed—understanding with respect to the new view of the subject field that it affords. It is too much to expect that the behavioral analyst, or anyone else, recognize the shadings of meaning in various evolving economic theories, the complex applications of the intricacies of wave motion, or the richness of nuance reflected in a Stravinsky composition.

Yet despite this two-culture problem—finding a match between the behavioral analysts and the disciplinary scholars—we still find that an expectation is being created for early behavioral identification of essential outcomes.

(Individuals who are concerned with producing hard data reflecting educational outputs would run less risk of dampening innovation if they were to enter the curriculum development scene in a more unobtrusive fashion—and later—than is sometimes the case. The curriculum developer goes into the classroom with only a poorly articulated view of the changes he wants to make. Then he begins working with children to see what he can do. He revises. He develops new ideas. He continually modifies as he develops. *After* he has produced a program that seems pleasing, it might then be a productive exercise for the behavioral analyst to attempt with the curriculum developer to identify *some* of the ways in which children seem to be behaving differently. If this approach is taken, I would caution, however, that observers be alert for long-term as well as short-term effects, subtle as well as obvious inputs.)

A third basic point to be emphasized relates to the question of instructional priorities, mentioned earlier. I think I have indicated that there is a vast library of goals that represent possible outcomes for any instructional program. A key educational task, and a task that is well handled by the effective teacher, is that of relating educational goals to the situation at hand—as well as relating the situation at hand to educational goals. It is impractical to pursue all goals thoroughly. And it does make a difference *when* you try to teach something. Considerable educational potential is lost when certain concepts are taught didactically. Let's assume that some third-grade teacher considers it important to develop concepts related to sportsmanship. It would be a rather naive teacher who decided that she would undertake this task at 1:40 PM on Friday of next week. The experienced teacher has always realized that learnings related to such an area must be stressed in an appropriate context, and the context often cannot be planned.

Perhaps there is no problem in accepting this view with respect to a concept like sportsmanship, but I submit that a similar case can be made for a range of crucial cognitive outcomes that are basic to various subject-matter fields. I use science for my examples because I know more about this field than about others. But equilibrium, successive approximation, symmetry, entropy, and conservation are pervasive ideas with a broad range of application. These ideas are taught with the richest meaning only when they are emphasized repeatedly in appropriate and varied contexts. Many of these contexts arise in classroom situations that are unplanned, but that have powerful potential. It is detrimental to learning not to capitalize on the opportune moments for effectively teaching one idea or another. Riveting the teacher's attention to a few behavioral goals provides him with blinders that may limit his range. Directing him to hundreds of goals leads to confusing, mechanical pedagogic style and loss of spontaneity.

A final point to be made in this paper relates to values, and it deals with a primary flaw in the consumption of much educational research. It is difficult to resist the assumption that those attributes which we can measure are the elements which we consider most important. This point relates to my first, but I feel that it is essential to emphasize the problem. The behavioral analyst seems to assume that for an objective to be worthwhile, we must have methods of observing progress. But worthwhile goals come first, not our methods for assessing progress toward these goals. Goals are derived from our needs and from our philosophies. They are not and should not be derived primarily from our measures. It borders on the irresponsible for those who exhort us to state objectives in behavioral terms to avoid the issue of determining worth. Inevitably there is an implication of worth behind any act of measurement. What the educational community poorly realizes at the moment is that behavioral goals may or may not be worthwhile. They are articulated from among the vast library of goals because they are stated relatively easily. Again, let's not assume that what we can presently measure necessarily represents our most important activity.

I hope that in this paper I have increased rather than decreased the possibilities for constructive discourse about the use of behavioral objectives for curriculum design. The issues here represent a few of the basic questions that seem crucial enough to be examined in an open forum that admits the possibility of fresh perspectives. Too much of the debate related to the use of behavioral objectives has been conducted in an argumentative style that characterizes discussions of fundamental religious views among adherents who are poorly informed. A constructive effort might be centered on identification of those issues which seem to be amenable to resolution by empirical means and those which do not. At any rate, I feel confident that efforts of the next few years will better inform us about the positive as well as negative potential inherent in a view of curriculum design that places the identification of behavioral objectives at the core.

The Elementary Science Program

INTRODUCTION

The science program in the elementary school should be planned and structured, just as is done in the other areas of the elementary school curriculum. All too often elementary science programs have been either non-existent or else very loosely planned and structured. In such cases the elementary science textbook would usually serve both as science program and curriculum guide for the teachers. Sometimes a school system would list the science topics and concepts to be learned for each grade and include a number of suggested activities for teaching these topics and concepts.

In recent years there has been a steadily increasing trend to planned, structured programs, developed cooperatively by the teachers with the help of administrators and science supervisors, educators, and scientists. When planning such programs the first step invariably consists of identifying and clearly delineating the objectives of science teaching, expressed in behavioral terms.

The program, whether it be a local program or a large-scale curriculum project, should be process-oriented and should stress the discovery approach to the teaching of science. In the large-scale elementary science curriculum projects, a highly significant feature of their programs is the unprecedented involvement of large numbers of scientists in the development of the programs. Scientists have initiated and directed almost all of the new curriculum study projects, and the impact of their process philosophy and discovery method of operation is quite noticeable. An examination of the new program reveals strong similarities in the statements of their objectives, in the methods they use for teaching science, and in the kinds of materials they have produced.

The elementary science program should be organized and structured so that it has adequate scope. The science topics that make up the program should be chosen with quality in mind rather than quantity. The program should have balance, so that the child is given the opportunity to explore in the areas of biological, physical, and earth sciences.

The program should have a well-developed sequence. Today's programs reflect the current thinking that the elementary science program should be organized around a unifying framework of conceptual schemes. Consequently, the present trend in sequence seems to be that each topic is taken up just once, and the topics are incorporated under broader related content areas associated with these conceptual schemes. As a result, fewer topics are taken up in each grade, but each topic can now be explored in greater depth and in more satisfying detail. Not only is there a greater opportunity for more concepts to be learned at one time, but also the relationships between these concepts as part of a major conceptual scheme can now be developed more easily, in a number of ways and from more than one direction.

The Elementary Science Program *

NATIONAL SOCIETY for the STUDY of EDUCATION

The following is an excerpt from Chapter 7, "Developing Science Programs in the Elementary School," of the Fifty-ninth NSSE Yearbook, Part I, Rethinking Science Education. Members of the committee who wrote this chapter include Glenn O. Blough, Paul E. Blackwood, Katherine E. Hill, and Julius Schwartz. The committee describes how successful programs have their origins in a variety of sources: (1) the child, (2) the environment, (3) the sciences, and (4) the total school program. All these sources must be considered when planning the program. Also, the properly organized program should have structure and sequence.

How the Selection of Subject Matter Is Made

Experience in the teaching of science in the elementary school has demonstrated that the most successful programs have their origin in a variety of sources: (a) the *child*, with his emotional, intellectual, and physical needs; (b) the *environment*, both natural and man-made, in which the child lives; (c) the *sciences*, especially biology, chemistry, physics, and astronomy; and (d) the *total school program*, as it relates to the needs of *society* for informed citizens, capable of participating in social living.

Curriculum-planning has sometimes drawn heavily upon one of these sources without due regard to the others. Thus, in some localities, science has been made an adjunct to social studies, whereas in others the science program has leaned heavily on selected features of the local environment. In some instances, the science program of the elementary school has been designed as a "simplification" of junior and senior high school science. This "watered-down" approach, while generally rejected at this time, crops up sporadically in some "crash" programs which attempt to "scale down" upper-school apparatus, experiments, and ideas to "fit" young people.

Science programs drawn chiefly from one source are sometimes helpful in demonstrating the limitations of such programs. Today, however, there seems to be widespread agreement that the most vital programs are those based on the needs of the child in his environment, programs which are in harmony with the total school program and mindful of the needs of

*REPRINTED FROM *Rethinking Science Education*, Fifty-ninth Yearbook of the National Society for the Study of Education, Part I (Chicago: University of Chicago Press, 1960), pp. 119–125, 128–129, by permission of the publisher.

society and which utilize the materials, concepts, and methods unique to science. The process of curriculum development involves the exploration of *all* these sources to find in them the content and the methods for the science program. Curriculum projects as designed are generally prepared by teams of classroom teachers, supervisors, curriculum specialists, and personnel from teacher-training institutions and community organizations.

Owing to recent developments such as those noted, elementary school science is now for the first time achieving full and independent status; it is no longer to be found on the periphery of other subjects in the elementary-school program; nor is it regarded as a downwind extension of upper-grade science. Elementary science is now beginning to develop its own structure. It is discovering its own setting and its own problems as it develops programs drawn from each of the four enumerated sources. Let us explore individually these sources.

THE CHILD. The curriculum in science is based on the nature and needs of children: on their delight in sensory experiences, their sense of humor, their curiosity, their concerns, their ability to generalize and to apply principles, and their urge to create. It recognizes that children are different—varying in rate of growth, in manual dexterity, in kinds of experience they have had, in the depths of their interests, and in their capacity for learning.

Children respond with enthusiasm and understanding when they are provided with wire, batteries, switches, and electrical devices like bells, lights, and toy motors and are encouraged to experiment with these materials.

Children get deep satisfaction from firsthand experiences with the forces of nature. They sense the spirit of science when their curiosity is rewarded with discovery.

As teachers, we get clues to science content when we listen intently to children's questions. We get other clues from our observations of toys they play with, the way they spend their afternoons, the television programs they watch, the books they select for reading, the sports and hobbies they engage in, the responsibilities they accept at home, and the pets they take care of.

The science program should encourage creativity and originality in the activities of children. These traits may be fostered by providing materials and situations which permit children to investigate problems and practices which are new to them, and which encourage creative expression reflecting their individual talents and capacities.

THE ENVIRONMENT. As has been indicated earlier, one of the important values of science in the elementary school is that it contributes to the child's understanding of his immediate environment at a time when he is most curious about it and most ready to explore it. The typical questions asked by children illustrate this breadth of curiosity.

It follows that each school should build into its curriculum the peculiar features of its own environment. The nearby river, the "empty" lot, the park, the brook, the swamp, the tree on the street, the vegetable market, the bakery, the flower shop, the large gas tanks, the school bus, all these are resources that can be utilized.

THE SCIENCES. We have observed how elementary science stems from the needs of children and how it flourishes when it is rooted in their environment. However, the uniqueness of elementary science is derived from the content of organized knowledge and the methods of discovery inherent in the formal sciences.

In designing the elementary-science curriculum we look to the basic sciences for both answers and questions. We look to biology, physics, chemistry, geology, and astronomy for answers to questions arising out of the total life of the child; we seek answers that furnish facts, concepts, principles, techniques and materials, approaches and methods. We look to these sciences also for key questions which will lead children into the structure of organized science. Science gives information; it furnishes concepts and principles; it suggests techniques and materials; and it provides approaches to problems and methods of thinking. Science asks questions. While rejecting the idea that elementary science is a watered-down version of the science of higher levels, we should not disregard the opportunities which present themselves for using guidelines which may help lead young people into the formal sciences. When, for example, we encourage children to discover that shape has something to do with buoyancy, we are starting them on the way to an understanding of the principle of flotation. When children are led to uncover, layer by layer, the disintegrating leaves of a forest floor, they are on the road to understanding the cycles which make life on earth possible. When they experiment to find out how to make their electromagnets more powerful, they are acquiring concepts which will be useful when they study electromagnets in advanced courses.

We find the clues to problems like these by looking for them in the structure and history of the various sciences, in their methods of discovery, and in the important concepts and principles which run through them. Incidentally, the study of the history of science is especially fruitful in suggesting many experiments which represent great triumphs of scientists, yet which children of today can perform and understand.

The search for these guidelines to the sciences is facilitated when curriculum teams include individuals who have had training in the various sciences. For example, personnel from high school and college should be included; perhaps doctors, engineers, geologists, and chemists of the community may help; so, too, may representatives of scientific, technical, and business institutions. From the use of teams of such diversified membership a broader understanding of the problems at all levels may result.

In the last decade there has been a strengthening of the sequence for science from Kindergarten through Grade XII. Articulation between the various levels is being advanced as the elementary schools look more intently at the science content of the upper grades and expect to include these observations in their planning. Articulation is also strengthened as the philosophy of the junior and senior high school embraces more of the educational values which the elementary schools have found so invigorating in the last three or four decades.

THE TOTAL SCHOOL PROGRAM. A basic premise underlying the science program is that it should be in harmony with the total program of education. This implies that elementary science is an integral part of the fabric which includes social studies, language arts, music, mathematics, art, and health education. Science brings new strength to the elementary schools. Its methods, its approach to problem-solving, and its informational content enrich the whole program and give it new scope and depth.

Social studies, which in Kindergarten through Grade VI includes geography, history, and civics, is, of all subjects, the one most closely allied to elementary-school science. Its concern with problems of living and working together in the home, school, neighborhood, community, or country makes social studies a good background for many science activities. Communication, transportation, food, clothing, shelter, water supply, are topics which are shared by social studies and science.

"If in the social studies, for example, a class is studying the buildings and building construction in their neighborhood, questions with science implications will undoubtedly arise. The children will want to know about some of the materials used—wood, rock, iron, glass, bricks, sand, cement— their origin, their preparation for use, their qualities. . . . They may be interested in some of the machines—wheels, levers, gears—that move things. They may explore the ways in which buildings are protected from the weather. As they watch men at work connecting utilities to the building, they learn about water, sewage, electricity, and telephones."[1]

But supplying information is only one of the contributions that science makes. Science vitalizes units by encouraging children to raise questions and to find ways of answering them. When children are permitted to experiment with materials and to find out, for example, why steel bridges and iron fences are painted, how concrete is made and used, why a lever makes some kinds of work easier, why water rises in the pipes of a tall building, or why electric wires are insulated, they are doing more than talking about science; they are living it.

Science is allied to mathematics because of its emphasis on measurement, accuracy, and numerical relationships and because it suggests many uses for mathematics in real life situations. Using instruments such as the

[1] *Science, Grades K-6,* Curriculum Bulletin #3, 1958–59 Series. New York City Board of Education.

thermometer and the rain gauge and making calculations required in planning models for a planetarium are illustrations of the use of mathematics in science.

Science makes use of language arts and art skills. Reading, writing, listening, speaking, painting, and sketching are essential tools in elementary science. Here again, the necessary skills are developed by the science program as the child needs them.

The foregoing observations do not mean that science serves only to enrich other areas. Science is the center for many units of planned, coordinated experiences, organized around central scientific themes and problems. These science-centered units draw on skills and knowledge from the other curriculum areas as need indicates; but their over-all focus is on science.

Organizing the Program

THE STRUCTURE. The National Society's Forty-sixth Yearbook pointed the way to the organization of the elementary-science program, stressing the importance of acquainting pupils with the broader areas of the physical and biological environment by introducing such subjects as the universe the conditions necessary to life, living things, physical and chemical phenomena, and man's attempts to control his environment.[2]

During the last decade, elementary-school science has succeeded in developing many vital experiences for children within these broad areas and in suggesting sequences of unifying concepts from the kindergarten through the sixth grade. A wealth of content in science is emerging as a result of the efforts of classroom teachers, science specialists, curriculum workers, college teachers, and writers of children's books. Although science programs vary markedly from place to place, content areas such as the following appear in many curriculums: living things, earth in space, communication, transportation, resources of the earth, magnetism and electricity, weather, machines, changes in the earth, and health.

These areas—or similar ones—are broad enough to serve as centers for organizing many experiences and activities to meet the needs and interests of children and, at the same time, are rich enough in science content to provide for sequential mastery of science concepts and principles.

Different schools and school systems allocate content to individual grades in different ways, depending on various factors, such as basic philosophy or the nature of the experience of their teachers. Some have divided the content to provide specific teaching materials for each of the grades, Kindergarten through Grade VI. Other schools or school systems

[2] "Organization of the Curriculum in Science," *Science Education in American Schools,* pp. 75–76. Forty-sixth Yearbook of the National Society for the Study of Education, Part I. Chicago: Distributed by the University of Chicago Press, 1947.

have organized the content for groups consisting of two or more grades, as for example, Kindergarten-II, III-IV, and V-VI. This broader grouping permits great flexibility in developing science instruction while providing for a measure of continuity.

ADVANTAGES OF STRUCTURED PROGRAM. Those who advocate an unstructured program in elementary science argue that teachers should be guided solely by the interests of the children. They regard a course of study as stultifying and unnecessary. There is no question but that some excellent teaching has been done without a structured program in a number of small school systems, particularly in those in which science consultants were available or in which the teachers have had an unusual background in science. However, the claims for a structured program are more compelling.

1. A structured program provides a framework of science principles which can help teachers unify their own experiences and give them confidence in meeting difficult classroom situations that arise. The answer suggested a decade ago to children's questions—"I don't know, but let's find out together"—is not sufficient for all of today's needs.
2. A structured program does not have to be a rigid one. Within the broad content areas, there are many choices which permit the teacher to adapt the program to the needs of the class. Both the unit approach and the provision of a variety of materials and situations which foster children's creativity and originality are possible within a structured program.
3. The freshness engendered by the use of unanticipated incidents is not lost in a structured program. Indeed, the incident becomes more significant because the teacher sees it as part of the whole and thus may be able to convey its importance to the pupil. A structured program helps the teacher anticipate, identify, and incorporate into the program the many incidents which arise during the school year.
4. While it is true that children come to school with many interests, it is also true that interest can be aroused and cultivated by what takes place in school.
5. A structured program makes it easier for children to acquire the science concepts essential for their understanding of the complex world they live in.
6. A structured program is a democratic one: many can share in building it and in changing it. It provides a common framework for testing and evaluation by the children as well as by the teachers.

THE SEQUENCE. Elementary science can serve the general purposes of elementary education, as well as its own unique purposes, if its content provides for children's growth in their understanding of science concepts and principles. Studies of children's development provide clues to the

order of complexity of science concepts. Some of the following generalizations have been found helpful in guiding the organization of sequence:

1. The child's view of the world begins with the here and now and extends
   to the far away and long ago.
2. The child grows in ability to reason, to generalize, to apply principles,
   to see cause-and-effect relationships.
3. As the child develops physically he is able to participate in activities
   requiring greater strength and dexterity.
4. The child's increasing capacity for comprehending such dimensions as
   time, distance, size, speed, direction, or weight may influence sequence.
5. Strong motivation provided by current interests and the special character
   of the local environment may sometimes outweigh other considerations
   in the determination of sequence.
6. Sequence will be influenced by the desirability of taking into account
   the science to come in the upper grades.

Sequence is something that must be tested and judged in the setting of
the entire program. Continuous experimentation and careful observation
are fundamental to growth in knowledge about what is most appropriate
at a specific level.

Research and Development of
Science Programs:
Dimensions for Consideration*

LAWRENCE F. LOWERY and JERRY S. CARLSON

*Dr. Lowery and Dr. Carlson set forth the central question which science
educators must ask: "What tangibles should serve as guides for future
practical applications in early childhood science programs?" The authors
turn to three areas of scholarly endeavor which might serve as useful guidelines: (1) the research findings of child development, (2) the organized
ways of knowing and learning within the science discipline, and (3) recent
developments in research on the teacher and instruction. The authors believe that these three areas could help produce a theoretical and research
framework for a needed new era in early childhood science education.*

*REPRINTED FROM *School Science and Mathematics*, Vol. 68, No. 6, June 1968, pp.
554–564. Reprinted by permission of the authors and the publisher. Dr. Lowery is
Assistant Professor of Education at the University of California; Dr. Carlson is Assistant
Professor of Education at the University of California, Riverside.

Today we realize more than ever the significance of early childhood education. Unfortunately our interest, though keen, has produced only a few programs in science education which are both soundly constructed and designed for the young child. Although the academic marketplace is now being besieged by commercial firms, and "packaged" programs are becoming popular items of educational hardware the desired qualitative development has not taken place. The central question which we, as science educators, must ask is: "What tangibles should, indeed could, serve as guides for future practical applications in early childhood science programs?"

To find useful guidelines, one might turn to several areas of scholarly endeavor. Three particular areas come first to mind. They are: (1) the research findings on the many horizons of child development; (2) the organized ways of knowing and learning within the science disciplines themselves; and (3) the recent developments in research on the teacher and instruction.

These three areas, if carefully explored, examined, and properly understood, could help produce a theoretical and research framework for a needed new era in early childhood science education.

The Learner

The vast quantity of research in this area prohibits an inclusive review of the literature. Instead, only a few strands of significant research and theory can be discussed and analyzed. Such a discussion can, then, only set the stage for further thinking and work, but it may serve as a necessary starting point for rethinking elementary school science education.

The work of Jean Piaget and his associates in Geneva has aroused interest in developmental psychology and in the thinking processes of the young child. Though Piaget's methodological approach, clinical findings, and the theoretical formulations are open to criticism, they can serve as a starting point for consideration of children's thinking and cognitive development.

Piaget views intelligence as the individual's ability to act in certain ways and perform certain logical mental operations. Intelligence is a form of adaptive behavior which allows the individual to cope more effectively with his environment by organizing and reorganizing basic units of thought and action. The child, then, takes in and processes new information in the context of past experiences which has, by-in-large, control over his existing mental structures or, in Piagetian language, schema.

For Piaget, cognitive development occurs in substages, stages, and periods, with each subordinate subdivision forming the basis upon which a number of supraordinate stages and periods can be built. The "mental structures" or "organizations" that exist at any time are constantly being modified by impinging environmental stimuli, and the growth of intelligence is a dynamic process which actively develops. Briefly, Piaget's approach has resulted in the construction of an image of cognitive development. This image suggests that cognitive development takes place sequentially in distinctive, yet overlapping and interdependent stages. The ages posited by Piaget are approximations and subject to variance from one child to another. The stages are, however, sequential and, as a child develops he must necessarily move in a unitary direction with the process reflecting a consistent order and with more mature behavior having its roots in the earlier stages. Full maturity is the final and total integration of all preceding stages.

The following, though brief and condensed, summarizes Piaget's taxonomy of developmental stages of the growth of intelligence. It is, perhaps, science education's best guideline to date.

Period I: The Period of Sensory-motor Intelligence (0-2 years of age).

In this period the child's organization is physical rather than symbolic. He adapts to his environment via sensory-motor means. Within this period Piaget posits six stages of development, with substages within these.

Period II: The Period of Concrete Intelligence (2-11 years of age).

This period, significant at the elementary school level, encompasses three important stages plus numerous substages.

The *preconceptual stage* (ages 2-4) occurs when the child attempts to regard objects in a symbolic sense. Symbolic representation and language development form the basis of this stage.

The *stage of intuitive thinking* (ages 4-7) is marked by the rudimentary development of logical thought. Objects can now be grouped into classes according to the child's perceptions of similarity and dissimilarity. The child now can act on the verbal instructions of others as well as his own covert speech. He is still, however, perception bound and cannot separate cause from effect.

The *stage of concrete operations* (ages 7-11) is marked by the child's ability to be logically consistent and to conserve. In the earlier substages the child can conserve in some, but not all, instances. However, by the time the child has reached the last substage, the "principle of invariance" is firmly entrenched. One must note, however, that the child can apply the "principle of invariance" only to concrete situations. He is unable to deal logically in the symbolic abstractions of language.

Period III: The Period of Formal Operation (11-15 years of age).

At this level the child can "operate with operations" and engage in such cognitive activity as hypothesis generation and testing at a purely symbolic level. In short, the child has the cognitive tools for inductive and deductive reasoning, and can think as adults do when they operate abstractly.

The question "What does all this mean for early childhood science education?" is a real one and deserves our attention. Some research designed to test out and extend Piaget's work may serve as guidelines which can direct our thinking and help us understand the cognitive processes and development of the young child. It must be noted, however, that although a great deal of work has been done in the area of young children's thinking, many basic questions still remain as we are still searching for definitive answers to basic and complex questions. But, let us begin.

Research designed to test out the stage-wise development, as posited by Piaget, has generally supported his views. Interestingly enough, though the stages may differ slightly with respect to the ages Piaget suggested, the general sequence has found support regardless of the cultural background of the children. This fact, though certainly important, is not sufficient, as it is more descriptive than explanatory and does not really aid our understanding of the hows and whys of cognitive growth and development. The seminal question of "How does a child at various stages of cognitive development learn?" is vexing and not thoroughly understood. But, we do have some leads worthy of consideration.

1. CONCEPT ATTAINMENT.   Piaget stresses the importance of the child's direct activity vis-a-vis the content. To Piaget, the development of thought (ergo, logical operations) is not due to the "stockpiling of information" or "insight" but based on the child's own activity. Thus, he views conceptual development as essentially the development of the schemata of action in which perception only plays a part.

The Geneva School, though not primarily interested in didactic technique or trition, does definitely place major emphasis on direct activity on the part of the child. It is felt that from direct and manipulative experience, logical inconsistencies would result in cognitive reorganization and development if the child had already formed the prerequisite systems of mental operations. Consequently the effects of external reward on the acquisition of behavior are not particularly important, as dissonance reduction, due to the development of logically appropriate cognitive structures, serving as an internal reward.

While Piaget (1926) stresses activity and manipulation of objects, he minimizes the importance of language as a variable of functional importance for cognitive development and concept attainment. In other words, Piaget seems to separate thoughts from words as, for him, concepts are formed from action and language can then "make use of them."

Recent work (Carlson, 1967) has shown that basic cognitive structures are subject to the effects of trition and the efficacy of the verbal mediation model is upheld. However, this work was done with seven year old children and perhaps younger children are not capable, or at least as capable, of verbal mediation as older children. The work of T. Kendler (1960) did show that improvement of reversal shift learning (increased use of verbal mediation) did take place for children whose ages ran from three to ten years. The percentage increased gradually to 62 per cent by age ten. Also, the percentage of children who responded inconsistently, decreased from 50 per cent for three year olds to 10 per cent for ten year olds. Subsequently, Kendler formulated the hypothesis that if relevant mediation were supplied, age differences would diminish or disappear. The Kendlers (1961), using four and seven year olds, found that those children who verbalized relevant information did significantly better than those who verbalized irrelevant information. The younger children (age four) did not, however, generally do as well as the seven year olds. They concluded that younger children are less responsive to their own verbalization than older children.

What are we to make of this? First, it would appear that all mediation is not verbal and, in fact, a postural or gestural mediation may precede and then lay the basis for later verbal control. At least this seems to be the case, and this definitely should be considered when planning or selecting early childhood science experiences.

A second major implication stems from consideration of the stagewise cognitive development which is central to Piagetian theory, as the stages may be considered as boundaries that limit, though perhaps to a lesser degree than Piaget envisages, the capability of the child to learn and perform a given task. This would imply that the curriculum's activities be analyzed in terms of the logical operations inherent in them, and decisions must be made as to whether or not the child, at some particular age and developmental level, can operate at the cognitive level that the operations demand.

A further implication of developmental psychology for early childhood science education arises from the view that intelligence develops through the dual functioning of the invariants of assimilation and accommodation.

This would imply that the spacing of learning activities is a very important factor in planning an instructional program. In other words, Piagetian theory suports the use of the "spiral" curriculum even at the unit stage.

2. HUMAN LEARNING. Finally, the psychology of learning should be considered, as many decades of work have led to a deeper understanding of human learning. Most representative of this are the associationist approach to learning and the research on reinforcement theory.

Psychologists have contributed to our understanding of how particular kinds of learning take place. Of particular importance has been the approach Gagné has taken. Gagné (1965) views learning as hierarchical, with one step or stage forming the prerequisite for further learning and for more difficult and complex behaviors. The hierarchical approach has the advantage of forcing the teacher or researcher to first decide upon what he expects the child to be able to do, and then to set the conditions of learning, starting from where the child is, so that the desired behaviors can be reached and assessed.

This approach offers an alternative proposal for the explanation of Piagetian cognitive development (Gagné, 1966) as *learning* plays a fundamental role and is distinguished from development even though they are certainly related. Gagné's model stresses the cumulative effects of learning which can account, at least within certain limitations, for behavioral development. The general hierarchical sequence may be summarized as follows.

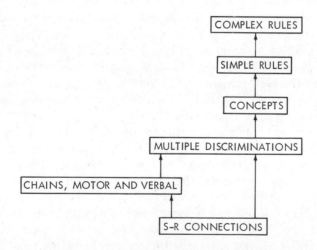

The main point here is that perhaps a highly general principle such as conservation of substance may be analyzable in terms of learning conditions rather than the unfolding or development of logical structures and the like.

As discussed by Jensen (1966), there has been a movement within these areas to extend the simple S-R model to paradigms that involve various mediational processes and hierarchies of association chains. Rohwer (1966) has helped to illuminate the role of language through work on serial and paired-associate learning tasks. Although many researchers have shown the importance of language to cognitive development of the individual's ability to use potential verbal mediators is still open to question. The writings of Luria (1957; 1961) and Vygotsky (1962) view "the word" as a hastener of mental processes and development. Or, as Brown (1956) has pointed out, words can serve as a "lure to cognition."

There are several ways in which the research guidelines in this section might be woven together.

One way is suggested by Whiteman (1964) who has attempted to interrelate the concepts of factors from psychometrics, learning set from learning theory, and operation from Piaget's work. His interrelations build around two characteristics of mental functioning: consistency and hierarchical organization of levels.

A second way might be through a "whole child" approach as described by Frank (1963). Frank suggests that the physical and mental dimensions of the growing child can be viewed as a dynamic configuration which cannot be particled without losing or destroying understanding of the basic processes involved.

A third way might be through Langer's assumption that man is most characteristically a user of symbols. To Langer (1958) man's humanity rests upon his ability to use symbols in order to produce whatever meanings there are in living, and through these symbols to communicate these meanings to his fellow man.

3. **AFFECTIVE OR MOTIVATIONAL FACTORS.** This area of research has been receiving more and more attention, as it is now realized that such factors as the individual's concept of self, and his attitudes towards school and learning are largely derived from the culture in general and his social and familiar milieu in particular. For example, the work of Wilson (1963) gives us insights into the influences of the child's peers, and Coles (1963) points out clearly how one's evaluation of self and society are affected by the social position in which one finds himself. And, as Bloom (1964) pointed out, the younger the individual, the greater effect environment will have on his subsequent development.

In answering the question "How does early experience work?" Hebb (1949) wrote that it "operates to establish perceptual elements." These elements, in Hebb's scheme, could be organized in the various senses, and modes for the foundation of all later environment would be laid. But, regardless of how early environment works, we know it strongly affects the individual, his aspirations, and his attitudes.

The complex and subtle ways in which the home environment affects educational achievement has only lately been the subject of systematic research. Only part of the educational achievement of children can be explained by status characteristics of the home, which is the aspect at which people most generally look. For example, Kahl (1953) found parental aspiration to be a more crucial factor than social class in explaining educational achievement. Further work attempting to delineate certain process variables within the home and correlate these with general scholastic achievement and intelligence was done by Wolf (1963) and Dave (1963).

Dave hypothesized six relevant home environment variables that would probably be relevant to educational achievement. The variables were:

a. Achievement Press.
b. Language models in the home.
c. Academic guidance in the home.
d. The stimulation in the home to explore various aspects of the environment.
e. The intellectual interests and activities in the home.
f. The work habits emphasized in the home.

The six variables were broken down into twenty-two process characteristics which were used to summarize and rate the mother's responses to an interview schedule. Dave obtained an overall correlation of .80 with the total score on an entire achievement test battery.

More work needs to be done in this area, for the tremendous importance that the environmental milieu has for individual development, especially at the early ages, mandates its consideration. To achieve the desired outcomes of early science education, we must consider the environment (both macroscopic and microscopic) from which the child comes.

The Discipline

It has been suggested by Phenix (1958) and Schwab (1964) that the scholarly disciplines can be viewed not only as sources of what is "known" but also as sources of ways of "coming to know." That is, the disciplines serve the dual function of (a) an organized body of knowledge and (b) a method of arriving at, validating, and developing further that knowledge. As Kuhn (1962) pointed out, the combination of the duality gives a paradigm for understanding and dealing with nature and natural phenomena, and the questions that one asks are largely determined by the paradigm employed which, in turn, dictates the type of answer that is meaningful and consistent within the framework of the problematic situation. Thus the solution to any problem is tentative. That is to say, it rests upon, or is derived from, a matrix of changing paradigms, different problematic situations, and a relativism that encompasses the entire process.

Relating the idea of the scientific explanation to early childhood science education places an emphasis not on a complete or "true" understanding of nature, but on those understandings which can be meaningful to the child at his particular age or stage of development (both experiential and psychological). In other words, the explanation is relative—relative to the child, his experiential and maturational development, the problematic situation as defined by the child, the operations used, and the context within which the concepts involved were developed. An explanation then is meaningful only in a timeplace setting, and that which constitutes an explanation for one child at any given time may not for another child at the same time.

Several attempts have been made to utilize the "ways of knowing" within frameworks of child development research.

1. *The Science Curriculum Improvement Study* (SCIS). This study is designed to lead children into the exploration and conceptualization of the physical world in ways that deliberately parallel Piaget's stages. Children experiencing the project are first asked to describe, compare, and classify static objects in their world by their physical properties. Such experiences form the basis for later work with measurements, interactions, and systems of objects.

2. *The American Association for the Advancement of Science* (AAAS). This program places an emphasis upon the processes by which information is gathered and manipulated. Through carefully planned hierarchies, children receive sequential experiences that lead to carefully defined behavioral objectives.

3. *Beginning Science—A Modern Approach*. This program for very young children (Holt, Rinehart and Winston, Inc.) combines a Piagetian framework with a hierarchical sequence of process experiences within the major science fields.

Millie Almy's work (1966) may give some guidelines as to the value of these and other such programs. Her work is presently attempting to measure changes in children's logical thinking as a result of exposure to the SCIS and AAAS programs.

Important at this point is the need for longitudinal research and ongoing evaluation of the many new programs.

The Teacher

In attempting to seek the important elements that compose instruction, one is first confronted with the problem that not enough of the good instructional techniques have been identified, described, or organized in a way that will allow one to reproduce more of them on a consistent basis.

Secondly, one is not even sure what the necessary elements are or if some still need to be created.

Unfortunately the science of instruction is still in a very primitive state. Major studies have attempted to correlate teaching "methods" with various teacher characteristics of student outcomes. To date, the results from these studies have proved inconclusive.

Bellack and Davitz (1965) have suggested that researchers begin to systematically describe what it is that takes place between teachers and students in different types of early childhood science programs. They feel that we need to know the ways in which teachers structure classroom experiences—especially the kinds of responses that are solicited from students and the kinds of operations students are asked to perform.

Along this line, some descriptive research has been started. The work by Flanders (1960), Hunter (1966), and Amidon (1967) have been the most promising by providing observational techniques and categories of instruction for analysis. Although scaling varies among the authors, the basic technique remains constant.

Unpublished as yet is Mary Rowe's (1967) work at Columbia University. Utilizing a simplified self analysis technique to aid and train teachers in science-micro-teaching situations, the training presently consists of a teach, feedback, and analysis sequence followed by a reteach, feedback, and analysis sequence. Analysis is made of verbal behavior through teacher collaboration and a modified Flander's observation-coding system.

The unpublished work of Frank Carus at the University of California, Berkeley, opens new directions in an attempt to evaluate and change teachers' modes of instruction. His research utilizes the video-taping of classroom performances with self evaluations coupled with a psychogalvanic skin response device that measures emotional reactions and verbal interpretations pertaining to performances.

Interest and research in the act of teaching and the total learning environment is growing. As it does, we, as science educators, should begin utilizing the many theories and studies which give us clearer understandings of the many dimensions which make up effective instruction. We should be seeking the kinds of materials, procedures, and settings which can not only be preplanned and provided for by teachers, but which will have a high probability concerning the fruitful development of the human potential in all children.

References

Almy, Millie, and E. Chittenden. *Young Children's Thinking: Studies of Some Aspects of Piaget's Theory.* New York: Bureau of Publications, Teachers College, Columbia University, 1966.

Amidon, E., *Improving Teaching; The Analysis of Classroom Verbal Interaction.* New York: Holt, Rinehart and Winston, Inc., 1966.

Bellack, A. A., and J. R. Davitz. *The Language of the Classroom: Meanings Communicated in High School Teaching.* Cooperative Research Project No. 1497, U.S.O.E. New York: Institute of Psychological Research, Teachers College, Columbia University, Part I, 1963; Part II, 1965.

Bloom, B. S. *Stability and Change in Human Characteristics.* New York: Wiley, 1964.

Brown, R. W. "Language Categories." In J. S. Bruner, J. J. Goodnow, and C. A. Austin (eds.), *A Study of Thinking.* New York: Wiley, 1956

Carlson, J. S. "Effects of Instruction on the Concept of Conservation of Substance." *Science Education,* 1967, 51, 46-51.

Coles, R. *The Desegregation of Southern Schools: A Psychiatric Study.* New York: Anti-Defamation League of B'nai B'rith, July, 1963.

Dave, R. H. *The Identification and Measurement of Environmental Process Variables That Are Related to Educational Achievement.* Unpublished Ph.D. Dissertation, University of Chicago, 1963.

Flanders, N. A. *Teacher Influence, Pupil Attitudes, and Achievement: Studies in Interaction Analysis.* Cooperative Research Project No. 397. Minneapolis: University of Minnesota, 1960.

Frank, L. K. "Human Development: An Emerging Scientific Discipline." In A. J. Solnit and Sally A. Provence (eds.), *Modern Perspectives in Child Development.* New York: National Universities Press, 1963.

Gagne, R. M. *The Conditions of Learning.* New York: Holt, Rinehart and Winston, Inc., 1965.

Hebb, D. O. *The Organization of Behavior.* New York: Wiley, 1949.

Hunter, Elizabeth, and E. Amidon. *Improving Teaching.* New York: Holt, Rinehart and Winston, Inc., 1966.

Jensen, A. R. "Verbal Mediation and Educational Potential." *Psychology in the Schools,* 1966, 3, 99-109.

Kahl, J. A. "Education and Occupational Aspirations of 'Common Man' Boys." *Harvard Educational Review,* 1953, 23, 186-203.

Kendler, H. H., and Tracy S. Kendler. "Effect of Verbalization on Reversal Shifts in Children." *Science,* 1961, 134, 1619-1620.

Kendler, Tracy S. "Learning Development and Thinking." In E. Harms (ed.), *Fundamentals of Psychology: The Psychology of Thinking, Annals of New York Academy of Sciences,* 1960, 19, 52-65.

Kuhn, T. S. *The Structure of Scientific Revolutions.* Chicago: University of Chicago Press, 1962.

Langer, Susanne K. *Philosophy in a New Key: A Study of the Symbolism of Reason, Rite and Art.* Mentor Books, New York: New American Library, 1958.

Luria, A. R. "The Role of Speech in the Formation of Temporary Connections." In B. Simon (ed.), *Psychology in the Soviet Union.* Stanford, California: Standford University Press, 1957.

Luria, A. R. *The Role of Speech in the Relation of Normal and Abnormal Behavior.* London: Pergamon Press, 1961.

Piaget, J. *The Language and Thought of the Child.* New York: Harcourt Brace, 1926.

Phenix, P. H. *Realms of Meaning: A Philosophy of the Curriculum for General Education.* New York: McGraw-Hill, 1958.

Rohwer, W. D., Jr. "Mental Mnemonics in Early Learning." Paper presented to the University of California Extension Seminar on Pre-School and Early School Enrichment, Berkeley, March, 1966.

Rowe, Mary. "Use of Micro-Teaching Situations to Train Elementary Teachers in a New Science Program." Unpublished paper presented to the North Eastern Regional Conference of the N.S.T.A., November, 1967.

Schwab, J. J. "Problems, Topics, and Issues." In S. Elam, *Education and the Structure of Knowledge*. Fifth Phi Delta Kappa Symposium on Educational Research. Chicago: Rand McNally, 1964.

Vygotsky, L. *Thought and Language*. New York: Wiley, 1962.

Whiteman, M. "Intelligence and Learning." *Merrill-Palmer Quarterly*, 1964, 10.

Willson, A. H. "Social Stratification and Academic Achievement." In A. Passow (ed.), *Education in Depressed Urban Areas*. New York: Teachers College Bureau of Publications, 1963.

Wolf, R. M. "The Identification and Measurement of Environmental Process Variables Related to Intelligence." Unpublished Ph.D. Dissertation, University of Chicago, 1964.

Prerequisites of an Effective Elementary Science Program*

EDWARD VICTOR

The following is a portion from Chapter 3, "The Elementary Science Program," of Science for the Elementary School. Edward Victor cites in great detail the necessary prerequisites for an effective elementary science program. The program must be planned and structured. It should be a coordinated part of an overall K–12 science program, and correlated with the rest of the elementary curriculum. It should emphasize both the content and process of science. It should have scope and sequence, and a balance of content from all the sciences. There must be a variety of activities, provision for individual differences, provision for necessary materials, sufficient time, and help and encouragement for the teacher. Finally, the program must be evaluated continuously if it is to be an effective one.

In recent years an increasing number of local science programs for the elementary school have been emerging. These programs are the result of

* REPRINTED FROM *Science for the Elementary School, 3rd Ed.* (New York: Macmillan Publishing Co., Inc., 1975), pp. 35–45, by permission of the publisher. Dr. Victor is Professor of Education at Northwestern University.

cooperative efforts of classroom teachers, supervisors, administrators, and science specialists.

These new programs are rich in content and process, and provide for an abundance of learning activities. These activities are directed specifically at giving the children an opportunity to investigate and explore so that effective learning takes place and desirable behavioral outcomes emerge. Provision is made for all kinds of learners: slow, average, and fast. Teachers are supplied with source materials and with necessary equipment. Competent supervisors or specialists are available for assistance.

Science programs may vary somewhat in their science content, learning activities, and teaching or unit format. However, all programs should meet the following prerequisites, if they are to be effective and successful.

Planning

A science program should be planned. When science was first taught in the elementary school, and for some time thereafter, there was no such thing as a planned science program. Science learning was organized around incidents that occurred in the classroom. If a child brought a magnet, whistle, unusual-looking rock, queer insect, or pretty leaf into class, a lesson or unit in science was developed around the incident. Often the lesson was quite brief and ended the same day. Usually this kind of lesson tended to stress identification, nomenclature, and the learning of facts rather than major science concepts. If there were no incidents, there were often no lessons in science.

There is no question that incidents arising in the classroom can be a tremendous motivating experience for the children. Under the direction of experienced and skillful teachers with a good science background, such incidents can be used to produce excellent teaching and learning. However, incidents alone are not sufficient to ensure an adequate science program for the elementary school. Nor would the teachers even think of teaching other areas in the elementary curriculum solely on this basis.

One of the most significant forward trends in science education today is the general agreement that the science program should be planned and structured, just as the programs in the other areas of the elementary school curriculum are planned and structured. A planned program not only provides a steady progression of science learning in all grades, but also gives the teacher a definite background and framework of basic science information with which to work in the classroom.

A properly organized program will not discourage incidents that occur, but rather will welcome them as an additional means for producing more effective learning in the classroom. In fact, a planned program now makes it possible for the teacher to create deliberately the kinds of incidents that will instill in the children a desire for exploration and investigation. And when unusual or important incidents do arise, such as sending a satellite or astronaut into space, the planned program can be flexible enough to provide time for these incidents to be taken up in detail.

A planned program should provide for and be guided by the interests of the children. An effective program takes into consideration the children's interests and uses them to motivate learning in science. At the same time it permits the children to help plan and carry out the daily and long-range work in science.

A Coordinated Part of a K–12 Science Program

Science in the elementary school should be planned and coordinated so that it is part of an overall K–12 science program. In this way haphazard teaching, unnecessary repetition, overlap, and flagrant omissions are eliminated. Instead, a steady progression of learning takes place at each grade level, building upon knowledge from previous grades and leading to further knowledge in the following grades. The science content to be learned will proceed steadily from the very simple to the abstract, as the children grow in maturity. At the same time, the children will become progressively more proficient in the process of science, proceeding from the simpler to the more complex operations of science and the scientist. In addition, the children will gradually acquire experience in solving problems and in thinking critically and creatively.

Correlation with the Elementary Curriculum

The elementary science program should correlate science, wherever possible, with other phases of the elementary school curriculum. The science program is only one part of the entire elementary school curriculum. However, learning can be more effective when all phases of the curriculum are integrated. The study of machines in science, for example, can be correlated very effectively with the study of transportation in social science. The study of light and sound can be correlated with the study of communications. The study of plants, animals, water, soil, air, and minerals can be correlated with the study of conservation and the control of environmental pollution. There are many opportunities in science to use measurements and other aspects of mathematics.

Arts and crafts are especially suited for correlation with science in the lower grades. One ingenious teacher had her children make an effective mobile when studying weather. The sun and moon were made of cardboard and then painted with appropriate colors. Stars were made or purchased in the stationery store. A jagged arrow, cut from cardboard and painted white, represented lightning. Modes of snowflakes were drawn and cut out. For rain the children used strings of pearls and beads. Each pearl, representing a raindrop, was separated by a glass bead that was shaped like a narrow, hollow tube.

Finally, a constant correlation can be made between science and the language arts. Reading, writing, and talking are also involved when learning science. These are language arts activities. Thus, science learning can help reinforce learning in the language arts.

Care should be taken, however, when correlating science with the rest of the curriculum, that the learning of science is not lost in the process. Real science learning cannot take place in a combined social studies—science unit on "Communications," when teachers take up the social aspects in great detail and merely talk about the science portion. Moreover, although it is good educational practice to correlate science when possible with the rest of the curriculum, it is also impractical and unwise to insist that all science be integrated with other areas. There are many phases of science that are learned best alone. Also, there are times where it is more logical to integrate the other areas with science rather than integrate science with the other areas.

Scope and Sequence

The science program should have scope and sequence. *Scope* refers to the content in the program, and *sequence* refers to the grade level or levels where the content will be allocated. The science program should be broad in scope so that the children will have ample opportunity to learn major concepts and basic principles that affect all the principal aspects of their environment. These broad understandings should be drawn from all areas of science, and their introduction should begin as early as kindergarten, then be developed and expanded through the elementary grades. This will help enable the children to acquire a greater understanding of their environment, of how man strives to use and control his environment, of how living things adapt and adjust to their environment, and of how living things are or may be interdependent and interrelated.

An examination of the current elementary science textbooks and science programs shows a fair amount of agreement on the scope of science content to be taught in the elementary school. However, this agreement is not true of sequence. Both textbooks and science programs vary widely and consistently in their grade placement of science topics. Some research is being conducted to determine the age levels or grades where selected science topics or understandings can be taught successfully. The findings generally tend to show that children at any grade level can learn something about all areas of science, provided the concepts are within the children's level of maturity and comprehension.

It is becoming more obvious that any attempt to develop one universal science program with a rigid or fixed grade-placed sequence, is virtually impossible. Children can and do differ widely in ability between schools in the same community, and also between schools of different communities. It is not uncommon for a teacher to find that the children differ in ability from year to year even in the same grade.

Yet it is equally obvious that some kind of sequence is necessary. In every science topic the concepts range from the very simple to the more complex. Some topics involve concepts that are more abstract than others. Whatever topics are assigned to a lower grade level will contain concepts that cannot be developed fully, regardless of the children's ability. Further development of these concepts will be needed later to ensure complete comprehension and learning.

Earlier science programs attempted to solve the problem of sequence by adopting a spiral pattern where the same topic—such as Sound or Heat—was taken up periodically. This would provide for a steady spiral of concepts to be developed, progressing from the easily understandable to the more difficult ones. New and more difficult concepts would be built upon previous learned ones, and from this a major conceptual scheme would emerge. In each case, previous knowledge about the topic was to be reviewed briefly, and then this knowledge was to be extended further. Repetition thus would serve to reinforce learning and to associate the old concepts with the new. Some schools used a spiral pattern where the same topic was taken up twice in grades K–6: once in grades K–3, and again in grades 4–6. Other schools preferred to take up the same topic three times: once in grades K–2, a second time in grades 3–4, and a third time in grades 5–6.

Today's programs reflect the current thinking that the elementary science program should be organized around a unifying framework of conceptual schemes. Consequently, the present trend in sequence seems to be that each topic is taken up just once, and the topics are incorporated under broader related content areas associated with these conceptual schemes. As a result, fewer topics are taken up in each grade, but each topic can now be explored in greater depth and in more satisfying detail. Not only is there a greater opportunity for more concepts to be learned at one time, but also the relationships between these concepts as part of a major conceptual scheme can now develop more easily in a number of ways, and from more than one direction.

Provision for teaching science in the kindergarten varies. Some schools assign specific science units to the kindergarten. Others suggest only that the teacher scrutinize her daily program of activities closely for science implications, then plan accordingly for experiences in science. Still others provide for both planned science units and incidental activities arising from the questions that children will ask.

Exact grade placement of science content in the science program is usually an individual concern, left to the decision of those working with the program. The grade placement may vary from school to school within the same community, or from community to community. Allocation of concepts will depend upon the children's intellectual development and the ability to understand cause-and-effect relationships, to recall and rationalize, and to grasp abstract ideas. Most concepts allocated for a specific grade level can be learned with equal success in one grade level immediately above or below the specified grade. However, difficulties are more likely to arise when the difference in allocation of concepts involves two or more grade levels.

The following suggestions may be helpful in organizing the sequence of topics and concepts for a science program. To begin, many individual topics can be related and incorporated to form broader content areas. Magnetism, static electricity, and current electricity, for example, can be combined to constitute one content area. Similarly, machines can be combined with friction, heat with fire and fuels, water with weather and climate, soil with rocks and minerals, and air with planes and space travel.

Some science topics might be placed in the same grade because they are all concerned with a common conceptual scheme. For example, an understanding of the theory of molecular motion will explain many of the phenomena of heat, sound, and physical states of matter. If the molecular theory is allocated to a certain grade level, the placement of these topics in the same grade level may save needless repetition and at the same time ensure a greater understanding of the theory because it was approached from different directions. Also, when the atomic theory is allocated to a certain grade, magnetism, static electricity, and current electricity could also be profitably placed in the same grade.

Finally, the science program should evaluate its sequence continuously, not periodically. Only if the effects of a particular sequence on learning in the classroom are carefully observed, and the sequence constantly reshuffled whenever the grade placement appears to be unsuited, can a well-organized and effectively structured science program emerge.

Balance

The science program should have balance. A well-balanced program should provide opportunities for children to explore regularly in each of the three major areas, which include the earth and the universe, living things, and matter and energy. Equal emphasis should be given to the physical and the biological sciences in the overall program. A balance in the length of units might be desirable so that some would be long and others would be shorter. There should also be balance in the number of units taught each year. The present trend is toward the adoption of a relatively small number of units per year, however, with provision for greater depth in science content.

Emphasis on Concepts and Conceptual Schemes

The science program should be concerned with more than technology. Too many science programs place undue emphasis upon how science helps us in our daily life, and not enough emphasis upon the underlying science concepts. The result is that the children, our future adult citizens, acquire a distorted image of science. They tend to view science primarily as an agent for developing useful gadgets and appliances, thus making our lives more pleasant and comfortable. The science program should provide children with ample opportunity to learn some of the key concepts and conceptual schemes that play such an important part in their daily lives, their environment, and the world in which they live.

Emphasis on the Process of Science

The science program should make children aware that science is a way of life—an exciting process of inquiry and discovery that man uses to explore, discuss, and explain the natural phenomena of the world in which he lives. Consequently, wherever possible, the children should be given an opportunity to learn and gain proficiency in the use of the key operations of science and the scientist. They should be given practice in learning how to solve problems and how to think critically and creatively. As they perform these operations they will learn concepts and conceptual schemes, and they will develop such desirable behavioral outcomes as scientific skills, attitudes, appreciations, and interests.

Variety of Activities

The children should have ample opportunity to use a large number of diversified activities when learning science. Some children seem to learn better or more easily from one kind of activity than another. They should have a chance to do experiments and demonstrations, read, give reports, participate in discussion, take field trips, listen to resource persons, use audio-visual materials, do research, and work on projects. There should also be activities that reinforce learning for the slow learner, and activities that challenge and extend the knowledge of the fast learner. At the same time, opportunities should be provided for children to investigate incidents or problems that arise and are not part of the planned program.

Provision for Individual Differences

The science program should provide for the individual abilities, needs, and interests of the children. It should offer a wide range of learning activities that will help the individual growth of children in science. The children should be given an opportunity to work in large groups, in small groups, and individually. It will allow slow learners to participate actively with the other children and to learn from them, yet permit them to work individually or in small groups for remedial purposes. It will enable fast learners to share their knowledge and ability with the other children, thus helping them, and yet it should permit the fast learners to extend their own knowledge and to explore further in areas which interest them.

Some schools have made changes in the organizational pattern of the classroom, claiming that one of the advantages of such changes is the greater opportunity to provide for individual differences in children.

One such organizational change is the nongraded classroom. Most schools have self-contained classrooms, where each classroom is under the direction of one teacher for one full year or grade. The nongraded classroom disregards single grade levels. Instead the children are placed in flexible groups on the basis of several related factors. They spend three years, and occasionally two or four years, in one group before moving on to the next group. Consequently, the children have a better opportunity to progress at their own individual and optimum speed at a time when maturation and growth in children is notoriously uneven and unpredictable.

Some schools have adopted team teaching, where two or more teachers are assigned to a group of pupils. This arrangement calls for different schedules and different allocations of time and space for teaching and learning. Team teaching lends itself to differences in grouping, thus providing for large-group, small-group, and individual learning activities as needed.

Other schools have departmentalized their science (and other) programs, so that a teacher with a good science background and with expertise in the teaching of science is responsible for the learning of science by all the children in one or more grades. This background and expertise presumably enables the teacher to provide more and better learning activities that will take into consideration the individual differences of the children.

Provision for Necessary Materials

It is useless for a science program to include "doing" learning activities unless the necessary supplies and equipment are made available. Thus an annual budget must be allotted to the elementary school for science materials so that the science program can function successfully. Moreover, each classroom should have its own science library, and the school library should have an adequate selection of science books. Provision must also be made for easy accessibility to films, filmstrips, and television programs.

Help and Encouragement for the Teacher

Giving the elementary teacher as much help as possible is an important facet of any planned science program. An examination of current elementary science textbooks shows that approximately 33 per cent of the content is in the area of biology, 33 percent is in the area of physics, 20 percent is in the area of geology, 8 per cent is in the area of astronomy, and 6 per cent is in the area of chemistry. (Meteorology is incorporated into the area of geology.) Thus to teach science effectively in the elementary school, the teacher should have a certain measure of knowledge and proficiency in these five areas. Unfortunately, this knowledge and proficiency requires a greater science background than most elementary school teachers receive in their pre-service training. It is generally agreed, and is verified by the findings of research, that most elementary school teachers have inadequate science backgrounds. Consequently, many of these teachers are reluctant to teach science.

Therefore, if teachers with an inadequate science background are given units that do not contain the basic science information, the teachers will be reluctant to use the units. This situation is easily understandable because all teachers realize that, unless they are at least moderately qualified to teach any subject, they may eventually be put into the embarrassing position of appearing inept before the children. A teacher does not mind saying "I don't know" occasionally to the children. But, when she has to say "I don't know" repeatedly, she soon stops teaching the particular topic or subject that places her in this awkward position. The teacher prefers to teach subjects in which she feels competent, comfortable, and secure.

If one of the objectives of science is to help the children understand and learn key concepts and conceptual schemes, it is imperative that the teacher be well informed about the science content and process that is being studied. Otherwise the teacher will not be able to guide the children's learning profitably.

Teachers can be given help in several ways. Providing them with science textbooks on both the junior and senior high school level can do much to upgrade their limited science background. A large number of reference books on individual science topics at the elementary school level are now available. The teachers can be provided with excellent professional books, sourcebooks, and curriculum materials on elementary science. In-service education in science content and process, in the form of workshops or courses, can be offered.

Many of the larger school systems are beginning to employ science supervisors or coordinators. These persons, proficient both in science and in working with children, can do much to strengthen the science program and the morale of the teachers. They can plan with the teachers, suggest additional learning activities, frequently do demonstration teaching, locate and order equipment, and conduct local workshops.

Some school systems employ full-time science supervisors or coordinators. They are given either a limited teaching schedule or none at all so that they can spend most of their time working on the program or with those teachers who need help. Other school systems may have a supervisor or coordinator on a part-time basis. Sometimes school systems use a competent junior high school teacher, who is given only a half-time teaching load so that the rest of the time can be devoted to the elementary teachers. Sometimes they use a science-minded elementary school teacher, letting someone else take over her class part of the time while she works with the other teachers in her building. Some school systems have a science educator come periodically to furnish advice and assistance to the teachers. Planned science programs in the elementary school are still comparatively new, and the position of elementary science supervisor or coordinator is even newer. The trend, however, seems to be quite definitely toward the increased use of full-time supervisors or coordinators.

Sufficient Time

There is definite agreement that science should be a regular part of the daily program, and have adequate time within the program. Both interest and learning are lost if science is scheduled only once or twice a week. Opinions vary, however, as to how much time should be allotted to science, daily or weekly. The general feeling is that more time should be devoted to science in grades 4–6 than in K–3. Some schools require that a definite amount of time be devoted daily to science. One recommended time allotment is 20–30 minutes per day for K–3 and 30–40 minutes per day for grades 4–6. Some schools set aside three days a week for science, with an average of 40–60 minutes per day. Other schools merely stipulate a definite amount of time per week, usually 120–180 minutes, and let the teacher allocate the time as needed throughout the week. Still other schools require that science be taught, but leave the time allotment to the discretion of the individual teacher.

Continuous Evaluation

To be effective the science program should be evaluated continually, with everyone involved in the program participating in the evaluation. The scope of science content must be examined for corrections, additions, or deletions. The sequence must be evaluated to ensure optimum grade placement. Activities should be scrutinized critically to see whether they are achieving maximum learning of content and process. Newer, more productive activities should be substituted as they appear in text, reference, and resource books. Initiating activities may be evaluated for greatest possible motivating and problem-raising potential. Even the evaluation techniques themselves should be examined regularly to see whether learning is taking place in the classroom.

Programs of the Elementary Science Curriculum Projects*

EDWARD VICTOR

The author describes the purposes and characteristics of the following curriculum projects: Science—A Process Approach (SAPA), Elementary Science Study (ESS), Science Curriculum Improvement Study (SCIS), and Conceptually Oriented Program in Elementary Science (COPES). Also included are brief descriptions of the Elementary School Science Project (ESSP), the Minnesota Mathematics and Science Teaching Project (MINNEMAST), and the Stony Brook Quantitative Approach in Elementary School Science Project. The author offers suggestions to schools regarding steps to take, and guidelines to follow, that will help them decide which project's program to select.

The decade of the 1960's will be long remembered as that period when elementary science became such a major concern that it received national attention. This period was marked by the initiation and development of a large number of elementary science curriculum projects that were designed to revise and improve the science program in the elementary school.

These curriculum projects are the most exciting things that have happened to elementary science in a long time. They have been widely publicized because heavy financial support, for the most part by the National Science Foundation and to a lesser extent by the United States Office of Education, made possible the large-scale involvement of scientists, science educators, teachers, and children in these projects. This financial support

*REPRINTED FROM *Science for the Elementary School,* 3rd Ed. (New York: Macmillan Publishing Co., Inc., 1975), pp. 52–58, by permission of the publisher. Dr. Victor is Professor of Education at Northwestern University.

also enabled the projects to print and disseminate a variety of bulletins and other descriptive literature that publicized the project's objectives, characteristics, and progress.

All these projects are actively concerned with teaching science in the elementary school as a process of inquiry. This method is often called the inquiry or discovery approach to the teaching of science. Exercises, units, materials, and teacher's guides have been produced that stress this approach. For guidance and direction in developing their programs, the projects turned to the research and theories of child development psychologists, especially Piaget, Gagné, and Bruner, on how children develop intellectually and learn.

Although all the curriculum projects agree that elementary science should be taught as a process of inquiry, they do not agree on the role and emphasis as well as scope and sequence of the science content in their programs. This difference in agreement ranges widely, from the belief that the science program should be designed primarily to develop the skills of science to the belief that the science program should be organized so as to have as its unifying principle the major conceptual schemes of science.

Regardless of this difference in agreement, the curriculum projects have served to bring sharply into focus the need for teaching process as well as content in elementary science. This need has existed for a long time and the projects will do much to ensure that process will now receive the emphasis it has so long deserved and that it will assume its rightful place in the elementary science program.

The following is a brief description of the purpose and characteristics of some of the well-known elementary science curriculum projects.

Elementary Science Study (ESS)

The Elementary Science Study, a branch of the Education Development Center (EDC), was established in 1960 in Newton, Massachusetts. Its goal is to develop meaningful science materials for use by children in grades K–9. The program consists of more than 50 units designed to make children curious about some part of their world and to encourage them to learn more about it.

Although science processes such as observing, measuring, classifying, inferring, predicting, and experimenting are an integral part of the program's units, the units do not aim solely at teaching individual skills and illustrating particular concepts or processes. Instead, the units provide the children with an opportunity to explore interesting problems that extend their knowledge, their insight, and their enjoyment of the physical and natural world.

The units do not make up a sequential science program. Instead, each unit is separate and, for the most part, unrelated to the others. Schools and school systems are invited to make up their own science programs, incorporating all or part of the Elementary Science Study units.

The program's units and materials are marketed by the Webster Division of McGraw-Hill Book Company, Manchester Road, Manchester, Missouri.

Science—A Process Approach (SAPA)

The Commission on Science Education, sponsored by the American Association for the Advancement of Science (AAAS), was established in 1962 in Washington, D.C. Its goal is to improve science education at all levels. Its elementary science project has implemented the ideas of Gagné to develop a K–6 program that stresses teaching the processes of science.

The program breaks the complex set of skills used by the scientist when conducting an investigation down into a number of processes and has developed a number of units designed to improve the children's skills in using these processes. A total of thirteen processes, eight basic and five more complex, are identified. The basic processes are taught in the primary grades, the more complex ones in the intermediate grades. These processes are named, as follows:

PRIMARY GRADES	INTERMEDIATE GRADES
Observing	Formulating Hypotheses
Classifying	Controlling Variables
Measuring	Interpreting Data
Communicating	Defining Operationally
Inferring	Experimenting
Predicting	
Using Numbers	
Using Space/Time Relationships	

The program has also developed a hierarchy chart for each process. The charts identify the behaviors that the child is expected to acquire from the activities of the program. These behaviors are arranged in a sequential hierarchical order of increasing complexity. The charts show not only the relationships among the behaviors within a single process but also the relationships among behaviors of the other processes. The procedure for developing these behavioral hierarchies is based upon the findings of Gagné that there is a greater probability of learning a higher, more complex, behavior when the learner first masters those behaviors that are subordinate to this higher behavior.

The program's units and materials are marketed by Xerox Education Division, 600 Madison Avenue, New York City.

Science Curriculum Improvement Study (SCIS)

The Science Curriculum Improvement Study was established in 1962 at the University of California at Berkeley. Its goal is to develop scientific literacy in children. This involves (1) an understanding of the basic concepts in both the physical and the life sciences, which is necessary for effective participation in twentieth-century life; and (2) the development of a free, inquisitive attitude and the use of rational procedures for decision making. The program consists of a sequential series of units that uses the common experiences of children in grades K–6 to develop a real understanding of science concepts.

The theories of Piaget and Bruner have been integrated into the program. There are two sequences, one in physical science and one in life science, each having six levels, as follows:

PHYSICAL SCIENCE SEQUENCE	LIFE SCIENCE SEQUENCE
Material Objects	Organisms
Interaction and Systems	Life Cycles
Subsystems and Variables	Populations
Relative Position and Motion	Environments
Energy Sources	Communities
Models: Electric and Magnetic Interaction	Ecosystems

The units in the physical science sequence are concerned with the fundamental concepts involving change and interaction. The units in the life science sequence are concerned with organism-environment inter-actions. The procedure in all the units involves free or guided preliminary exploration with the materials, "invention" lessons that introduce new concepts, and "discovery" lessons that develop applications of the concepts.

The program's units and materials are marketed by Rand McNally & Company, P.O. Box 7600, Chicago, Ill.

Conceptually Oriented Program in Elementary Science (COPES)

The Conceptually Oriented Program in Elementary Science was established in 1965 at New York University. Its goal is to develop a K–6 program using interrelated major schemes of science as unifying principles. Consequently, five conceptual schemes have been selected, around which the program has been developed. These conceptual schemes are as follows:

The Structural Units of the Universe
Interaction and Change
The Conservation of Energy
The Degradation of Energy
The Statistical View of Nature

The program is structured so that all five conceptual schemes are interwoven in a logical hierarchy. All five schemes are developed concurrently and presented spirally by grades. The activities in grades K–2 are devoted primarily to introductory materials designed to provide children with the skills and conceptual framework needed for entering the main sequences, which start at grade 3. The concepts intended to develop the five conceptual schemes are spread through grades 3–6. Sometimes a concept is related to a single conceptual scheme, but many concepts are related to two or more schemes.

Other Well-Known Curriculum Projects

The Elementary School Science Project (ESSP) was established in 1960 at the University of Illinois. Its goal is to revise the astronomy program in grades 5–9 so that it presents accurately the concepts, theories, and methods used in modern astronomy.

The Minnesota Mathematics and Science Teaching Project (MINNE-MAST) was established in 1961 at the University of Minnesota. Its goal is to produce a coordinated science and mathematics program for grades K–6 and to develop in-service teacher training materials to go along with the program. Its program is built around the following six processes of science: observation, measurement, experimentation, description, generalization, and deduction. These processes are developed from both the scientific and the mathematical point of view and are organized into a spiraling program that takes up each process at each grade level. The emphasis varies according to the age and the abilities of the children involved. (Unfortunately, curtailment of funds made it necessary to terminate the program after grade 3.)

The Study of a Quantitative Approach in Elementary School Science Project was established in 1964 at the State University of New York at Stony Brook. Its goal is to develop lessons on natural science topics based on measurement and quantitative analysis for grades 1–6.

The Oakleaf Individualized Elementary School Science Project was established in 1964 at the University of Pittsburgh. Its goal is to develop materials that will allow children in grades K–6 to work independently on individually prescribed laboratory activities.

Suggestions for Selecting a Curriculum Project Program

Most school administrators and curriculum directors probably would prefer to develop an elementary science program specifically designed to meet the individual backgrounds, learning characteristics, abilities, and needs of the children in their schools. If it is to be done well, developing such a program can be long and arduous, involving a considerable amount of time, effort, and personnel. Consequently, if a decision is made to use a curriculum project instead, it is imperative to select a program that will coincide most closely with the school's philosophy and goals, that will most successfully promote and facilitate learning by the children, and that will put the teachers most at ease when conducting the lessons and units.

There are certain steps that schools or school systems may take that will help them decide which project's program to select. The companies that market such programs can provide informational literature. Their units and materials can be purchased and tried out by individual teachers. Schools will often try out two or more different programs at the same time in different classrooms, then compare the reactions of teachers and children to the programs. The companies that market the programs will usually send representatives to speak to the teachers of interested schools and to demonstrate the use of their program's materials.

Projects that are not yet marketed will welcome inquiries and will also provide informational literature. If given advance notice, these projects will be glad to have groups visit their headquarters and may even arrange for visits to demonstration classrooms.

State departments of education usually know which school systems in the state are using the various programs. Arrangements can be made to visit these schools, discuss the programs with the teachers who are involved, and see some of the programs in action in the classroom.

There are also certain guidelines that schools or school systems can follow that will help them in selecting a program. One such guideline has to do with the main focus of the program. This main focus varies for the different programs. SAPA focuses on the development of specific process skills, and evaluation is made in terms of the attainment of these skills. Concepts are a necessary part of the program, but the program does not focus on them, and the concepts have no control in how the objectives of the units in the program are sequenced. SCIS and COPES focus on conceptual schemes more than on the development of process skills. These projects believe that the conceptual schemes should be the basis for explaining a large number of natural phenomena and, in the process, help develop process skills. ESS focuses on environmental phenomena and uses nondirected exploration, first to raise questions about the causes and effects of these phenomena and then to find ways of obtaining answers to these questions. Although ESS does not provide for the development of process skills, it believes that its program can be used for this purpose, if desired. MINNEMAST focuses on combining the teaching of processes and concepts of science and mathematics at the same time.

A second guideline is the examination of the teaching strategy of the program. All the programs use an inquiry and discovery approach for teaching their individual units. They suggest procedures for introducing and conducting the lessons and for developing successful attainment of the objectives. In all the programs the role of the teacher is primarily a nondirective one, and the children are encouraged to inquire, discover, explain, and apply what they have learned on their own. However, the programs do vary in how closely the teacher should follow the suggested procedures and how uniform the approach should be for the lessons. SCIS specifies a single procedure of instruction for most of its units. SAPA, ESS, COPES, and MINNEMAST suggest different instructional procedures for different units and encourage the teachers to develop their own procedures if they are dissatisfied with the recommended ones. SAPA, however, does qualify its encouragement of alternative procedures by insisting that whatever procedure is selected, the outcome must be consistent with the behavioral objectives set for the unit.

A third guideline has to do with the sequencing of the lessons and units in the programs. The programs vary in the degree in which learning in one lesson of a unit depends upon successful completion of learning in a previous lesson. Also, programs vary in their degree of flexibility in allowing a teacher to determine or change the order in which the lessons and units will be taken up in class. These factors will also have an influence on how easily a program can be adapted to a school's existing program. SAPA and COPES specify clearly the sequencing of individual units. SCIS and MINNEMAST also specify sequencing, but recognize and encourage the occasional need to resequence lessons as the need arises. ESS does not specify a sequence at all for any of its units, but it does indicate which units are appropriate for the primary grades and which ones are best suited for the middle grades.

A fourth guideline has to do with the possibility of being able to coordinate the programs with required existing science programs or textbooks. This is a factor in areas that have state-adopted textbooks or curriculum guides that must be followed. ESS seems to have the only program whose materials can be incorporated into an existing program or text. The programs of the other projects are sequenced in such a way that incorporation into existing programs or texts would be difficult and undesirable.

The Impact of Experimental Programs on Elementary School Science*

SHIRLEY A. BREHM

In this article Shirley A. Brehm describes some of the causes for the emergence of several new experimental programs in elementary science. She points out that these programs have a number of features in common. The programs are experimental, emphasize process, evoke a new role for the teacher, give a new importance to the development of concomitant mathematic skills, introduce abstract concepts at an early level, emphasize children's activity, and emphasize science as a "skill" subject. Finally, Dr. Brehm discusses the impacts which these programs are making on the teaching of elementary science.

Elementary school personnel are experiencing an unusual situation today concerning curricular innovations. While a few years ago curriculum changes were developed primarily by teachers themselves, the curricular possibilities of the 1960's have evolved through the cooperative work of academic experts and highly qualified, select classroom teachers. It is general knowledge that elementary school science and mathematics have been experimented with more extensively than have other curricular areas in the elementary school. For the most part elementary science and mathematics curricula of this decade have been written, taught in sample classrooms, tested, re-written, taught again, and often revised again. Furthermore, the composition of several groups working in the various writing conferences has been national in scope as opposed to either regional or local.

Causes for New Programs

THE INFLUENCE OF HIGH SCHOOL REVISIONS

To understand more fully the implications of the experimental curricula, it is necessary to examine some of the causes for the emergence of the trial programs. One of the most prominent stimulators of experimental elementary curricula was the wide acceptance of science programs developed since 1955 for the high school age group. These can no longer

*REPRINTED FROM *Science Education*, Vol. 52, No. 3, April 1968, pp. 293–298. Reprinted by permission of the author and the publisher. Dr. Brehm is Professor of Education at Michigan State University.

be considered experimental today. The Biological Science Curriculum Study (BSCS), the Physical Science Study Committee (PSSC), the School Mathematics Study Group (SMSG), to mention only a few, are well known examples of high school curriculum developments. Innovators at the secondary school level became more and more concerned that students entering high school should have a better and a different type of background in science and mathematics than students had had previously. It was felt that the lower school preparation should not revolve around added quantity of science or mathematics per se, but it should reflect a deeper insight into the structure of the subject and the very method of inquiry unique to that subject. These innovators, who represented academic specialties in the sciences and education, began to investigate means of revising the elementary school programs. As a result several elementary curricular experiments grew in downward trend, while others began with kindergarten and grew upward.

EXPLOSION OF KNOWLEDGE

A second cause for the experimental work in elementary science and mathematics was the veritable explosion of knowledge resulting from, and contributing to, the scientific era we are experiencing. The older emphasis on the accumulation of factual knowledge for its own sake could no longer remain valid because of the plethora of this knowledge and the rapidity with which factual knowledge was outdated. It became evident that quantity alone would not do, but that a qualitative revision of the early work in science and mathematics was required. Unlike the weeding out process of the 1890–1910 era revision in elementary arithmetic in which complex and difficult "problems" were discarded, this present revolution in science and mathematics emphasized a shifting of focus away from social utility toward two closely related objectives: a comprehensive investigation of major ideas called the structure of discipline; and the ability to act as a scientist acts called the process of inquiry of the discipline.

NEW ADVANCES IN LEARNING THEORY

Closely related to these were the concerns of cognitive psychologists [1] for how one learned best and retained best those things learned. Early indications from psychological studies emphasized the position taken by the experimental curriculum builders: one retains learning best if it follows a pattern—but this pattern or structure is unique to the subject matter and to the learner's way of structuring the subject. Another psychological premise underscored the manner in which persons learned— the process of involvement. Interestingly enough, both of these ideas have been part of the stock-in-trade of highly competent teachers. While most teachers have tended to operate on an intuitive plane concerning either or both of these ideas, it has taken the learning psychologists to initiate the placement of the ideas into the more formal, logical pattern and thus enable the educators to examine and implement these ideas more fully.

SPEEDING UP THE "GRASSROOTS" PROCESS

A fourth factor in assessing the advent in elementary curricular innovations, oddly enough, was the very procedure used in developing curricular programs prior to the experiments of the 1960's. This writer recognizes the need to fully explore the pros and cons of teacher involvement in curriculum building, and admits a strong bias toward teacher involvement. Yet this article is neither the time nor the place for such an extended discussion. The point to be made here, however, is that despite the positive aspects inherent in a philosophy of grassroots curriculum development, the factor of social lag had become extremely significant. According to many persons involved with the rapid transformation of knowledge and ways of knowing, there was not time to permit a thorough realignment and education of all personnel in terms of content, psychology, and educational methodology for persons to become experts in each and every speciality. It followed that these tasks, then, could not remain the sole responsibility of school personnel, who may be competent in one specialty only—methodology, with secondary competencies in other areas such as content. More and more the fact had become evident that what was needed was a broadly based team approach with several specialists brought together to share solutions to common problems. The Woods Hole Conference [2] held in 1959 was a good example of this approach to problem-solving in curricular development.

However important the grassroots program was concerning curriculum development, it fostered a diversity that could be typified as unevenness in the emergence of sound programs. Furthermore, under the guise of grassroots curriculum, many schools left the elementary science program almost entirely to the interests of the individual teacher who may have had limited resources and interests to bring to bear in solving this problem. This resulted, often-times, in a fragmented, factually oriented program in elementary science, and a dull, routinized, mechanical operation in mathematics with the textbook as the sole arbitrator of both methodology and content.

THE NEED TO KEEP IN TOUCH WITH EMERGING KNOWLEDGE

Where curriculum committees did exist in local school systems, these were composed almost exclusively of public school personnel—teachers, administrators, consultants—who themselves were not close enough to the emerging knowledge in the several disciplines. This is not meant to castigate curriculum committees for not including the scientific specialists earlier: these scientists and academic specialists had spurned any commitment they might have had to the broader field of public education for they were committed solely to their discipline. So the situation evolved wherein the public school curriculum committees tended to rework the older content of the curriculum and to emphasize the comfortable pattern of subject matter in elementary science based on the biological sciences for the most part, with some inclusion of the physical and earth sciences. The outcome of this situation was a heavy stress upon the acquisition of factual information.

Then, too, these same committees knew only too well the complex task faced by elementary teachers in the self-contained classroom as they implemented the many curricular areas: the subtle weaving together of experiences and concepts drawn from social studies, science and the skill involved in the language arts-mathematics spectrum into meaningful classroom learning experiences. The elementary classroom teacher typically has focused major attention on the development of the child, and in so doing she has utilized subject matter content as a vehicle for accomplishing this goal.

As a result of concerns more immediately connected with children in the elementary classroom, a lack of close contact with emerging knowledge a point of view consistent with assisting individuals to develop through the older curricular patterns, the grassroots type of curriculum development was slow and intermittent. Communities which developed science curriculum guides tended to follow two or three basic patterns. These in turn were not too different from basic patterns established in elementary science textbooks. Segments of subject matter were apportioned out to the several grades, either in a spiral pattern or a block-and-gap pattern, or modifications of one or the other. In the more unfortunate communities, the textbook might well have constituted the elementary science curriculum, which in turn was essentially a reading program because the teachers lacked equipment, know-how, or scientific background sufficient to involve children in science activities.

SCIENTISTS ENCOURAGE CURRICULAR CHANGE

In the meantime, while educators were pleading with boards of education for released teacher time to do curriculum development or to get the necessary inservice education essential to update the curriculum, scientists were developing grave concerns for the outcomes of the then extant science curricula throughout the elementary and junior high schools, in keeping with the earlier concerns for secondary school science and mathematics. Knowledge was being "produced" at a rate that made "learning the facts" an impossibility. Furthermore, scientists have long felt that the end product of science knowledge was only part of the picture. Another significant factor was the ability to do science, to "science" as it were. Thus the emphasis, in the eyes of scientists, should swing toward the process of science and away from the facts. The end product of knowledge could not be eliminated nor should it—but the way in which one finds knowledge became as important as what was found, particularly for elementary age children. The impossibility of predicting what one might need to know in the future has led scientists and educators alike to view education as a life-long operation, and the function of formal education to provide basic learning tools to enable the learner to continue to learn for himself.

The scientists recognized some similarities between the native curiosity of the child and the intellectual quest of the scientist. However, they noted that where the scientist was sophisticated in applying his disciplined mind to assist him in pursuing problems when the going got difficult, the child tended to drop his quest when his curiosity was satisfied. It was upon this need for knowing inherent in child and scientist alike, along with the realization that the knowledge of an educated person could no longer be encyclopedic, that prompted scientists to engage in curricular ventures, first at the secondary school level, and increasingly since 1960, at the elementary school level.

Common Features of New Programs

Numerous experimental programs in elementary school science have been developed. These have several features in common. In the first place all programs are *experimental*. This means that they are being tested, re-written, and tested again. In some, the testing is very rigorous, and the very nature of the program is carefully controlled. It is a tribute to educational research, and particularly curriculum research, that the testing is as rigorous as it is. Educational experimentation, in some programs, is approaching an exactitude found in the physical sciences [3]. These same experiments, as with all experiments, may prove or disprove the hypothesis being tested. This must be kept in mind. The experimental programs, as they now stand are not designed as a national curriculum in elementary science or in elementary mathematics. The manner in which the experimental curricula may influence regional and local developments will be discussed in a later section of this essay.

A second feature found in common with the experimental programs is the general emphasis on the teacher as a guide and director, rather than a font of knowledge. This role, in which the teacher sets the stage for learning ("structures the situation") may be somewhat upsetting to teachers who view science and mathematics teaching as having only one correct answer. Facts are not ends in themselves. The teacher can no longer operate in a dogmatic, "sole-source" manner in which she places greatest emphasis on "telling" children about science information.

This brings about a third similarity. This is the emphasis on process or "scienceing" mentioned earlier. Subject matter is taken from different sources than one would previously have found in elementary science programs. For example, one might observe how insect larvae behaves under certain circumstances. It is not as important to learn specific facts about specific larvae as it is to learn how to observe, to collect data and to interpret these data [4].

A fourth similarity in the experimental programs is reflected in the importance given to the development of mathematical skills and understandings concurrently with the science. Heretofore, elementary science was not quantitative, only descriptive. As a result, some of the experimental science programs introduce advanced mathematical concepts and skills at a stage much earlier than typically experienced in the elementary school.

A fifth similarity between the experimental programs is the tendency to introduce more abstract content earlier into the program. The several programs are not uniform in any way as far as the content is concerned, yet the overall approach to content selection varies from the traditional appointment of subject matter mentioned earlier. The experimental programs also vary from the use of the science unit typical in many elementary classrooms in which science is related to reading, social studies, arithmetic, written expression, and so forth. For example, one program utilizes the abstract idea that what one perceives is relative to the position of the perceiver in time and space.

A sixth similarity between the several programs is the emphasis on child activity. The child is not a passive listener, but instead he becomes an active participant. In many programs the activity tends to be open-ended, in that there is no one answer, nor is there a preconceived answer. In several of the programs there is no children's text. This removes the possibility of science remaining solely a "reading about science." Instead, the child must engage in activities under the guidance of the teacher. It is this role, that of the guide not the teller, that is often the most difficult for some teachers to assume. It causes one to reorient one's philosophy away from the direction-giving philosophy of teaching with the emphasis on teacher activity, toward the discovery on the part of the learner philosophy with the emphasis on learner involvement. A direct result of this approach is the disquieting fact that not everyone will arrive at the same answer, not at the same time, nor even in the same manner!

A seventh similarity between these experimental programs is the change in emphasis from science as a content subject to science as a "skill" subject as well. The skill in this case has been variously labeled critical thinking, problem-solving, discovery approach, or even creative thinking in science. This is closely related to the sixth point particularly when it comes to the implementation of this approach within a real classroom.

Impact of New Programs

The impact of the experimental elementary science programs has begun to be felt. One outcome already apparent is the sense of respect for the specialties of the various professionals whether scientist or classroom teacher. Overheard at one recent summer writing conference was the comment made by a biologist team member concerning several elementary classroom teachers also on the team. He said, "There are some excellent elementary teachers here. They are real pros and we can be proud to work with them." The mutual respect and admiration for excellence in classroom or laboratory are bound to break down barriers in communication previously evident.

Another likely impact of these programs on the elementary school will be that teachers and school administrators will need to take time to thoroughly study the programs in depth before committing themselves to a given course. Once committed, inservice education will be needed to bring teachers into contact with the unique methodology required. A different kind of science teaching will, of necessity, emerge.

A third impact of the experimental curricula, whether these ever go beyond the testing state or not, will be the influence upon elementary science textbook materials. Some textbooks are already beginning to show evidence of the concepts and methodologies similar to those developed in experimental programs. This may be due for the most part because the science educator authors have had experience in the writing conferences. And as a result, the excitement of the curriculum experiments has been great enough to have spilled over to science educators beyond the confines of the writing teams. This in itself will be a marked impact inasmuch as the particular stimulation for a new direction has been lacking for some time in elementary science curriculum development.

The involvement of team members from several disciplines has been mentioned earlier. Cognitive psychologists and classroom teachers are sharing a new relationship involving the theoretical and the practical aspects of closely related ventures. Teachers in curriculum development have a new role, which if they become competent enough in that role to earn the respect of scientists—behavioral as well as biological and physical —they will certainly elevate themselves to a new status. Part of this new role is that of a team member who knows a great deal about the practical aspects of teaching children; who is secure enough to try new ideas that may not be her own; who is also secure enough to admit her ignorance when she does not know a fact; who is intellectually alert to devise ways of utilizing the best the new has to offer. In a sense, then, the greatest impact of experimental programs may well be felt through the redefinition of the teacher's job beyond the telling or arbitrator stage, to a fully competent guide for learning.

References

1. See works of Gagné, Bruner, Piaget, and others.
2. Bruner, J. S., *The Process of Education*. Cambridge: Harvard University Press, 1961.

3. See both the *Commentary for Teachers* of the AAAS Science—A Process Approach and J. R. Suchman's work on inquiry training for details of experimental design and controls.
4. Education Development Center, *Elementary Science Study Sampler*, "Behavior of Mealworms."

The Teaching of Elementary Science

INTRODUCTION

Planning is essential for successful teaching and learning in the classroom. This may not be readily apparent when one is observing an experienced and skillful teacher at work, because so often the science lesson seems to have developed quite extemporaneously. However, as the lesson progresses, it becomes quite evident that learning is taking place in a logical, well-ordered manner. Problems are raised. The teacher and children together discuss and decide how to solve these problems. Appropriate learning activities are selected and performed. The supplies and equipment needed for these activities appear or are available at just the right time and in just the right place. The reading materials necessary for finding information or for checking conclusions are either present or easily accessible. All this happens because of careful planning and preparation. This makes it possible for the teacher to guide and direct the children's learning so that they discover science concepts and develop process skills.

When helping children to learn science, the teacher should always keep in mind that there is no one best method of teaching science. No single method is superior to any other, and one method should not be used constantly in preference to others. A variety of methods is desirable because some methods lend themselves better to a learning situation than others. However, the current thinking is that wherever possible the discovery approach to teaching science should be used. In the discovery approach the children acquire knowledge by discovering it for themselves.

Science teaching and learning are always more effective when the learning begins with a problem that arouses the curiosity and interest of the children. The problem may come from a number of different sources. It may come from the teacher, the curriculum guide, the textbook, a current event, or even the children themselves. Planning ways and means of solving this problem will help determine the appropriate method to be used and will also help decide the selection of suitable learning activities.

Provision should be made for the use of a wide variety of learning activities. The children should be given the opportunity to do experiments, to read, to give reports, to participate in discussions, to take field trips, to consult resource persons, to use audio-visual aids, to do research, and to work on projects. All these activities are the means whereby the children are given the opportunity to perform the key operations of the scientist, and in the process learn science concepts.

Provision must also be made for individual differences. For the slow learner there should be additional activities that will either ensure or reinforce his learning. For the fast learner there should be activities that will challenge his intellectual ability and extend his knowledge. With increasing attention being focused today on the problem of teaching the culturally deprived child, specially designed science learning activities may be both necessary and desirable.

When teaching elementary science, care should be taken that the planning does not become rigid. Planning is necessary, but it should be flexible enough so that as new or unexpected problems arise, they can be easily incorporated into the lesson. In this way the children's investigation can digress at any point, if necessary, without disorganizing the general pattern of learning.

As innovations in education appear, they are quickly adapted wherever possible for use in the teaching of elementary science. Some widely publicized teaching innovations in recent years are educational television, team teaching, programed instruction, individualized learning, the ungraded classroom, and the open classroom. Although programed instruction has been introduced with some success in the secondary school, adaptations for its use in the elementary school have been very limited to date.

Some Observations and Reflections About Science Teaching in the Elementary School*

GLENN O. BLOUGH

Glenn Blough briefly describes the real progress being made in the teaching of science in the elementary schools. Today there is more and better science. The author presents a number of fundamental considerations which the teacher must keep in mind when the children are learning science. Two of these considerations are worth noting: (1) it is still all right to read in science, and (2) subject matter is still important. It is imperative to stop the rote memorization of facts, but to de-emphasize or disregard the importance of acquiring a knowledge of science is not the alternative.

Most observers would probably agree that we are making real progress in the teaching of science in the elementary schools, since many teachers are more confident, venturesome, and enthusiastic in their science teaching. There are new curricula and projects that spur us on to bigger and better things. There's more science and there's better science. Children are getting a better deal in science. An analysis of these circumstances appears to reveal certain fundamental considerations that apply in any situation where learning is going on in elementary classrooms.

Our objectives demand our undivided attention, no matter if they are stated as behaviors or in some other fashion. Stating them is not enough. They must influence our selection of subject matter, methods of teaching, and procedures for evaluation, and children as well as teachers should be aware of them. Our progress depends on this.

Science is part of the total elementary school program and exists only because it furthers the objectives of this total program. It cannot and should not be planned to exist outside this framework.

Children cannot make all of the decisions. Leadership by teachers who use their experiences and backgrounds to guide children into meaningful experiences is fundamental to a good program. When we urge children to make decisions for which they have no background we are often wasting time and frustrating both ourselves and the children.

*REPRINTED FROM *Science and Children,* Vol. 9, No. 4, December 1971, pp. 9–10. Copyright, 1971, by the National Science Teachers Association, Washington, D.C. Reprinted by permission of the author and the publisher. Dr. Blough is Professor of Education Emeritus at the University of Maryland.

The fact that children are active and involved does not in itself necessarily make a good program. How purposeful and meaningful these activities and involvements are determine whether or not they can be used as a measure of success. Let us keep asking ourselves, "What meaning have these experiences for children?" An activity without meaning to children is taking up valuable time in an already too crowded curriculum.

It is still all right to read in science. Granted, we have overdone reading, but this is hardly a reason to abandon one of the greatest avenues to the attainment of knowledge, attitudes, and skills. Children cannot discover everything through first-hand experience anymore than teachers can.

We cannot hurry discovery. In our haste to get on with the show and because of the pressures of time we may be inclined to overtax children to show results quickly and in so doing violate the real spirit of science.

Teachers must themselves possess interest and appreciation for the science of their environment if they are to impart these traits to children. There are no records of children being inspired by teachers who themselves are not inspired.

It is still all right not to solve the problem. There are countless examples of problems children tackle that they cannot solve for almost as many reasons. There is often more real science learning taking place when children realize that "We have gone as far as we can but we still cannot be sure." Let us hope they may continue to be interested at a later time when they again encounter the problem.

Teachers, as well as children, live in the "age of science" or the "space age," or the "age of the computer," etc., and because of this, they need to achieve the general objectives for science teaching. A teacher who does not understand and use the processes of discovery probably cannot help children understand how to use them.

We will never help children formulate hypotheses or theories if we do not listen to them and encourage their best thinking. They may be, and often are, wrong but it is through these attempts that they grow in ability to express ideas. An environment in which children are belittled either by the teacher or other children is not one in which children can grow in ability to hypothesize.

Science classes should be occasions for questioning by children as well as teachers. Who asks most of the questions in our class?

Open-endedness is in itself not the sole criterion for successful science experiences. The emphasis on open-endedness may lead into avenues that are neither interesting nor appropriate to the situation. This concept is important but now and then we need to evaluate the effectiveness of the process.

Subject matter is important. In our zeal to curtail the emphasis on having children memorize unrelated facts we may have gone overboard, and may have de-emphasized the fact that knowledge of science is essential to understanding the world we live in. Stop the rote memorizing of facts, yes, but to disregard the importance of learning the information is not the alternative.

When teachers have told the answers, problem solving, investigating, discovering, and other similar processes come to a screeching halt. Sometimes in our zeal to demonstrate that we know, to "save time," and for other reasons we talk too much!

Children learn best when they are involved but the involvement is most productive when it is purposeful. Children can be active and still be wasting time. "Having fun" is not necessarily the prime purpose for the science lesson.

Techniques for Developing Discovery Questioning Skills*

ARTHUR A. CARIN

Arthur Carin maintains that the heart of teaching and learning science by discovery is in questions properly asked and answers to them properly used. He lists a number of purposes for which teachers should ask questions. Although unplanned questions are important, premeditated questioning is essential for a starting point in a creative discovery science program. The author puts premeditated questions into two categories: convergent questions and divergent questions. Finally, he offers a list of pertinent suggestions to teachers who wish to start improving their own questioning skills.

It has been accurately observed that we live in an *answer-oriented* world. This trend must be reversed if we are to help children learn scientific processes along with scientific facts, concepts, and principles. Emphasis must be refocused on finding answers rather than merely on the answers themselves. Teaching-learning science by discovery is an approach that stresses involvement of the learner in seeking answers.

The heart of teaching-learning science by discovery is in questions properly asked and answers to them properly used. Not only do teachers ask too many questions, they more often than not ask the *wrong* kinds of questions. Surveys indicate that over 90 percent of all questions teachers

*REPRINTED FROM *Science and Children*, Vol. 7, No. 7, April 1970, pp. 13–15. Copyright, 1970, by the National Science Teachers Association, Washington, D.C. Reprinted by permission of the author and the publisher. Dr. Carin is Associate Dean of Education at Queens College.

ask call merely for reproducing what was just read, heard or seen by children. These questions require only the lowest level of thinking by children—memorization.

There are unlimited opportunities in a science program to use stimulating questions: discussion, laboratory experiences, demonstrations, student worksheets, films, etc. However, before entering the classroom, teachers should know specifically what they want to teach, why they ask questions, what types of questions they want to ask, and the responses they will accept.

One of the most important considerations for planning effective questioning techniques is for the teacher to know specifically what it is he wants the children to learn. Selection of specific questions will then follow from the goals and objectives he hopes to guide the children to achieve.*

Why do teachers ask children questions? One of the most important reasons teachers ask questions is to find out what their pupils know and do not know. These questions are very valid for they assist the teacher in planning and modifying his science program according to the needs of his class. He can avoid going over material the children already know or presenting material too difficult for their backgrounds. In a similar vein, by knowing the direction his children are going in a lesson, the teacher can redirect or focus by the questions he asks. Questions can be utilized for keeping the lesson relevant to the investigation at hand.

In addition to the above, teachers ask questions for these purposes:

1. To arouse interest—motivating children to actively participate in a lesson.
2. To evaluate a pupil's preparation and to see if his homework or previous work has been mastered.
3. To review and summarize what is taught.
4. To develop insights by helping children see new relationships.
5. To stimulate critical thinking and development of questioning attitude.
6. To stimulate pupils to seek out additional knowledge on their own.
7. To evaluate the achievement of goals and objectives of lesson.

Premeditated Questions

Although unplanned "on the spot" questions are important in science education, little true long range creative teaching-learning is possible on such a hit-and-miss basis. Premeditated or planned questioning is essential for a starting point in a creative discovery science program. Two kinds of preplanned questions are *convergent* and *divergent* questions.

*For examples of levels of questioning which increase depth of thinking processes, see David R. Krathwohl, Benjamin S. Bloom, Bertram B. Masia, *Taxonomy of Educational Objectives: The Classification of Educational Goals*. (David McKay Company, Inc., New York City. 1964) pp. 186–193.

CONVERGENT QUESTIONS

Some questions cause children to move toward closure or to summarize and draw conclusions. They are called *convergent* questions. Recall questions fall into this category. "What is the annual rainfall for Arizona?" is a convergent question. There is only one answer. Although their importance is limited, convergent questions are nevertheless necessary. Robert Gagné has cautioned that discovery could be undertaken only after the individual acquired a store of broad and critical knowledge. When convergent questions are overused, however, more advanced and creative thinking is inhibited. An excess of the question-answer, stimulus-response questioning can be destructive to developing process thinking in science. Convergent questions rarely lead to further investigation.

DIVERGENT QUESTIONS

Some questions, on the other hand, cause children to ask further questions, plan and carry out experiences with science equipment, and do library or other research. These are called *divergent* or productive questions.

In contrast to the convergent question, "What is the annual rainfall for Arizona?" the following is an example of a divergent question:

Mr. Goodman gave an atlas to each of two children. He then asked them to look over the Annual Rainfall Map of the United States. After a few minutes Mr. Goodman asked: "You'll notice by the colors used that some states receive over 89 inches of rainfall annually, while others receive under 10 inches. *Why do you suppose this is so?*"

Divergent questions go further than convergent questions. They stimulate the learner to find out what is to be. The learner is encouraged to broaden or deepen the area to be studied. He is required to gather facts, evaluate them, and to engage in higher creative thinking processes in order to answer divergent questions. Because of their broadening effect, divergent questions are referred to as *open-ended* or *productive*.

Improving Teacher Questioning Skills

The following suggestions are presented for teachers who wish to start improving their own questioning skills:

1. Write down specific wording of 6–8 questions in your lesson plan *before* coming to class.
2. Ask your questions as simply, concisely, and directly as possible. Avoid such unnecessary introductions as, "What do you think about . . . ," "How many of you can tell me . . . ," etc.
3. Ask your questions before designating which child should answer. Pause briefly after asking the question so that all children have time to think about the question.
4. Ask an individual child to respond to your question. Total class

shouting out of answers could result in classroom discipline problems for the teacher.

5. Ask questions of as many children as possible during the science lessons—volunteers and non-volunteers, slow and bright, etc. Gear the difficulty to each child's interest, science background, and ability.

6. Ask a question about the most obvious part of the investigation for your first question. Such a question might be, "How much weight did the hamster gain since last week?"

7. Ask as many questions that stimulate creative thinking processes as possible from among these categories:

    (a) comparison   (f) criticism
    (b) summarization   (g) making assumptions
    (c) observation   (h) collection and organization of data
    (d) classification (grouping)   (i) evaluation
    (e) interpretation

8. Ask questions that give children practical experience with science process thought questions. These include:

    (a) designing an investigation—i.e., How would you find out?
    (b) hypothesizing or predicting—i.e., What do you think will happen?
    (c) making an operational definition—i.e., How would you define that?

9. Ask questions in a variety of ways in addition to "what," "how," "why," so that students are asked to:

    (a) illustrate or show how   (f) interpret
    (b) explain   (g) evaluate
    (c) discuss   (h) contrast
    (d) justify   (i) summarize
    (e) trace

10. Ask questions that lead to actual experimentation on the children's part such as:

    (a) Questions that present a discrepancy in anticipated outcome to excite curiosity. (While pouring juice from a can with only one hole punched in it, ask: "Why does the juice plop out instead of run out?")
    (b) Questions that suggest possible tests for solution ("How are metals affected by a magnet? What metals are attracted by a magnet?")
    (c) Questions that are specific and not too broad or general (*Poor:* How do seeds sprout? *Better:* What conditions are needed for seeds to sprout?)
    (d) Rather than "How" questions (which lead to frustration) ask "What will happen if we . . . ?" Will it work more or less quickly with . . . ? What might we do if we want this one to . . . ? Can anyone think of a way we might work to get the plant to . . . ?"

11. *Avoid* asking questions that inhibit investigations:

    (a) Questions where the answer is obvious and foregone conclusion
    (b) Yes-No questions (*Poor:* Are all trees the same size and age? *Better:* How do trees vary in size, shape, and age?)

(c) Questions in which teleological phenomena or object is given purpose or will (*Poor:* Why does nature abhor a vacuum? *Better:* Why is maintaining a vacuum so difficult?)

(d) Anthropomorphic questions (*Poor:* Why do electrons want to leave the metal? *Better:* What causes the electrons to move?)

(e) Vague questions (*Poor:* Tell us about light. *Better:* What are some of the characteristics of light?)

(f) Tooth pulling questions (*Poor:* Come on, you can think of a third kind of acid. *Better:* We seem to have difficulty in thinking of a third kind of acid. What kind of acid did we find in orange juice?)

(g) Statements that suddenly turn into a question. (*Poor:* The growth of your plants with fertilizer since last month was what? *Better:* How much have your plants with the fertilizer grown since last month?)

(h) A battery of questions (*Poor:* What is weather, how is it different from climate, and how can a weather man help predict it? *Better:* What are some of the elements that make up weather?)

(i) Asking for information children cannot be expected to know (*Poor:* How does a Geiger counter work? *Better:* If a charged particle like a proton comes into the Geiger counter tube, what should take place?)

12. *Avoid* **repeating children's answers.**

In summary, questioning must begin to reflect concern with scientific processes along with content. Before entering the classroom, teachers must know specifically what they want to teach. The teachers then will ask questions to find out what their students do and do not know, to arouse interest, to evaluate pupil progress, to guide higher level thinking processes, and to review and summarize. Convergent questions lead to closure while divergent questions cause children to ask further questions and to plan and carry out further investigations.

Some Ways of Helping Children to Learn Science*

BEATRICE HURLEY

Beatrice Hurley discusses some of the kinds of activities which can serve as channels through which children may learn science. This discussion includes such activities as direct observation, field trips, reading, experi-

*REPRINTED FROM *Science for the Eights-to-Twelves,* Copyright, 1964, Bulletin No. 13A of the Association for Childhood Education International, 3615 Wisconsin Avenue, NW, Washington, D.C., pp. 23–32, by permission of the author and the publisher. Dr. Hurley is Professor Emeritus of Education at New York University.

menting, and using audio-visual aids. It is intended as a guide for those who seek ways of helping each child learn how to go on learning science for the rest of his life. This article is a portion of a larger article, "What Is Science?" which appears in an Association for Childhood Education International Bulletin entitled Science for the Eights-to-Twelves.

Children learn science in a wide variety of ways. Obviously, there is no one blueprint which should be followed by all teachers. The activities selected for and by children should take several factors into account. Greater effectiveness in the teaching-learning process is almost always achieved when there is a challenging problem to be solved—one that children feel is worth solving. At times, the problem to be solved comes from a child's proposal; at others, the selection of the problem is the teacher's. And at still other times children and teacher jointly select it. Who makes the selection matters little, if all involved accept the problem as one worthy of solution.

When the solution of a problem is accepted as genuinely important enough to work on, planning must be done and accurate information gathered from many sources. There must be a period of exploration, time for proposals as to how and when the work shall get done and by whom. Shall the entire group be involved in each step, or shall small groups or individuals take responsibility for portions of the work and report their findings to the large group? Well-guided discussions are essential throughout the entire planning and working times. For example, let us suppose that a group of children are finding answers to the question, "What do plants need in order to grow?" This general topic might well be broken up into smaller segments:

What does soil have to do with plants' growing?
What does water have to do with plants' growing?
What does temperature have to do with plant growth?
What does light have to do with the growth of plants?

Children working in small groups or individually could work effectively upon one or another of these questions. One group might suggest experiments which would yield evidence concerning the needs of plants for growth. Another might suggest going to books to find out. Another might suggest a trip to a greenhouse, a farm, a botanical garden to talk to persons involved in successfully growing many kinds of plants.

Children should carry on activities within the large problem area which they are able to tackle with a reasonable expectation of success. Provision for individual differences in interest and maturity should be carefully assessed as decisions of work assignments are made.

It is desirable to use a variety of procedures for finding out. Not all individuals learn equally well, nor do they take the same things from any one experience.

Direct Observation

Whenever possible, and within the bounds of safety, children should be given opportunity to learn about their world through direct observation of it. What a learner learns through seeing, feeling, smelling, tasting and hearing gives him much firsthand knowledge of the nature of things in the local environment. With the use of certain instruments such as a telescope, observations of more distant phenomena can be made.

Young children learn much of what they know through keen use of their senses. Older children should be encouraged to continue to learn in this manner. Skill in observation is perhaps one of the most useful tools a person can acquire. Teachers can enrich the lives of boys and girls by helping them learn how to see and interpret their environment. Children who know where the first crocuses are to be found, when the spring migration of warblers takes place, what stream is best to fish to catch the biggest trout, which kinds of clouds bring clear weather are usually children who have learned to be keen observers of what goes on around them.

Learning is made more vivid and pleasurable through numerous direct observational experiences. The goal worth striving for is growth in accuracy of one's observations and in reporting them to others. The ability to observe accurately is a part of all other activities in science. Without it, experiments are of no value. Excursions benefit children more when blinders have been removed from eyes and children are helped to see what spore cases look like on the underside of fern leaves; how a robin's flight habits differ from those of a hawk; what the buds on a tree look like in midwinter; how a mullein leaf differs from a plantain leaf in the way it feels in your hand.

Taking Field Trips

Some of the most valuable learning situations occur outside the classroom. The distance covered from school to the place to be visited is not the measuring stick for the value of an excursion. Every local environment holds numerous possibilities for fruitful observational experiences. There are inexhaustible resources for teaching science in any community, even in one that at first may appear to hold few possibilities for direct learning through trips.

Within the school building itself investigations could be made that might include:

How our school is heated.
How electricity comes to our building.
Where the fuse box is.
How the intercommunication system works.

How food is prepared in the cafeteria.
How garbage is disposed of.

A study of the schoolyard has much value for learners. Suggested investigations are:

Places where soil is being eroded or where grass grows best.
Do animals live on the schoolground? If so, what do these animals find to eat?
Where do they make their homes?
What kinds of trees and other plants are there that can be studied throughout the four seasons?
What machines are used in play equipment on the playground?

Exploration of these things helps bring science into the lives of children.

Moving away from the school and schoolground, there is the community to explore—persons, places and things. Trips to fields, farms, bogs, a vacant lot, a zoo, a park, a stream, an excavation or an abandoned quarry can acquaint children with a great variety of living and nonliving things and give them knowledge of how these living and nonliving things are inter-related. Return visits to places help children realize the changes that occur as seasons pass. Likewise, trips to processing and manufacturing plants, a telephone exchange, newspaper printing plant, TV station or water purifica-tion plant can reveal much of man's use of technological advances.

Almost any community has resource persons who can offer enrichment to the school curriculum. A teacher's source file of such persons will help children to benefit from the talents of special people in the community. There may be an amateur astronomer, a naturalist, a conservationist, a geologist, a photographer with color films and slides, a tropical fish keeper, a physician or a world traveler, who would be glad to share knowledge and experiences with boys and girls.

Trips into the community should be carefully planned ahead of time. Children should know the object of taking the trip, what they wish to find out while there. They should keep records on the spot, make sketches or take pictures if these activities are appropriate. One of the goals the teacher should hold in mind is to make more careful observers of children. Also, children should learn to check their observations of natural-phenomena with reliable sources, a necessary operation which requires the use of books.

Reading

Through reading children learn about the ideas of others. Books are useful tools for learning science. It is important to recognize that factual textbooks and trade books should be used to add information to a topic under consideration and should be consulted when unanswered questions are hanging fire. Under these conditions, children go directly to that part of the book dealing with their specific concerns. The learner may have any of several reasons to consult a book. He may wish to check his own conclusions; to get added information; to learn how to do an experiment; or to answer a question.

Using factual books in this manner helps children learn to use books effectively and efficiently. Skill in using encyclopedias is not quickly learned, but teachers who guide children in using their science textbooks and single-volume factual books as research tools build basic skills for using encyclopedias and other complex reference books.

Many teachers have in the classroom library factual books and other reading matter relating to science topics, chosen with concern for the varying reading abilities of a group of children. Assignments of topics can then be made for the individual child, using books neither too hard nor too easy. Developing skill in reading and learning science can go hand in hand if the teacher guides children well in their selection of books and other reading matter.

Thoughtful, deliberate reading of science material often sparks discussions that further enhance children's understanding of a given topic and of new topics as well. Varying points of view of authorities may cause children to question authoritative sources. Lack of agreement may also help children sense the tentative nature of much that is now known and thought to be fact. This, in itself, is a valuable experience. A healthy skepticism is a wholesome attribute.

From the foregoing, it must be evident that books and reading have an important role to play in the science program. It must also be clear that "Open the book to page 34 and read to page 39" is an undesirable kind of assignment.

Sometimes an interest catches fire in the classroom that leads children to search for new information not readily found in textbooks.

Such a search engaged the energies of a group of sixth-graders. As an offshoot of a study centering around the concept that "we are caretakers of the environment," these children learned that some animals once numerous are now extinct and that others are on the way to becoming so.

Committees set to work to find out which animals had already died out and why; which ones were threatened with extinction; and what was happening to correct the situation. This search led children to magazines, bulletins, daily papers, movies, TV programs and books for information about whooping cranes, the condor of California, the bald eagle now scarce in this country, and other scarce animals throughout the world. The children were stunned to learn that giraffes are still being slaughtered, not for food, but for their tails which are marketed as flyswatters; and that the rhinoceros are killed for their horns which are ground into a powder that is an aphrodisiac.

The New York Times of December 22, 1963, carried a story of the killing of 351 rare, gray seal calves on an island in the North Sea by marksmen from the Ministry of Agriculture, Fisheries, and Food. Fishermen had complained that the calves were damaging their nets and eating their fish. The children were puzzled at the wanton destruction of seal calves by a body of men engaged in the conservation of wildlife. Was this not a shortsighted act on the part of these men? "Aren't there wiser ways to keep nature in balance?," they asked. Many more questions were asked.

But the children's faith in human nature was somewhat restored as they learned of the exciting wildlife survival centers being set up in many zoological parks for breeding stock of endangered species. Children's letters to persons planning these centers brought replies with many details concerning which animals were to be protected.

If it is true that concepts govern actions, this vital science enterprise may well have conditioned the behavior of these sixth-graders in matters pertaining to the responsibility of each as a "caretaker of his environment."

Among the concepts that the teacher sought to advance in this experience were the following:

Countless species of plants and animals that once lived on Earth are nowhere to be found today.

Once a species has died out, it is never likely to develop on Earth again.

Thoughtless acts may cause great damage.

Sometimes men have helped to cause the extinction of some living things.

Sometimes men have helped to save species of living things from extinction.

Boys and girls not only need to learn about the living things in their environment, but they also need to learn the importance of their actions in bringing about change.

Part of this understanding about the importance of individual acts can be gained by studying some of the changes which have occurred in the past.

Each individual is responsible to some degree for the care of his environment.

Concepts of such magnitude clearly illustrated that this teacher was not concerned with pouring in a mass of small facts. To be sure, a great number of facts were uncovered and utilized, but it was not the memorizing of small content that guided the teacher as she worked with the boys and girls. Her goals were changes in behavior, deepening of understanding, appreciation of the vital role of each individual in enjoying and protecting the environment. The teaching of science that aims at changes in behavior is quite different from that which is set out to be learned, such as covering the book and passing the test.

Experimenting

An experiment is an activity intended to supply information in solving, or helping to solve, a problem. It is a means to an end rather than an end in itself. Experimentation is conducted primarily for learning something that the experimenter does not already know.

Let us suppose a fourth-grade child asks, "Where is the attraction of a magnet strongest?" He asks because he doesn't know the answer. This is the moment for the teacher to suggest that he go to the storage cupboard, get a magnet and experiment to find the answer he seeks.

Equipment for most experiments done in elementary school should be simple. A paper bag can be used as successfully as a bicycle pump and tire to show that compressed air can do work. Occasionally, the use of simple materials stimulates children to improvise equipment from materials at hand; often such improvisation is ingenious and quite creative.

In guiding experiments done by children, the teacher needs to bear in mind that the factor of *control* is very important; that is, all conditions must be the same except for the experimental one, called the *variable*.

For example, a child might set about to find out "what would happen to green plants if there were no more sunlight." One way to find out is to plan an experiment. Since the answer is not known, the situation is truly experimental.

The child decides to use two potted green plants. He chooses the same kind of plant, in the same-sized pots, growing well in the same kind of soil; that is, he attempts to get plants as nearly alike as possible.

He allows one plant to continue to grow under ordinary conditions just as it has been doing. This is his control. He places the other plant in a completely dark place. Otherwise, he keeps conditions as identical as possible. The factor of light is the variable.

Periodically, he examines both plants. He notes and keeps a careful record of any changes that take place. At the end of ten days, dramatic differences have developed. Since all other aspects of the experiment are the same, the experimenter concludes that the differences may be ascribed to the difference in the amount of light available to the two plants. This is the answer to his question, "What would happen to green plants if there were no more sunlight?"

But this answer must be considered tentative only. It may not be the final answer. There is always the possibility that the results obtained were only accidental. Perhaps another plant kept in darkness would not react in the same manner.

He might try more than two plants—perhaps ten—keeping five in darkness and the rest in the light. He repeats the steps used earlier. At the end of ten days, he finds that the plants in the dark reacted in a similar manner to the one used in the first experiment.

If this happens, he has a sounder basis for his conclusion. Even so, he should check his conclusions with an authoritative source.[1]

Not all situations call for experimentation. Many answers are to be found by direct observation of phenomena, by asking others, by reading books. Doing experiments when the answer is already known, not only by the teacher but by the students as well, is a dull and unproductive use of time.

Audiovisual Aids

Although personal, firsthand experiences furnish the richest ways for acquiring correct concepts in science, they are not always possible. Glaciers and geysers can seldom be visited. Hence the teacher seeks another source to help children learn about glaciers and geysers.

Often visual or auditory aids can be profitably used, such as colored photographs, slides, filmstrips, movies and recordings. Many schools now budget for the purchase or rental of such materials. Catalogs of major distributors of audiovisual materials should be available to teachers. Often the school librarian is custodian of the audiovisual aids, which are kept in the library and checked out as books are loaned.

Museums sometimes have dioramas and mounted exhibits to loan to neighborhood schools. Many commercial and industrial plants have exhibits that can be had for the charge of mailing them back to their owners. Models, such as a model of the human body, can be profitably used.

For example, in discussing geometrical shapes, children in a fourth grade had become interested in Pythagoras and the introduction of geometry into Greece. The name of Socrates was mentioned in answer to the question, "What other famous men lived in Ancient Greece?" Then it was brought out by the teacher that a favorite saying of Socrates was "Know thyself."

The children pondered on what "Know thyself" really meant. Someone suggested that it was important to know what is in our bodies, and this launched the class on a study of the human body.

Through much research in encyclopedias, trade books and many texts, children found that the smallest part of a healthy body is a cell. After initial total class discussion, individual and small groups of children worked on their own to delve into this study, under the guidance of the teacher. Various activities included:

Taking apart the large model of the human body (and putting it together again).

[1] Gerald S. Craig and John Urban, Teachers Manual for *Science Today and Tomorrow: Facing Tomorrow with Science* (Boston: Ginn and Company, 1958), p. 12.

Learning about the bony framework, joints, and organs.
Writing reports and drawing figures.

As well as "knowing themselves," children developed vocabulary and research skills in their study of the human body.[2]

Perhaps one of the most exciting innovations now being used in schools is the tape recorder. There is no end to the possibilities for enriching classroom living through carefully prepared tapes. Recordings of talks by specialists in any number of areas can be made and re-used. Discussions of children concerning scientific matters are frequently worth taping and re-using, often as an evaluative device wherein children examine their own ability, or lack of it, to think critically. Recordings of bird songs, of sounds at a pond, of porpoises communicating in a tank, of animals when in danger are among other uses of tapes.

Needless to say, the same careful planning for using auditory and visual aids that characterizes uses of other materials is essential for the best results.

There are, then, many types of activities which can serve as channels through which boys and girls may learn science. The choice of the particular activity, or activities, depends upon the goals to be achieved. Whatever is chosen, that activity should promote understanding, interest and appreciation in science. It should make science concepts and principles more vivid, more clearly understood. As was said earlier in this bulletin, science experiences should help children construct a comprehensible and orderly system of explanations for natural phenomena and build a basis for intelligent control and utilization of the natural world.

The Unit*

EDWARD VICTOR

Edward Victor presents a comprehensive discussion of the components of a planned and structured elementary science unit. These components include the overview, teacher's and pupil objectives, initiating activities, learning activities, materials, bibliography, vocabulary, culminating activities, evaluation, and work sheets. Dr. Victor describes the purpose of each

---

[2] Highview School, Hartsdale, N.Y., Fourth Grade.
*REPRINTED FROM Science for the Elementary School, 3rd Ed. (New York: Macmillan Publishing Co., Inc., 1975), pp. 105–124, by permission of the publisher. Dr. Victor is Professor of Education at Northwestern University.

component, and shows how the components may be incorporated into the teaching unit, resource unit, and textbook unit. This excerpt on the unit is taken from Chapter 5, "Planning for Science in the Classroom," of Science for the Elementary School.

Concomitant with the need for planning is the need for organizing the elements of good planning into a suitable framework, through which the teaching-learning situation in the classroom has scope and sequence. A highly effective means of organizing such a framework is the unit.

The unit is a logical division of class work or activity. When constructed, the unit becomes an *anticipated* plan for using a wide variety of activities, involving inquiry and discovery, so that learning can take place. The objectives of the unit are to help the children learn content and process, and to develop such behavioral outcomes as scientific skills, attitudes, apprehensions, and interests. Thus, the unit presents a plan for providing learning activities that will achieve the objectives of the unit.

Sometimes beginning teachers are told that a good teacher does not have to plan the unit carefully and rather should try to build from questions, conversations, arguments, or other sporadic incidents that occur in the classroom. This method is not as simple as it may sound. Definite readiness is required for this kind of emerging lesson or unit. First, the teacher must have a competent science background so that she is familiar with the topic under discussion. Then the teacher must be acquainted with a wide variety of experiments, demonstrations, and other learning activities suitable for teaching the understandings associated with the topic. Finally, the appropriate supplies, equipment, references, and other materials must be easily or already available. Once the teacher has this background of science knowledge, activities, and materials, she is in an excellent position to convert questions and incidents into worthwhile learning situations. The same readiness is also necessary for experienced teachers. A science lesson or unit can emerge from incidents in the classroom only when the teacher has the necessary knowledge and tools to take advantage of the situation.

Construction of a unit entails careful planning and preparation, but the rewards are great, namely, effective teaching and learning. When units bog down or collapse, the failure is generally due to a lack of adequate planning and preparation. A very hastily prepared or poorly constructed unit will create "dead spots" in a learning situation, which cannot ordinarily be remedied by the teacher's ingenuity or ability to think quickly. When this situation occurs often—and sometimes one unfortunate experience suffices—the teacher is likely to reject all unit construction as a "waste of valuable time," and thus discards what is generally considered a most valuable and effective teaching technique.

Initial attempts to construct units are often slow and time-consuming, as are other valid teaching techniques when planned and presented for the first time. The teacher may spend a lot of time in finding the best sources for collecting the science concepts and learning activities, and an equal amount of effort in coordinating all the unit components into an effective working plan. However, once the pattern becomes familiar, the time and effort involved lessens considerably, and the results become increasingly satisfying and rewarding.

When planning and constructing the unit, the teacher or curriculum committee selects the objectives, develops the means for arousing pupil interest and problems, anticipates a logical sequence of learning activities, provides for the necessary laboratory and reference materials, and even gives consideration to the possibilities for evaluating both the learning and the behavioral outcomes that the children will gain. The teacher or committee strives at all times to give the unit suitable scope and sequence.

The unit should never be rigid. It must be flexible enough to permit digression at any point, if necessary, without interrupting the broad pattern of learning anticipated by the unit. It is necessary to plan the day's work in advance, but the plan should be pliable enough to include and incorporate new situations and questions as they arise.

What to include in a unit is always a matter of discussion. Proponents of the various types of units differ somewhat about content and organization. However, it is generally agreed that a unit should contain most—if not all—of the following:

1. Overview.
2. Objectives.
3. Initiating activities.
4. Learning activities.
5. Materials.
6. Bibliography.
7. New science vocabulary.
8. Culminating activities.
9. Evaluation.
10. Work sheets.

A discussion of each of these components of a unit follows.

Overview

The purpose of the overview is to describe the nature and scope of the unit. Some teachers or school systems, when constructing units, omit the overview. However, the overview can serve a definite purpose. When a school system develops a science program and constructs units, it is likely that a science committee is given the responsibility of preparing the units for the rest of the teachers in the school system. This preparation will result whenever a school system is large and has so many elementary school teachers that it becomes impossible to involve all the teachers in constructing every unit for each grade level. Furthermore, with the consistent rapid turnover of elementary school teachers, there will always be new teachers or beginning teachers who have started teaching after the units have been constructed. In such cases, whenever units are presented to teachers who have had no part in constructing them, it is always helpful to provide an overview with a brief description of the nature and scope of the unit. Even when the teacher makes her own unit, an overview can be of real service when shown to administrators, parents, or other teachers who visit her class and need a quick briefing on what is going on.

One highly effective way of presenting an overview is to give it in written form, consisting of two or three paragraphs. The overview might begin by describing the importance of the unit topic in our daily lives, for both child and adult. Then it might list the key concepts, and conclude by giving some general values and desirable behaviors that the children will derive from the unit.

An example of this kind of overview, for a unit on "Leaves," is as follows:

Leaves are important to the daily life of both children and adults because they are the primary sources of food for all living things. Leaves and grass contain chlorophyll and can manufacture food, and from green leaves and grass we get all our food—either directly or indirectly. Hence, the study of leaves can be basic to the understanding of life and how it exists on earth. In addition, leaves give us one of the several signs of the change of seasons in many parts of the country.

This unit hopes to teach (1) the kinds of leaves and how they differ from one another, (2) the parts of the leaf, including its external and internal structure, (3) the function of the leaf, with special emphasis on photosynthesis, and (4) the change in color of leaves in the fall.

From the learning activities in this unit the children may gain a better understanding of leaves and their function, and an appreciation of the beauty and the way leaves are constructed. The children will develop further their ability to observe carefully and accurately, to listen intelligently, and to read science books for information. They will be asked to draw conclusions from what they have learned, and to apply these conclusions to life situations. Finally, they will learn how to express themselves more effectively, to participate more ably in class discussion, and to work cooperatively with their peers.

Teacher's Objectives

In general, the teacher has two main objectives: (1) to help the children learn science content—the product of science, and (2) to help the children learn the key operations of science and the scientist—the process of science. Both objectives are vital, and one is meaningless without the other. Consequently, definite provision must be made to incorporate both objectives into the unit. Otherwise the unit will fail to accomplish its purpose.

Some school systems develop only a scope and sequence chart, leaving the construction of units to the individual teacher. Other school systems appoint a science curriculum committee, which, under the guidance of a science supervisor or consultant, constructs a comprehensive set of units for all the teachers. An analysis of science units which have proven to be highly successful, and which have enabled the teacher to achieve effective learning in the classroom, shows that they all have one factor in common. In all cases, the units contain an outline or list of the science concepts that the children are expected to learn while the units are in progress. And it seems that the more specifically the concepts are expressed in behavorial terms, the more successful are the units.

The preparation of an outline or list of concepts for inclusion in the unit helps the teacher in two ways. First, regardless of whether the unit is constructed by the teacher or by a committee, such an outline can be of great help as a guide when the learning activities are selected for the unit. Second, the outline serves as a check to make sure that the teacher will have the necessary science background for the topic being studied.

If the teacher's school system has a detailed curriculum guide, she will have some indication of what science concepts to teach. If there is no such guide, the selection of concepts will have to be left to the judgment of the teacher. In this case she may have to simplify the wording of these concepts (without losing their scientific accuracy) to meet the vocabulary level of her class, and organize them into what she thinks will be a logical sequence of learning. The latter is very important because one set of understandings will lead easily into another set of understandings, and in this way learning can take place more quickly and efficiently.

The learning of science content, then, is one of the teacher's two major objectives. The second major objective is the learning of science process, accompanied by the development of desirable behaviors. These behaviors include scientific skills, attitudes, appreciations, and interests. They also involve how to think critically and creatively, and how to solve problems. These behaviors emerge from the learning activities that are conducted while the unit is in progress. The behaviors may be either immediate or long-range behaviors. Examples of these behaviors have already been described in Chapter 2, "Objectives of Elementary Science."

The learning of process and the development of behaviors will depend to a large extent upon the kinds of learning activities that will be selected. Each learning activity, as a rule, will call for the use of certain operations and the development of certain behaviors. Consequently, if process is to be taught effectively, the teacher must become completely familiar with all the key operations of science and the scientist and with all the desirable behavioral outcomes. The teacher can then examine each learning activity closely to determine which operations and behaviors are associated with that activity. Provision for the inclusion of a wide variety of learning activities in the units will ensure ample opportunity for the children to develop proficiency in any or all of the desired operations and behaviors.

Many units include a list of those key operations and behaviors that will constitute one of the objectives for the unit. These operations and behaviors should be incorporated with the concepts and expressed in specific behavioral terms that lend themselves to proper observation and evaluation. In most units the behavioral objectives are written in the form of statements. In some units they are written as questions.

Pupil Objectives

Units often include pupil objectives. These objectives are the anticipated pupil questions or problems that will emerge from the initiating activities. The questions and problems are stated as the children might raise them in the children's own vocabulary. Pupil objectives thus also remind us that the children's aims may be quite different from those of the teacher. The teacher may want the children to learn about heat expansion. The children, however, will want to know why cracks are intentionally put into concrete sidewalks. The teacher is interested in electrical circuits; the children want to learn how to connect a dry cell, wires, and a porcelain socket containing a bulb so that the bulb will light up. The teacher is interested in the laws governing vibrating strings; the children want to know what can be done to make the musical note from a violin or guitar higher or lower. The teacher is primarily concerned with the learning of basic science information and the development of desirable behaviors. The children want to know "why," "what," "how," "when," "what will happen if," and so forth.

If the initiating activities are properly selected, the pupil objectives will emerge easily. However, because the pupil questions and problems in the planned unit are anticipated, if the children should fail to raise them, the teacher may ask them instead. Actually, the children often raise better or more questions and problems than those anticipated by the teacher. The wise teacher incorporates these questions and problems into the unit.

Initiating Activities

The purpose of initiating activities is to involve the children in the unit; these activities are the means whereby pupil interest and curiosity are aroused. In the process, questions and problems are raised that, when answered or solved, will help achieve the teacher's objectives. The main purpose of initiating activities is to raise questions or problems, the answers to which the children do not know but will find out as they proceed with the learning activities in the unit. Because the children do not know the answers, their curiosity is piqued and their interest in finding out the answers is aroused.

GENERAL OR OVERALL INITIATING ACTIVITY.   Usually a general or overall initiating activity is used to introduce or "initiate" the entire unit to the children. There are several ways of initiating the entire unit. Sometimes a previous unit will lead the children quite naturally into a new unit. If the class has just finished a study of magnets, for example, it will require very little effort to motivate the children for the study of electromagnets. Units can also be initiated by books and stories. Sometimes, merely the announcement of the next topic or problem may be sufficient to arouse pupil interest and problems.

Another way to initiate a unit is to set the stage for the unit. A good example is an attractive bulletin-board display, accompanied by thought-provoking questions. To initiate a unit on "Evaporation and Condensation," a teacher may plan to put on the bulletin board a series of pictures showing evaporation and condensation taking place. This display can include pictures of a puddle of water on a concrete sidewalk under the warm sun, sheets or towels drying on the clothesline, droplets of water on a bottle of soda pop or on the sides of a pitcher of lemonade, fogged-up windows, a person's breath visible on a cold, wintry day, and so on. Under the pictures can be questions such as "How does the water get into the air?" "How does water come out of the air?" "How can we make water go into or come out of the air more quickly or more slowly?"

Another way to set the stage for a unit is to have a display of materials on a table with accompanying questions. Materials for display can include pictures, books, models, or specimens. When initiating a unit on leaves, it will be natural to have a variety of leaves on display, especially in the fall. Typical questions that can be asked would be "Are these leaves alike?" "How are they different?" "How many parts does each leaf have?" "What do leaves do?" "Why do leaves change color in the fall?"

A thought-provoking demonstration is an excellent way to initiate a unit. A teacher can initiate a unit on "How Does Heat Travel" by simply placing a spoon in a cup of hot water. Pupil interest and curiosity will be raised about why the part of the spoon that is out of the water also becomes hot.

Even a thought-provoking discussion can initiate a unit. In temperate climates most children are quite familiar with the effects caused by static electricity, especially on a cold, dry day. The teacher can initiate a unit on such a day by first asking the children to describe personal experiences with static electricity and then leading into an on-going discussion about the characteristics of and reasons for this phenomenon.

INITIATING ACTIVITIES DURING THE UNIT.   There are some who believe that one good general or overall initiating activity is sufficient to sustain pupil interest and motivation for the entire unit. They feel that the one activity will raise enough questions and problems to ensure the learning of all the science content and process in the unit. On the other hand, there are many who think that additional initiating activities are necessary, as the unit progresses. These additional activities may be necessary, especially when a unit extends over two, three, or even more weeks. Interest and motivation may flag over a period of time for even the most enthusiastic children.

Also, in those units which include an outline or list of science concepts, the concepts seem to arrange themselves into related groups. These groups differ sufficiently among themselves to have their own initiating activities. Thus, the unit will need enough initiating activities to raise pupil questions or problems involving all the understandings involved in the outline or list of science concepts. Usually one initiating activity is needed for each group of related concepts.

Thus, additional initiating activities—other than the general or overall initiating activity—may be used at various intervals as the unit progresses. The most effective activities are thought-provoking experiments and demonstrations, questions or series of questions, and discussions. Occasionally, one or more frames of a filmstrip can be used as an initiating activity. Often the general or overall activity can also be used as the initiating activity for the first group of related understandings in the outline or list of concepts.

Films, field trips, and speakers should rarely be used as initiating activities. The purpose of initiating activities is to raise questions or problems, the answers to which the children do not know, which then necessitates special learning activities to find the answers. Films, field trips, and speakers as a rule not only raise questions, but also usually provide the answers to the questions immediately afterward. This procedure defeats the purpose of initiating activity.

Similarly, because the initiating activity raises questions instead of giving answers, the initiating activity is almost never used as the first learning activity. The purpose of the learning activity is to obtain answers whereas the initiating activity is designed only to raise questions. However, the initiating activity can be used to advantage as an evaluation technique later in the unit. If the children have really learned the science understandings in the subsequent learning activities, they should now be able to answer the questions or solve the problems raised by the initiating activity.

The selection of good initiating activities is perhaps the most difficult phase of unit construction. Very often, many pupils are able to explain what were intended to be thought-provoking experiments or demonstrations. Thus, the initiating activities have not fulfilled their purpose and are valueless. The curriculum committee or teacher should not become discouraged, but must discard the unsuccessful initiating activities and continue to search for new and better ones.

Learning Activities

Learning activities are the means by which the children learn both the content and process of science. Using inquiry and discovery, the children acquire understandings that enable them to answer the questions or problems raised by the initiating activities, gain proficiency in doing the processes of science, and develop desirable behavioral outcomes. The teacher uses a wide variety of learning activities to accomplish this purpose. All the techniques suggested in Chapter 4, "Methods of Teaching Science," are utilized. These include experiments, demonstrations, observation, reading and study, discussion, oral and written reports, films, filmstrips, speakers, models, charts, posters, planning, and so forth.

Many teachers have a tendency to use many more learning activities than are necessary to ensure satisfactory learning. This excessive use tends to prolong the unit unnecessarily, slow down learning, and dull pupil interest. The experienced teacher employs her learning activities wisely and economically, especially when teaching for science understandings. She realizes that sometimes one activity is enough for an understanding to be learned. Occasionally one good learning activity will suffice to produce the learning of more than one understanding, especially if the understandings are simple or are related to each other. Other times, when an understanding is difficult or abstract, more than one activity may be necessary to obtain adequate learning. Slow learners usually learn better when more than one activity is used.

The grade level may also influence the number of learning activities needed. In the lower grades, where the children's attention span is small and their ability to think abstractly is not well developed, more than one activity is often necessary to obtain satisfactory learning of an understanding. However, in the upper grades one well-chosen activity is usually sufficient.

In all cases the best procedure is for the teacher to use as many—but *only* as many—activities as are necessary to ensure satisfactory learning. And if the teacher finds that there is a surplus of activities, they can always be used as additional activities for slow and fast learners.

Materials, Bibliography, New Science Vocabulary

Units usually list all the materials that will be needed for the learning activities. This list includes supplies, equipment, textbooks, reference materials, films, filmstrips, and other learning aids. In this way the teacher can begin to accumulate the necessary materials and have them ready and available as the activities require them.

Most units contain a bibliography of the textbooks and other reference materials that will be used during the unit. This bibliography includes materials for both the children and the teacher. The pupil list contains those references that the children will use to answer questions, solve problems, learn how to do an experiment, check conclusions, and find additional information for reports, and so forth. Wherever possible, the pupil list should include duplicate references on the same topic, but on different grade (reading) levels. Thus, there will be available reading materials for slow and rapid learners. The teacher list should contain those references that will provide the teacher with more detailed information about the science topic or about the experiments and demonstrations the teacher plans to conduct.

For clarity, the pupil and teacher references should be listed separately. Each reference should include the title, author(s), publisher, place and date of publication, and grade level (if it is part of an elementary science textbook series). Films and filmstrips should be included in the bibliography, usually under a separate listing. Besides listing the title and the producer, it may be helpful to include such information as the running time, whether it is in black and white or color, and so forth.

With the development of concepts and understandings, the children regularly will encounter new words and terms. This new vocabulary must be thoroughly explained and understood for maximum learning to take place. Many units include a vocabulary list of the new science terms that will be learned and used during the unit. This list reminds the teacher to give full attention to the learning of the terms when they appear for the first time.

Culminating Activities

A culminating activity is an activity that concludes the unit. It should be a logical part of the unit and a natural outgrowth of the work in the unit. It should appear when the objectives of the unit have been achieved. The culminating activity helps summarize the learnings and brings the high points of the unit into focus.

Culminating activities can be many things. They can be films, filmstrips, field trips, or speakers. They can be exhibits, science fairs, news letters, or reports. They can even be discussions, programs, assemblies, or dramatizations. However, the teacher should always keep in mind that culminating activities are primarily for the benefit of the children, even though others may profit from them as well.

Certain precautions should be noted about the use of culminating activities. They should not try to summarize every science understanding in the unit because this procedure would make the activity much too long, with the resulting loss of interest and educational value. Not every unit needs a culminating activity. Some units do not lend themselves well to such activity, and to have one arbitrarily would make the activity highly contrived and artificial. Also, sometimes a culminating activity can actually hinder the children from continuing quite naturally to another unit. Finally, tests and other evaluative techniques are not culminating activities and should not be used as such.

Evaluation

Evaluation should be continuous while the unit is in progress. The teacher must determine how well the children have learned science content and process and have developed desirable behavioral outcomes. Since evaluation is an ongoing continuous process, it is impossible to complete the evaluation section of a pre-planned unit. However, the unit can indicate the kinds of evaluation techniques that may be used while the unit is in progress. It can also indicate specific places in the unit outline where the learning activities lend themselves particularly to the development of certain behaviors.

The children themselves can—and should—participate in much of the evaluation. They can evaluate their work, their daily progress, and their learnings and behaviors as well. The various techniques for evaluation that can be used by both teacher and children are described in Chapter 8, "Evaluation of Science Learning in the Classroom."

Work Sheets

When units are constructed, careful consideration must be given to how the work of the children and teacher will proceed. Once the unit is in progress all the components of the unit must be coordinated and utilized to achieve maximum learning. At the same time provision must be made for evaluation of the work that is being done. Consequently, the working period is the vital part of the unit and, as such, must be thoroughly integrated. For in the working period lies the success—or failure—of the unit.

There are several forms in which the working period can be presented. Of these forms, two are most commonly used and both involve work sheets. One form makes use of a single running column. This single column contains in varying order of sequence the science concepts, initiating activities, anticipated pupil questions or problems, learning activities, culminating activities, necessary laboratory and audio-visual materials, and reading materials for the teacher and the children.

In the other form all unit components are placed in a varying number of parallel columns. In these parallel columns the corresponding science concepts, anticipated pupil questions, learning and culminating activities, laboratory and audio-visual materials, teacher and pupil bibliography, and even evaluative techniques are all placed side by side. By using adequate spacing in the parallel columns, the work sheets provide the teacher with a horizontal row of related components, all clearly delineated.

Kinds of Units

When looking for guides or models for constructing units, the local curriculum committee or teacher will encounter in the literature what seems to be a large variety of units. Curriculum experts, all interested in good teaching and learning, have proposed or described units with the following names: teaching units, experience units, resource units, problem units, activity units, textbook units, center of interest units, topical units, survey units, and so forth. To add to the confusion, the term *unit* has become so popular that teachers use it very loosely to describe almost any kind of teaching-learning situation.

However, a closer examination of these units will reveal that many are quite similar, differing in varying degrees with regard to style or format. Accordingly, all these units can be classified into one of three basic kinds of units: **resource units**, **teaching units**, and **textbook units**.

RESOURCE UNITS

A resource unit usually consists of an extensive collection of objectives, activities, and materials dealing with a science topic. The resource unit contains many more suggestions for study than any single classroom can pursue. The idea is to provide the teacher with the opportunity to select from the resource unit the learning activities that will best fit the needs, abilities, and interests of the children, yet still achieve the objectives of the unit. This is why the resource unit is organized in such a broad and flexible fashion.

The contents of the resource unit may be arranged in a number of different formats. One very common format divides the contents of the unit into four broad sections, as follows:

I. Objectives
    A. Key Science Concepts and Understandings
    B. Behavioral Outcomes
    C. Anticipated Pupil Objectives or Problems
II. Activities
    A. Initiating Activities
    B. Learning Activities
    C. Enrichment Activities
    D. Culminating Activities
    E. Evaluating Activities
III. Bibliography
    A. Teacher Bibliography
    B. Pupil Bibliography
IV. Materials
    A. Science Supplies and Equipment
    B. Audio-Visual and Other Materials

Resource units found in school system curriculum guides often begin with an overview of the unit. In some curriculum guides the suggested learning activities are placed under or beside the pertinent science concepts. Almost all the curriculum guides urge the teacher not to use all the suggested learning activities, but rather to select only as many as are needed to achieve the objectives of the unit. Otherwise the unit will become overly long and repetitious. The teacher is also urged to take full advantage of the suggested teacher bibliography to become thoroughly familiar with the concepts, experiments, and demonstrations listed in the unit.

TEACHING UNITS

A teaching unit differs from a resource unit in that the teaching unit contains only those objectives, activities, materials, and bibliography that the teacher and children will actually use during the unit. It is a highly developed detailed plan for teaching and learning in the classroom. Curriculum guides that contain resource units usually suggest that the teacher use these resource units to prepare teaching units. Some curriculum guides bypass resource units and instead contain teaching units that have been constructed cooperatively by all or part of the teachers in the school system.

In a teaching unit the teacher carefully selects the science concepts to be learned, then organizes them into a logical learning sequence. Specific learning activities are chosen that will enable the children to learn these concepts. At the same time these learning activities are carefully examined to determine which key operations of science and the scientist will be involved, and also which behaviors can be developed when the children do the activities during the unit. Provision is made for evaluating the learning of science content and process, and for evaluating the development of the behaviors. Additional activities are selected and included for slow and fast learners. Then the science and audio-visual materials that will be needed for all the activities are listed.

A general or overall initiating activity is selected to stimulate interest in the unit as a whole. Additional initiating activities which will raise pupil questions or problems are added, and these anticipated questions or problems are also incorporated into the unit.

The teaching unit contains a bibliography of only those pupil and reading materials that will be used during the unit. Some teaching units also add a supplementary bibliography to be used for enrichment purposes as needed. Many teaching units even include a vocabulary list of the new science words and terms that will be learned during the unit. Finally, an overview is often included, especially in those units that appear in curriculum guides.

One of the predominant characteristics of most teaching units is the work sheets. These work sheets indicate precisely how the teacher anticipates the work in the classroom will proceed as the unit develops. To accomplish this, the unit components are usually placed in a number of parallel columns. Using parallel columns involves much more work, but it helps greatly by providing the teacher with a comprehensive view of all the unit components, placed side by side and delineated clearly.

Teaching units vary in the number of parallel columns they contain and in the order in which the columns appear in the work sheets. One format, using six columns, is described here in detail, as follows:

Initiating Activities and Pupil Objectives	Basic Science Information	Learning Activities	Supplies and Equipment	Texts and References	Evaluation

TEXTBOOK UNITS

When properly utilized, the elementary science textbook can become the basis for an effective teaching unit. Most elementary science textbook series today are quite well organized. They are developed around a nucleus of key concepts and conceptual schemes. Each textbook in the series contains a comparatively small number of chapters, permitting a science topic or area to be treated with some degree of depth and detail. The science content has been organized into a logical learning sequence. Consideration has been given to the children's levels of understanding and reading ability. A variety of activities are presented, and an effort is made to teach process as well as content. The teacher's edition often provides additional science background for the teacher and suggests additional activities for the children.

When preparing a textbook unit, the first step is to construct an outline of science concepts for the unit. The science content for a topic in the textbook should be examined closely, and a list made of all the concepts already taken up in the topic. Some elementary science textbook series may have already prepared such an outline and included it in the teacher's manual. This list of concepts must be carefully checked to see whether it is inclusive enough, and whatever additional concepts that seem to be pertinent and necessary should be added. Then all the concepts should be rearranged, if necessary, and organized into a logical learning sequence.

The next step is to look for and select a wide variety of additional learning activities. These activities will be needed not only for the new concepts that have been added to the outline, but also for many of those concepts that were originally in the textbook and for which there were either inadequate activities or no activities at all. Provision should be made in the unit to present these additional activities in such a way that the children also learn the process of science and develop desirable behavioral outcomes. Finding additional activities will be no problem because today there are a goodly number of sourcebooks of science experiments and other activities for the elementary school on the market. Additional reading materials for the children may also be provided.

To complete the unit, a number of initiating activities should be selected that will arouse interest in the unit and also raise pupil questions or problems. Then a list must be made of all the science materials and audio-visual aids that will be needed for these additional learning and initiating activities. When completed, the textbook unit becomes quite similar to the teaching unit.

Team Teaching in the Elementary School: Implications for Research in Science Instruction*

ABRAHAM S. FISCHLER and PETER B. SHORESMAN

In this article seven basic assumptions about the efficacy of the self-contained classroom are challenged by the team-teaching approach to instruction of children. The authors define team teaching as an effort to improve instruction by the re-organization of teacher personnel, involving the assignment of two or more teachers to a group of pupils. This reorganization forces new roles for teachers, ranging from specialist to observer. Two models of team teaching are described, and the impact of the team-teaching approach on curriculum organization and sequence and on grouping for instruction is discussed.

For many school systems team teaching has become more than an enticing phrase: many communities have now initiated the utilization of new personnel patterns to which the label "team teaching" might be applied. Generally, the organization of these various teams has consisted of a group of two or more teachers working together, within or without a formal hierarchy, to plan for, initiate, accomplish, and evaluate the instruction of the same group of children.

Before introducing two models of team teaching and some of the problems which need to be researched, the structure of the self-contained class will be examined. It is hoped that this review will help clarify some of the assumptions which new personnel organizations are now challenging.

*REPRINTED FROM *Science Education*, Vol. 46, No. 5, December 1962, pp. 406–415, by permission of the authors and the publisher. Dr. Fischler is President of Nova University of Advanced Technology and Research, Fort Lauderdale, Florida. Dr. Shoresman is Professor of Education at the University of Illinois.

Self-Contained Classroom Organization

In the self-contained classroom organization, the elementary school principal assigns twenty to forty students to a class, either homogeneously or heterogeneously grouped. If homogeneous, the assignment is usually on the basis of I.Q. and/or reading ability. The principal is also responsible for the supervision of all the teachers in the building and for curriculum coordination, pupil discipline, and public relations.

The elementary school class itself is usually under the direction of one teacher who provides instruction in the four basic areas of the elementary school curriculum: language arts, social studies, mathematics, and science. Teachers are expected to have knowledge and skills in all of the major areas and, furthermore, to be equally enthusiastic and competent in their presentation of each subject. They are expected to provide for a wide range of individual differences; this is usually accomplished by dividing the class into three groups: "high, average, and low." The teacher is also responsible for many non-teaching duties such as lunchroom supervision, bus duty, collecting milk money, and other tasks of a similar nature. The beginning teacher, just out of college, assumes *full* responsibility for her class; she assumes as much responsibility for instruction as teachers who have been teaching for twenty years. There is little chance during the school day for communication between this beginning teacher and teachers with many years of experience. The only time for extended communication is during the noon hour or before and after school.

Within the structure of this organization there is no career pattern for the young teacher who aspires to increased responsibility, increased prestige, and increased salary. Since all teachers are on the same salary schedule, which calls for increments on the basis of education and longevity of service, there is usually no provision made for higher salary based on increased responsibility. In this situation there seems to be no career pattern within the teaching profession for those who wish to remain in the classroom. If a teacher is seeking increased prestige or more responsibility, he usually moves into the field of administration. This removes him from actual teaching which, hopefully, is the reason he initially entered the profession.

Assumptions Challenged

The following are seven basic assumptions which are being challenged by the team teaching model:

1. That all teachers are approximately of the same quality, with the result that the superior teacher never moves (as teacher) to a position of greater influence over a large number of learners.

2. That each teacher should enjoy individual instructional autonomy; that is, that he has a right to be an absolute "king of his classroom."
3. That the assignment of differential reward and status leads to poor morale and lower productivity.
4. That the employment of part-time and/or sub-professional personnel will somehow have undesirable effects.
5. That the ideal class size approximates thirty.
6. That pupils can relate to only one teacher.
7. That values accrue from having one teacher teach all subjects.

Definition of Team Teaching

Team teaching, as we envision it, is an effort to improve instruction by the reorganization of teaching personnel. It involves the assigning of two or more teachers to a group of pupils. This involves different schedules for teachers as well as changed allocations of time and space for instruction. It eliminates the rigid grouping based on one or two criteria and allows for variations in student grouping depending upon the outcomes being sought. It allows for teachers to observe other teachers teach the same group of learners. It *forces* teachers to communicate in planning for the same group of learners. It allows for a variety of period lengths, sub-groups, and part-time teachers with special competencies, as well as for programmed instruction. Evaluation of students is based upon the common observations of several teachers. Team teaching, furthermore, encourages teachers to become specialists in one or more areas. The particular model which we are researching provides for a hierarchy of positions which are based on expertness and responsibility. It allows for increased salary and prestige accompanying greater knowledge and responsibility. The model also provides for the use of non-professional help as well as for the use of part-time professional help, lay readers, and other individuals who might aid in the learning process.

Different Organizational Patterns

There are several types of organizational structures built on different value systems. We shall discuss two of them.

1. Two "master" teachers (at increased salary) plus one teacher-aide are assigned to a group of seventy-five pupils. In order to keep the cost stationary the teacher-aide is employed instead of a third regular teacher. In the self-contained class structure, the ratio of teacher to pupil is approximately one to twenty-five, the same as above. Thus, by rearranging the budget, we are able to pay additional salary to the two teachers and still have funds with which to pay the salary of the aide. Implied in the value

structure of this organization is that the cost will not be greater to operate a team teaching school than it was to operate a traditional school.

Among the duties of the teacher-aide is the assistance of pupils as they work individually. A variety of lessons are taped, programmed or individualized, so that pupils can work with a minimum of verbal teacher direction. The teacher-aide, a semi-professional person, circulates among the pupils to answer questions and offer any necessary help. In addition, she helps with such details as typing worksheets, collecting milk money, and supervising the playground.

2. A second organizational structure necessitates a higher budget. This model assigns six teachers and one teacher-aide to approximately one hundred and fifty children. The team is organized on a hierarchical basis. At the top is the Team Leader who receives $1,000 to $1,500 more than the regular teacher. This additional salary is given for increased responsibility as well as greater competency in an area of instruction.

On this same team there might be one or more Senior Teachers who receive from $500 to $1,000 more. These individuals have acquired competency in one or more subject fields. Usually both Team Leader and Senior Teacher have had three to five years of teaching experience in the elementary school.

The regular teachers on the team are trained elementary school people capable of teaching the normal elementary school curriculum. They usually teach in all of the subject areas, but begin to specialize in one or two if they aspire to become Senior Teachers.

The teacher-aide has the same type of responsibilities mentioned in the previous organization.

In the ideal situation the Team Leader and Senior Teachers would complement each other by having competencies in different areas. In addition, these people should be capable of curriculum development in their particular strengths; of giving in-service education to members of their team; of supervising classroom interaction between teacher and pupil; and of aiding in the articulation of their subject area with others. Thus we have a small "school of education" built into the team.

The total school program is coordinated by the principal who heads two cabinets: an *administrative* cabinet composed of the Team Leaders which is responsible for policy decisions; and an *instructional* cabinet composed of the Team Leaders, Senior Teachers, and other specialists in the school, which coordinates and integrates the total school curriculum.

Insights and Implications

During the past two years, the authors have been engaged as science consultants and research personnel to work with the staff of a Lexington, Massachusetts, team teaching elementary school organized along the lines mentioned in pattern 2. Although it is felt that our short experience with team teaching does not, and cannot, entitle us to make any definitive statements as to what can and cannot be done, how certain tasks should be performed, or how specific problems should be solved, it has provided us with a number of problems and questions necessitating serious soul-searching on the parts of both ourselves and the teachers involved. Comparisons are still being made between this school and a control school in the same town, but evaluation is far from complete with so many problem areas still to be resolved.

While we have encountered many problems in our work so far, many seemingly inherent in a personnel structure where it is both *necessary* and *desirable* for a number of teachers to work closely together, the problem areas outlined below are unquestionably crucial ones for the instruction of science within the team teaching organization.

Curriculum Organization and Sequence

1. *Does the teaching of science within the context of team teaching require a reorganization of the traditional "content-topic" oriented curriculum?*

It has been our experience that the pattern of team teaching cannot find its most effective expression unless the curriculum utilized is modified or reorganized in the light of the unique aspects of flexibility which are afforded by this personnel structure. The following aspects seem especially worthy of mention:

1. The possibility of utilizing groups of different sizes, from large groups where two hundred children are taught by one teacher to small discussion, laboratory, and project groups where an almost one-to-one tutorial type of instruction can be afforded.
2. The associated possibility of deploying and redeploying a number of teachers according to the nature and size of the pupil groups formed.

    Given the two preceding attributes inherent in the team teaching model, the limitations imposed upon the experimental and discovery approaches in the self-contained classroom because of lack of adequate supervision need no longer comprise obstacles to an exciting and creative science program for elementary school children.

The preparation and presentation of extremely worthwhile demonstrations and experiments is now economically feasible time-wise, since not only will the senior teacher in science be allotted adequate time to prepare such presentations, but also since it will be necessary to offer these presentations only once—via the medium of the large group lesson. The structure, wherein many teachers must plan together to develop a science curriculum, also necessitates that the "incidental science" curriculum so typical of many elementary school classrooms be replaced to a large extent by a *planned* and *sequential program* of science experiences. Perhaps, the team teaching pattern will provide conditions conducive to releasing the elementary school's current preoccupation with the "products and things" of science and raising to its proper position of emphasis, and to a more appropriate balance with the former, the consideration and practice of the "process" of science and "sciencing."

2. *How can the coordination of the science curriculum of an entire teaching team be reconciled with the flexibility of instruction necessary for individual groups?*

The team teaching structure provides opportunities for the following: the utilization of large group instruction, the periodic regrouping of students as the situation and their own individual needs indicate, the deployment and redeployment of teaching staff as necessary, the administration of cooperatively developed, team-wide instruments of evaluation, and many more important adjuncts to the learning process. If, however, the flexibility of team teaching is to be utilized to a maximum degree, it then becomes imperative that the efforts of every teacher teaching science within the team be coordinated to a considerable extent. This coordination is further necessitated by scheduling considerations which often require that all science (and this is true for other subjects as well) within a specific team be taught during the same time interval in the course of the school day. This procedure is necessary to facilitate pupil regrouping and the presentation of large group lessons.

However, it is quite important that individual teachers be provided with the degree of freedom necessary to plan, or modify, within the context of the team's science program, content and activities which are appropriate for the pupils within their own group. Despite the apparent contradiction which the terms may connote, it does seem possible to provide for "coordination" on the one hand, and "flexibility" on the other, without subordinating either one to the other. For example, let us suppose that a particular topic may most suitably be presented through the medium of a large group lesson. It is necessary that the room required for this lesson (for example, the cafetorium) be scheduled in advance because of the program demands for this space which might also be made by the other teams operating within the same building. If it is to be anticipated that most of the pupils in the team are to be present at this large group lesson, it is necessary to agree upon the goals to serve as a foundation for this lesson. If agreement has been reached a week or so in advance of the lesson, it would seem that each individual teacher should attempt to guide her own pupils toward some realistic goal which would provide them with the degree of readiness necessary to make the large group lesson as meaningful as possible. It is certainly quite unrealistic to expect that all children in a team should be approaching the same goal at the same time; however, if given sufficient time and adequate planning, by teachers, it is *not* unreasonable to expect that some commonality of general goal attainment be achieved by a certain time. This requirement places heavy responsibility upon the shoulders of individual teachers, for they must not only carefully assess the readiness of the students in their own group and devise the most appropriate program to bring them to a certain general level in the curriculum by a certain time, but they must also plan considerably further ahead than they are accustomed to do. For some teachers this may mean carefully selecting key points of content upon which to concentrate exclusively; for other teachers it may mean developing a wide variety of enrichment activities to occupy profitably the time of those students who have completed the essential core of science material to be studied by each group.

3. *What is the proper place of teaching machines and other programmed materials in science within the team teaching structure?*

Within most classrooms utilization of teaching machines and other programmed materials (such as programmed textbooks) has considerable promise for providing greater opportunities for individualizing instruction in the various subject matter areas. The evidence available in the literature suggests that programmed instruction can be used to good advantage for certain specific learning tasks. If we accept the fact (upon which much additional research must be done in relation to the specific applications of this technique) that programmed instruction supplies another possible approach to learning by children, while also providing for greater economy of time in learning—both in regard to actual classroom time required and to the assignment of professional teaching personnel, then it would seem that for specific purposes this economy would find maximum expression and realization in the large groups possible within the structure of team teaching. Most likely, what can be taught by programmed materials in a group of thirty children could be taught just as effectively in a group of two hundred children.

In the field of science, programmed materials might be utilized for purposes of review and evaluation, drill and practice, and for learning subject matter which required rote memorization (such as science vocabulary words or formulas) or the learning of the steps in the tight logical development of a concept or of the procedures involved in a technological process (such as the extraction of various metals from their ores). However, before we plunge into programming various aspects of elementary school science, it is necessary that serious consideration be given to specifying those behaviors which we expect pupils to acquire as a result of utilizing our programs.

It should be stressed, however, that the possible contribution of programmed instruction to science teaching is only one complementing the contributions of a myraid of other approaches. It is the feeling of the authors that this approach may be somewhat limited in its application. This is especially true if the current philosophies of elementary school science education, based upon providing opportunities for children to seek answers about natural phenomena by having actual manipulative experiences with these same phenomena, are not to be lost.

4. *What implications does team teaching have for the development and utilization of various teaching "techniques"?*

It is to be hoped that serious thought related to the goals of elementary school science education and to the concepts which we wish to develop will improve the various teaching "technologies" which have been traditionally used in the small group of the self-contained classroom. It is also hoped that new and appropriate instructional aids will be developed. However, the possibility of large group instruction which is afforded by team teaching makes it imperative that considerable effort be expended in transforming the instructional aids designed for use in the small classroom to a form which will be appropriate for their utilization in a very large group. Two criteria, at least, must be satisfied for materials which are to be used with large groups:

1. The materials must be easily seen from all locations in the room where the lesson is to be held; where large rooms and very large numbers of children are involved, the materials—models, projected images, and so on—must be LARGE. We have experienced considerable success utilizing the overhead projector as a "chalkboard substitute" as a light source for a shadow-graph effect, for projecting the images of various semi-transparent, translucent and opaque objects (such as marbles, iron filings, colored solutions in Petri dishes, etc), and for projecting both commercially-made and teacher-made multi-overlay transparencies.
2. The materials should possess certain "dynamic and dramatic" qualities such as moving parts, unexpected behavior and appropriate contrasting coloration.

Many more qualities have been shown through experience to be necessary ingredients but lack of space prohibits their mention here.

5. *What is the proper place of the science textbook within the team teaching model?*

As has been intimated in preceding sections, team teaching allows for an unprecedented flexibility and wealth of different science activities. These, in turn, should obviate the former reliance which has been placed in the elementary school science curriculum on the information-dispensing properties of one or two commercial textbooks or trade books. Within the model proposed above, teachers qualified to teach science will be available for the purpose of guiding learning in the area of science as will be sufficient professional staff to supervise experimentation and other activities by students. It is hoped that the textbook in this situation will assume its proper function as another adjunct to learning and will not continue to be the sole dispenser of information about science so common in many elementary school classrooms. Within team teaching it is possible for the textbook to find its proper niche as a resource or reference to which the children should have ample opportunity to turn when their own investigations or classroom discussions indicate that specific or general information available from this source is necessary.

Grouping for Instruction in Science

1. *If greater flexibility in inter-class and intra-class grouping is one of the main attributes of team teaching, what rationale, criteria, or predictors should be utilized to determine the formation of groups of appropriate composition and size for various diverse purposes?*

In approaching this question, we should explore the possibility that certain subject matter, and the activities suitable for the presentation of such subject matter, indicate the means by which the total team should be broken down to form the most appropriate "instructional units." For example, does Subject Matter A (e.g., the study of heat phenomena) with appropriate Activities A' (e.g., the laboratory investigation of the expansion of different solids, liquids, and gases) indicate that the team be broken down into small sub-groups of approximate Size X (e.g., manipulative ability)? (e.g., 3 to 4 children per sub-group on the basis of criterion M). Or perhaps, the grouping criterion might more suitably be I.Q., manifested pupil interest, reading ability, or previous knowledge of the area being studied.

We might also ask the question whether small groups which are homogeneous with respect to a specific criterion are more suitable for certain activities than are small groups of heterogeneous composition which have been formed purely from the advantages accruing from their small size. So far our experience has not provided us with any criterion which we have found highly successful for grouping in science, although we have tried random heterogeneous groups and groups whose composition has been determined by the results of an experimental science vocabulary test which was administered to all the children in one team late last fall.

2. *What factors govern the time and method of regrouping for instruction in science?*

This problem is related to the preceding one. It is obvious that usable criteria must also be found for regrouping as well as for the initial formation of instructional sub-groups. These criteria might very well be the same. One generalization which has arisen from our experience is that the composition and size of initially established groups must be flexible and that approximate regrouping should occur periodically according to the needs of the teaching-learning situation and of the students themselves.

Perhaps, regrouping may be accomplished by merely transferring a single child from one group to a more appropriate one after evaluation of the total situation by the teachers concerned. On the other hand, it may be discovered that the underlying rationale for the initial organization of the various science groups of a team has been faulty; in this case, an over-all reorganization of all of the instructional units of the team may be necessary.

3. *For what purposes and to what ends can large group instruction best be utilized?*

In viewing the optimum utilization of large group instruction, a wide variety of possibilities confronts us. For example, can large group instruction (involving groups of approximately two hundred pupils) best be utilized for the purpose of (1) introducing a unit of study, (2) motivating pupils toward the study of a specific sub-topic of a unit, (3) presenting a teacher or pupil demonstration, (4) hearing a guest lecturer, (5) viewing a particularly outstanding visual aid, (6) raising additional problems for consideration, (7) clarifying a particularly difficult concept which most of the teachers of the team cannot explain adequately, or (8) summarizing a unit or sub-unit at the end of a topic? Perhaps, it is possible that one type of unit, for example, one in astronomy and space travel, might be completely or almost entirely taught in large groups, whereas this approach would not be appropriate for the study of a unit dealing with rocks and minerals. Perhaps (and we do not have experimental evidence to refute this contention) it is possible that *most* science at certain grade levels (for example, the intermediate level) may be taught in large groups of approximately sixty pupils per group regardless of the subject matter being considered.

Another question which must be considered under this sub-problem is whether large group instruction in science is more appropriate and applicable to certain ability levels than to others. Perhaps the bright, independent child will be stimulated by the presentation of subject matter in large groups and by the relative individual freedom accruing to him from the nature of the group size, whereas the slower child, needing both to receive considerable individual attention from the teacher and to proceed through the curriculum at a slower pace, will not be able to progress as rapidly with this method of instruction as he might in a smaller instructional unit. As a matter of fact, subjective evaluation by one of the authors seems to have confirmed the statement of the situation presented in the preceding sentence. The slower children become very restless in large group lessons and do not seem to derive much benefit from what does occur within these groups. In discussion groups immediately following the large group lessons, these children are often unable to recall even the general nature of what has occurred during the preceding period.

We must also ask ourselves, and obtain an answer to, the following important question: "Where do the great majority of school children—

those who fall within the range of 'average' academic ability—fare better (for a particular objective), in the large group or in a group of smaller numerical size?

It is also necessary to ask how large group instruction may most profitably be articulated with the total instruction pattern which has been established for science. How should children in the various individual science classrooms be prepared for a large group lesson? How should the content of a large group lesson be followed up? Should all children attend every large group lesson regardless of their needs, abilities, and interests? Several points have become increasingly evident during the course of our experience with team teaching: (1) Large group lessons must be planned well in advance. This is necessary so that the teacher presenting the lessons can either meet with, or distribute a summary sheet to, the other teachers in the team so that they, in turn, are aware of and can prepare their students for the content to be considered therein. (2) In many instances, if follow-up of the large group lesson is advisable or imperative, the teachers who are to lead subsequent small discussion or laboratory groups must take the responsibility either to attend the large group lesson themselves or to discuss the lesson with the teacher who presented it. Too often the maximum effectiveness of stimulating and provocative large group lessons has been lost because the other teachers who teach science did not know what had transpired during the lesson and, therefore, could not develop appropriate follow-up experiences. (3) It has become quite obvious that a single large group lesson cannot be all things for all children. The bright children may have already discussed and mastered the material considered. The slower children may not be ready to consider the concepts being developed or may not be capable of understanding what is being presented at the level at which it is being presented. A possible alternative to requiring all children in all groups to attend a certain large group lesson would be to provide one-to-several "splinter" groups—for example, one for the bright children for whom the lesson would be just a review and another for the slower children who would not benefit greatly because of their current lack of readiness. Teachers "released" by the teaching of the large group could be assigned to these splinter groups, where activities more appropriate to the needs and interests of certain children could be offered.

Utilization of Teaching Members of the Team

1. *Under what patterns of teacher deployment and redeployment within the team teaching model can the objectives of science instruction best be served?*

There are many questions which relate to the many possible ways in which teachers might be deployed and redeployed to yield optimum learning conditions in science. Careful consideration and research might be directed to the following questions: (1) Can one teacher successfully teach a total group lesson to sixty youngsters at one time? If so, for what purposes and under what circumstances? (2) What criteria might be utilized to enable us to select the most appropriate teacher for a particular group of children? (3) For certain activities, can the flexibility provided by the team organization be utilized to good advantage? For example, if laboratory or individual project work requiring close supervision is indicated at a particular point in a unit of study, would it be possible and appropriate to break a group of sixty children down into smaller units, each supervised by a separate teacher who, for that particular class and activity, has been especially redeployed to this classroom? The students of the redeployed teachers might, in turn, be regrouped and assigned to one teacher who would supervise a lesson of programmed study.

For the most part, in the school where we have worked, one teacher has been assigned to twenty-five or thirty pupils for laboratory and discussion sessions. For most teachers, this method of assignment has not proved very satisfactory. Although considerable use has been made of the intra-class "buzz group" discussion technique, adequate supervision has still been lacking for an active experiment and project oriented science program. Collaborative teaching by two and three teachers with groups of thirty to sixty has proved much more successful. The added supervision made available by this technique has provided opportunities for extensive and intensive laboratory work and teacher-guidance involving a great majority of the children in the groups concerned.

2. How can time be made available to the senior teacher science specialist of the team so that he has an opportunity to discharge the functions inherent in his role?

If, according to the model presented above, the team's specialist in science is to have responsibilities related to the initiation, development, coordination, evaluation, and supervision of the program in science, he must have time during which to perform these functions. It was mentioned in the first part of this paper that the specialist should be released from the responsibility of teaching at least one subject matter area. Thus, some time is made available in the course of the school day for the discharging of his responsibilities related to science. However, it also seems necessary to release the science specialist from the teaching of a regularly scheduled science class at times so that he may observe the other members of the team teach science, so that he may participate in collaborative teaching with various of the team members, and so that he may provide special guidance, supervision, and instruction for special pupil groups (for example, those working on a special project, those setting up a school science display, etc.). Some serious thought must then be given to appropriate scheduling to permit this flexibility. Only two alternatives were utilized this past year in regard to this problem: (1) One of the authors assumed responsibility for the specialist's class several times while he was engaged in classroom visitations with the team; and (2) the members of the specialist's science class were divided equally among the other five science classes for the period. This latter approach has not proved to be desirable or effective for several reasons; especially contributory to this outcome is the fact that very intelligent, highly verbal students were necessarily placed in classes consisting of considerably less gifted students.

Evaluation

It is evident that the problem of adequate evaluation is not unique or peculiar to the team teaching pattern. However, the entire process of evaluation, especially certain mechanical aspects, is made considerably more difficult because it must be developed in a situation where a number of teachers must work together cooperatively to determine what approaches are to be utilized. The following questions, then, which are undoubtedly applicable to many types of personnel organization found in the elementary school, are especially pertinent to the team teaching structure.

1. *What should be the main emphasis in the evaluation of science instruction within the team teaching model?*

We have mentioned in an earlier section of this article that it is rather unrealistic to expect all of the children in a team to have acquired a certain amount of science knowledge or to have attained a certain level of science sophistication by a certain point in time. Within the team structure, where individual science groups may be proceeding through only limited portions of the science curriculum via different methods of approach, is it educationally desirable for us to evaluate all youngsters by a method which assumes that they have considered the same subject matter in the same way? Perhaps not. Let us only say at this point that it is very necessary for us to review the major goals for which we are teaching science in the elementary school and then to determine the outcomes which we wish to have assessed by our instruments of evaluation. In any case, an understanding of the process or methods of science should undoubtedly serve as a more prominent target for evaluation than in the past, while the current emphasis solely on retention of scientific fact should be moderated accordingly.

2. *What are some of the characteristics of an adequate testing program in science within the structure of team teaching?*

The characteristics of an adequate testing program in science within the model proposed above should not be very much unlike those of an adequate testing program in any good elementary school, regardless of the personnel structure. There are many obstacles standing in the way of good testing programs in elementary school science, in general. The most important and significant of these obstacles is serious lack of availability of a variety of different kinds of standardized tests for the various elementary grades. A survey of current elementary school science tests does not provide a very impressive list of up-to-date and carefully devised instruments designed to evaluate the child's science interests, his understanding of science as a process, the nature of the scientific enterprise and of the scientists, and his factual knowledge in various specific content areas. Some adequate tests designed to evaluate the scientific reasoning of children are available, however. It is evident that appropriate tests designed to evaluate the areas mentioned immediately above are urgently needed.

It is also important for teachers within the team pattern, as well as elsewhere, to learn to devise effective teacher-made tests. Generally, the science test questions asked by many elementary school teachers of their students are of a purely factual nature or are worded in an exceedingly ambiguous and frustrating (for the children) manner.

Perhaps within the team structure, where several teachers might be deployed to a single classroom, evaluation procedures other than those utilizing paper and pencil tests might be employed. For example, the responses of individuals or of small groups of children to an original problem depending for its solution upon an experimental approach might provide carefully observing teachers with important information of an evaluative nature.

3. How might evaluation procedures best be developed within the team structure?

As has been mentioned, evaluation, within the team structure, of both the students involved and of the total effectiveness of the science program, is a cooperative and collaborative endeavor. Although individual teachers might find it desirable at times to develop evaluation instruments for use within their own classes, valuable ideas are to be gained by consultation with the science specialist and with fellow team-mates. Unit-end and year-end evaluation of all the students in a team necessitates the cooperation of all those teachers involved in teaching science within the team. The experience of the teachers of individual science classes must be pooled in order to develop an instrument which will be as valid as possible for all children of the team. A paper and pencil test might consist of a series of "difficulty ranked" items some of which could be answered by the members of even the "lowest" science group. The group of items as a whole should represent, in an equitable fashion, all of the major goals and objectives for which science is being taught. In any case, it has been found fairly effective to ask individual teachers to submit a series of questions which they would consider appropriate for their own class to a sub-team assigned to construct the evaluation instrument. These questions are then "hashed over" and refined in subsequent meetings of the sub-team. The questions are then resubmitted to all the teachers involved in teaching science within the team. After a final discussion and revision of all of the items by the former group, the finished instrument is then produced by the sub-team.

Periodic and end-of-the-school-year evaluations of the total science program of a team should incorporate the efforts of all team members. These evaluations might consider the appropriateness and effectiveness of content, methods utilized, staff utilization, and pupil evaluation. It seems that only in this way can a science program be restructured and developed in a direction which is consistent with both the philosophies of the majority of the team members and with the facts gleaned from the evaluation instruments administered. Hopefully, a cooperative evaluation program of this nature will eventuate in the provision of better conditions for learning and more appropriate and stimulating experiences in the area of science instruction.

National Assessment Findings in Science 1969-1970: What Do They Mean?[*]

NSTA TEAM to STUDY NAEP FINDINGS in SCIENCE[1]

The following is an abridged report of the NSTA Study Team appointed to examine and interpret the findings of the National Assessment of Educational Progress (NAEP) in science. In this NAEP assessment, various science exercises were administered to persons aged 9, 13, 17, and 26–35. The NSTA Study Team consisted of James Raths (Chairman), Julian R. Brandou, Wilmer W. Cooksey, Fred D. Johnson, Richard Kay, Morris R. Lerner, Richard J. Merrill, Joseph A. Strothers, Leslie W. Trowbridge, James R. Wailes, and Charles N. Wilson.

Introduction

The National Assessment of Educational Progress (NAEP) is a census-like survey of the knowledge, skills, understandings, and attitudes of young Americans. Its two major goals are:

*REPRINTED FROM *Science and Children*, Vol. 11, No. 1, September 1973, pp. 23–30. Copyright, 1973, by the National Science Teachers Association, Washington, D.C. Reprinted by permission of the publisher.
1 The views expressed in this summary do not necessarily represent the positions of the National Science Teachers Association, the United States Office of Education, or the National Assessment of Educational Progress.

1. To make available the first comprehensive data on the educational attainments of young Americans.
2. To measure any growth or decline which takes place in selected aspects of the educational attainments of young Americans in certain subject areas.

By gathering the first national information about the "output" of education in the United States, the National Assessment of Educational Progress hopes to assist those who are responsible for planning, implementing, and evaluating the educational programs of the schools. Science was one of the first subject areas assessed by NAEP. This report deals with the data collected in science during the first round of assessment 1969–1970.

SPONSORSHIP OF NAEP
National Assessment of Educational Progress is a project of the Education Commission of the States (ECS). ECS is composed of representatives of 47 states and territories, whose purpose is to discuss mutual educational problems and to act together to achieve goals. Representatives include governors, legislators, chief state school officers, and lay people. The Steering Committee of ECS is the ultimate policy-making group. Since its inception in 1964, financial support for NAEP has come from three main sources: the Carnegie Corporation of New York, the Ford Foundation's Fund for the Advancement of Education, and the U.S. Office of Education. USOE provides most of the project's current funding, which is at the level of about $6 million per year.

SAMPLING
In the first round of NAEP assessment, science exercises were administered to persons aged 9, 13, 17, and 26–35. The sample included about 28,000 in each of the three younger groups, and about 10,000 young adults, for a total of over 90,000 individuals. More than 2,500 schools participated in the first assessment by allowing the project staff to administer exercises to the student sample. Young adults and out-of-school 17-year-olds were assessed individually in their homes.

ADMINISTRATION OF EXERCISES
The approximately 450 different science exercises were divided among 47 "packages," each of which also contained exercises assessing writing and citizenship. About 50 of the science items were administered to more than one age group. Thus each package included 10 to 12 science exercises. Only one package, taking less than one hour, was administered to each adult, but several packages were sometimes administered to out-of-school 17-year-olds. Most items administered in schools were given to groups of no more than 12 students. Some items administered to students, and all items

given to out-of-school 17-year-olds and adults, were individually administered. Each item administered at ages 9, 13, and 17 had about 2,000 respondents, and each adult item had between 650 and 900 respondents.

In the administration of each package, the effect of reading difficulty was minimized by having the items read aloud to the participants, who also had printed copies before them. In the individually administered exercises involving equipment, the assessee was presented with the equipment and given oral instructions. Ample time was provided to complete all exercises.

DEVELOPMENT OF OBJECTIVES

The major criteria established by the National Assessment of Educational Progress for objectives on which the exercises are based are that they be (1) considered important by scholars in the field, (2) accepted as an educational task by schools, and (3) considered desirable by thoughtful lay citizens. Educational Testing Service drafted tentative statements of objectives, which were reviewed and revised by a committee of prominent scientists and science teachers and educators named by NSTA and later endorsed by 11 independent panels of laymen. ETS also developed most of the items used in the first science assessment. The science objectives for the 1969–70 survey were organized into the following categories:

I. Know fundamental facts and principles of science.
II. Possess the abilities and skills needed to engage in the processes of science.
III. Understand the investigative nature of science.
IV. Have attitudes about and appreciation of scientists, science, and the consequences of science that stem from adequate understandings.

STUDY TEAM REPORTS

While the NAEP has conscientiously dedicated itself to collecting appropriate data to assess educational progress, it has assiduously refrained from interpreting the findings. To contribute to this task, the National Science Teachers Association under the leadership of NSTA President Morris Lerner and Executive Secretary Robert Carleton named a study team to examine the NAEP findings in science. The study team was to answer the broad question: What do the results of the science assessment mean? The undertaking was funded by the U.S. Office of Education through the Education Commission of the States.

The complete report of the study team has been published by the NSTA and is available to the public through the organization's regular publication outlets.[1] The full report is composed of four major sections: a description of the goals and methods of the NAEP; a summary of the findings of the 1969–70 assessment; a collection of judgments and summary

[1] Stock no. 471–14656; $5.

statements concerning the findings endorsed by the study team; and a series of appendices. Included in the appended materials are the following: a profile of study team members; a description of some of the changes made in the national assessment procedures from 1969 to 1972; a copy of all the released items and the results for those items based on a national sample of 9-year-olds, 13-year-olds, 17-year-olds, and adults; a series of recommendations the study team is making to the NAEP concerning its procedures; a bibliography with selected annotations of references dealing with NAEP; and a position paper summarizing the similarities in findings noticed among the various subject areas reported to date. This abridged report includes only the statements of findings and the concluding remarks. Persons interested in a more complete analysis of the methods, procedures, and findings of the science assessment are urged to make use of the unabridged report and to review some of the many references found there.

Findings of the First Assessment

This section of the abridged report describes selected findings of the first science assessment, 1969–70. The information reported here does not begin to exhaust the enormous amount of data collected by NAEP in its first effort. In addition, a second assessment has been completed since our study team initiated its work in the fall of 1972. We hope that the findings reported here will encourage readers to seek out additional information from the professional literature.

OBJECTIVE I—KNOWLEDGE OF SCIENCE

Sixty-nine percent of the exercises in the NAEP instruments were directed toward assessing Objective I—knowledge of fundamental facts and principles of science. The NAEP analysis roughly divided the items into biological science, physical science, and other. The findings for the former two subgroupings as well as the overall results are reported below in Table 1 for each age group. The percentage of respondents within a particular

Table 1. Median P-values (percentage correct) for the national sample of nine-year-olds, thirteen-year-olds, seventeen-year-olds, and young adults on Objective 1—Knowledge of Science.

AGES	PHYSICAL SCIENCE	BIOLOGICAL SCIENCE	ALL ITEMS[a]
Nine	66.5	77.7	70.3
	(61 items)	(33 items)	(96 items)
Thirteen	56.5	58.2	57.4
	(43 items)	(31 items)	(75 items)
Seventeen	44.6	53.9	47.6
	(60 items)	(29 items)	(89 items)
Adult	52.1	55.8	54.4
	(46 items)	(38 items)	(85 items)

[a] Some items not classified as either physical science or biological science.

age group getting an item correct was used to rank all the items. The median value of this set is reported as the median P-value of a collection of items. Thus, if the median P-value for 9-year-olds is given as 66.5, it means that if all the items given to 9-year-olds in that classification were ranked according to the percentage of respondents getting the item correct, the median of such values is 65.5.

- In terms of percentage correct values, the 9-year-olds performed highest, followed by the 13-year-olds, the young adults, and finally the 17-year-olds. (It should be noted that for the most part, the different age groups were responding to different items. These data do not take into account differences in the inherent difficulties of the items.)
- Percentage correct values tended to be higher for items classified as assessing knowledge in the biological sciences than in the physical sciences, with the largest discrepancy in the 9-year-old group.

OBJECTIVE II—ABILITIES IN THE PROCESS OF SCIENCE

Twenty-one percent of the exercises in the NAEP instruments were directed toward assessing Objective II—abilities and skills needed to engage in the processes of science. In a manner similar to that used above for Objective I, the findings relevant to Objective II are reported in Table 2 for each age level assessed and for the subgroupings of items (biological science and physical science) and for all items.

Table 2. Median P-values (percentage correct) for the national sample of nine-year-olds, thirteen-year-olds, seventeen-year-olds, and adults for Objective II—Processes of Science.

AGES	PHYSICAL SCIENCE	BIOLOGICAL SCIENCE	ALL ITEMS[a]
Nine	64.3 (16 items)	59.1 (10 items)	66.5 (29 items)
Thirteen	59.1 (23 items)	60.7 (7 items)	59.1 (31 items)
Seventeen	45.1 (18 items)	55.6 (3 items)	52.4 (24 items)
Adult	51.2 (16 items)	70.0 (6 items)	51.1 (24 items)

[a] Some items not classified as either physical science or biological science.

- In terms of percentage correct values for all the items assessing Objective II, the 9-year-olds performed highest, followed by the 13-year-olds, the 17-year-olds, and finally the young adults. (Again, the subsamples were in the main responding to different items. These data do not take into account the inherent difficulties of the different items.)

OBJECTIVES III AND IV

The National Assessment of Educational Progress project also made some effort to assess two other objectives. Objective III was aimed at the understanding of the investigative nature of science. Objective IV was geared to the development of attitudes about and appreciations of scientists, science, and the consequences of science that stem from adequate undertsandings. Only 6 percent of all items found in the NAEP instruments were directed at Objective III, and another 6 percent were written toward Objective IV. The number of items were too few, in the opinion of the study team, to report those findings.

OVERLAP ITEMS

One difficulty associated with interpreting the findings reported in the previous paragraphs is that they are derived for the most part from different sets of exercises. The variability in the scores may be accounted for more by the difficulty of the items than by attainments in school. To throw some light on this area, the NAEP design did provide for some overlap items which were administered to subjects at more than one age level. Table 3 illustrates some of the topics included in the overlaps and the relative performances of three age groups.

Table 3. Illustrations of performances of thirteen-year-olds, seventeen-year-olds, and adults on selected exercises.[a]

Exercise Content	13s	17s	Adults
	percent correct		
Analyzing tables to determine weight of object	62	81	63
Result of repeated scientific measurement	69	72	57
Timing a pendulum	38	56	49
Characteristics of air masses in predicting weather	59	77	85
Effect of changing a member of an ecosystem	[b]	68	52
Adrenaline, a heart stimulant	[b]	56	70
Function of plaçenta	[b]	41	45
Purpose of a fuse	[b]	49	64

[a] Reference 1, p. 12.
[b] Not asked of this age level.

- On 13 items addressed to Objective I and given to both the 13-year-olds and the 17-year-olds, the latter group outperformed the former in each case. The released items covered the topics of comparative animal structures, health, and body functions. On 10 items assessing higher objectives, the 17-year-olds again outperformed the 13-year-olds in each case.
- On 27 items given both to young adults and to 13-year-olds addressed to Objective I, the adults did better than the younger respondents on 19 of the items. The one item of the 8 exceptions that was released dealt with the movement of molecules in hot water as opposed to their movement in cold water. For 14 items measuring achievement at objectives higher than knowledge, the adult group outperformed the 13-year-olds on

all but two of them. The one released item in this latter category dealt with the expected imprecision of scientific measurements. More adults expected all measures to be exactly the same.

- On 36 items addressed to Objective I and given to both the 17-year-olds and to young adults, the 17-year-olds did better on 21 of them. The adults did better than the 17-year-olds on items dealing with the time of release of the egg in the human female menstrual cycle, the purpose of the fuse in an electric circuit, heart stimulant, function of the placenta, and estimating the velocity of a boat moving in a current. On 20 overlap items given to both 17-year-olds and to young adults addressed to objectives higher than Objective I, the 17-year-olds did better on all of them except one. This one item was not released.
- There were 6 exercises given to 13-year-olds, 17-year-olds, and young adults. In 5 of the 6 items the 17-year-old group outperformed the other two groups. The young adults scored high on an item dealing with weather predicting.
- When these items were compared with the data for the 13-year-olds, it was found that the 13-year-olds outperformed the 9-year-olds on all 14 of the exercises given to those two groups. The topics treated in the released exercises included health and body functions, weather, and the processes of science.
- The young adults outperformed the 9-year-olds on all 11 of the overlap items addressed to Objective I for those two groups. None of these items was released. The young adult group also performed higher than the 9-year-olds on two items assessing higher objectives.
- Adults used the "I don't know" response more often than did any of the other groups.

MALES AND FEMALES

The National Assessment reports detailed observed differences between performances of males and females. To determine the differences, the percentage of females performing correctly on an item was subtracted from the percentage of males successfully answering the item. These differences were then ranked, and the median difference was identified for each age group. (See Table 4.)

Table 4. Median male-female differences in percentage correct at four age levels.

Ages	Median Differences on All Items
	percent
Nine	0.5
Thirteen	1.7
Seventeen	3.0
Adult	9.7

- For items dealing with the biological sciences, the median of the differences between the sexes favoring the males remained small at all four age levels, rising from 0.1 percent at age 9 to 2.3 percent for young adults.
- The average male advantage on physical science exercises rose from 0.8 percent at age 9 to 14.2 percent for young adults.
- An exception to the overall trend was found on items dealing with knowledge of human birth and reproduction. In this area, females did appreciably better than males, especially at the young adult level.

RELATIVE PERFORMANCE OF BLACKS

The NAEP arranged to assess the relative performance of Blacks in our society by comparing their performance with the national median. At the time of testing, the color of each respondent was determined by the exercise administrator as answer sheets were collected. Color was reported as Black or non-Black. To describe the relative standing of Blacks, the national percentage correct responses for each item was subtracted from the Black percentage correct for that item. Within each age level, the distribution of differences was inspected and the median was identified. The median value was taken as the estimate of the relative standing of Blacks within each age level.

Table 5. Median relative performance by Blacks for exercises under Objective 1, Objective II, Total Exercises, and Total Exercises (balanced) at four age levels.

	Age Levels			
	9	13	17	Adult
	percent	percent	percent	percent
Objective I	−15.5	−15.0	−10.9	−14.8
Objective II	−17.7	−18.7	−19.6	−17.8
Total (All exercises)	−14.5	−15.0	−11.8	−15.8
Total (Balanced)	−10.2	−11.0	− 7.7	−10.9

- Blacks performed between 12 percent and 16 percent below the national average at the four age levels: 9, 13, 17, and adults.
- Statistical procedures applied to the data by National Assessment analysts to estimate what the relative performances of Blacks might have been if they were represented proportionately in differing types of communities, in differing levels of parental education, and in various regions of the country moderated the observed differences somewhat. This statistical method, called "balancing" by NAEP, does not take all characteristics of respondents into account. For instance, economic status was not measured directly, although this factor is reflected in some of the other variables taken into account, such as size and type of community, level of parents' education, and others. [3]

GEOGRAPHICAL REGIONS

A breakout of the data was also performed by dividing the United States arbitrarily into four regions, Northeast, Southeast, Central, and West. The specific states that are included in each of the regions are listed in the NAEP literature. [1] The purpose of this analysis was to estimate regional effects as reflected in the performances on the National Assessment exercises. A regional effect for each item was defined as the difference between the percentage correct for that region and the national percentage correct. By ranking all the items in terms of their effects, the NAEP determined the average effect by taking the median of the distribution of item effects. The findings of this analysis are reported in Table 6.

Table 6. Median differences in P-values (percentage correct) between regions and the national performance for four regions of the United States at four age levels.

| | REGIONS | | | |
AGES	NORTHEAST	SOUTHEAST	CENTRAL	WEST
	percent	*percent*	*percent*	*percent*
Nine	2.2	−5.1	1.6	0.0
Thirteen	2.0	−4.8	1.9	−0.6
Seventeen	2.4	−4.8	0.0	1.7
Adult	0.7	−5.1	0.6	2.6

- In general, performance of the Northeast region at each age level was higher than the national performance.
- The performance value of the Southeast region at each age level was lower than the national performance.
- The median values of the West region showed the greatest variability in estimated effects—between that of the 13-year-old group and the adult group.

It was also found that respondents in the Northeast region tended to perform better on Objective II items than on Objective I items, and respondents in the Southeast region did relatively better on items addressed to Objective I than to items written toward Objective II.

SIZE AND TYPE OF COMMUNITY

Another of the breakouts of the NAEP data related to the size and type of community in which the respondents lived. Several arbitrary classifications were made, including the following: extreme inner city; inner city fringe; extreme affluent suburbs; extreme rural communities; and others (Table 7). The precise bases for these classifications are found in NAEP literature. [1, 2] The data in Table 7 are similar to those reported in other sections of this report. They were determined in the following way. First, the national percentage correct for each item was subtracted from the percentage correct received by the membership of a particular subgroup. Next, all the differences for a particular subgroup were ranked, and the median was entered in Table 7 as an estimate of the effect of membership in that subgroup on performance.

Table 7. Median effects by size and type of community for four ages.[a]

Size of Community	Size and Type of Community	9	13	17	Adult
Big City		− 4.8	− 4.7	−2.6	− 2.4
	Extreme inner city	−15.1	−13.7	−7.4	−10.2
	Inner city fringe	− 2.6	− 3.8	0.3	− 2.9
Urban Fringe		3.0	3.4	2.4	3.2
	Extreme affluent suburb	7.2	6.3	5.1	10.9
	Suburban fringe	2.7	2.9	1.0	0.8
Medium City		0.8	1.1	0.8	0.4
	Medium city	0.8	1.9	1.2	0.4
Smaller Places		− 1.2	− 1.1	−2.1	− 2.8
	Extreme rural	− 6.3	− 6.1	−3.5	− 4.7
	Small cities	0.9	0.5	−1.4	− 2.7

[a] Reference 3, p. 51.

- In the Big City category, data for respondents of age 17 showed a deficit of 2.6, but when this category was broken down into Extreme Inner City and Inner City Fringe, the deficit appeared to be 7.4 for the former and a 0.3 advantage for the latter. The disparate results indicate the degree of variance found with the four gross classifications of size of community.
- Respondents from the Extreme Inner City showed large deficits when compared to national measures.
- The performance gap between those from the Extreme Affluent Suburbs and the Extreme Inner City is largest at age 9, decreased at the 13- and 17-year-old levels, and increased sharply for the adults.
- The differences cited above seem to hold over various classifications of items: for physical science, for biological science, and for all objectives assessed in the 1969–70 cycle.
- When statistical procedures are applied to the data to balance different proportions of population characteristics, the effects found in Table 7 are essentially reduced 50 percent. Such manipulations, however, do not affect the deficit shown by Extreme Rural Adults.
- The discrepancies between subcategories were the lowest at the 17-year-old level with the Extreme Inner City respondents having the smallest deficit at that age and the Extreme Affluent Suburban respondents having the smallest advantage. It is interesting to note that this narrowing of differences occurs at an age when most children have been recently exposed to formal science instruction.

PARENTAL EDUCATION

Findings of the National Assessment of Educational Progress project were analyzed in terms of the education levels of parents. Categories included the following: (a) education level of parents not ascertained: (b) neither parent educated beyond eighth grade; (c) either mother or father had some high school; (d) either mother or father completed high school but neither educated beyond high school; and (e) either mother or father educated beyond high school. The data were treated as follows: Within each age level, the national percentage correct for an item was subtracted from the percentage correct of a particular subgroup cited above. The difference estimated the effect on that particular item of belonging to that subgroup. The effects of all the items were then ranked from high to low for the subgroup, and the median of the effects was taken as an estimate of the average effect of subgroup membership over all the items. The results of this analysis are presented for each age group in Table 8.

Table 8. Parental education effects or differing levels of parental education for each of the age levels.[a]

Ages	No High School	Some High School	Graduated High School	Post High School
Nine	− 7.2	−4.8	.6	5.8
Thirteen	−11.8	−6.2	−1.3	5.2
Seventeen	− 8.4	−7.6	.1	5.1
Adults	− 7.9	−1.6	3.0	9.1

[a] As in previous tables, students at the various age levels were administered different items so that comparisons across age groups are difficult to make.

- At the four age levels tested, 9, 13, 17, and adult, the respondents neither of whose parents were educated beyond eighth grade showed average effects ranging from −7.2 to −11.8.
- At the four age levels, the respondents whose parents had received some high school education manifested average effects which ranged from −1.6 to −7.6 percentage points.
- At the four age levels, the respondents whose parents had graduated from high school showed average effects from −1.3 to +3 percent.
- At the four age levels, the respondents whose parents had received some post high school education demonstrated an average effect that ranged from +5 to +9 percentage points.

PERFORMANCE ITEMS

Included within the assessment exercises were a few items that differed qualitatively from the others. These items asked respondents to perform a task with simple equipment (rather than to choose the best response from a set of alternatives). For example, some of the items required respondents to operate a beam balance, to calculate the density of an object, or to time the swings of a pendulum. Curriculum developers during the last decade have given emphasis to performance skills as an outcome of science instruction; it is appropriate that performance items were included in the assessment. The number of such items in the 1969–70 assessment was small—3 released and 8 unreleased exercises at the age levels 13, 17, and adult—approximately 8 percent of the total.

- The absolute level of performance on these 11 items which required skills such as measurement, graphical analysis, and making inferences concerning operations with concrete materials was low; less than half of all the respondents showed these competencies.
- Respondents in the Affluent Suburbs displayed a substantial advantage in these tasks over Inner City populations.
- Non-Black respondents showed a large advantage over Blacks on these items.
- Males outperformed females on the performance items included in the assessment.

EXPECTATIONS

One of the problems in interpreting the results of the national assessment is that it is difficult to know what performances should be expected on particular items. All teachers know that test items assessing the same specific objective can vary in difficulty because of characteristics of the item. Distractors in the tests can be shaded or nuances introduced to make items which appear to be very similar actually be very different in difficulty. An example of this problem in operation is found in comparing the performances of the various age groups. Overall the performance of the 17-year-olds in terms of percentage correct is lower than that for other age groups, and yet on the items that were overlapped across age groups, the 17-year-olds did generally better than did the other groups. One explanation for this apparent discrepancy is that the items given to the 17-year-olds were generally more difficult in a technical sense. The study team examined each of the released items and for each age level classified them according to a general level of expectation. Some items were judged as measuring performances that all persons of that age group "should" have acquired. Other items were judged as measuring performances that approximately half of a particular age group "should" have acquired. Finally, some items were judged to be measuring performances that only very few of a particular age group "should" have acquired. An analysis was run to compare the actual performances of the various age levels with the expectations defined by the study team. The comparisons are reported in Table 9. The rows of Table 9 define intervals of observed percentage of correct responses on items within each age level. Three classifications are included in the table: those items for which the national percentage correct was between

75 and 100; those items for which the national percentage correct was between 50 and 74; and the items for which the national percentage correct was between 0 and 49. Extreme care needs to be given to the interpretation of these findings.

There was a great deal of disagreement among the study team members in their judgments about expectations. Second, most of the study team had had an opportunity to peruse the findings related to each item before they were called upon to make their judgments. There is no estimate of the bias this factor may have introduced into the process.

- The 9-year-olds performed closest to the study team's expectations, with the 13-year-old group performing next closest to expectations.
- The 17-year-old group was the most discrepant in deviating from the study team's expectations.
- Expectations of the study team tended to exceed actual performance, especially in the 17-year-old and young adult subgroups.

Table 9. Number of released exercises classified by expectation level as judged by the NSTA study team and by the national percentage correct for each age level.

| | | EXPECTATION LEVELS | | |
| | | VERY FEW "SHOULD" RESPOND CORRECTLY | ABOUT HALF "SHOULD" RESPOND CORRECTLY | ALMOST ALL "SHOULD" RESPOND CORRECTLY |
AGES	PERFORMANCE LEVELS			
	percent correct			
Nine	75 - 100	0	5	18
	50 - 74	1	16	3
	0 - 49	7	8	0
Thirteen	75 - 100	0	0	15
	50 - 74	0	10	4
	0 - 49	4	14	0
Seventeen	75 - 100	0	0	9
	50 - 74	0	10	11
	0 - 49	9	11	4
Adult	75 - 100	0	1	8
	50 - 74	0	7	10
	0 - 49	9	12	2

Judgments and Concluding Statements

JUDGMENTS

The following statements represent the specific judgments the members of the study team felt were warranted at this time. Specific recommendations to NAEP based on these concluding remarks are found in Appendix V of the full report.

1. One of the most striking findings of the science assessment has to do with the comparatively poor performance of females compared to males. It is made especially noteworthy by the fact that in all the other assessments available to the study team at this time, science is the only area in which males outperformed females. (See Appendix VI of the full report for further comparisons among assessment findings.) While other industrial societies apparently make full use of their female citizens to meet the demands for highly skilled technicians and scientists, the United States is lagging in this regard. The findings here do nothing to make us optimistic about the future involvement of women in the sciences. Science teachers must become especially sensitive to their behaviors that may turn women away from science and science achievement.

   The NSTA should appoint a committee to review the progress that has been made by females in the science areas and to identify systematic factors that may be impeding the progress of women in the study of science.

2. On 21 out of 36 overlap items, the 17-year-olds did better than did the young adult group. It may be that much of science content is recondite —and subject to rapid forgetting on the part of students. Teachers need to inspect their goals to identify those which are especially narrow. For items that are deemed important, efforts need to be made to find methods of teaching that will contribute greater retention.

   One approach is to concentrate on science methods which have a high probability of making every student an autonomous learner. Instead of relying on teacher lectures and canned programs, more effort could be expended toward inviting students to participate in independent learning activities which involve the science content thought to be important.

3. Assuming that the objectives assessed by the National Assessment of Educational Progress are appropriate to the general student population found in the public schools and not to an elite group, it is clear that something systematic is preventing these objectives from being attained in equivalent ways by Blacks, by rural students, by Southeastern students, by inner-city students, and by females. While many factors may contribute to the observed differences, it is important that science teachers take the following into account:

   a. The range of scores within each of the subsamples reported in the NAEP publications shows that, either singly or in combination, none of the factors of being a girl, being Black, being a student in the Southeast, is an absolute barrier to high achievement in science.

   b. While one goal of schools is to widen the differences found in children—to promote intellectual diversity rather than conformity—it is counter to the goals of education in their most profound sense and to the ideals of the American society for the diversity to be systematically accounted for by factors of color, sex, or neighborhood. It is commonly assumed that teachers will take steps to ensure that their teaching methods and their attitudes, conveyed by what they do and what they say, transmitted formally or informally, do not discriminate against subsamples of students.

4. An examination of those items assessing knowledge in the area of sex education indicated that the 7-year-olds, as a group, did poorly and the adults performed only somewhat less poorly. One inference to be made from these findings is that sex education is needed in our schools. With the rather poor showing of the adults, there may be a basis for believing that parents may not know enough about sex education to be competent teachers of their children in this area.

CONCLUDING STATEMENTS

The study team is aware of the rather bland nature of these judgments. We had hoped that an examination of the data would allow us to write recommendations suggesting practical and profound changes in funding, in teaching practices, in curricula policies, and in other significant aspects of the science teaching enterprise. We perceive now that none of the statements we have drafted is particularly fresh or insightful. Policy-making groups will probably not be able to act on our recommendations to the benefit of science students throughout the nation. An explanation for our failure to date to identify great significance in the data may lie in the various contexts in which the study team was operating and in which the National Assessment of Educational Progress project was carried out. Those contexts seem worthy of discussion here.

CONTEXT OF TIME. The National Assessment of Educational Progress must be seen as a long-term effort. From its outset, the project was designed to assess changes in the attainments of young Americans *across time*. In this light, it is perhaps premature to seek interpretations of the results of the first testing. The importance of the NAEP findings may not become clear until the fourth or fifth cycle of testing. To become impatient after only one or two rounds is seemingly to misjudge a significant character of this project: testing across several time periods.

Accepting this view, the study team anticipated what might be said about similar findings even if several data points over time were available. Our thinking included the following points:

1. Approximately 60 percent of the items used in the 1969 administration were repeated in 1972. For those items, differences between administrations can be taken as measures of trends. For instance, perhaps more children will be able to handle a beam balance in 1972 than could do so in 1969. While two data points hardly provide definitive support for a trend, points found in subsequent assessments should be of some interest to science educators.

2. We can anticipate that the percentage of correct responses for a given

item will fluctuate over time. However, as changes are identified, it will be difficult to identify the casual factors which account for the changes. The data reported by NAEP are not being collected in a laboratory— but in the real world. There are many variables which can be considered as reasonable explanations for the differences observed in the NAEP findings over time—television, systematic changes in school curricula, influences of dramatic scientific achievements, to name only a few. Additionally, these variables and many others not named here must not only be assessed in terms of their direct effects on the NAEP findings, but also as they interact with each other to alter the educational attainments of our young citizens.

3. As changes are identified over the cycles of assessments that are to take place in the next several decades, it must be remembered that it is not the case that increased achievement on an item is *ipso facto* good and a decreased achievement level is bad. A downward shift in some areas and on some items might signal a welcome change away from teaching trivial bits of information while an increasingly high performance on an item might be an indication that our schools are still teaching in old and unwanted ways.

In sum, it may be the case that the possible significant contributions of NAEP cannot be discerned at this time; that the assessment project will gain in significance and importance only after a series of measures are taken. It was not clear to our team, however, that much could be made from such trends—even if they were quite definitive.

CONTEXT OF MEASUREMENT STRATEGIES. Many advocates of the National Assessment of Educational Progress undertaking argued initially that the project will provide legislators, policy makers, professionals, and citizens of this country with reliable information about the educational enterprise. Armed with this valuable information, the various publics to which the educational establishment is accountable would, it was hoped, be in a better position to make decisions necessary for the provision of quality education. While the exact form of the information to be provided by NAEP was not clear, allusions were made to the formulation of a complex indicator of the status of education, a statistic similar to that of the Gross National Product. While few citizens can define explicitly the variables that are included in the formulation of the GNP and even fewer can identify the weightings that are applied to combine the variables into an index, nevertheless, the Gross National Product is apparently a very meaningful measure. The literature discussing the potential payoffs of the NAEP almost always implied that such an index would be one of the useful products emanating from this effort.

However, the conception of the assessment task on the part of the professionals has been from the beginning based generally on a behavioristic tradition—a school of thought that rejects the formulation of constructs. Item writers, from the first, were not asked to develop exercises that would contribute to the measurement of such constructs as "educational quality" or "knowledge of science." Instead, each item was to stand as important by itself. It follows from this position that the findings, including the breakouts of the performances of the various subgroups, were to be considered important in their own right—and not as they contributed to the validity of a grand index or construct on the scale of GNP.

Giving stress to the importance of each item, not as it contributes to a larger more meaningful index but only as it stands by itself, may have blunted the incisiveness of our judgments. (This point is discussed in the recommendations sent to NAEP.)

CONTEXT OF COMPARISONS. The comparisons the National Assessment of Educational Progress did choose to make in its reports might be another source of the difficulties our study team experienced. Knowing that Blacks score higher than non-Blacks on a particular item—or that males score higher than females on another—is not as edifying as other comparisons might have been. For instance, if students could have been grouped by science curricula, or by years of receiving science instruction, to name two, perhaps more meaningful statements could have been made at this time. The comparisons reported seem on the whole rather gratuitous. For instance, we wonder how teachers could make use of the information that one section of the country scored higher than another. (This question is one of those included in the recommendations made to NAEP.)

CONTEXT OF CONTROVERSIES IN EDUCATION. A final context which may account in part for our difficulty in finding more important recommendations to advance after studying the NAEP results lies in current conflicting views of the educational enterprise. By placing a focus on the outputs of the educational process, the National Assessment of Educational Progress seems to be accepting a technological metaphor, viewing education through a separation of ends and means. One of the obstacles facing our study team was the difficulty on the part of some members of accepting the view that the quality of education can be assessed by the examination of multiple choice test results.

It is our fervent wish that after baseline data lines are established and with the addition of the second round results, more specific and meaningful recommendations may be gleaned from the NAEP results.

References

1. National Assessment of Educational Progress. *Report 1. 1969-70 Science: National Results and Illustrations of Group Comparisons.* Education Commission of the States. Denver, Colorado, July 1970. Appendix B.

2. National Assessment of Educational Progress. *Report 4. 1969–70 Assessment: Sex, Region, Size of Community.* Education Commission of the States. Denver, Colorado, April 1971. Appendix B-1.

3. National Assessment of Educational Progress. *Report 7. 1969-70 Assessment: Color, Size and Type of Community; Parental Education; Balanced Results by Region and Sex.* Education Commission of the States. Denver, Colorado, December 1971. Page B-10.

An Analysis of Research Related to Instructional Procedures in Elementary School Science[*]

GREGOR A. RAMSEY and ROBERT W. HOWE

The Educational Resources Information Center (ERIC) comprises a network of decentralized clearinghouses in various locations throughout the United States. The ERIC clearinghouse for science education is located at Ohio State University and is designed to help teachers keep informed of new instructional techniques and materials. The following contains that portion of an article which refers specifically to an analysis of recent research related to instructional procedures in elementary science. Eleven research categories, together with an extensive bibliography, are included: (1) Comparative Studies: Traditional vs. Nontraditional, (2) Audiovisual Aids, (3) Programed Instruction, (4) Individualized Instruction, (5) Ability Grouping—Socioeconomic Status of Students, (6) Use of Reading Materials, (7) Critical Thinking, (8) Process: Inquiry in Science, (9) Problem Solving, (10) Creativity, and (11) Concept Development.

The purpose of this article is to report to the profession an analysis of recent research related to instructional procedures used to teach elementary school science. The reviewers found it necessary to place arbitrary limits on the studies reviewed so that the field could be contained in manageable form. In general, only studies reported after 1960 were examined, and from these only those studies which attempted some objective evalua-

[*]REPRINTED FROM *Science and Children*, Vol. 6, No. 7, April 1969, pp. 27–36. Copyright, 1969, by the National Science Teachers Association, Washington, D.C. Reprinted by permission of the authors and the publisher. Mr. Ramsey is a Retrieval Analyst for ERIC. Dr. Howe is director of ERIC and Chairman of the Faculty of Science and Mathematics Education at Ohio State University.

tion of the outcomes of an instructional sequence are discussed in detail in this article. Likewise, studies which were designed to test various aspects of learning theory, although they may have used a novel instructional procedure to do this, were ignored. Learning theory forms an important basis for designing an instructional procedure, but it has only an indirect effect on classroom teaching.

The studies are reviewed in terms of whether they focused on the instructional procedure, e.g., inductive or deductive, individualized instruction, programed instruction, or whether the studies focused on outcomes, e.g., development of concepts, attitudes, problem-solving skills, creativity, or understanding content. It was surprising to find the outcome category "development of psychomotor skills" void, since it might be expected that this would be an important area to be developed in elementary school science. No information was obtained concerning what manipulative skills in science can be developed in elementary school children, nor whether a hierarchy of such skills can be identified. This area requires much more basic research.

A number of "status" studies were identified. School systems were surveyed for procedures used, e.g., Snoble (113)[1] and Swan (120), or wider surveys of national practices were made, e.g., those by McCloskey (79), Moorehead (83), Smith and Cooper (111), Blackwood (13), Stokes (116), and Melis (81).

These status studies are in reviews themselves and provide sound statements of the position in the areas mentioned. They are not discussed further in this article, but are cited as useful sources for the interested reader.

Only one study was identified which attempted evaluation of one of the newer course improvement projects in elementary science. This study was undertaken by Walbesser, *et al.* (126) and the American Association for the Advancement of Science in their comprehensive study of *Science—A Process Approach*. An evaluation model was posed which described expected learner behaviors and established what might be accepted as evidence of learner accomplishment. Evaluation in these terms allows for objective comparisons of courses, gives objective evidence that learning has occurred, and makes independent replication of the findings possible.

The behavioral objectives of each instructional sequence were clearly identified, and they were evaluated by determining the percentage of pupils acquiring a certain standard percentage of specified behaviors, and comparing this to an established level of expectation. From this information, feedback to improve the instructional sequence was constantly available. For example, an arbitrary 90/90 (90 per cent of students acquire 90 per cent of the prescribed behaviors) was chosen as the standard. If the standard attained by pupils were lower than this, then modifications were made to the instructional sequence.

---

[1] See references.

Specific findings of the evaluation were too varied and far reaching to be described in a review of this nature; however, it is the model provided by the evaluation, rather than the results which are important. Much has been said and written about the efficacy of stating objectives in behavioral terms. This study gives concrete evidence that this is so.

Comparative Studies: Traditional vs. Nontraditional

In this section are reviewed those studies which compared outcomes obtained when the same body of content is taught by two methods. A "conventional" or "traditional" method was the usual standard of comparison, although what researchers meant by these terms was not always clear. Methods investigated included "inductive," "directed self-discovery," a "field method," "democratic," and "problem solving." It was in this area of comparison studies that the reviewers had the most concern regarding the research design. It is extremely difficult in such circumstances to control all the variables which may affect instruction. A study by Brudzynski (16) illustrates this point. He compared an inductive method where pupils learned concepts by "directed self-discovery" in a pupil-centered atmosphere to a "lecture-demonstration" teacher-centered one. The "inductive" method favored above-average students while the "lecture-demonstration" method favored average and below average students in the fifth- and sixth-grade population studied. These differences need not be ascribed to the particular instructional method. Teacher expectation may have been far more important. The less-able students may not be "expected" by the teacher, perhaps subconsciously, to perform as well in a self-directed situation. He may act in the classroom accordingly and this subconscious expectation could affect the outcomes of the students more than the instructional procedure used.

Anklam (5) identified the teachers who liked to use "democratic" instructional methods and those who preferred a more "autocratic" approach. No significant differences in achievement motivation existed between the groups of pupils taught in each of these environments. This finding points clearly to the importance of teacher characteristics and behaviors to the whole instructional procedure, and the danger of imposing a particular procedure upon teachers who do not have the personal characteristics to teach it. In this study, the teachers investigated had adopted a style of teaching which suited them. Even though the simplicity of the democratic-autocratic dichotomy may be doubted, the study did show that teachers performing within a frame of reference which they have built for themselves, motivated students equally. What is needed is research into determining instructional procedures which suit different personality types rather than research directed to finding one procedure "best" for all teachers.

Other studies where no significant differences were found between methods used included Gerne (51) who compared a traditional textbook method with a method utilizing a specially designed board to teach electricity and magnetism, and one by Bennett (10) who compared a field method with a classroom method for teaching ecology. Smith (110) compared a lecture-demonstration style of teaching carried out in a classroom to teaching in a planetarium for presenting a lesson on astronomy concepts to sixth-grade pupils. Children in the classroom achieved significantly higher than those taught in the planetarium. These studies suggest that the use of any visual aid or direct experience will not necessarily of itself produce significant outcome gains in children.

Carpenter (24) used fourth-grade pupils to compare a "textbook recitation method" with a "problem method." In effect, the textbook method included no demonstrations while the problem method was based on classroom demonstration and experimentation. Achievement of content gains were strongly in favor of the problem-solving method for teaching units on "magnetism" and "adaption of animals." This finding was even more definite for the slower learners—who were, in general, poor readers.

Pershern (91) investigated student achievement outcomes obtained by integrating industrial-arts activities with science instruction in grades 4, 5, 6. He used electricity and machines as his content vehicles and found significant gains in favor of integration for the electricity unit, but no significant differences for the machines unit. Integration seems to add an important dimension to instruction, and may prove a useful approach for further research.

It is difficult to generalize from comparison studies, however, it seems that pupil activity and pupil-performed experiments are important prerequisites to the effective learning of science concepts. Instructional procedures where the responsibility for the conceptual leap is placed upon the child, as in problem solving and inductive methods, do seem to bring about more significant achievement gains than do those methods where the teacher or the text material provides the concept. It appears that for these inductive methods to be fully effective, the teacher must have a certain teaching philosophy and a certain set of personal characteristics.

Audiovisual Aids

The bulk of the research in this area involved the use of television and movie film in the classroom. How these aids can best be used in an instructional situation, what their effect is on student achievement and attitudes, and how they can improve classroom instruction are all questions to which research has been directed. Much of the research was of the "direct-comparison" type where control of all variables is extremely difficult. Conclusions based on such studies should be viewed with some caution.

Bickel (12), Decker (36), and Skinner (109) investigated changes in attitude, achievement, and interest in children following television instruction. Bickel (12) found no significant differences in the learning outcomes of his fourth-, fifth-, and sixth-grade pupils taught science by closed-circuit television incorporating a "talk-back" facility and teacher follow-up, when compared with students taught science without the aid of television.

Skinner (109) compared two television presentations for two separate groups of fifth graders. In one presentation a problem was identified, and many questions were posed which were not answered in the lesson. In this way, it was hoped that pupils' curiosity and interest in science would be aroused. The other presentation included the same materials, but used a direct expository teaching style with very few questions. Teacher follow-up of these lessons was either a modified inquiry session where the teacher answered only pupils' questions or a typical discussion session with teacher and pupils participating fully. Skinner found that pupils who experienced the television presentation with unanswered questions, regardless of teacher follow-up, achieved significantly higher than pupils who viewed "explanation" on television.

Decker (36), like Skinner, also worked with fifth graders and followed a somewhat similar procedure. He prepared two sets of ten half-hour television programs using the same materials for each. One set stressed providing information, concepts, and generalizations while the other stressed the posing of problems. No significant differences in pupil achievement were detected, so Decker concluded that the problem-solving method was as effective as the information-giving method in teaching natural science.

These conflicting results of Skinner and Decker, where one finds a significant difference in one and no significant difference in the other, point clearly to the difficulties associated with these direct-comparison type studies. They oversimplify the learning process and do not take into account how individual student needs, interests, and abilities interact with instruction. An instructional method which may be in tune with the profile of characteristics of one group of students in the class may be out of tune with another, so any gains obtained with one group will be offset by the losses in the other, and no significant differences are detected. Research on instructional procedures must be increasingly multi-dimensional, since no one method of instruction can be considered "best" for all students.

Bornhorst and Hosford (15) investigated television instruction at the third-grade level by comparing the achievement of a group of television-taught pupils with a group who had only classroom instruction. The television group achieved significantly higher results on tests than the control group, and it was felt that the "wonder-box" where children placed questions arising from the television lessons for future discussion was an important factor.

Allison (3) investigated the influence of three methods of using motivational films[2] on the attitudes of fourth-, fifth-, and sixth-grade students toward science, scientists, and scientific careers. He adapted the Allen attitude inventory[3] for use with these elementary school children. Allison concluded that the films did change the attitudes of the students favorably toward science, scientists, and scientific careers, and that these changes in attitude were not related to mental ability, science achievement scores, sex, science training, or the economic status of parents.This study suggests that film sequences can be devised which will effectively bring about a desired attitude change. More research in this area is needed particularly in the development and evaluation of material.

Novak (87) describes the development and use of audiotape programed instruction for teaching first- and third-grade elementary science. Cartridge tape recorders and projectors with simple "on-off" switches were used. Some of the problems associated with setting up such a program included vocabulary difficulty, pace of audio instruction, difficulty of task to be performed, density of information to be presented, inadequacies of filmloops, and unexpected distractions. Four to eight revisions of each program sequence were necessary to be sure that students could proceed with very few apparent difficulties.

Evaluation of the program was highly experimental. Individual interview using loop films, display materials, and appropriate questioning was found too time consuming. Pencil and paper tests using drawings, administered orally to the whole class, were then tried. Also, several suggestions as to future possible avenues of evaluation were developed along with other ways the materials may be used. The study leaves little doubt that audiotutorial instruction is feasible in grades one, two, and three, and should be looked on as a useful way to individualize instruction.

Programed Instruction

The role of programed instruction in the elementary school has had some attention from researchers. This is understandable since such programs encourage individual student work, and free the teacher from direct instruction to perform other tasks.

Hedges and MacDougall (61) investigated the effectiveness of teaching fourth-grade science using programed science materials and laboratory experiences. The study had three phases. In phase one, the purpose was to establish the possibility of programed instruction as a teaching method. This was done by observing students using the materials, and determining student and teacher attitudes. The information was used to revise and

2 "Horizons of Science." Films produced by Educational Testing Service, Princeton, New Jersey.
3 Allen, Hugh, Jr. "Attitudes of Certain High School Seniors Toward Science and Scientific Careers." Teachers College, Columbia University, New York City. 1960.

rewrite the programs as part of phase two of the study. The final report on the evaluative phase (phase three) has not yet come to the reviewers' attention; however, the intention was to compare innovative ways of using the materials with a more traditional approach under the headings: achievement, interest, problem-solving ability, ability to generalize, and retention. This three-phase method of determining feasibility, refining materials and methods, and evaluating student and teacher outcomes outlines a promising sequence for the development of instructional procedures.

Blank (14) investigated developing inquiry skills through programed-instruction techniques. The programs trained children to ask questions about the relative dimensions of problems before attempting to solve them. He found that the children given inquiry training asked significantly more questions (as well as a lower proportion of irrelevant ones) on oral and written criterion tests than did students in control groups. This improvement in inquiry skills was not at the expense of other achievement criteria, so it was found possible to introduce inquiry training without affecting progress in regular course work.

Dutton (41) investigated achievement using programed materials on heat, light, and sound with fourth graders. He found that children did proceed at different rates and that they could perform simple science experiments with little teacher supervision. Pupils using the programed materials learned concepts more efficiently than did those in classes taught in a conventional way.

Crabtree (30) studied the relationships between score, time, IQ, and reading level for fourth-grade students by structuring programed science materials in different ways. Linear programs seemed preferable to branched versions since the same amount of material was learned in less time. Other findings were of the "no significant difference" type, although there was some evidence that multiple choice type response requires a higher reading ability than other response forms.

Taylor (122) investigated the effect of pupil behavior and characteristics and teacher attitudes on achievement when programed science materials are used at the fourth-grade level. Teacher attitudes, combinations of pupil and teacher attitudes, pupil intelligence, interest, and initial knowledge of science, along with other selected personality and performance factors all contribute significantly to pupil final achievement. The study indicates that any given set of programed science materials cannot meet the needs of all the students at any given grade level.

Individualized Instruction

Instruction may be classified as individualized if experiences are specifically designed for each individual child, taking into account such factors as background, knowledge and experience, reading level, interests, and intelligence. There have been several attempts at individualizing which have tried to allow for the individual needs of children in the instructional design.

Baum (8) prepared materials to test the feasibility of individualizing science experiences for fifth-grade pupils. He devised a series of pretests of skills and knowledge so that pupil deficiencies could be identified. Each pupil was then assigned a kit specially designed to help him acquire the skill or competency shown to be deficient on the tests. This method was found suitable for helping pupils achieve curricular goals in the area of science. Evaluation was carried out by observing pupil reactions to this instruction, and though the evaluation was subjective, the strengths of the program in terms of desired outcomes clearly emerged.

O'Toole (89) compared an individualized method with a teacher-centered approach in the teaching of science to fifth graders. He found no significant differences between his groups in achievement, problem-solving ability, or science interest. The teacher-centered program stressing problem solving as a major objective was more effective in developing the ability to identify valid conclusions while the individualized program was more effective in developing the ability to recognize hypotheses and problems.

It is likely that group methods of instruction will develop some outcomes more effectively than individualized methods, while other outcomes will develop more effectively in an individualized situation. This study was the only one which attempted to identify what some of these outcome differences might be.

Schiller (102) used activity booklets and data sheets to individualize instruction for sixth-grade pupils. The materials were designed to give children an opportunity to complete some science experiments and other activities which were in addition to the formal instructional program. Much of the evaluation was subjective, but students were eager to participate in the activities and seemed to gain from them.

Other attempts at individualizing instruction were undertaken by La-Cava (69) who used the tape recorder as an aid in individualizing, Carter (25) who developed a science experience center, and Lipson (74) who developed an individualized program by coordinating audio-tapes to simple science kits. These studies, in general, support the contention that individualizing instruction is possible and educationally desirable at the elementary level. To date, however, evaluation has been highly subjective.

A more rigorous evaluation of an individualized program was undertaken by Gleason (54). He measured pupil growth in areas of general science knowledge, liking for science, and learning to generalize. Although he found no specific advantages in favor of individualized self-study activity in science, pupils learned as much content by themselves as they did when taught by a teacher.

An important project related to individualizing instruction is the Oakleaf Project for Individually Prescribed Instruction discussed by Lindvall and Bolvin (72). Here, the Oakleaf Elementary School is used as a laboratory for testing the feasibility of individualizing instruction, developing suitable programs, and evaluating the effects of such instruction.

Ability Grouping—Socioeconomic Status of Students

Three studies investigated the effects of socio-economic status on achievement in elementary school science. Some of the findings have clear implications for instruction.

Rowland (98) compared the science achievement of sixth-grade pupils of high socio-economic status with those of generally low status. He found that given equal intelligence and equal science background experiences, higher socio-economic status pupils show greater science achievement than do lower groups, and these differences carry over to all the various types of science achievement measured. He found that it is of great importance that lower socio-economic status pupils have opportunities to manipulate and study simple science materials, and this should precede experience with more complex types of commercial science aids. Also, these students should engage in concrete science experiences before being expected to learn from reading or discussing science material.

Wagner (124) compared the responses of economically advantaged and disadvantaged sixth-grade pupils to science demonstrations. Pupil responses to the demonstrations were obtained by getting them to either write about, tell about, or construct pictorially, using predesigned plastic templates, suitable applications of the demonstrations. Advantaged pupils were significantly superior in written and oral responses, but no differences were detected in the construction responses. This finding suggests that disadvantaged pupils understand and can communicate their understandings of science concepts when placed in situations requiring limited language response.

Becker (9) investigated the achievement of gifted sixth-grade students when segregated from, partly segregated from, or homogeneously mixed with students of lower ability. No significant differences were detected between the groups, and no special advantages accrued when gifted children were placed in special groups. Unfortunately, the description of the design of the study did not mention some important aspects, one of which was the length of time students were placed in these various arrangements. This time factor is likely to be highly significant in such a study.

These studies point to the great importance which must be placed on student characteristics in the design of instructional procedures. Selecting one factor, e.g., ability, from the whole range of factors which influence learning, and then separating instructional groups on the basis of it, is unlikely to significantly improve student outcomes. The factors involved in determining the outcomes of instruction are much more subtle than this.

Use of Reading Materials

Little research was detected on investigating ways reading materials may be used in an instructional situation. Some very interesting studies, however, were identified.

Fryback (48) evaluated some elementary science curriculum materials which had been written to accommodate five different reading levels in a fifth-grade class. Other variables in the design included whether the students performed experiments or not, and the extent of class discussion. He found that the provision for different reading ability levels and class discussion did not show any significant influence on achievement. Only when pupils worked experiments were significant achievement gains noted. The provision of different reading levels and class discussion may have a motivational effect for later work and may affect other outcomes, but these data indicate that the provision of experiments to be performed individually by pupils is important.

Bennett and Clodfelter (11) investigated student learning of earth-science concepts when the science unit was integrated within the reading program of second-grade children. For the integration, a "word-analysis" approach was used. In this method, the child was given a basic list of words to be used in the new resource unit on earth science, and then introduced to their meanings before presentation of the unit. The "word-analysis" group showed greater achievement gains than the control groups where the science was taught in the traditional way. The study demonstrated that certain earth-science concepts can be learned at the second-grade level.

Williams (128) rewrote sixth-grade science materials to a third-grade level of readability, and used them with his sixth-grade pupils. Gains in reading speed and comprehension seemed to occur when the materials were used, but the duration of the study was far too short for differences in learning outcomes to be evaluated.

Research in the area of the use of reading materials is indeed thin. More and more textbooks and other materials directed to the elementary pupil are coming onto the market, yet the role of reading materials in science instruction has had little recent evaluation.

Critical Thinking

Over the period of review, only one study was identified which investigated the development of critical thinking in children. Mason (78), in a two-year study, developed materials for teaching critical thinking in grades K–6. The first year was devoted to developing materials and providing inservice seminars for the teachers who would eventually teach the course. Basic assumptions were that children should have planned experiences in science rather than incidental ones, they should have direct experience with both content and methods of science, and that experiences can be identified to give students direct training in the acquisition of scientific skills and attitudes. Evaluation of the course was subjective for grades K–3 because of the lack of suitable instruments; but, in grades 4–6 significant gains in critical thinking were made over the period of a year. The materials were particularly effective at the fifth-grade level where maximum gains were made.

It seems quite clear that instructional sequences can be devised which will develop pupils' powers of critical thinking. Only by evaluating the outcomes of the experiences can the effectiveness of these materials be assessed. There is a lack of activity in this area, particularly in grades K–3.

Process: Inquiry in Science

Much emphasis has been placed on the development of science process skills and the use of inquiry methods to develop certain cognitive abilities by the new elementary science course improvement projects. Less research has been reported in this area than might have been expected if one judges from the significant sums of money spent on developing these programs.

Raun (95) investigated the interaction between curriculum variables and selected classroom-student characteristics using the AAAS *Science—A Process Approach* materials. He was interested in the changes in cognitive and affective behavior brought about by children using some of the strategies of science. Some of the factors investigated included problem solving, perceptual closure, verbal fluency, ideation fluency, tested intelligence, achievement, and attitudes toward science and scientists. The strategies of inquiry selected for performance evaluation after five months instruction were classifying, observing, using number relations, and recognizing space-time relations. He found limited evidence of significant grade differences between behaviors and performance in the strategies of inquiry in science, and that there was no consistent pattern of behavioral change among grades. In fact, on many of the factors investigated, grades 5 and 6 showed regressive tendencies which support the argument that there is rather slow development of science process skills beyond grade 5.

Price (93) investigated whether students who had manipulated objects and materials to gather empirical data in an elementary classroom would transfer this manipulative process behavior to a test situation outside the classroom. It was found that children rarely sought data by overt manipulative processes in the test situations, even though verbal responses to them indicated high motivational interest. Also gifted children showed no greater tendency to empirically gather data to solve problems than students in the normal range of intelligence.

Scott and Sigel (106) used grades 4–6 to investigate the effects of inquiry training in physical science on creativity and cognitive style. Pupils receiving inquiry training learned science concepts as well or better than children in conventional classes, and no significant differences were found between boys and girls. Cognitive styles did seem to be influenced by the inquiry process, and some differences in the development trends of cognitive styles of boys compared to girls were apparent.

More studies like the above are needed if instructional procedures are to be developed which meet the individual needs of students at each stage in their development. Inquiry methods and methods designed to have children working with the processes of science are likely to produce different outcomes than conventional procedures. These new procedures are becoming more carefully controlled, and with the development of more sensitive evaluative instruments, a clearer idea of what these differences may be is starting to emerge. Increased research on ways the new materials may be used and the outcomes obtained seems essential.

Problem Solving

A number of studies investigated problem solving in elementary children. Dyrli (42), Gunnels (55), and Harris (59) all made some analysis of the problem-solving behavior of children at various grade levels. Only Schippers (103) extended what is known about problem solving into a suggested instructional sequence.

Dyrli (42) wished to discover whether instruction had any effect on the length of transition period from the stage of concrete operations to more formal patterns of thought in the Piagetian developmental sequence. Gunnels (55) also investigated cognitive development based on the Piagetian stages of intuitive, concrete, and formal thought. He used an interview technique to study the development of logical judgments in science of successful and unsuccessful problem solvers in grades 4–9. In general, the Piagetian order of development was confirmed that successful problem solvers operate at a higher level of operational thought than do unsuccessful problem solvers; however, even though a child is at a given chronological age, this does not guarantee a definite level of thought process skills.

Harris (59) used sixth graders and investigated the usefulness of pupil drawings in developing a problem-solving approach to learning science concepts. He identified two kinds of problem-solving behavior; verificational and insightful, but his study concentrated on the verificational aspects which seem most often encountered in school. He made an intensive individual analysis of the problem-solving processes of eighteen children. Some of his findings are pertinent to the development of instructional procedures. He found that children do not use consistent patterns of thinking in different problem situations, and that the confidence of the child in his ability to solve problems is an important factor in his success. Also instruction in science, which includes drawing of concepts in a tangible form by the learner, was not significantly related to growth in the ability of the learner to use these concepts in problem-solving situations. A particularly significant finding relating to the evaluation of an instructional sequence was that pencil and paper tests did not provide an adequate means for evaluating problem-solving processes in individual children.

Schippers (103) designed materials and a procedure to teach sixth graders a problem-solving instructional method using a multi-reference activity base. Three steps in the instructional process were identified: first, establish the background situation; second, understand the problem; and third, work out a solution. Supervision and the use of illustrative lessons were found important if inexperienced teachers were to use the method effectively. Evaluation of student outcomes was largely subjective.

Creativity

Only two studies were identified which made an attempt to develop materials and procedures for encouraging creativity and creative thinking in students.

DeRoche (37) used creative exercises with sixth-grade pupils to see if these produced any gains in creative thinking and achievement not seen in classes doing more traditional work. The experimental group had creative exercises in 26 space science lessons and four "brain-storming" sessions, while control classes either had 30 space science lessons without the exercises or no space science instruction at all. The *Minnesota Tests of Creative Thinking* and specially prepared content achievement tests were used to evaluate outcomes. For high intelligence students, the experimental method was significantly superior to the control in developing creative factors like verbal fluency, flexibility, originality, and elaboration. This trend was less marked for average and low ability students. No significant differences on the achievement tests were found between the "creative" group and the "traditional" group taught space science.

Tating (121) studied ways of developing creative thinking in elementary school science. Creative thinking was defined operationally as divergent and original thinking measured in terms of questions asked and hypotheses given. More divergent responses were obtained with the trained groups than with the control, but the number of divergent responses decreased if pupils were given instructions to be original. Tating "primed" creative thinking by getting pupils to write down as many questions as they could about a particular demonstration, which, if given a "yes-no" answer by the teacher, would help the child understand why a given event occurred. Another method of priming used to get students to write down a number of words in response to a given word.

Although the asking of questions could be primed, the development of hypotheses was not as responsive to training. The formulation of hypotheses in science is a highly complicated mental process, and the formation of an original hypothesis probably requires more time than is needed to think of questions.

The evidence is mounting that creative exercises can be designed to increase creative responses in children without any losses in content achievement. Teachers are constantly being urged to teach science creatively, and more research needs to be done to estimate the effectiveness of various forms of instruction.

Concept Development

Many of the studies in this area were concerned with concept development as part of research into learning theory, rather than evaluating different instructional procedures for their efficiency in developing concepts.

Voelker (123) gives an example of pertinent research on the developments of concepts within the field of science education. He compared two instructional methods for teaching the concepts of physical and chemical change in grades 2–6. Using essentially similar lesson procedures and materials in both cases, he found that formulation and statement by the teacher of the generalization to be learned was not superior to a procedure in which the pupil individually formulated the generalization concerning physical and chemical change. An interesting sidelight of the study was that although sixth-grade pupils were significantly better verbalizers of the concepts, if the criterion of understanding was simply to classify observed phenomena, no significant differences could be detected among grades 2–6. In this study, where teaching method and materials were carefully controlled, there did not seem to be any significant advantages of an "inductive-discovery" approach over a "deductive" one on the outcomes selected. Unfortunately, the concept of physical and chemical change appeared rather difficult except for pupils in grade 6.

Salstrom (100) compared concepts learned by sixth-grade pupils in two types of guided discovery lessons. The same experimental lessons were presented as a science game to each of his groups. Following this, one group had an oral inquiry session while the other received a battery of cards which on one side had printed questions a pupil might ask in an inquiry session and on the other, the answers to those questions were printed. In the card group, each pupil could draw only cards that would yield information needed to solve the problem. They were then ordered by the pupil to give a solution to the problem posed in the lesson. The card treatment group showed greater gains in concept development than the oral inquiry group, supporting the contention that the more guidance that can be given each pupil in an oral inquiry session helps concept development.

Three studies were directed at finding the relationship between the child's level of maturity and the understanding of a particular concept. Carey (21) investigated the particle nature of matter in grades 2–5, Haddad (56) investigated the concept of relativity in grades 4–8, and Helgeson (62) investigated the concept of force. Maturity studies like these are extremely useful in helping course developers decide the level to which a particular concept may be unfolded with pupils at a particular stage in development. The studies suggested that there was almost as much variation in maturity within a grade level as there was between grade levels. These data question the grouping of children by grades if the aim is to provide a group of children at the same stage of mental development.

Kolb (66) investigated integrating mathematics and science instruction with fifth-grade pupils to determine if such integration would facilitate the acquisition of quantitative science behaviors. He used *Science—A Process Approach* materials and found that such integration with mathematics did significantly increase achievement. Integration seems a promising way to reduce the time spent in developing concepts which have elements common to both mathematics and science, and this aspect should be pursued further.

Ziegler (132) investigated the use of mechanical models in teaching theoretical concepts regarding the particle nature of matter to pupils in grades 2–6. They found that children who had not previously learned to use such a model could learn to do so with suitable instruction, and those who had some knowledge of such models improved their ability to use them. These concrete experiences with mechanical models helped pupils form theoretical concepts to explain expansion, contraction, change of phase, and mixtures by the time they completed grade 4.

Studies like this and those of Carey (21), Haddad (56), Voelker (123), and Helgeson (62) should be extended into other concept areas so that a more complete picture of the concepts which may be developed at any given level may emerge. From this, suitable instructional procedures using mechanical models and other devices can be developed. Until this is done, courses of instruction in elementary schools will be based on subjective opinion and feeling about what can be accomplished at any given grade level or stage of development, rather than on a soundly researched experimental base.

Summary and Conclusions

Reviewing the available research into the outcomes of instruction in elementary science has revealed a number of areas where little in the way of a planned attack on the problems has been initiated. Such areas include the development of psychomotor skills, critical thinking skills, creativity, and work in the affective domain on the development of attitudes toward science and scientists. Only in the field of understanding concepts can one see steady progress being made.

The tentative nature of the findings of much educational research and the massive qualifications which surround any generalizations made by researchers often appear confusing to the classroom teacher. In light of this, the reviewers have decided to outline a number of tentative conclusions which seem to emerge from the research reviewed.

1. **Instructional procedures, whether in the classroom or in the research situation, should be based on some clearly defined model of what constitutes the instructional process.** The major criteria for such a model should be that it is useful in helping understand the components of instruction and that the instruction develops desired behavior changes in pupils.

2. **For teachers skilled in handling them, problem-solving or inductive methods or instructional procedures designed to improve creativity can bring about gains in outcome areas which are greater than if more traditional approaches are used.** This is not achieved at the expense of knowledge of content.

3. **Audiovisual aids and reading materials should be carefully integrated into the instructional sequence for a definite instructional purpose, otherwise little effect on achievement outcomes will be noted.**

4. **Pupil activity and pupil performed experiments are important prerequisites for the effective learning of science concepts.** This seems true for all levels of ability.

5. **Instructional procedures can be devised to bring about specific outcomes, provided these outcomes are clearly defined. Both problem-solving skills and creativity can be developed.**

6. **Individualized instruction is a satisfactory alternative to total class instruction.** Even very young children can work alone on preplanned experiences using quite sophisticated aids with minimal teacher help.

7. **Elementary children can learn by using programed-instruction materials.** Outcomes from these are enhanced if they are integrated with laboratory experiences.

8. **Each child should have the opportunity to develop science concepts and process skills in both individual and group situations.** The out-

comes of one kind of instruction will complement rather than parallel the other.

9. **Verbalization of a concept is the last step in a child's understanding of it.** He can demonstrate aspects of his understanding in concrete situations long before he can verbalize them.
10. **Any given class in elementary school is likely to contain children who are in at least two stages of cognitive development—that of concrete operations and formal thought.** These two groups require quite different instructional strategies.
11. **Ability grouping has little effect on the achievement of high ability students.** Other student characteristics are just as significant as intelligence in the learning process.
12. **Educationally disadvantaged students can communicate their understanding of science concepts if the response mode is by a means other than language; e.g., pictorial representation.**
13. **Integration of mathematics and science saves time.** Where common concepts are being developed, achievement in both areas seems to be enhanced.
14. **Educationally disadvantaged children need even greater recourse to simple materials and individual experiments if they are to develop the desired science concepts to the level of other children.**
15. **Teachers should decide on instructional procedures which suit their own personal characteristics and philosophy.** Modification of firmly established patterns of teaching can only occur if there is a corresponding modification of personal characteristics and behaviors.

References

1. Ainslie, D. S. "Simple Equipment and Procedures in Elementary Laboratories." *The Physics Teacher*. September 1967.
2. Allen, Leslie Robert. "An Examination of the Classificatory Ability of Children Who Have Been Exposed to One of the 'New' Elementary Science Programs." (M)[4]. 1967.
3. Allison, Roy W. "The Effect of Three Methods of Treating Motivational Films Upon the Attitudes of Fourth-, Fifth-, and Sixth-Grade Students Toward Science, Scientists, and Scientific Careers." Pennsylvania State University, 1967.
4. Anderson, Ronald D. "Children's Ability To Formulate Mental Models to Explain Natural Phenomena." *Journal of Research in Science Teaching*. December 1965.
5. Anklam, Phoebe Anne. "A Study of the Relationship between Two Divergent Instructional Methods and Achievement Motivation of Elementary School Children." (M). 1962.
6. Barker, D. "Primary School Science—An Attempt to Investigate the Effects of the Informal Use of a Discovery Table on the Scientific Knowl-

[4] (M) denotes University Microfilms, Ann Arbor, Michigan.

edge of Primary School Children." *Educational Research.* February 1965.

7. Barrett, Raymond E. "Field Trip Tips." *Science and Children.* October 1965.

8. Baum, Ernest A. "Report of the Individualization of the Teaching of Selected Science Skills and Knowledges in an Elementary School Class-room with Materials Prepared by the Teacher." (M). 1965.

9. Becker, Leonard John. "An Analysis of the Science and Mathematics Achievement of Gifted Sixth-Grade Children Enrolled in Segregated Classes." (M). 1963.

10. Bennett, Lloyd M. "A Study of the Comparison of Two Instructional Methods, the Experimental-Field Method and the Traditional Classroom Method, Involving Science Content in Ecology for the Seventh Grade." *Science Education.* December 1965.

11. Bennett, Lloyd M., and Cherie Clodfelter. "A Study of the Integration of an Earth Science Unit Within the Reading Program of a Second Grade by Utilizing the Word Analysis Approach." *School Science and Mathematics.* November 1966.

12. Bickel, Robert F. "A Study of the Effect of Television Instruction on the Science Achievement and Attitudes of Children in Grades 4, 5, and 6." (M). 1964.

13. Blackwood, Paul E. "Science Teaching in the Elementary School: A Survey of Practices." *Journal of Research in Science Teaching.* September 1965.

14. Blank, Stanley Solomon. "Inquiry Training Through Programed Instruction." (M). 1963.

15. Bornhorst, Ben A., and Prentiss M. Hosford. "Basing Instruction in Science on Children's Questions: Using a Wonder Box in the Third Grade." *Science Education.* March 1960.

16. Brudzynski, Alfred John. "A Comparative Study of Two Methods for Teaching Electricity and Magetism with Fifth- and Sixth-Grade Children." (M). 1966.

17. Brusini, Joseph Anthony. "An Experimental Study of the Development of Science Continua Concepts in Upper Elementary and Junior High School Children." (M). 1966.

18. Buell, Robert R. "Inquiry Training in the School's Science Laboratories." *School Science and Mathematics.* April 1965.

19. Butts, David P. "The Degree to Which Children Conceptualize from Science Experiences," *Journal of Research in Science Teaching.* June 1962.

20. Butts, David P. "The Relationship Between Classroom Experiences and Certain Student Characteristics." University of Texas, February 1967.

21. Carey, Russell LeRoy. "Relationship Between Levels of Maturity and Levels of Understanding of Selected Concepts of the Particle Nature of Matter." (M). 1967.

22. Carlson, Jerry S. "Effects of Instruction on the Concepts of Conservation of Substance." *Science Education.* March 1967.

23. Carpenter, Finley. "Toward a Systematic Construction of a Classroom Taxonomy." *Science Education.* April 1965.

24. Carpenter, Regan. "A Reading Method and an Activity Method in Elementary Science Instruction." *Science Education.* April 1963.

25. Carter, Neal. "Science Experience Center." *Science and Children*. February 1967.
26. Caruthers, Bertram, Sr. "Teacher Preparation and Experience Related to Achievement of Fifth-Grade Pupils in Science." (M). 1967.
27. Chinnis, Robert Jennings. "The Development of Physical Science Principles in Elementary-School Science Textbooks." (M). 1962.
28. Cobun, Ted Charles. "The Relative Effectiveness of Three Levels of Pictorial Presentation of Biological Subject Matter on the Associative Learning of Nomenclature by Sixth-Grade Students." (M). 1961.
29. Cox, Louis T. "Working with Science in the Kindergarten." *Science Education*. March 1963.
30. Crabtree, J. F. "A Study of the Relationships Between 'Score,' 'Time,' 'IQ,' and 'Reading Level' for Fourth-Grade Students Using Programed Science Materials." *Science Education*. April 1967.
31. Crabtree, Charlotte Antoinette. "Effects of Structuring on Productiveness in Children's Thinking: Study of Second-Grade Dramatic Play Patterns Centered on Harbor and Airport Activities Under Two Types of Teacher Structuring." (M). 1962.
32. Cunningham, Roger. "Implementing Nongraded Advancement with Laboratory Activities as a Vehicle—An Experiment in Elementary School Science." *School Science and Mathematics*. February 1967.
33. Cunningham, John D. "On Curiosity and Science Education." *School Science and Mathematics*. December 1966.
34. Dart, Francis E., and Panna Lal Pradham. "Cross-Cultural Teaching of Science." *Science*. February 1967.
35. Davis, Joseph E., Jr. "Ice Calorimetry in the Upper Elementary Grades." *Science and Children*. December 1966.
36. Decker, Martin George. "The Differential Effects Upon the Learning of the Natural Sciences by Fifth Graders of Two Modes of Teaching over Television and in the Classroom." (M). 1965.
37. DeRoche, Edward Francis. "A Study of the Effectiveness of Selected Creative Exercises on Creative Thinking and the Mastery of a Unit in Elementary Science." (M). 1966.
38. Dietmeier, Homer J. "The Effect of Integration of Science Teaching by Television on the Development of Scientific Reasoning in the Fifth-Grade Student." (M). 1962.
39. Downing, Carl Edward. "A Statistical Examination of the Relationship Among Elementary Science Achievement Gains, Interest Level Changes, and Time Allotment for Instructional Purposes." (M). 1963.
40. Drenchko, Elizabeth K. "The Comparative Effectiveness of Two Methods of Teaching Grade School Science." (M). 1966.
41. Dutton, Sherman S. "An Experimental Study in the Programming of Science Instruction for the Fourth Grade." (M). 1963.
42. Dyrli, Odvard Egil. "An Investigation into the Development of Combinational Mechanisms Characteristic of Formal Reasoning, Through Experimental Problem Situations with Sixth-Grade Students." (M). 1967.
43. Eccles, Priscilla J. "Research Reports—Teacher Behavior and Knowledge of Subject Matter in Sixth-Grade Science." *Journal of Research in Science Teaching*. December 1965.
44. Elashhab, Gamal A. "A Model for the Development of Science Curricula

in the Preparatory and Secondary Schools of the United Arab Republic."
(M). 1966.

45. Engelmann, Siegfried, and James J. Gallagher. "A Study of How a Child Learns Concepts About Characteristics of Liquid Materials." EDRS, National Cash Register Company, 1966.

46. Fischler, Abraham S. "Science, Process, The Learner—A Synthesis." *Science Education*. December 1965.

47. Fish, Alphoretta S., and Bernice Goldmark. "Inquiry Method—Three Interpretations." *The Science Teacher*. February 1966.

48. Fryback, William H. "Evaluation of Multi-Level Reading Materials, Intra-Class Discussion Techniques and Student Experimentations on Achievement in Fifth-Grade Elementary Science." (M). 1965.

49. Garone, John Edward. "Acquiring Knowledge and Attaining Understanding of Children's Scientific Concept Development." *Science Education*. March 1960.

50. Gehrman, Joseph Leo. "A Study of the Impact of Authoritative Communication of Expected Achievement in Elementary School Science." (M). 1965.

51. Gerne, Timothy A., Jr. "A Comparative Study of Two Types of Science Teaching on the Competence of Sixth-Grade Students to Understand Selected Topics in Electricity and Magnetism." (M). 1967.

52. Glaser, Robert. "Concept Learning and Concept Teaching." Unversity of Pittsburgh, Learning Research and Development Center. 1967.

53. Glaser, Robert. "The Design of Instruction." National Society for the Study of Education Yearbook, 1966.

54. Gleason, Walter Patterson. "An Examination of Some Effects of Pupil Self-Instruction Methods Compared with the Effects of Teacher-Led Classes in Elementary Science of Fifth-Grade Pupils." (M). 1965.

55. Gunnels, Frances Goodrich. "A Study of the Development in Logical Judgments in Science of Successful and Unsuccessful Problem Solvers in Grades Four Through Nine." (M). 1967.

56. Haddad. Wadi Dahir. "Relationship Between Mental Maturity and the Level of Understanding of Concepts of Relativity in Grades 4–8." (M). 1968.

57. Harris, William, and Verlin Lee. "Mental Age and Science Concepts—A Pilot Study." *Journal of Research in Science Teaching*. December 1966.

58. Harris, William. "A Technique for Grade Placement in Elementary Science." *Journal of Research in Science Teaching*. March 1964.

59. Harris, William Ned. "An Analysis of Problem-Solving Behavior in Sixth-Grade Children, and of the Usefulness of Drawings by the Pupil in Learning Science Concepts." (M). 1962.

60. Haugerud, Albert Ralph. "The Development of a Conceptual Framework for the Construction of a Multi-Media Laboratory and Its Utilization for Elementary School Science." (M). 1966.

61. Hedges, William D., and Mary Ann MacDougall. "Teaching Fourth-Grade Science by Means of Programed Science Materials with Laboratory Experiences." *Science Education*. February 1964.

62. Helgeson, Stanley Leon. "An Investigation into the Relationships Between Concepts of Force Attained and Maturity as Indicated by Grade Levels." (M). 1967.

63. Hinmon, Dean F.. "Problem Solving." *Science and Children*. April 1966.

64. Johnson, Mervin LeRoy. "A Determination of Aerospace Principles Desirable for Inclusion in Fifth- or Sixth-Grade Science Programs." (M). 1966.

65. Karplus, Robert. "Science Curriculum Improvement Study." *Journal of Research in Science Teaching.* December 1964.

66. Kolb, John R. "Effects of Relating Mathematics to Science Instruction on the Acquisition of Quantitative Science Behaviors." *Journal of Research in Science Teaching.* 1968.

67. Korey, Ruth Anne. "Contributions of Planetariums to Elementary Education." (M). 1963.

68. Kraft, Mary Elizabeth. "A Study of Information and Vocabulary Achievement from the Teaching of Natural Science by Television in the Fifth Grade." (M). 1961.

69. LaCava, George. "An Experiment via Tape." *Science and Children.* October 1965.

70. Languis, Marlin, and Loren L. Stull. "Science Problems—Vehicles To Develop Measurement Principles." *Science Education.* February 1966.

71. Lansdown, Brenda, and Thomas S. Dietz. "Free Versus Guided Experimentation." *Science Education.* April 1965.

72. Lindvall, C. Mauritz, and John D. Bolvin. "Individually Prescribed Instruction—The Oakleaf Project." University of Pittsburgh, Learning Research and Development Center, February 1966.

73. Lipson, Joseph I. "Light Test—Comparison Between Elementary School Children and College Freshman." University of Pittsburgh, Learning Research and Development Center. February 1966.

74. Lipson, Joseph I. "An Individualized Science Laboratory." *Science and Children.* December 1966.

75. Livermore, Arthur H. "The Process Approach of the AAAS Commission on Science Education." *Journal of Research in Science Teaching.* December 1964.

76. Lowery, Lawrence F. "An Experimental Investigation into the Attitudes of Fifth-Grade Students Toward Science." *School Science and Mathematics.* June 1967.

77. Los Angeles City Schools. "The Art of Questioning in Science—Summary and Implications." Los Angeles City Schools. 1967.

78. Mason, John M. "The Direct Teaching of Critical Thinking in Grades Four Through Six." *Journal of Research in Science Teaching.* December 1963.

79. McCloskey, James. "The Development of the Role of Science in General Education for Elementary and Secondary Schools." (M). 1963.

80. McKeon, Joseph E. "A Process Lesson in Density." *Science and Children.* December 1966.

81. Melis, Lloyd Henry. "The Nature and Extent of Reading Instruction in Science and Social Studies in the Intermediate Grades of Selected School Districts." (M). 1964.

82. Mermelstein, Egon; Edwina Carr; Dorothy Mills; and Jeanne Schwartz. "The Effects of Various Training Techniques on the Acquisition of the Concept of Conservation of Substance." U.S. Department of Health, Education, and Welfare, February 1967.

83. Moorehead, William D. "The Status of Elementary School Science and How It Is Taught." (M). 1965.
84. Nasca, Donald. "Effect of Varied Presentations of Laboratory Exercises Within Programed Materials on Specific Intellectual Factors of Science Problem-Solving Behavior." *Science Education.* December 1966.
85. Neal, Louise A. "Techniques for Developing Methods of Scientific Inquiry in Children in Grades One Through Six." *Science Education.* October 1961.
86. New York State Department of Education. "Tips and Techniques in Elementary Science." Bureau of Elementary Curriculum Development. 1966.
87. Novak, Joseph D. "Development and Use of Audio-Tape Programed Instruction for Elementary Science." Purdue University, February 1967.
88. O'Toole, Raymond J. "A Review of Attempts to Individualize Elementary School Science." *School Science and Mathematics.* May 1968.
89. O'Toole, Raymond J. "A Study to Determine Whether Fifth-Grade Children Can Learn Certain Selected Problem-Solving Abilities Through Individualized Instruction (Research Study Number 1)." (M). 1966.
90. Perkins, William D. "The Field Study as a Technique in Elementary School Science." *Science Education.* December 1963.
91. Pershern, Frank Richard. "The Effects of Industrial Arts Activities on Science Achievements and Pupil Attitudes in the Upper Elementary Grades." (M). 1967.
92. Pollach, Samuel. "Individual Differences in the Development of Certain Science Concepts." (M). 1963.
93. Price, LaMar. "An Investigation of the Transfer of an Elementary Science Process." (M). 1968.
94. Ramsey, Irvin L., and Sandra Lee Wiandt. "Individualizing Elementary School Science." *School Science and Mathematics.* May 1967.
95. Raun, Chester Eugene. "The Interaction Between Curriculum Variables and Selected Classroom Student Characteristics." (M). 1967.
96. Reese, Willard Francis. "A Comparison of Interest Level and Problem-Solving Accuracy Generated by Single Concept Inductive and Deductive Science Films (Research Study Number 1)." (M). 1966.
97. Riessman, Frank. "Education of the Culturally Deprived Child." *The Science Teacher.* November 1965.
98. Rowland, George William. "A Study of the Relationship Between Socio-Economic Status and Elementary School Science Achievement." (M). 1965.
99. St. John, Clinton. "Can Science Education Be Scientific? Notes Toward a Viable Theory of Science Teaching." *Journal of Research in Science Teaching.* December, 1966.
100. Salstrom, David. "A Comparison of Conceptualization in Two Types of Guided Discovery Science Lesson." (M). 1966.
101. Sands, Theodore; Robert E. Rumery; and Richard C. Youngs. "Concept Development Materials for Gifted Elementary Pupils—Final Report of Field Testing." Illinois State University. 1966.
102. Schiller, LeRoy. "A Study of the Effect of Individualized Activities on Understanding in Elementary School Science." (M). 1964.

103. Schippers, John Vernon. "An Investigation of the Problem Method of Instruction in Sixth-Grade Science Classes." (M). 1962.
104. Shulz, Richard William. "The Role of Cognitive Organizers in the Facilitation of Concept Learning in Elementary School Science." (M). 1966.
105. Scott, Lloyd. "An Experiment in Teaching Basic Science in the Elementary School." *Science Education*. March 1962.
106. Scott, Norval C., Jr., and I. E. Sigel. "Effects of Inquiry Training in Physical Science on Creativity and Cognitive Styles of Elementary School Children." U.S. Office of Education, Cooperative Research Branch, 1965.
107. Scott, Norval C., Jr. "Science Concept Achievement and Cognitive Functions." *Journal of Research in Science Teaching*. December 1964.
108. Scott, Norval C., Jr. "The Strategy of Inquiry and Styles of Categorization." *Journal of Research in Science Teaching*. September 1966.
109. Skinner, Ray, Jr. "An Experimental Study of the Effects of Different Combinations of Television Presentations and Classroom Teacher Follow-up on the Achievement and Interest in Science of Fifth Graders." (M). 1966.
110. Smith, Billy Arthur. "An Experimental Comparison of Two Techniques (Planetarium Lecture-Demonstration and Classroom Lecture-Demonstration) of Teaching Selected Astronomical Concepts to Sixth-Grade Students." (M). 1966.
111. Smith, Doyne M., and Bernice Cooper. "A Study of the Use of Various Techniques in Teaching Science in the Elementary School." *School Science and Mathematics*. June 1967.
112. Smith, Robert Frank. "An Analysis and Classification of Children's Explanations of Natural Phenomena." (M). 1963.
113. Snoble, Joseph Jerry. "Status and Trends of Elementary School Science in Iowa Public Schools, 1963-1966." (M). 1967.
114. Stapp, William Beebe. "Developing a Conservation Education Program for the Ann Arbor Public School System, and Integrating It into the Existing Curriculum (K-12)." (M). 1963.
115. Stauss, Nyles George. "An Investigation into the Relationship Between Concept Attainment and Level of Maturity." (M). 1967.
116. Stokes, William Woods. "An Analysis and Evaluation of Current Efforts to Improve the Curriculum by Emphasis on Disciplinary Structure and Learning by Discovery." (M). 1963.
117. Stone, Ruth Muriel. "A Comparison of the Patterns of Criteria Which Elementary and Secondary School Teachers Use in Judging the Relative Effectiveness of Selected Learning Experiences in Elementary Science." (M). 1963.
118. Suchman, J. Richard. "Idea Book—Inquiry Development Program in Physical Science." Science Research Associates, Inc., Chicago. 1966.
119. Suchman, J. Richard. "Inquiry Training: Building Skills for Autonomous Discovery." *Merril-Palmer Quarterly*. 1961.
120. Swan, Malcolm D. "Science Achievement as It Relates to Science Curricula and Programs at the Sixth-Grade Level in Montana Public Schools." *Journal of Research in Science Teaching*. June 1966.
121. Tating, Marcela Tionko. "Priming Creative Thinking in Elementary School Science." (M). 1965.

122. Taylor, Alton L. "The Influence of Teacher Attitudes on Pupil Achievement with Programed Science Materials." *Journal of Research in Science Teaching.* March 1960.

123. Voelker, Alan Morris. "The Relative Effectiveness of Two Methods of Instruction in Teaching the Classification Concepts of Physical and Chemical Change to Elementary School Children." (M). 1967.

124. Wagner, Bartlett Adam. "The Responses of Economically Advantaged and Economically Disadvantaged Sixth-Grade Pupils to Science Demonstrations." (M). 1967.

125. Walbesser, Henry H. "Science Curriculum Evaluation—Observations on a Position." *The Science Teacher.* February 1966.

126. Walbesser, Henry H., et al. "Science—A Process Approach, An Evaluation Model and Its Application—Second Report." American Association for the Advancement of Science, AAAS Miscellaneous Publication 6814. 1968.

127. Washton, Nathan S. "Teaching Science for Creativity." *Science Education.* February 1966.

128. Williams, David Lee. "The Effect of Rewritten Science Textbook Materials on the Reading Ability of Sixth-Grade Pupils." (M). 1964.

129. Wilson, John Harold. "Differences Between the Inquiry-Discovery and the Traditional Approaches to Teaching Science in Elementary Schools." (M). 1967.

130. Wolinsky, Gloria F. "Science Education and the Severely Handicapped Child." *Science Education.* October 1965.

131. Zafforoni, Joseph. "A Study of Pupil-Teacher Interaction in Planning Science Experiences." *Science Education.* March 1963.

132. Ziegler, Robert Edward. "The Relative Effectiveness of the Use of Static and Dynamic Mechanical Models in Teaching Elementary School Children the Theoretical Concept—The Particle Nature of Matter." (M). 1967.

The Evaluation of Elementary Science

INTRODUCTION

If the elementary science program is to be effective, the program should be evaluated continuously. Definite and adequate provision should be made to ensure that the evaluation is dynamic and continuous rather than perfunctory and sporadic. All those who participate in the science program should be involved in the evaluation, and not just a small committee of teachers specifically appointed for that purpose. This is especially important when the elementary science program is part of a total K–12 program. Then the program should be evaluated by the elementary and secondary school teachers, by the science supervisor or consultant, and by the curriculum director, because all these persons are responsible for determining the content of the program.

If there is a curriculum guide, it too should be evaluated continuously. Teachers should be encouraged to evaluate the contents of the guide critically as they use it, and to forward criticisms and recommendations to the persons or committee responsible for conducting the evaluation and revision of the guide. The science content of the guide should be examined carefully for corrections, additions, or deletions. The sequence of topics in the guide should be checked for appropriate placement. Initiating activities should be evaluated for motivating and problem-raising potential. Learning activities should be tested critically to see if they are producing maximum learning, and should be replaced by newer, more creative activities as they appear in text and reference books. Even the evaluation techniques themselves should be scrutinized regularly.

In the classroom good teaching and learning call for continuous evaluation by both the teacher and the children. The teacher should constantly evaluate the content being learned, and also the methods and materials being used, to see if the children are achieving the objectives of the science program. The children should be encouraged to evaluate continually their strengths and weaknesses, their progress and growth in science learning, and their proficiency with the key operations, or processes, of science and the scientist.

Evaluation in the classroom can be used for a variety of purposes. First, it can be used to appraise achievement, by determining how well the children have learned science concepts and how competent they have become in performing the operations of the scientist. Second, it can be used for diagnostic purposes. As such, it can help identify the children's strengths and weaknesses. It can determine how well the children can work individually and in groups. It can be used as a pretest to learn how much the children already know about a topic before they begin the study of this topic. It can be used to diagnose the effectiveness of the teaching methods being used. Sometimes one method is more effective than another for different groups of children. Third, evaluation can be used for predictive purposes, where the teacher attempts to predict the children's behavior and achievement in the future or under different conditions.

There are a variety of methods of evaluation which the elementary school teacher can use. These methods are grouped into three categories: oral methods, written methods, and observation methods. Teachers may vary in their preference, but there is no one single best method of evaluating science learning. Actually, the objectives to be evaluated are more important than the method used, and very often the desired objectives or outcomes of learning will help determine which method should be selected. Also, the teacher should keep in mind that good test questions can be difficult and time-consuming to prepare, so tests should be constructed with much thought and care.

The Evaluation of the Elementary Science Program [*]

NATIONAL SOCIETY for the STUDY of EDUCATION

A total elementary science program must be evaluated by all who participate in the program. Such evaluation must include children, teachers, supervisors or consultants, and administrators. Evaluation should be planned and should be a constant process. It can take place only after the characteristics of a good program are established. The following article presents eight such characteristics and the criteria for their evaluation. This article is an excerpt from Chapter 7, "Developing Science Programs in the Elementary School," of the Fifty-ninth NSSE Yearbook, Part I, Rethinking Science Education. Members of the committee who wrote this chapter include Glenn O. Blough, Paul E. Blackwood, Katherine E. Hill, and Julius Schwartz.

A program in elementary science can be effectively evaluated only when the objectives of a program are clear and have been accepted by the teachers and administrators in charge of the program. Too often the goals of a program are listed by a committee, printed at the beginning of a course of study, and then forgotten. Once goals have been accepted, they should be used as a basis for the selection of subject matter and the methods of teaching. If this is done, the adequacy of the program may be evaluated, at least in terms of its goals. Such appraisal may lead to redefinition of purposes and the establishment of new goals, which in turn may reasonably be expected to lead to experimenting with different teaching methods and subject matter. This is a process by which educational programs can be improved continuously.

Many curriculum guides and resource units include suggestions for evaluation. Some of the manuals for the development of courses of study that have been produced by state departments of education contain excellent suggestions for evaluation. However, few systematic attempts at evaluation of elementary-science programs have been reported.

WHO EVALUATES? If the evaluation of a total program in elementary science is sought, then all who participate in the program should be involved in the evaluation of it. Too often segments of the program have been evaluated in discrete units only by those most closely connected

*REPRINTED FROM *Rethinking Science Education*, Fifty-ninth Yearbook of the National Society for the Study of Education, Part I (Chicago: University of Chicago Press, 1960), pp. 129–135, by permission of the publisher.

with the particular parts examined. For example, fifth-grade teachers in a school system have regularly evaluated the science taught in the fifth grades only. At times, the evaluation has been limited to the appraisal of the elementary-school program in science by the elementary-school faculty. This is too limited a group to evaluate elementary science as an integral part of a science program extending from the Kindergarten through Grade XII. A total science program must be assessed by elementary- and secondary-school teachers, by consultants in elementary science if they operate in the system, and by those administrators who are responsible for the development of curriculum. These are the persons primarily responsible for the selection of methods and content. All must be involved in the evaluation of the acceptability of the elementary-science program.

But the learner must not be forgotten. He must have a part in the evaluative process. Involving elementary-school children in assessing the *program* in science is a different undertaking, since their appraisal is apt to be related only to their most recent science experiences. Even so, the judgment of children may lead to reappraisal of a program. Older children, especially those in the upper-elementary grades and in the secondary school, may be used in helping the teaching and curriculum staffs find strong and weak features of the elementary-science program.

A third group sometimes involved in judging the merits of a program in elementary science is composed of parents and other members of the community. Often, they make judgments of the value of various aspects of the science program. At times, their judgments result in pressure being applied to influence school programs. The evaluation by members of the community may contribute to the over-all evaluation of the elementary science program.

The teacher and adminstrator have the responsibility of weighing and coordinating the various evaluations of the elementary-science program. Children, teachers, and other members of the community all express their views about the program. To make a difference, however, evaluations must affect the program. To use evaluations to modify and improve programs is a task for the administrators, who are responsible for the development of programs of elementary science.

WHEN AND HOW SHOULD EVALUATION TAKE PLACE? If a program in elementary science is to be dynamic, if it is to make a difference in the lives of children, then that program must undergo careful and constant scrutiny. But, planning for the evaluative process must also be an integral part of the program in elementary science. This process must not be left to chance, to be considered in a cursory manner every few years by a committee of teachers. Ongoing and thorough examination of a science program should be considered part of the educator's responsibility, and there should be adequate provision for meeting this responsibility.

A description of the procedure for involving responsible personnel in evaluating the program follows: In one local school a group of three teachers, one who taught five-, six-, and seven-year-olds, one who taught eight- and nine-year-olds, and one who taught ten- and eleven-year-olds were the nucleus of a committee for the evaluation of the science program in each elementary school. These three teachers had the responsibility for gathering information from their co-workers each eight weeks. Such information was gathered verbally or in writing and included responses to the following questions: What content, methods, or materials have you used or would you like to use? Have you evidence that your present group of children is making use of previous experiences? Have you evidence that your children are strengthening their insights and expanding their interests in science? If so, what is making this possible? What improvements would you like to see made in our total school program in science?

Such information is invaluable in appraising a school's science program and as a basis for its improvement. With such information, committees of teachers and administrators can plan a series of meetings with the total teaching staff. Such meetings can lead to continuing improvement of the science program in the elementary school.

For such important curriculum work, leadership is needed to organize the evaluation and to find means to insure that the outcomes of the evaluative process are reflected in the developing program. Adequate periods of time must be planned for evaluation, and administrative and secretarial assistance should be provided to facilitate the work of the committees. The machinery must be set up so that representatives of various groups of teachers and administrators can work together on evaluation.

SOME CHARACTERISTICS OF A GOOD ELEMENTARY-SCIENCE PROGRAM. Each teacher, each elementary school, and each school system is responsible for determining the goals toward which science teaching and learning are directed. It follows that each teacher, school, and school system must be intimately involved in judging the appropriateness of the goals and the methods and materials employed in reaching those goals. Science programs will vary from community to community and certainly will change with the passage of time. It seems appropriate, however, to present the following characteristics of a good elementary science program, together with the criteria for evaluation in the hope that they will be of specific aid to educators in judging their programs.

CHARACTERISTICS OF A GOOD ELEMENTARY-SCIENCE PROGRAM	CRITERIA FOR EVALUATING AN ELEMENTARY-SCIENCE PROGRAM
Elementary science should be recognized as an important part of the total elementary-school curriculum. Science experiences should be a part	Is sufficient time for science provided in the program? (Some educators are suggesting that one-fifth of the elementary program be devoted to sci-

CHARACTERISTICS OF A GOOD ELEMENTARY-SCIENCE PROGRAM	CRITERIA FOR EVALUATING AN ELEMENTARY-SCIENCE PROGRAM

of the total school experiences at each grade level. Elementary-school science should be an integral part of a K–12 science program.

ence, one-fifth to social studies, one-fifth to language arts, one-fifth to expressive and graphic arts, and one-fifth to the development of skills related to learning.)

Has a curriculum in elementary science been developed for your school?

Do the science experiences at each grade level build upon experiences in previous grades and lead to experiences in subsequent grades? Is an administrator responsible for assisting teachers in developing the science program from the Kindergarten through Grade XII? Are parents regularly informed of the achievement of their child in science?

A program in elementary science should be provided for *all* children.

Do the teachers and administrators view science as important in the life of each child?

Realizing that all citizens must be aware of and understand the importance of science in a democracy, is a science program provided for all children?

Is opportunity provided to extend the horizons of those children who are especially fascinated with science?

The development of scientific attitudes is basic in a good elementary science program.

Do teachers provide time for the exploration of ideas verbally and with materials?

Is there evidence that scientific attitudes are becoming a part of the behavior of children?

An elementary-science program should provide a balanced content in science.

During each one- or two-year period, do children have an opportunity to explore in each of the several large areas of science, such as (a) our earth, its composition, and the changes occurring on it; (b) our earth in space; (c) the living things on the earth, how they grow, change, survive, and die; (d) the physical and

CHARACTERISTICS OF A GOOD ELEMENTARY-SCIENCE PROGRAM	CRITERIA FOR EVALUATING AN ELEMENTARY-SCIENCE PROGRAM
	chemical forces man uses; (e) man's place in his changing environment?
Children need to have an opportunity to participate in a variety of activities in elementary science.	There is no one best way to develop elementary-science experiences. A good elementary-science program is characterized by a variety of challenging experiences.
	Do children have a chance to participate in experiments, demonstrations, field trips, construction projects, library research, group discussions, and discussions with informed members of the community?
	Is the curriculum flexible enough to provide time for investigating important science questions not provided for in the planned program in elementary science?
Adequate materials are provided to carry on a good elementary-science program.	Are appropriate manipulative materials provided as regular equipment in each classroom?
	Is provision made for exploration of the out-of-the classroom environment?
	Is each classroom provided with a science library of at least two different books per child?
	Is there a selection of science books in the school library?
	Are films, film strips, TV programs, slides, records of bird songs, etc., readily available?
Expert help is available to the classroom teacher, who is the key to a good elementary-science program.	Are professional books and curriculum materials in science provided for teachers?
	Is some one administrator responsible for aiding teachers in the development of a program in elementary science?
	Is a consultant in elementary science available for each group of 18 to 24 classroom teachers in the school system to aid them in their work? Is this

CHARACTERISTICS OF A GOOD ELEMENTARY-SCIENCE PROGRAM	CRITERIA FOR EVALUATING AN ELEMENTARY-SCIENCE PROGRAM
	consultant trained both in working with elementary-school children and in science content?
	Are opportunities available to classroom teachers for in-service education in science?
Ongoing evaluation is a part of a good program in elementary science.	Is provision made for constant and thorough analysis of the elementary-science program?
	Has the program in elementary science been improved substantially during the last two years?

These are some characteristics of good elementary-science programs. Committees of elementary-school teachers and administrators working in cooperation with teachers and administrators from other schools in the school system can use those characteristics to examine and evaluate their programs of elementary science. Such evaluations can lead to the continuing improvement of children's experiences in this important area of the total elementary-school program.

A Suggested Checklist for Assessing a Science Program*

U.S. OFFICE of EDUCATION

This checklist, prepared by Specialists for Science at the U.S. Office of Education, is designed to help identify the strengths and weaknesses of a science program. The checklist can be used at all grade levels, in schools of different sizes, and by teachers of varying degrees of experience. Suggestions are offered on how to provide for broad participation in the evaluation of ten areas of the science program. A chart is provided for making an evaluation profile of these areas, to decide which science program problems are most pressing.

*REPRINTED FROM A *Suggested Checklist for Assessing a Science Program*, U.S. Office of Education, Document OE-29034A, 1964, pp. 1–19.

Many persons in all parts of the country are concerned about the quality of their schools. Taxpayers want to know whether their tax dollars are well spent. Administrators want to know what they can do to strengthen their school programs, and conscientious teachers and supervisors want to know how well they are doing in light of present efforts to improve teaching.

How to go about assessing a school program is a problem, particularly in science where content and methods are changing rapidly—perhaps even more so than in other subjects.

To evaluate a program some kind of yardstick is needed. This publication contains a suggested checklist that can help identify the strong points of a science program as well as those that need to be strengthened. The checklist may be used at all levels, in schools of varying sizes, and by teachers of varying degrees of experience. Therefore, the following suggestions on the use of the list are not all applicable to every situation. Many have come from individual teachers and supervisors and have been found useful by them; and there are, among the suggestions, some which will be of use to any school undertaking an evaluation of its science program.

This service bulletin has been prepared by the U.S. Office of Education at the request of many schools. This fifth revision, which results from extensive field use over the past several years, has been submitted to competent specialists of science, professors of science education, science teachers, and others for comments and editorial suggestions. We wish to thank all who have had a part in making this checklist an improved instrument for the evaluation of a science program.

Broad Participation

The broader the participation of science teachers, supervisors, principals, and superintendents in the science program evaluation, the more satisfactory the results. To initiate it, each science teacher of a given school might fill out a copy of the suggested checklist. Then all the science teachers in each school of the district or system might, as a group (again using the checklist), evaluate their particular school's science program and prepare a composite checklist. Finally, the proper authorities could, in the same way, evaluate the science program of the entire school system. From the evaluations, a profile would emerge of the school system's strengths and weaknesses in science teaching. This profile would be the basis for setting up priorities in a plan to improve the science program.

Recency of Content and Methods

When using a checklist keep in mind the importance of *recency*. For example, a library collection in science cannot be considered up to date if few of the books, especially in rapidly developing science areas, have been published within the past 5 years. Similarly, a teacher's science background should be modern. Unless it has been updated by science refresher courses or independent study during the last few years, it too is out of date.

Teaching methods for science should be as modern as the content itself. It goes almost without saying these days that *how* children and young people learn is as important, really, as *what* they learn. Who would gainsay that they must be equipped to find answers to problems as well as to manipulate verbal and mathematical symbols in the three R's?

Merely to memorize facts is no longer considered sufficient in education. It has become increasingly clear that the apparent validity of a fact cannot be assured for any given length of time. But scientific methods of inquiry into the nature of things will stand the test of time and are as necessary to other areas of learning as they are in science.

In good science programs, pupils do not use the laboratory merely to confirm textbook statements or to follow step-by-step written procedures. Rather, they participate in activities that stimulate scientific creativity in identifying problems, stating hypotheses, designing experiments, and evaluating data from many sources Open-end activities, where the pupil can continue an individual investigation in greater depth, have been designed for both elementary and secondary grades; and reports concerning them have been published. In science many resourceful teachers use pupil-teacher planning to develop their own unique investigative experiments.

A Profile for Determining Priorities

Everything cannot be done at once—outline a science curriculum for junior high school, develop an inservice education program for elementary teachers, plan a program for academically talented senior high school students, provide individual laboratory work in general science, and arrange a science fair. Confronted by all these urgent problems, decide which ones in your own school are most crucial. How to decide?

One help in deciding might well come from making an evaluation profile from the data provided from this checklist of the science program. At the end of this publication is a suggested chart for such a profile which ties in with the immediately preceding suggested checklist. When the profile chart is filled in from the answers appearing on the checklists, it will become apparent which science-program problems are most crucial and pressing. These problems would naturally be given top priority and, as such, could then serve as the starting point to plan improvements in the program.

How to Use the Checklist

The checklist items are merely suggestions. Many of the items are general statements because local school systems vary greatly. A school may want to revise them to fit local needs. In any case, it would want to examine each item—as it now stands or after revision—to make certain that when the entire list is applied to the local program it does in fact draw an accurate profile of that program.

More specific checklists will be required for followup use after this general checklist has been completed by the local schools. Such checklists will be available soon from the U.S. Office of Education for *elementary school science, junior high school science,* and *senior high school sciences* (biology, chemistry, and physics). These will search more intensively and more deeply into items which pertain especially to the levels mentioned above.

The checklist is provided with four answer columns, which may be used as suggested below, or the individual schools can write in their own headings, geared to local requirements.

Check (✔) the column most applicable:

3—There is *much* evidence that the practice exists
2—There is *some* evidence that the practice exists
1—There is *little* evidence that the practice exists

Insert O in column headed "other" if the item *does not exist*
Insert X in column headed "other" if the item *does not apply*

	3	2	1	other
1. (Item)				
2. (Item)				
3. (Item)				
etc.				

An alternate method of using the checklist is to place a check in one of the first three columns that answers the item as in 1, 2, or 3 below.

3—Yes, there is *much* evidence that the practice exists
2—Yes, there is *some* evidence that the practice exists
1—No, there is no evidence that the practice exists

A SUGGESTED CHECKLIST FOR ASSESSING
A SCIENCE PROGRAM[1]

The items marked with an asterisk (*) may be considered as being of major importance or most desirable for a minimum basic science program. If a school wishes to change or add to these basic items, it may do so.

I. Foundations for Local Program Planning	3	2	1	other
*1. Has a local science advisory committee been established?				
*2. Have such representatives of the local community as scientists, engineers, school and lay personnel been involved—to the extent of action—on the local advisory committee?				
3. Has a survey or a listing been made of local science-related resources available for improving science teaching?				
4. Have resources of local business and industry been utilized, e.g., field trips, classroom presentations, and science materials?				
5. Are scientists from the local area *regularly* invited to participate in the school's science program?				
6. Are scientists and science educators from nearby colleges and universities invited to serve as consultants and speakers for the school's science program?				
*7. Are measurements made of factors such as changes in enrollment and interest in science classes and activities which might be significant in planning for facilities, staff, budget, and curriculum?				
*8. Is there coordination to insure that conservation, health, safety, aerospace, and other like areas are being adequately included in the science program and at the same time are not being duplicated?				
*9. Is attention being given to coordinating the science program with the mathematics, English, social studies, and other programs?				
10. Is there provision for two-way communication be-				

[1] Adapted by permission. *School Management* Magazine, Inc., copyright 1959.

tween the community and school about changes in the science program, whether through the advisory committee or by some other means?

11. Has an effort been made to develop adjunct science activities within the community, such as a junior museum, nature trail, or wildlife preserve?

II. Public Responsibility and Goals

*1. Has the local board of education and the school administration evidenced a sensitivity for the responsibility for public education in science:
   a. By establishing policies which are consistent with local, State, and national needs, such as providing for an education adequate to give the background needed for future scientists, engineers, technicians, and scientifically oriented non-science citizens?
   b. By providing an opportunity for every child to study science at every grade level?
   c. By providing for the identification, encouragement, and development of boys and girls with special science talent?
   d. By considering the need for a science program for students with below-average ability?
   e. By recognizing that specific facilities and equipment as well as properly trained science teachers are a basic requisite to a good program, and by making plans to adequately finance such a program?

*2. Have consistent long-range goals in harmony with the present American culture (as implied in the preceding statements) been established for your science program?

*3. Do long-range goals give emphasis to the processes of scientific inquiry, e.g., problem recognition, assumption recognition, hypothesizing, observations as comparison and measurement, experimental design and conduct, data analysis and interpretation, and the extension and relating of understandings to new problems?

4. Are the long-range goals for the science program used in determining short-range immediate objectives?

5. Has competent outside professional guidance, both educational and scientific, been sought in the development of the long-range goals for your science program?

6. Do the long-range goals consider the nature and importance of the history, philosophy, and lives of men of science as a major cultural influence?

III. Curriculum

*1. Does the content of science courses taught provide a valid impression of science as it exists today both in terms of major ideas and the evidence upon which these ideas are based?

*2. Have criteria, based on long-range goals, been established for the selection and organization of course content?

3. Are broad integrating themes used as the basis for developing an understanding of science?

*4. Is science scheduled as a regular subject and is it available to each pupil at every grade level?

*5. Is the amount of class time scheduled for science at every grade level sufficient for the full attainment of the desired goals?

*6. Are open-ended and problem-solving-type activities used extensively as a means of developing:
   a. Scientific attitudes?
   b. Skills in the processes of scientific inquiry?
   c. Functional understandings of scientific concepts?

*7. Do science courses provide frequent opportunities for each pupil to engage in laboratory work and other firsthand experiences?

8. Are double laboratory periods or extended class time scheduled each week for the science courses offered in grades 7 to 12?

9. Are the school's science laboratories and/or project work areas available to science talented pupils for independent projects and research outside of regular class time?

3	2	1	other

	3	2	1	other
10. Are the pupils who have shown interest in science careers provided opportunities to take at least 4 years each of science and mathematics in grades 9 to 12?				
11. Is every secondary school pupil required to take a minimum of 2 years of laboratory science, at least 1 each of biological and physical science, for graduation?				
*12. Does the curriculum at all grade levels give emphasis to the historical, biographical (men of science), and philosophical aspects of science?				
13. Have the following been utilized in the development of science curriculum materials:				
a. State department of education personnel?				
b. Science supervisor?				
c. Local teaching and administrative staff?				
d. College and university scientists and science educators?				
e. Business and industry personnel?				
f. Representatives of lay organizations, e.g., county farm agents, health department, hospital, and clinic personnel?				
14. Is there a trend in curriculum revision in your school to cover fewer topics (subject matter areas)? Are those areas that are selected for study covered in greater depth?				

IV. Teaching-Learning

	3	2	1	other
*1. Are pupils at all levels given opportunities to:				
a. Learn and practice skills in scientific observation?				
b. Design, set up, and carry out controlled experiments to test hypotheses?				
c. Formulate and delimit problems?				
d. Recognize assumptions?				
e. Prepare and discuss hypotheses regarding the solutions to problems?				
f. Use appropriate instruments for making measurements?				
g. Use proper statistical and mathematical procedures for handling measurements?				
h. Evaluate and interpret evidence they have collected?				

i. Learn the value of withholding judgment until sufficient evidence has been collected.

j. Recognize the nature of any conclusion and modify this conclusion on the basis of new evidence?

*2. Do pupils at all levels have the opportunity to discover science principles through participation in experiences rather than through mere reading or talking about science?

*3. Does the laboratory work consist of working on real problems which are genuinely thought-provoking rather than performing "cookbook" types of exercises?

4. Are teacher and pupil-teacher demonstrations used to promote critical thought and discussion rather than just to serve as illustrations of science principles?

*5. Are pupils encouraged to question evidence, challenge loose thinking, and develop hypotheses as an accepted part of classroom behavior?

6. Do science activities seek to relate new learnings to previous learnings?

7. Are pupils encouraged to develop investigations on their own?

V. Evaluation

Evaluation of Pupil Performance

*1. Does the evaluation program make use of a variety of techniques and instruments such as the following:
   a. Anecdotal records?
   b. Performance tests?
   c. Objective tests?
   d. Essay examinations?
   e. Observations of laboratory procedures?
   f. Rating scales?

2. Are inservice or other opportunities available for teachers to discuss and prepare evaluation materials and procedures?

3 2 1 other

Evaluation of the Science Program   3 2 1 other

*1. Are criteria for evaluation available which are based on the stated goals for the science program?

2. Are materials (books, sample tests, and national norms) available within the school to help teachers evaluate pupil learnings in science?

*3. Is there specific evidence that attempts are made at all grade levels to evaluate growth in the processes of scientific inquiry?

4. Are efforts made to follow up the graduates of high school to determine whether or not the science program has met the needs of:
   a. Those who plan to follow careers in science?
   b. Those who plan to become science teachers?
   c. Those who plan to become science technicians?
   d. Those who do not plan to pursue science-related careers but who will become scientifically literate citizens?

*5. Are teachers encouraged and given the opportunity to evaluate their own teaching procedures?

VI. Youth Activities

*1. Does your school science program include one or more of the following?
   a. Science clubs?
   b. Science seminars?
   c. Annual science exhibits?
   d. Participation in a statewide or national organization?
   e. Participation in the Junior Academy of Science?
   f. The Westinghouse Science Talent Search?

2. Do the secondary school science pupils conduct research projects which may be exhibited at science fairs or science congresses?

3. Do pupils prepare and read scientific and research papers at science congresses, junior academies of science, and other scientific meetings?

*4. Do projects for science students emerge from and, in part, contribute to the on-going classroom activities?

5. Are the science youth organizations affiliated with:
   a. Local organizations?
   b. State organizations?
   c. National organizations?

6. Are the faculty sponsors of science youth activities given either compensatory time or a salary supplement?

7. Are science pupils encouraged to participate in:
   a. Summer science camps?
   b. Summer science institutes?
   c. Summer science expeditions?
   d. Summer employment in scientific laboratories?

VII. Staff

*1. Are the NASDTEC-AAAS[2] recommendations for preparation in science and mathematics met by a substantial portion of:
   a. Elementary school teachers?
   b. Junior high school science teachers?
   c. Senior high school science teachers?

*2. Have all science teachers completed at least:
   a. An undergraduate major in science?
   b. A master's degree in science?

3. Are inservice institutes conducted for science teachers as a regular part of their professional workload?

4. Have most of the science teachers attended summer or academic year science institutes within the last 5 years?

*5. Is consultant help available to all science teachers from:
   a. An elementary science consultant?
   b. A secondary science consultant?
   c. Scientists in local industry?

	3	2	1	other

[2] *Guidelines for Science and Mathematics in the Preparation Program of Elementary School Teachers*, National Association of State Directors of Teacher Education and Certification in Cooperation with the American Association for the Advancement of Science, 1515 Massachusetts Avenue, NW, Washington, D.C., 1963.

Guidelines for Preparation Programs of Teachers of Secondary Science and Mathematics, National Association of State Directors of Teacher Education and Certification in Cooperation with the American Association for the Advancement of Science, 1515 Massachusetts Avenue, NW, Washington, D.C., 1961.

	3	2	1	other

d. Scientists and science educators in a nearby college or university?

e. A State supervisor of science?

f. Academics of science?

*6. Do science teachers generally attend meetings of professional or scientific organizations at the:
a. Local level?
b. State level?
c. Regional level?
d. National level?

7. During out-of-school time do all science teachers strive to improve their professional, scientific, and general cultural backgrounds through:
a. Travel?
b. Study?
c. Work in science-based industry?
d. Engaging in scientific research?
e. Engaging in science education research?

8. Do all the science teachers subscribe to or read:
a. Educational journals?
b. Scientific journals?
c. Journals of research in science teaching?
d. Science teaching journals?

9. Are science teachers given assistance by means of one or more of the following:
a. Clerical help?
b. Paid laboratory assistants?
c. Volunteer laboratory assistants?
d. Free periods for planning activities and caring for and setting up equipment?

10. Does the guidance staff include counselors who are sensitive to the needs of pupils interested in science?

*11. Do science teachers assume professional responsibility for career guidance of pupils interested in science?

12. Do science teachers work with other staff members to effectively coordinate teaching-learning activities?

13. Do science teachers assist pupils or refer them to appropriate personnel for assistance in the improvement of reading and study skills?

VIII. Administration

	3	2	1	other

*1. Do the board of education and the administration have a policy to frequently review teacher assignments in terms of academic and other qualifications?

*2. Have the board of education and the school administration taken specific action to enable and encourage teachers to update their:
   a. Professional qualifications?
   b. Academic qualifications?

3. Are teachers on all grade levels encouraged to experiment with new content and techniques?

4. Are science teachers allowed time with pay to attend professional conferences related to the science program?

5. Does the school have a policy that provides for, encourages, and regulates:
   a. Local field trips?
   b. School journeys to special areas?
   c. Summer excursions for scientific studies?

6. Does the administration exert leadership to encourage science teachers and other teachers to work together for overall science program planning as part of their regular assignment?

7. Does the administration maintain close contact with and seek consultant help from the school district and State supervisors of science?

*8. Does the administration recognize that good science teaching requires more in the way of specific facilities and equipment than other academic areas and that science classes should not be scheduled in standard classrooms?

9. Does the school district provide transportation for science field trips for:
   a. Science pupils?
   b. Science teachers?

IX. Finances

*1. Does the budget[3] provide realistically and adequately for science:

---

[3] Charles L. Koelsche and Archie N. Solberg, *Facilities and Equipment Available for Teaching Science in Public High Schools*, 1958–59. Toledo, Ohio: Research Foundation, University of Toledo, 1959, p. 26.

	3	2	1	other

a. Apparatus?
b. Supplies?
c. Instructional material?
d. Teaching aids?
e. Library books?
f. Repair, maintenance, and replacement of equipment and materials?

2. Is science equipment purchased with the needs of specific science courses in mind?

3. Does the school science budget provide needed laboratory supplies for each student in every course throughout the year?

4. Is a petty cash fund or an equivalent source of money provided to purchase incidental science materials?

*5. Does the salary structure:
a. Attract well-qualified science teachers?
b. Include increments which will assure retention of well-qualified teachers?
c. Eliminate the need for additional nonprofessional employment?

6. Does the school provide money and/or leave for professional travel for science teachers?

7. Have NDEA Title III funds been used to the limit of Federal matching funds?

8. Are science teachers consulted in the establishment of budgetary procedures and the formulation of the budget?

X. Facilities, Equipment, and Teaching Aids

*1. Are the suggestions and recommendations of qualified science teaching personnel sought and incorporated in plans for new science facilities?

*2. Does each room where science is taught have the following characteristics:
a. Proper heat and ventilation (including fume hoods where needed)?

" . . . (a) breakdown of budgeted funds for the various enrollment categories revealed that the average amount per science student in the 1–199 size group was $3.90; 200–499, $2.80; 800–999, $2.50; and 1000-up, $2.26."

	3	2	1	other

b. Good lighting with supplementary lighting where needed?

c. Electrical wiring and outlets with voltage and amperage control where needed?

d. Gas supply and outlets where needed?

e. Running water taps and sinks where needed?

f. Proper acoustics for potentially noisy areas?

g. Room darkening facilities (blackout shades)?

h. Area suitable for photographic darkroom work?

i. Exhibit and display areas?

j. Space for individual pupil project work?

k. Suitable areas for maintaining living plants and animals near or in the biology laboratory?

l. Acid resistant tabletop and floor covering where needed?

m. Preparation area?

3. Are the following laboratory safeguards provided:
   a. Prevention and control of gas, chemical, and electrical fires (blankets or extinguishers)?
   b. Electrical equipment (fuses, breakers, etc.)?
   c. Emergency shower and eye fountains?
   d. "Hot lab" facilities for radioactive chemicals?
   e. First aid kits or cabinets?
   f. Properly placed exits?

4. Are the science facilities, furniture, and equipment suitable for and adaptable to:
   a. Individual experimentation by pupils?
   b. Long-term pupil experiments or projects?
   c. Teacher and pupil demonstrations?
   d. Small and large group work?
   e. Effective use of supplementary aids?
   f. Science clubs, fairs, and project activities?

5. Does each science teacher have facilities for effective performance of:
   a. Preparatory activities?
   b. Conference activities with pupils and parents?
   c. The use of reference books and materials?
   d. Desk and office functions?

6. Are adequate storage facilities provided in:
   a. The rooms where science is taught?
   b. Separate storage and/or preparation rooms?

7. Are equipment and supplies stored and organized for effective use in:
   a. Classrooms and laboratories?
   b. Storage facilities?

8. Are adequate inventory records and controls maintained for science equipment and materials?

9. Are the science rooms equipped with the following instructional aids or are they readily available:
   a. Overhead projector?
   b. Microprojector?
   c. 16 mm. movie projector?
   d. Slide and filmstrip projector?
   e. Closed circuit television?
   f. Programed learning devices?

*10. Are suitable[4] types of basic equipment and instructional aids provided and readily available to:
   a. Teachers for instructional purposes?
   b. Pupils for project work?
   c. Pupils for team work?
   d. Pupils for individual work, both during and outside of classroom time?

*11. Are adequate[5] quantities provided of the following:
   a. Textbooks with recent copyright dates?
   b. Science periodicals for teachers?
   c. Science periodicals for pupils?
   d. Science reference books for teachers?
   e. Science reference books for pupils?
   f. Professional science journals?

12. Are the following types of facilities available in areas where possible:
   a. A school pond or wild life area?
   b. An area where activities related to conservation may be carried out?
   c. A greenhouse?
   d. A weather station?
   e. A planetarium?
   f. An area where the environmental conditions—

Column headers: 3 2 1 other

---

[4] Should be interpreted as meaning sufficient for the full realization of the purposes and goals of the course.

[5] *Ibid.*

temperature, light, and moisture—can be controlled and varied?

*13. Is the library adequately equipped with books for a comprehensive science program?

14. Does the science staff request additional titles to supplement existing references?

15. Is the library effectively and regularly used by the:
a. Pupils?
b. Science teachers?

3	2	1	other

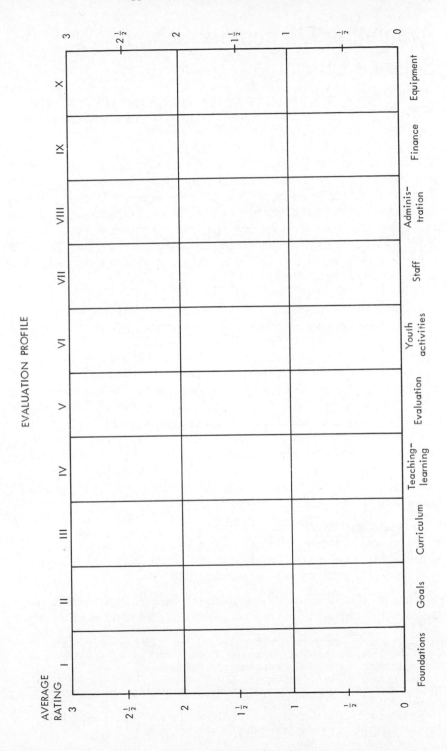

Evaluating Elementary School Science Curricula*

UNIVERSITY of OKLAHOMA SCIENCE EDUCATION CENTER[1]

The following article lists a set of sixteen evaluative criteria which can be used specifically to evaluate an elementary school science curriculum to determine whether or not it can lead children to achieve the purposes for teaching science in the elementary schools. These purposes are to permit and encourage every child to develop (1) the ability and confidence to inquire, (2) a command of the ten rational powers, and (3) an understanding of the changing nature of the environment in terms of matter, life, energy, and their interactions.

Today's elementary schools may lack some of the features, facilities, and opportunities the modern educator would like to see in them, but they do *not* lack curricula to select from. These curricula all claim to lead children to the objectives of the modern school. Within the last ten years "new" curricula in nearly every subject taught have become available. How good are these "new" curricula? How does a school know which curriculum to select? The answers to the foregoing questions are the same—it depends upon the purposes for which a particular subject is taught.

With that answer in mind, we wondered how the recent curricular innovations in elementary school science could be evaluated. If we were to devise criteria, we had to first state our purpose for teaching science in the elementary school. We believe that elementary school science should permit and encourage every child to develop:

- the ability and confidence to inquire
- a command of the ten rational powers[2]
- an understanding of the changing nature of the environment in terms of matter, life, energy, and their interactions.

What follows is a set of criteria which can be specifically used to evaluate an elementary school science curriculum to determine whether or not

[1] Kenneth Absher, Larry A. Darbison, Kay Giezentanner, Bari J. Herbert, Gail W. Hutton, Anton E. Lawson, John W. Renner, Beth N. Ridgway, Janet S. Stewart, George C. Worth.

[2] Educational Policies Commission. *The Central Purposes of American Education.* National Education Association, Washington, D.C. 1961. p. 5.

it can lead children to achieve the foregoing purposes. Someone else's purposes for teaching science in the elementary school, however, need not be the same as ours. But for these criteria to be useful to others in evaluating existing curricula and those which will become available in the future, their specific purposes must be stated.

There are a few basic, ground rules which may need explanation. Each criterion is written in the form of a question which must be answered "yes," "no," or "information to determine not available." This technique was deliberate because we believe that any evaluation instrument should yield definite information. The criteria are mutually independent, i.e., just because one is answered negatively does not invalidate all the criteria following it. It is not necessary to have only affirmative answers to weight the decision for a given program and/or unit. For example, if the work of the Elementary Science Study (ESS) were subjected to these criteria, criterion number eight will receive a negative response. (However, a teacher can build a structure from several ESS units even though a conceptual framework was not in the original design of the program.) Does that invalidate the work of that group? No—it does mean, however, that if a school system selects the ESS program that it may not lead a child to develop an over-all conceptual framework of science. The criteria were designed to provide schools with basic information which can be used to allow them to make science curriculum decisions. The number of "yes" and "no" answers the criteria provide about a curriculum is important *only* when that particular school's purposes for teaching science are known. The evaluative criteria follow.

Evaluative Criteria

1. **Does the unit emphasize the processes of science as well as the information acquired?**
   Teach science as science is, and science is process.

2. **Are the students actively involved?**
   a. Do the pupils do their own investigations?
   b. Do the pupils gather their own data?
   c. Are the pupils encouraged to perform experiments on their own?
   d. Are pupils led to form hypotheses?
   e. Is the primary responsibility for data interpretation and evaluation left to the pupils?

3. **Do the learning activities require the development of the rational powers?**
   The central purpose of American education as stated by the Educational Policies Commission in 1961 is to develop the ten rational powers, which they described as "the essence of the ability to think." The ten rational

powers are listed as: recalling, imagining, classifying, generalizing, deducing, inferring, evaluating, synthesizing, analyzing, and comparing.[3] The learning activities of the program under consideration should include activities in which the use and development of these powers is demanded. Only in this way can the student's ability to think be developed. In looking through the programs, examples of these activities should be apparent; classification of bottle caps, buttons, seeds, animals, or plants should be evident. There should be activities in which the students are called upon to imagine, experiment, synthesize hypotheses, and analyze and evaluate data which the experiments produce. Also instances of students comparing things such as animals, rocks, or any other variety of materials or data should be apparent. Students should be encouraged to generalize from their classroom experiences and experiments to out-of-class experience in order to discover the important relationships.

Because of the nature of the processes of science, if you are able to answer *yes* to question number one, in most cases, you will be impelled to answer *yes* to question number three.

4. Does the program fit the developmental level of the child?

The developmental level concept is based on Jean Piaget's model of learning.[4] Piaget calls the phase of development that children are in when they enter school *pre-operational*. Pre-operational thought is egocentric, irreversible, and perception bound. The child can make observations and report them, but doesn't have the ability to draw abstract generalizations about the relationships that exist among those observations. The *concrete operational* thinker (about ages 7–15) can do some abstract thinking but it is directly related to concrete objects. The last stage of Piaget's model is called *formal operational*; here, the learner can think not only in terms of reality but in terms of the possible. Because we feel that education should move children toward formal operations, a science program should fit into Piaget's learning model.

5. Does the unit contain a variety of materials which appear to interest the child?

Children should be given *concrete* objects which they can handle and experiment with. These materials allow the children to be involved as they analyze, compare and otherwise develop their rational thinking.

6. Does the unit contain a variety of activities which appear to interest the child?

Activities which interest the child will greatly increase the frequency and consistency with which his needs are met as he participates in the

---

[3] *Ibid.*, p. 5.

[4] These stages of learning have been outlined by Thomas A. Chittenden in his article, "Piaget and Elementary Science" (*Science and Children* 8:9–15; December 1970) and John Renner's article "Piaget Is Practical" (*Science and Children* 9:23–26; October 1971), and in numerous other sources.

learning experience. (In the accompanying diagram read → as "lead(s) to.")

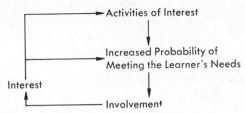

7. Are the teacher's guides explanatory as to purpose and methodology?

The value of any guide is that it provides a skeletal outline of *what* is to be achieved and *how* those achievements are to be accomplished. A useful guide would include stated objectives with exercises discussed and related activities given.

8. Does the entire program have a conceptual framework?

A conceptual framework is an expandable reference model (i.e., organizational scheme) which allows the learner to place and evaluate new information. A science program with a conceptual framework has a dimension which one lacking it does not have. That dimension adds depth to the program, in our belief, and allows the child to develop a structure in which to categorize ideas, concepts, and experiences. A conceptual framework gives direction to the ideas taught in the materials and methods being used.

9. Does the program reflect the structure of the discipline?[5]

Many programs in the past and some even today fall far short of the real goal of science education, which is to teach science. Science can and should be taught to help students think, solve problems, and become confident, but for a program to be truly successful it must remain true to the discipline. It must teach the underlying concepts of the field and not trivial items of passing interest upon which so much of some science textbooks are based.

10. Are the concepts each unit purports to develop clearly stated?

Since the teacher must have definite objectives in mind when selecting a science program, clear statements of the concepts of each unit will facilitate the selection process. In the teaching process, having the concepts of each unit clearly stated will allow the teacher to set goals and arrange priorities.

11. Does the program encourage the teacher to accept all sincere student answers as valuable?

---

[5] For an extensive discussion of the phrase "structure of the discipline" see Jerome Bruner's book *The Process of Education*. Harvard University Press, Cambridge, Massachusetts. 1963.

An answer is always valuable even if his answer isn't "correct." That answer may lead to more questions and the teacher can guide (by questioning or by the children experimenting) the pupil to conclusions supported by evidence. The material provided for the teacher should give clues for questioning and suggestions for leading the children to experimenting rather than outlining specific facts to be mastered.

12. Is the unit flexible enough to be adapted to the needs and interests of a particular class?

The unit should allow rearrangement, expansion, condensation, tangent activities and individual projects. The teacher should be encouraged to use his discretion in order to create the most dynamic learning situations and experiences for each individual child and the distinct (unique) class he is teaching. If the units are too formally or rigidly structured to allow them to maintain their effectiveness after necessary alterations are made, then they are not flexible enough to be adapted.

13. Can a child with limited reading ability succeed in the program?

Reading is extremely important, but achievement in science should not be dependent upon it.

14. Are the teaching and resource materials carefully integrated into the program?

If films, slides, or recordings are to be used with a lesson, the teacher needs to know what purpose these materials serve. Were they included to demonstrate something that couldn't be done by the class or would have been difficult to do successfully? Was the time that the material should be used for maximum effectiveness specified, or are the materials to be used at any convenient time? If the material has value then there is a best time for it to be used, and the teacher needs to know when that time is.

15. Is a format provided which allows the teacher to set up and teach each unit smoothly?

16. Are the costs, construction, mobility, durability, maintenance, and availability of materials reasonable and practical?

Whether or not the cost of a science program is reasonable and practical will be determined largely by the ability and willingness of the school to finance it. If the program requires the use of consumable items such as chemicals, seeds, and special solutions, their cost and availability must be considered. If the items are not common ones the students can bring from home, or which can be obtained locally, the price of the program is affected. With any elementary science program the teacher should be able to handle and move from place to place with a minimum of difficulty the materials that will be used.

The aim should not be to produce some numerical score using these criteria (although that could be done). Rather, after using the criteria on a particular science program, look at which of the criteria are answered positively and which negatively. When you compare these answers with the purposes of *your* program, then you will know which "no" and "yes" answers are most important to *you* in evaluating a curriculum.

Has the Objective
Been Attained *

RONALD D. ANDERSON

Ronald D. Anderson cites the three main reasons for evaluation, namely, (1) to find out how well the child is learning, (2) to find out how well the teacher is teaching, and (3) to report the child's progress to his parents. Dr. Anderson focuses his attention on the first two reasons, and discusses formal and informal evaluation techniques. He cautions teachers to be sure that all the objectives are given proper attention and that the measurement planned does actually measure the stated objectives.

Broad general objectives are important to give general guidelines, but if they are to serve as an adequate basis for planning either teaching or evaluation, they must be translated into specific objectives for each day. In fact, if specific objectives for the day are formed, a great deal of the planning for the teaching and evaluation already has been done. The evaluation, in particular, is aided by stating as part of an objective, the conditions under which the behavior is expected and the minimum acceptable level of performance.

Reasons for Evaluation

The most important reason for conducting careful evaluation of the science program is to locate learning difficulties that individual children are encountering and aid them in overcoming these difficulties. To accomplish this purpose, the evaluation must be a continuous activity that is done each day and not put aside until the end of a unit when a formal evaluation is made. It may be difficult in a large classroom, but the teacher

*REPRINTED FROM *Science and Children*, Vol. 5, No. 2, October 1967, pp. 33–36. Copyright, 1967, by the National Science Teachers Association, Washington, D.C. Reprinted by permission of the author and the publisher. Dr. Anderson is Associate Dean and Professor of Education at the University of Colorado.

must continually attempt to determine what obstacles, if any, each child is encountering.

A second important reason for careful evaluation is to enable the teacher to change and alter her teaching practices and procedures in the manner that will best improve the learning situation. The idea that appeared promising before trying it in the classroom may, in practice, be a complete failure in terms of the objective it was expected to accomplish. Or possibly the objective itself is unreasonable when viewed with respect to the classroom experience. An evaluation at the end of the unit should show if the promising idea "fizzled." Here again, the continuous day-to-day evaluation of the teaching techniques is important so that revisions can take place.

A third reason for evaluation is as a base for reporting a child's progress to his parents and other members of the school staff who work with him. Usually this is referred to as grading, although the report may include more than just a grade. Grading or reporting of student progress is a matter of importance but is not our major concern. Even though it is one of the reasons for evaluation in elementary school science, the focus of this article is on the evaluation itself.

Types of Evaluation

It might be helpful to discuss two types of evaluation which can be referred to as informal and formal. Formal evaluation refers to paper and pencil tests, or other devices such as individual tasks which are administered uniformly to all the children in the class. This type of evaluation will be discussed in detail in the following sections. Much of a teacher's evaluation is more informal and is based upon her observations while the usual classroom activities are underway. The responses that children make to the teacher's questions and the questions that children ask are noted by the perceptive teacher. In addition to verbal statements and questions, the actions of children as they work with equipment provide important information for informal evaluation.

It is important that the teacher's informal evaluation be centered on those behaviors which are her objectives and that she not be unduly influenced by unrelated behaviors of the children. If one of the objectives for the day's work is that children be able to formulate hypotheses concerning a particular phenomenon, such as the breaking of rocks during freezing weather, the teacher should be listening for statements that indicate that a hypothesis has been suggested. The central objective is for the children to develop their ability to formulate hypotheses. The behavior that is indicative of this should be of major concern to the teacher rather than verbal fluency or discussion of the breaking of rocks in freezing weather which is unrelated to hypotheses concerning the phenomenon.

Informal evaluation of the type described above is dependent upon a certain type of teaching. The teacher who does not have much student involvement (for example, the discussion of thought-provoking questions), often is not in a position to observe student behaviors which are indicative of whether or not an objective has been reached. This indicates clearly the close "tie-in" between objectives, teaching, and evaluation. Ample evidence is available to show that student involvement is important for science teaching, particularly for objectives related to the processes of science. This student involvement also is important for the informal evaluation in which a teacher evaluates on the basis of what students *DO* on a day-to-day basis. What is good teaching practice also is generally advantageous for evaluation.

Cover All Objectives

The more formal evaluations such as paper and pencil tests should be planned carefully to insure that all objectives are given proper attention and that the measurement planned actually does measure the stated objectives. The first step, specifying the objectives, was discussed in the first article. It is well to remember, however, that teaching is a very dynamic and flexible activity, and as a result of interaction with the children, the objectives may have been altered or given a different emphasis. Now that preparations are being made for the evaluation, it is time to consider again exactly what goals *have* been sought.

The next step is to weight the various objectives according to the relative emphasis given to them during the teaching. For example, if two days were spent on the measurement of temperature and one day on formulating hypotheses concerning the change of state of water from one form to the other, the former should receive twice as much emphasis in the evaluation. If it is a paper and pencil test, the number of items or questions should be in proportion to the time spent on the objectives which they are designed to measure.

A crucial step is the selection of the evaluation technique which will be used to measure the various objectives. The technique used is dependent upon the nature of the objective. Many teachers use a particular type, e.g., an objective paper and pencil test, regardless of their objectives. Sometimes a particular evaluation technique is appropriate; many times it is not. This teacher then asks herself, "What are some items that are related to the topics that have been considered?" There are at least two things wrong with this approach. First, the achievement of the objective at hand may not be measurable with this technique. Second, just because the test items chosen are on the same topic as the objectives, does not insure that the items actually measure the students' achievement of the specific objectives.

The first type of error is shown by the following example. One of the objectives for a unit is that children should be able to classify a group of leaves into three groups on the bases of color, size, or shape. Paper and pencil items are probably not the most appropirate means of evaluating whether or not this objective has been achieved. In this case, each child could be given a group of leaves and asked to classify them. It may be possible to devise paper and pencil items using pictures that test such an ability, but a teacher is more likely to devise a means of measuring the stated objectives by the above technique than by objective test items which she devises.

The second type of error is shown by a teacher's evaluation of the following objective: Given data showing the daily fluctuations in temperature over a two-week period, the child should be able to construct a graph which shows the relationship between time and temperature. In this case the teacher constructed this true-false item which referred to a graph of time vs. temperature: The graph above shows the relationship between time and temperature. This item was on the same topic as the objective, yet it was not a measure of the students' achievement of the objective. The item required that the student be able to determine what had been plotted on the graph, but the objective stated that the child should be able to construct a graph. In this case, it would have been more appropriate to give the student some data and ask him to construct a graph.

Variety of Formal Evaluation Techniques

Two main types of formal evaluation techniques have been referred to thus far—paper and pencil tests and the systematic use of situations in which individual children are presented a situation which includes the use of material objects. The latter type is used very extensively in the evaluation program of *Science—A Process Approach*.[1] Each child is individually presented with a standard and given specific directions for indicating his responses on a check sheet. Some of their items and the objectives they were designed to assess will serve as good examples of this evaluation technique.

One of the objectives for a lesson on color in Book One is that the child should be able to "identify the following colors by sight: yellow, orange, red, purple, blue and green."[2] A competency measure designed to assess the achievement of this objective has the following directions:

Show the child each of three blocks—a yellow (1), a red (2), and a blue (3) one, and say to the child, WHAT IS THE COLOR OF THIS BLOCK?

[1] Commission on Science Education, *Science—A Process Approach*, American Association for the Advancement of Science, Washington, D.C. 1965 and 1966.
[2] *Ibid.*, Book One, p. 1.

Repeat for all three blocks. One check should be given in the acceptable column for each correct name.[3]

In Book Four is a lesson on communicating entitled "Describing an Experiment." The objectives of this lesson are:

The child should be able to describe any one of the following portions of an experiment which he has just observed or conducted:
1. the question to be answered.
2. the method or approach used.
3. the apparatus and procedures used.
4. the results obtained, as observed.
5. the answer to the original question.[4]

The competency measure designed to assess the achievement of this objective is as follows:

Tell the child: I AM GOING TO EXPERIMENT TO SEE WHAT HAPPENS TO A PENCIL FLOATING IN WATER WHEN SALT IS ADDED TO THE WATER. I WANT YOU TO WATCH ME CAREFULLY SO THAT YOU WILL BE ABLE TO DESCRIBE WHAT I DID. Fill the test tube with water and place a pencil in the tube. Place test tube next to a ruler and record the reading either at the bottom or the top of the pencil. Pour salt (two tablespoons) into the test tube and record the reading again. (Change in level will be about one half centimeter.) Ask the child: WRITE DOWN OR TELL ME IN WORDS ALL THAT YOU CAN ABOUT THIS EXPERIMENT. Give him one check for each of the following steps that he includes:
1. question to be answered.
2. proposed method or approach.
3. apparatus and procedures required.
4. results obtained, as observed.
5. answer to the original question.[5]

Note some characteristics of these examples. In contrast to informal evaluation, this is a carefully defined standard situation which is the same for each child. There is a close correlation between the stated objectives and the items used for evaluation. It is apparent that the evaluation items were designed specifically to measure the corresponding stated objective. Also, these items are not dependent upon either the child's reading or writing ability. In both cases the child does not read anything. In the second example the child may write his answer but only if he prefers this method to telling the teacher his answer.

An obvious difficulty with this type of evaluation is the time required to

[3] *Ibid.*, Competency Measures, Parts One and Two, p. 11.
[4] *Ibid.*, Book Four, p. 95.
[5] *Ibid.*, *Competency Measures*, Parts Three and Four, p. 85.

administer the assessment to each child in the class individually. On the other hand, its freedom from dependence on writing and reading ability gives it an advantage over paper and pencil tests. The reading difficulty of paper and pencil tests is a major problem when employing them at the elementary school level. Both varieties of assessment devices have their advantages and disadvantages. In choosing between them the basic question should be, "What can I use that will determine if my objective has been attained?" As a result, an assessment of the student's achievement over a fairly long period of time will probably include some of both types.

The situation evaluation technique, with some modifications, can be used with groups of children rather than individuals. When used with groups, the children generally are required to give their responses on paper rather than verbally. This is a useful form of evaluation in that it combines the flexibility of the situation technique with the efficiency of paper and pencil tests. Because of these dual advantages, some teachers find this technique to be the most useful of all the evaluation techniques which they employ.

The higher the grade level, the more paper and pencil tests are likely to be employed. This is understandable, since as the child's reading and writing abilities increase, the better able he is to respond to this kind of examination. At present it is the most widely used type of evaluation for elementary school science. Since science is being tested, every effort should be made to reduce the influence of the child's reading ability upon his score. This influence is greater than most teachers realize. One helpful procedure is to project the test on a screen with an overhead projector and read each item to the children as they respond to the questions on their own copy of the test. With the modern equipment which many schools have today it is relatively easy to make an overhead projector transparency of any printed material.

The construction of good essay, matching, true-false, completion or multiple choice items is not a simple matter. An adequate discussion of this topic would require far more space than is available here. For helpful information on the construction of good items, the reader is referred to one of the many good books in this area such as those written by Stanley[6] or Ebel.[7] If the reader is not thoroughly familiar with the principles of constructing good test items, he should spend time studying the relevant chapter or chapters of such a book.

In summary, the key to good evaluation is carefully defining objectives and then devising a means of determining if the objectives have been achieved through informal and formal evaluation.

[6] Stanley, Julian C., *Measurement in Today's Schools*, Fourth Edition, Prentice-Hall, Inc., Englewood Cliffs, N.J. 1964.
[7] Ebel, Robert L., *Measuring Educational Achievement*, Prentice-Hall, Inc., Englewood Cliffs, N.J. 1965.

Evaluation in Elementary Science by Classroom Teachers and Their Supervisors*

HAROLD E. TANNENBAUM, NATHAN STILLMAN,
and ALBERT PILTZ

This article is intended by the authors to serve a number of different purposes in the area of elementary school science. First, it should be helpful to supervisors and administrators on the state and local levels in evaluating the effectiveness of the elementary science program. Second, it should enable teachers to do a more effective job of evaluating the growth of their students in achieving the goals of the science program. Third, it should provide supervisors with material for in-service teacher education programs in evaluation. Fourth, it should aid supervisors by giving them guiding principles for measuring the effectiveness of teachers. This article is an excerpt from the U.S. Office of Education Bulletin Evaluation in Elementary School Science.

"What," "how," and "how well" are key words introducing three of the major questions faced by every supervisor and classroom teacher in the formal education of students. The first, "What should children learn?" is concerned with both the long-term goals and the consequent immediate objectives of the educational enterprise. The second, "How should they learn?" related to the problem of method or of determining the most effective means of helping students achieve the objectives. The third, "How well have they learned?" involves ascertaining the degree to which the objectives have been achieved. It is this careful appraisal of where a pupil is and how well he is progressing that comprises "student evaluation."

Teachers generally and rightly consider evaluation as one of the most complex problems in teaching and one for which they have been inadequately prepared. This is especially true in the area of elementary school science, where curriculums are undergoing extensive revisions not only in relation to content but also with respect to scientific attitudes and prob-

* REPRINTED FROM *Evaluation in Elementary School Science*, U.S. Office of Education, Document OE-29057, Circular No. 757, 1964, pp. 19–52. Dr. Tannenbaum is Chairman of the Department of Curriculum and Teaching at Herbert Lehman (formerly Hunter) College, New York. Dr. Stillman is Professor of Education at Yeshiva University, New York. Dr. Piltz is Specialist for Elementary Science at the U.S. Office of Education, San Francisco Regional Office.

lem solving approaches. Standardized tests in elementary school science which would be appropriate for most schools are still nonexistent. Merely using a test labeled "science" could well result only in obtaining erroneous information about students and would be worse than not using tests at all. Thus, both the classroom teacher and the local personnel charged with the supervision of the elementary school science program are faced with the responsibility for learning how to develop, use, and interpret a variety of appraisal techniques for the purpose of furthering the teaching-learning process.

Measuring the outcomes of the teaching-learning process requires a great variety of evaluative techniques. For some purposes, testing devices such as objective tests or essay tests are not only satisfactory but even necessary. For example, objective tests can be used to determine if students can define such terms as "compound," "mixture," and "element"; essay tests can be used to determine if students are able to use these terms in formulating chemical explanations of natural or man-made phenomena.

Other kinds of achievement can be evaluated by nontesting techniques such as the rating of pupil-made products, or observation of a pupil's classroom performance, or the nature and extent of an individual child's behavior during selected science activities. Consider science fairs and the children's exhibits as an example. In addition to being excellent motivators, such activities can furnish the supervisor and teacher with many opportunities for evaluating how well given pupils are progressing towards pertinent goals of the science curriculum. Does the exhibit present scientific information clearly? Are the details of the exhibit relevant to the main concept? Can the student explain his exhibit so that it is obvious that he understands the principles involved? Such nontesting techniques are valuable in judging the progress of students and the effectiveness of programs.

Dependable evaluation is recognized as fundamental to both effective teaching and effective learning. Thus, evaluation procedures used by a teacher with his class can serve such functions as:

1. Providing feedback information for the teacher and helping him decide how effective a given amount of teaching has been.
2. Supplying diagnostic information concerning individual pupils.
3. Providing motivation for students. As pupils see progress toward established goals, they can be motivated to further learning.
4. Affording sound evidence for differentiating among pupils.

1. DEFINING OBJECTIVES
The first and most important step in evaluating teaching and learning is to define the objectives that are to be attained, and questions like the following may prove useful:

a. What problem-solving abilities is the student expected to achieve?

Can he describe what he saw when he watched a candle being snuffed as a jar covered it? Can he formulate hypotheses about the observed phenomena? Can he plan experiments to test his hypotheses?

b. What information is the student expected to acquire? Has he learned the components of air? Does he know about changes in percentages of these components depending upon altitude or other variables?

c. What skills is he supposed to display? Can he measure amounts of air that are consumed by a candle burned in a jar? Can he manipulate science equipment so that he can perform experiments with air?

d. How is he expected to reveal his attitudes? Does he defer judgment when he observes a demonstration? Does he consider the reliability of a source of information?

e. What applications of his knowledge is the student expected to make? Can he apply what he learned about candles burning in a jar to other problems involving combustion? Does he understand that rusting of iron is another form of oxidation?

All school programs have objectives, but too often these are stated in very general terms and are vague and unclear. Before a supervisor or teacher can determine whether a student has reached certain objectives, he must be able to identify specifically what the student was supposed to achieve. For example, "to help students develop a wholesome attitude toward science" or "to help students appreciate the methods of science" are purposes that have little meaning and would not be useful as guides for evaluation. Objectives must be clearly and specifically defined in terms of pupil behavior, and the performance expected of a student if the objective has been achieved must be specified. If a teacher is unable to list the characteristic behaviors of a student who has reached a particular objective, it is meaningless.

The job of defining objectives in terms of student behavior is recognized as an extremely difficult one, but it is basic to effective evaluation. For example, consider the long-term goal "to help children learn some techniques of problem-solving." Among the specific pupil behaviors that might be expected when this goal is achieved are the abilities to:

1. State a variety of hypotheses concerning the problem,
2. Plan experiments for testing these hypotheses,
3. Report observed phenomena, and
4. Generalize from what has been observed.

As a second example, the long-term science goal "to help children develop rational attitudes toward the world around them" may be cited. When this is specified in terms of pupil behavior, it might require that the child be able:

1. To identify certain superstitions, and
2. To identify sources of information and consider their dependability.

In every science unit, certain of the attitudes, skills, and techniques that have been defined generally must be spelled out so that they relate to the science to be taught. Thus, in a study of weather, growing out of the goal of identifying superstitions might be the following immediate objectives. The pupil can:

1. Distinguish between "weather superstitions" and "weather facts," and
2. Offer explanations for the origins of some "weather superstitions."

In a similar manner, the goal of identifying sources of information and considering their dependability might be formulated as the following objective. The pupil can:

Compare the reliability of weather information from such varied sources as the United States Weather Service and the *Farmer's Almanac*.

The examples cited above suggest only a few of the kinds of behavior which would indicate achievement of the desired goals. There are, in every case, many different kinds of behavior which could be examined. In fact, there are far too many behavioral characteristics for adequate consideration by teachers in elementary school classrooms, and some of the desired behaviors, while very important, do not lend themselves to evaluation in classroom situations. What the teacher must do is to choose those particular behavior patterns which he feels are important and measurable within the framework of his classroom, and use them as his criteria for evaluation.

2. ASSIGNING RELATIVE EMPHASIS TO OBJECTIVES

Every unit in elementary school science has a variety of objectives which students are expected to attain. However, all of the objectives are not of equal importance. If an objective has been assigned major emphasis, it should be allotted a greater proportion of the class time; other objectives, which have been assigned lesser emphasis, should be allotted relatively smaller amounts of time. Therefore, to simplify the process of planning a unit of study, the weight assigned to each objective should be specified. This can be easily accomplished by using the numerical scale of 100 and distributing numerical weights to each objective. Higher weights should be assigned to major objectives and lower weights to minor objectives. If the objectives are all determined to be of equal importance, equal weight should be assigned to each.

This simple system of assigning weights to objectives has real value for the teacher in planning both the content and the evaluation. He now has a measure for determining how much class time should be allotted to the achievement of each objective, as well as an index of the degree to which the objective should be emphasized in the evaluation process. For example, if major emphasis is placed on helping students learn to use the microscope, this should be emphasized to a similar extent in the total evaluation of the student's achievement. If identifying the parts of the microscope is considered a minor objective, it should receive relatively little emphasis in the appraisal process.

The procedure of assigning weights to objectives does not have to follow a rigid formula but may be as flexible as a teacher desires. The emphasis allotted in a classroom quiz may differ from the emphasis assigned in a weekly test. In addition, the distribution of emphasis may be modified from group to group, depending on such factors as the students' readiness for achieving certain objectives, their current interests, and the availability of necessary materials and equipment for developing particular areas of the elementary science program. But regardless of what evaluation procedure is used, the important factor is that the procedure be planned so that it achieves the purpose for which it was intended.

3. OUTLINING THE CONTENT

Once the objectives have been clearly specified and defined, the next important step in the evaluation process is outlining the content. The content of the unit or area of study becomes the actual means of achieving the objectives. The term "curriculum" frequently is defined as a means to behavioral ends. The content of a unit is the curriculum for attaining the specific behavioral objectives of that unit. By outlining the content, the teacher is able to relate the particular objectives to the method of achieving the objective. Frequently, the same content can be utilized in attaining several objectives; sometimes a variety of methods have to be developed for achieving a single objective. For example, if an objective of a science unit is to help children learn to use measuring instruments such as thermometers, the content might include activities like reading daily temperatures in and outside of the classroom, measuring temperatures in sun and shade, or measuring temperatures of hot and cold liquids. This content also could be used for achieving other objectives relating to heat absorption, heat reflection, heat transfer, or insulation.

Another way in which outlining the content can have value for the teacher is in predetermining the specific materials and equipment which must be available for achieving certain objectives. If children are to use thermometers, such instruments must be available in sufficient quantity so that each child may have several opportunities for using the instrument. If skill in doing reference work about geologic periods is in the objective, a variety of appropriate books on historical geology must be available so that each child may read from various sources and compare the information obtained.

Although this may appear to be a time-consuming task for the teacher, it actually can simplify the arduous job of preparing conventional lesson plans and, in addition, specify the evaluation procedure to be used in determining student progress toward particular objectives. A simple way of arranging objectives, content, and evaluation for a unit is to use a three-column table. The first column would contain the objectives; the second column would indicate the methods and materials necessary for achieving each objective; and the third column would specify the type of evaluation procedure to be used in determining student achievement of each objective.

In the first table one objective requires two procedures for evaluation:

Objective	Methods and Materials	Type of Evaluation
The ability to record and interpret temperature data from information gathered using outdoor thermometers	Make simple bar graphs of the daily temperature as found at noon in the shade next to the building.	Examine the charts prepared by each child. Does the chart show that the child can make an accurate and understandable table of data?
	Use the graphs to find significant temperature information; make comparisons among the days studied and also among reading made by different children.	Devise written questions to be answered by individual children, each using his own chart: Which day was hottest? Which day was coldest?
	Have sufficient supply of outdoor thermometers so that variations in readings can be observed.	On which two days was the temperature about the same at noon?
	Have necessary graph grids prepared so that each child has appropriate equipment.	

In the second table, two objectives may be evaluated through a single procedure:

Objective	Methods and Materials	Type of Evaluation
The ability to use library resources to do reference work	Introduce the use of the card catalog and encyclopedias, to show a) How to search out appropriate references; b) How to make summaries; c) How to make a bibliography.	Examine the summaries for accuracy of reporting, comparison of material found in different sources, completeness of bibliography, comprehension of content.

OBJECTIVE	METHODS AND MATERIALS	TYPE OF EVALUATION
The ability to prepare a summary of information found on the last glacial period in North America	Have each child find at least four appropriate references.	
	Make sure there are sufficient references for the children's use.	
	Make sure there are reading materials at the appropriate reading level for each of the children.	

Evaluation Techniques

The teacher who is concerned with evaluation will recognize that he must select appropriate evaluation methods for each of his educational objectives. For certain objectives, the overt behavior of the student—in the classroom situation, in the library, in the laboratory—would yield the most appropriate information. For other objectives, where opportunities for students to demonstrate their actual behavior are very limited or do not exist, pencil-and-paper tests would be more satisfactory. Some objectives are more difficult to measure than are others; for some, appropriate measuring devices have not yet been developed. However, because of the intimate relationship which exists between the objectives and evaluation, objectives must be stated in concrete and specific ways if evaluative results are to lend themselves to precise statements; objectives that are stated in vague and general terms result in evaluation methods that yield incomplete and inaccurate results.

The various kinds of evaluation—observation of student behavior, appraisal of student projects, and the variety of paper-and-pencil tests— yield a wide range of information. But unless sufficient use is made of the results of such observations, appraisals, and measurements, they become a waste of time both for the supervisor or teacher and for students. Such evaluative techniques have three basic uses. In the first place, they can provide a means for assessing the growth of individual students. Secondly, such devices can help each student know his strengths and weaknesses.

Finally, through the use of these techniques, a supervisor or teacher can learn how well the objectives of a program are being met.

It must be remembered, however, that the supervisor or teacher is the ultimate evaluator. A test or other evaluative device can gather information about a student or a program. But only the evaluator can look at this information, weight it, add and subtract related data, and come up with an appraisal of where a student is in relation to his potential, or how well a program is attaining its stated objectives.

1. SELECTION OF APPROPRIATE DEVICES

There is no single evaluation procedure which is best for judging student achievement. Each method has it advantages and limitations depending on the situation in which it is used. The key to selecting the most appropriate technique is the behavioral objective the teacher wishes to measure. How should a teacher appraise a child's ability to work cooperatively with others on a science problem? A written test for this kind of appraisal would be pointless. Observation of the students in a variety of classroom situations would seem more appropriate in determining progress toward this objective, but even "observation" has its limitations and must not be counted on for evaluating too many objectives. Two criteria for the effectiveness of observation as an evaluative technique are suggested:

1. Can the desired behavior be evoked in the classroom?
2. Has the teacher sufficient opportunity to observe and record what he sees?

Take another example: How should skill in setting up laboratory apparatus be measured? Often, teachers wishing to make such a determination give a written test and make their evaluations on the basis of such test results. A moment's consideration, however, shows that such tests are nowhere near as appropriate as having the student actually carry out the desired laboratory procedure. In fact, it is quite conceivable that students could answer correctly all the questions relating to the ways in which a Bunsen burner should be lit, but, placed in the actual laboratory situation, be unable to light the burner correctly and safely. Again, the kind of test that is given must be determined by the kind of behavior to be observed and evaluated.

Under what conditions, then, are pencil-and-paper tests appropriate? What can such tests indicate? If the teacher is concerned with determining how well students can explain certain phenomena, compare materials from several sources, make inferences, draw conclusions, or select significant factors, pencil-and-paper tests are appropriate vehicles.

It is also necessary to recognize that for measuring certain desired outcomes present devices for evaluating student behavior are still inadequate.

Results of attempts to evaluate such behaviors are highly unreliable and must be treated with this fact in mind. One such behavior pattern relates to the use of science information in the choice of a well-balanced diet. Obviously, young children are not in a position to purchase and prepare their own meals. Thus, the desired behavioral objective cannot be measured adequately at this time. In short, each teacher must recognize what he is trying to measure and to what extent his measuring device is effective.

2. VALIDITY AND RELIABILITY OF EVALUATION TECHNIQUES

There are two important factors that teachers must consider before using any procedure or instrument for determining student growth. The first and foremost factor is validity, the second is reliability. An instrument is valid insofar as it measures what it is supposed to measure. An instrument is reliable insofar as it measures accurately. A thermometer can be perfectly reliable in that it measures temperature accurately, but the thermometer alone hardly would yield valid results in measuring the caloric content of a substance.

The distinction between reliability and validity can be seen clearly when one examines the stated objectives of a given science program and then considers almost any of the currently available achievement tests in elementary school science. The tests all report high reliability. In general, these reports are true; the tests do measure accurately what they set out to measure. But an inspection of the content of these tests and a comparison of the items in the test to the stated objectives of a particular science class readily show that there is little relationship between the items found in the test and the objectives for which elementary science is being taught. Actually, the validity of these tests for measuring what is being taught in science classes is extremely low. The ideal evaluation technique must serve the purposes for which it is intended and it must yield information that is accurate.

Since validity is so important in evaluation, teachers must be very much concerned with this factor both in selecting commercial testing instruments for measuring the work of the students in their classes and in preparing their own instruments. The validity of any teacher-made instrument will depend on the degree of correspondence between the behavior that is to be appraised and the objectives that have been set for given instruction. It is for this reason that so much emphasis has been placed on identifying the behavioral objectives as the first step in the evaluation process. If the teacher can spell out the way in which a student will act after he has learned a given item or successfully mastered a given unit of work, he can then construct valid evaluative instruments by developing situations in which the student will be able to indicate how effectively he has mastered the desired behavior. For example, if it is desired that a student know the parts of an electric motor, a pencil-and-paper test which requires the student to describe these parts could be satisfactory.

However, suppose the stated objective of a unit is to develop an understanding of the interrelationships of the parts of an electric motor. A test which asks students only to identify or describe the parts of the motor would not be valid in relation to the stated objective. Some kind of test situation which determined the extent to which the student understood the interrelationships among the parts would be necessary. A valid test might ask the student to explain the relationship of the armature to the brushes. Or he might be asked to explain the relationship between the stator and the rotor. For the test situation to be valid, it must elicit responses that are very similar or identical to the objectives of the unit being studied.

Another important factor which teachers should be aware of both in selecting and in making valid instruments is the vocabulary used for the test situation. If a test or an item in a test is worded so that it can be understood by only a few students in the class, such an item is not valid for measuring the learning outcomes of the other members of the class. This is especially true in the primary grades, but also holds true for other groups in which there are wide variations in reading ability and comprehension.

Reliability of commercially prepared testing materials is generally not a problem. Such materials usually are carefully designed and controlled for reliability. But the reliability of teacher-made classroom tests depends upon a few special considerations. The usual and conventional methods of developing reliable tests of the standardized variety generally are impractical for teacher-made tests. However, since the major reasons for the low reliability of teacher-made tests are that such tests are either too short or too difficult, remedies can be found which will help teachers prepare more reliable tests.

First, teachers should include large numbers of items in the test; second, each test should include an adequate number of items which most students will be able to answer. For example, if a test is to be constructed to determine the ability of students to classify foods as proteins, carbohydrates, or fats, listing merely three foods—nuts, dried beans, and apples— would make a test that has little reliability and, incidentally, little validity. To improve the reliability of the test, large numbers of foods of each of the three categories would need to be included. Furthermore, among the items included would need to be simpler ones such as meat, butter, and sugar. Adequate samplings must be included if an evaluation device is to have high reliability and high validity.

Finally, adequate samplings are needed so that the teacher can determine how well—to what extent—a student is meeting the objectives which have been established for him and for the class as a whole. It is the student's performance on the samples included in a test that enables the teacher to judge the student's progress in the total area which has been studied. To obtain sound results for such evaluations, test samples must be sufficiently large and sufficiently varied in difficulty.

Categories of Classroom Tests

The classroom test is still the foundation of the day-to-day evaluation program of most schools. Yet many of these tests have poorly framed items, confusing directions, ambiguous statements, and other flaws that seriously impair the usefulness of the scores they yield. Some of the basic principles of test construction are summarized below so that teachers will be able to derive full value from the use of these instruments in evaluating student growth.

Classroom tests generally are classified into two broad categories, essay tests and objective tests. The essay or free-response examination permits the student to compose and express his answer in his own words. The response may range from a few sentences to several pages, and the accuracy and quality of the response is judged subjectively by a person who is competent in the field.

Objective tests restrict the student's response to a symbol, word, or phrase, and subjective judgment is practically eliminated in determining the accuracy of the answer. The term "objective" as applied to objective tests refers to the scoring of the response and not to the choice of the content. Objective-test items generally are classified as supply or selection items. In responding to a supply item, the student provides the necessary word, phrase, or symbol. In responding to a selection item, the student chooses a response from among those presented to him.

1. ESSAY TESTS

Essay tests have certain advantages that cannot be matched by any other form of evaluation. The chief merit of the essay item is that it provides the student with an opportunity to demonstrate the degree to which he can analyze a problem, select relevant information, present evidence, and organize his answers logically and effectively. In addition, since no answer need be completely right or completely wrong, it is possible for a teacher to determine the degree of correctness of a student's response.

Despite these distinct advantages, essay tests have come under considerable attack in recent years because of certain glaring weaknesses. Many essay tests, as they are currently used in various schools, measure nothing more than the ability to reproduce information. Merely phrasing a question in essay form does not automatically guarantee that progress toward such goals as recognizing causal relationships, applying principles, or making generalizations will be assessed. In addition to poor design of questions, the essay test frequently suffers from inadequate sampling, from highly subjective and inconsistent scoring, and from the influence of such extraneous and irrelevant factors as literary skill and handwriting. However, these are weaknesses that can be overcome, and the following guidelines are suggested to help teachers develop greater skill in designing appropriate items and in improving their methods of evaluating student answers.

a. Limit the use of essay items to those objectives that are measured most efficiently by the essay format. For example, the question:

What is the accepted composition of air at sea level? tests only for specific facts, namely, the percentages of various components of air. It illustrates inefficient use of an essay item. The essay item should be re-reserved for evaluating progress toward more complex educational goals than merely reproducing information. The following example, based on the same general topic, is more appropriate for an essay item:

Compare the composition of the air of a large community and a small farm community, and account for the differences.

In answering this question, the student would have to demonstrate his ability to use information to interpret data.

b. Improve effectiveness of essay items by requiring the student to use knowledge in situations that have not been discussed directly in class. Thus, if students have studied the use of the lever, inclined plane, and wheel, the following instruction might be appropriate:

There is a large stone in the playground which is too heavy to lift and carry away. Explain how you could use simple machines to remove the stone.

In this situation, the student would be using information learned in class to solve a problem that has not been discussed previously.

Another example providing the student with an opportunity to demonstrate his ability to apply principles might result from a study of the properties of metals. In this case, the student could be asked to:

Explain three ways in which you could test the "lead" in a pencil to determine if it is a metal.

Similarly, after a study of experimental procedures, the student could be presented with the following situation:

John heard that weak tea makes plants grow better than tap water. He set up an experiment to find out if this is true. First, he obtained two identical plants. He kept one plant on the shelf along the wall and the other plant on the window sill. He watered each plant daily. He used tap water on one plant and a weak tea solution on the other plant. He found that the plant which was given the tap water grew better than did the plant that was given a weak tea solution.

The student then could be asked any number of questions relating to this situation, such as:

On the basis of this experiment, should John conclude that tap water is better for plants than weak tea? Why?

or:

How would you perform the experiment to determine if weak tea is better for plants than tap water?

Naturally, the quality of the response would depend upon the grade level of the students, their familiarity with experimental methods, and their ability to make accurate inferences.

    c. Frame essay items that measure ability to apply principles, recognize relationships, or make generalizations more effectively by starting with such phrases as "Explain how," "Explain why," "Compare," "Interpret," "Show the relationships," and "Give reasons for." Essay items which start with such words as "what," "who," or "list" generally require that the student merely reproduce certain facts. Essay items that start with such phrases as "What is your opinion of" or "What do you think of" are usually inappropriate for measuring various facets of educational achievement. Frequently, the teacher who uses this type of phrase actually is concerned with the student's ability to analyze a situation or support a particular position and not with the giving of a personal opinion. Therefore, it would be preferable for the teacher to rephrase the question so that the desired response could be elicited.

    d. Word essay questions clearly so that the answers which students give will be limited to the specific objectives which are being measured. Too often essay items are so vague and ill-defined that pupils are forced to guess what the teacher wanted. If a student guesses wrong through no fault of his own, or if he interprets a question one way while the teacher wants a different interpretation, the responses become impossible to score, and the advantage of using essay items is lost. Thus, the question *What effect will atomic energy have on the world?* is much too broad and vague. The response could be limited to the destructive properties of atomic energy, or the constructive uses to which it can be set, or both. To be sure that each student will interpret it the same way, the following statement is better:

Plans are now being made for the peacetime use of atomic energy. Give two examples of how atomic energy could be used in agriculture.

In the rephrased statement, there is no uncertainty about what is wanted and about the specific areas to be discussed.

e. Allow sufficient time for students to answer essay questions. Since essay items are used to evaluate the more complex educational goals which require a good deal of thought, the student must have adequate time for analyzing the question, organizing his answer, and then writing it. When students are pressed for time, their responses frequently show careless thinking and sloppy writing.

f. Score every objective that is to be measured by the essay question independently. The grading of correct factual information should be judged separately from the grading or organization of material. If grammar, spelling, or writing style are included in the objectives of the unit, these areas should also be scored, but scored separately from the other educational objectives. If only a single score is given for an essay response, the student has no way of knowing how well he has progressed toward each of the objectives established for the particular science unit.

g. Prepare scoring guides in advance. By so doing, judging essay responses can be made more reliable. One of the chief disadvantages of using essay questions has been the inconsistency of the scoring methods. Not only have different teachers reading the same answer come up with divergent scores, but the same teacher reading the same answer has reported different scores on different days. To eliminate such inconsistencies, teachers can prepare a model answer in advance, indicating the factors that should be covered and the credits assigned to each factor. This guide can provide a more uniform basis for evaluating the written responses of each student.

h. Administer several essay tests during the school year to increase the sampling of subject matter. Generally, adequate subject matter sampling can be obtained more satisfactorily through the use of other measuring devices. However, where the essay test is the best instrument for measuring progress toward a goal, it should be used. In essay tests, adequate sampling of subject matter can only be provided for by increasing the number of essay items used. This is not feasible because of limitations of class time; therefore, several tests are necessary.

2. OBJECTIVE TESTS

The objective test was introduced into the classroom to overcome some of the weaknesses of the essay test. One obvious advantage of the objective test is that it permits extensive sampling of the topics covered, whereas the essay test tends to limit the amount of subject matter that can be sampled. Another advantage of the objective test is that the answers can be scored quickly and objectively. In the essay test, scoring is generally time-consuming and sometimes unreliable. The major complaint made against the use of the objective item is that it tends to measure bits of superficial and random information rather than broad understandings and more complex abilities. But this limitation, when examined carefully, seems to be more the fault of the person constructing the test items than of the inherent nature of the test itself. Items can be constructed that test not only for knowledge but also for the more complex abilities of understanding and reasoning. However, designing such items for an objective test is far more difficult than preparing similar items for an essay test.

It is no longer a question of which kind of test to use because both essay and objective tests can be used to advantage in the classroom. The most important factor is how well an item is constructed. A poorly constructed test fails to achieve its purpose and actually can interfere with the learning process. Therefore, certain guiding principles are offered here to assist the teacher in constructing objective tests so that greater benefits will be derived from the classroom evaluation program.

A. Supply Items. One major type of objective-test item is the supply item. In a supply-item test, the student is required to provide information, usually in the form of a word or a phrase. Generally speaking, there are two kinds of supply items, the short-answer and the completion item. If the problem is presented in question form, it is a short-answer item. If the problem is presented as an incomplete statement, it is a completion item. The following examples show how the same information can be elicited from both forms:

1. Short Answer: What is the source of energy in a flashlight?
   Completion: The source of energy in a flashlight is _____.
2. Short Answer: What is the atmospheric pressure at sea level in pounds per square inch?
   Completion: The atmospheric pressure at sea level in pounds per square inch is _____.
   or: The atmospheric pressure at sea level is _____ pounds per square inch.
3. Short Answer: What is the chemical formula for hydrochloric acid?
   Completion: The chemical formula for hydrochloric acid is _____.

Supply items emphasize recall of information and are satisfactory for measuring knowledge of specific facts, names, dates, and simple computations. In addition, supply items allow the teacher to sample a large body of subject matter in a relatively brief period of time. In a supply test, the probability of a student guessing the correct answer is reduced to a minimum. However, these items are not well suited for measuring the more complex abilities of understanding and reasoning.

Suggestions for Constructing Supply Items

1. Design items that avoid misinterpretation and require one correct response. The following shows how a poorly stated item can be improved:

Poor: The two most common gases in the air are _____ and _____.

Although the teacher expects students to respond with "oxygen" and "nitrogen," it would not be surprising to find some pupils responding with "invisible" and "important" or any two other qualities. It would be difficult to score such an answer since it is actually correct even though it is not the answer desired.

Improved: The names of the two most common gases in the air are _____ and _____.

2. Design items that require only one or two completions to be made in a statement. When statements are interrupted by many blanks, the meaning of the item is destroyed, and students are forced to resort to guessing.

Poor: A _____ is an _____ for measuring the _____ of the air.

Improved: A barometer is an instrument for measuring the _____ of the air.

3. Place blanks near or at the end of a statement. When blanks are placed at or near the beginning of statement, the student generally must read the statement twice before being able to supply the answer.

Poor: A(n) _____ measures the speed of the wind.
Improved: The speed of the wind is measured by a(n) _____.

4. Do not provide clues to the correct answer. In the previous example, the article is listed as "a" or "an" so that the student who does not have accurate information cannot guess at the correct response. In addition, the length of the blank should not offer the student a clue to the length of the word omitted. It is a good policy to make all blanks a uniform length, but long enough so that the child has room to write his answer.

5. Specify the units in which a numerical answer is to be given.

Poor: The freezing point of distilled water is _____ degrees.

Improved: The freezing point of distilled water is _____ degrees Fahrenheit.

B. SELECTION ITEMS. Another major group of objective tests is the selection item. In a selection test, the student is required to select a response from among those presented to him. Selection items are also referred to as recognition items and include true-false, multiple choice, and matching items.

1. True-False Items

The true-false test is perhaps the most widely used of all selection tests. It generally consists of a simple declarative statement to be judged true or false, such as:

True. False. It is the oxygen in the air which supports combustion.

A variation of the traditional true-false test is sometimes employed which requires the student to correct the item if it is false. The student must supply the correct answer in the blank provided, for example:

The sun is a planet. True. (False.) Star_____

This modified true-false item helps to reduce guessing, and thus provides the teacher with more valid information about the student's knowledge.

The chief advantage in using true-false tests is that the teacher can sample a large body of subject matter in a short period of time. However, the tests are appropriate only for measuring specific pieces of information, rather than broad understandings. True-false items are also very difficult to construct because they have to be limited to statements that are either completely true or absolutely false. As a result, many of the items that are seen on true-false tests are ambiguous and pose difficult problems, especially for the bright student. Another weakness of true-false tests is that they encourage guessing.

Suggestions for Constructing True-False Items

(a) Use statements that are completely true or absolutely false. One of the glaring weaknesses of true-false items is that the capable student generally can think of certain exceptions, and thus finds them difficult to answer, as in this example:

Poor: T. F.   The boiling point of water is 212° Fahrenheit.

Improved: T. F.   The boiling point of distilled water at sea level is 212° Fahrenheit.

In the first example, certain information related to atmospheric pressure and kind of water is omitted, which might pose a real problem for these students who see the need for additional qualifications before answering the statement as true. The second example takes these factors into account.

(b) Avoid using specific determiners that give students clues to the probable answer. Words that tend to identify a statement containing them as true or false are called specific determiners. For example, such words as "always," "never," "one," and "all" are found in statements that are likely to be false. On the other hand, words such as "sometimes," "may," "usually," and "could" are found in statements likely to be true, as for example:

T. F.   Evaporation *always* takes place more rapidly in summer than in winter.

T. F.   Evaporation *sometimes* takes place more rapidly in summer than in in winter.

In the above examples, a student without specific knowledge in the area could probably answer these statements correctly by using the specific determiners "always" and "sometimes" as clues.

(c) Avoid using negative statements. Negatives tend either to confuse students by complicating the meaning of the statement or to cause careless errors when students overlook them, as in the following:

T. F.   Mercury is *not* a metal.

(d) Avoid lengthy and involved statements. On the one hand, statements that are lengthy are frequently true. On the other hand, they needlessly prevent the pupil from readily recognizing the important factor in the item, for example:

T. F.   When a person moves from New York to Denver, he finds that the reduced atmospheric pressure at higher altitudes alters the forces exerted on water molecules, and as a result, water changes to steam at a lower temperature than along the seacoast.

(e) Avoid using statements that are partly true and partly false. This again leads to confusion and obscures the real purpose of the test item.

T. F.   Oxygen, a gas which supports combustion, was discovered by Newton in 1736.

2. Multiple-Choice Items

A second type of selection item is the multiple-choice test. In a multiple-choice item, the student is given an introductory statement, called the stem, and several alternative answers from which he must select the one that is most appropriate. The introductory statement or stem may be in the form of a question or an incomplete statement as follows:

Question form: Which of the following foods is the best source of vitamin C?

    (a) raisins   (b) grapefruit   (c) pears   (d) cherries

Incomplete statement: We get the most iron from a normal serving of

    (a) fish   (b) veal   (c) liver   (d) ham

Incomplete statement: We get the highest caloric value from one ounce of

    (a) lean beef   (b) banana   (c) white bread   (d) butter

In the above examples, four options are included for each stem. There is no fixed rule regarding the number of options used, but generally four or five possible responses are listed because guessing is then reduced to a minimum. With younger children, however, fewer options can be given without destroying the effectiveness of the item.

The multiple-choice item is considered the most valuable and most flexible of all objective items. It can be used to measure the degree to which a student can recall factual knowledge as well as measure the degree to which he can use the more complex abilities of understanding and reasoning. Many content areas can be sampled adequately even though the amount of time needed for answering multiple-choice items is greater than for true-false items.

The most serious drawback of multiple-choice items is that plausible distractors are difficult to construct. As a result, teachers sometimes use options that are obviously incorrect or resort to such alternatives as "all of these" or "none of these," which are more often wrong answers rather than right answers. It would be preferable for teachers to use fewer options than to weaken the multiple-choice item by presenting distractors that do not seem plausible to the student. Another limitation of the multiple-choice item is that it cannot measure the ability of pupils to organize and present their ideas.

Suggestions for Constructing Multiple-Choice Items

(a) Word the stem clearly and meaningfully. The stem should present a single problem adequately. Teachers who have had little experience in constructing multiple-choice items probably will find that it is easier to state the central problem when the stem is in the form of a question than when it is in the form of an incomplete statement. When an incomplete statement does not present a specific problem, the alternatives merely become a series of independent true-false statements with the student deciding which one is more correct than the others, for example:

> Poor: A study of plants tells us that
> 1) green plants store food only in leaves and stems
> 2) some green plants grow from bulbs
> 3) green plants need only air, heat, and water to stay alive
> 4) green plants and animals do not have common needs.

It is rather obvious that this item does not present a definite problem. Instead of the student being asked to select the best of four choices concerning a single problem, he actually is involved in deciding which of four somewhat related true-false statements is more true than the others. One suggestion which has been made for determining whether there is a central problem in the stem of a multiple-choice item is to cover the alternatives and see whether the stem, standing by itself, points to a definite problem. This would not be the case in the stem illustrated above. However, it could be improved as follows:

Improved: A study of the ways in which green plants react to sunlight shows . . .

(b) Include in the stem as much of the item as is possible and especially any words that would otherwise have to be repeated in each alternative. Thus, items are improved because after reading the stem, the student knows exactly what to look for before he examines the alternatives, as in the following:

The temperature of the water for sterilizing baby bottles at home should be 1) 112° F., 2) 212° F., 3) 100° F., 4) 312° F.

(c) Design distractors that are plausible to students. The distractors should appear to be reasonable answers to students who do not have the knowledge required by the item. When some alternatives are obviously incorrect, students with inadequate understanding of the material can arrive at the correct response by the process of elimination, for example:

Poor: The process of nuclear fission normally is started in a nuclear reactor by
1) neutrons hitting atomic nuclei
2) earthquakes
3) releasing electrons
4) volcanic explosions

This item can be improved by substituting for the implausible responses 2) and 4) new responses that are more closely related to the others, such as:

Improved: The process of nuclear fission normally is started in a nuclear reactor by
1) neutrons hitting atomic nuclei
2) uniting atomic nuclei
3) releasing electrons
4) neutralizing protons

(d) State the problem in positive form. The use of negatives tends to confuse the student and causes careless errors.

Poor: Which of the following is not an element?
1) mercury 2) oxygen 3) salt 4) hydrogen

Improved: Which one of the following is an element?
1) mercury 2) peroxide 3) salt 4) hydrocarbon

(e) Construct responses that are grammatically consistent with the stem. A correct sentence should be formed when each alternative is attached to the incomplete statement. Cues resulting from grammatical inconsistencies should be avoided.

Poor: The voltage in an alternating current circuit can be stepped down by a
1) transformer
2) induction coil
3) oscillator
4) alternator

Improved: The voltage in an alternating current circuit can be stepped down by a
1) transformer
2) rectifier
3) magneto
4) condensor

The grammatical inconsistency in the first example could also be remedied by removing the article "a" from the stem and using the appropriate article with each option.

(f) Use situations that the student has not previously encountered in class when designing items to measure such abilities as reasoning, problem solving, or any of the other higher mental processes. If students are presented with items that have already been used in the text or discussed in the classroom, the teacher may be measuring only rote memory rather than thinking ability.

3. Matching Items

A third type of selection test is the matching-item test. Typically, such a test consists of two columns of items which are to be associated on some directed basis. The first column is called a list of premises and the second column a list of responses. In the simplest form, the two columns have the same number of items, but the matching test can be made more complex by increasing the number of responses or requiring the use of more than one response item for some items in the list of premises. For most elementary school programs, however, the simpler test is more appropriate:

Directions: In the space next to each item in Column I, place the letter of the phrase in Column II which defines it best.

Column I	*Column II*
_____ 1. Force	A. The rate of doing work
_____ 2. Energy	B. A push or pull
_____ 3. Power	C. Capacity for doing work
_____ 4. Speed	D. Rate of change of position

Matching tests are particularly well-suited for measuring a large body of factual information in a relatively short period of testing time. Matching tests can show whether a student is able to associate events with persons or places, terms with their definitions, principles with examples, and chemical symbols with names of chemicals. Matching items can be scored quickly and objectively, and when the items are well-designed, guessing is reduced to a minimum. The major disadvantage of the matching test is that its use is restricted to a limited number of subject areas. Since the items must bear some relationship to each other, it is often difficult and even impossible to find a sufficient number of related items in all areas of subject content. Another weakness of the matching test is that good items that are not completely obvious are hard to construct.

Suggestions for Constructing Matching Items

(a) The items in the list of premises and the items in the list of responses should be as homogeneous as possible. One method for determining homogeneity is to see whether all of the items in a column can be described accurately by one term. In the following example, this cannot be done:

Poor: *Column I*

_____1. mammal

_____2. insect

_____3. scientist

_____4. gas

Column II

A. Pasteur

B. cat

C. mosquito

D. hydrogen

It is obvious that the problem presented in this example could be solved by students with the most superficial knowledge merely by the process of elimination. The items are so heterogeneous that no item in Column I could in any way be related to more than a single item in Column II. In the next example, only homogeneous items are used:

Improved: *Column I*

_____1. anemometer

_____2. barometer

_____3. hygrometer

_____4. thermometer

Column II

A. measures atmospheric pressure

B. measures temperature

C. measures wind velocity

D. measures humidity

(b) The directions should specify clearly the basis for matching the items. The purpose in providing explicit directions is to avoid confusion and clarify for the student the task he is to perform even in situations where the basis for matching seem obvious.

Poor: Match items in Column I with Column II.

Improved: The following problem presents a column listing weather instruments and a column listing what they measure. In the space next to each item in Column I, place the letter of the phrase in Column II which defines it best.

(c) The premises and responses should be arranged in logical order whenever possible. If dates are used, they should be arranged chronologically, and if names are used, they should be arranged alphabetically. This simplifies the task for the student and reduces the amount of time needed for answering these items.

C. **OBJECTIVE TESTS USING PICTURES.** Objective test items based upon pictorial material can be adapted to measuring a variety of objectives including ability to recall information, interpret data, and apply principles. Furthermore, they are versatile enough to be used in all grades of the elementary school and especially for students with limited reading comprehension. Since relatively few words are needed for this sort of item to be understood, the teacher can give the instructions orally. Test items based upon pictures can provide the student with clear and unambiguous problems that are interesting, novel, and realistic. It is true that there are certain topics that do not lend themselves to pictorial representation and that some teachers may be poor artists. Nothing can be done about the first problem, but teachers who have little skill in art can find appropriate material in books and magazines which they can either copy or trace. Just using pictures is of little value unless the pictures improve the test item and communicate the problem more effectively than the words they replace.

The following are examples of objective-test items which are based upon pictorial material:

Directions: Mark an **X** across the picture that shows a complete circuit.

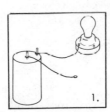   

This is an example of a multiple-choice item based on pictorial material. It has been successful in first and second grades with the teacher reading the directions orally.

Directions: Here is a picture of a tree with names of some of its parts printed on it. (See p. 334.) Use these names to complete the statements about the tree.

1. The food for the tree is made in the _____.
2. The tree is held in the ground by the _____.
3. Water is taken into the tree through the _____.
4. The sap is carried to the branches through the _____.
5. The food for the tree is stored in the _____.

This is an example of a completion item using pictorial material. It has been used successfully in second and third grades. Where children have difficulty reading the statements, the teacher reads the statement orally and the children copy the appropriate word from the picture.

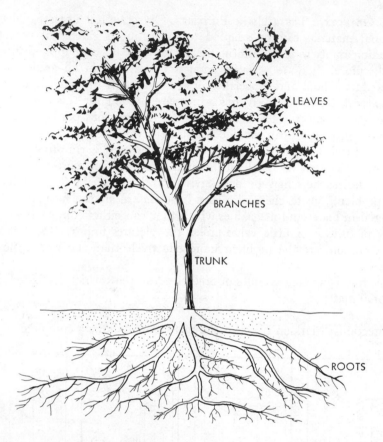

Directions: Look carefully at this picture of a sailboat being moved by the wind. (See p. 335.) There are two statements about the boat listed below. Mark an X across the word which makes each statement true.

1. This boat will move because the wind is pushing the ＿＿＿＿＿＿.
    SAIL   WATER   AIR
2. This boat will move toward ＿＿＿＿＿.
                          A.   B.   C.

This is another example of a multiple-choice item using pictorial material.

Summary Suggestions for All Testing Procedures

a. Check test items against the objectives of the unit to insure that the items relate to the goals and that the test items adequately cover all of the goals. One method of assuring a proper distribution of items is to use a simple coding system. Each objective can be numbered, and as each test

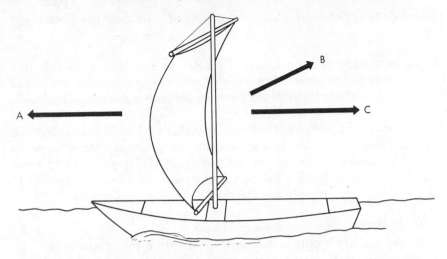

item is constructed, it can be related to the objective by assigning it the appropriate number.

b. Check the reading level of each item so that students who are being evaluated in science are not penalized for deficiencies in reading speed or comprehension.

c. Arrange test items in order of difficulty. This provides for more efficient use of the testing time. When difficult items appear first, many students use up most of their time with a few questions and never have time to answer easier questions which may appear later. Furthermore, students who have difficulty at the beginning of a test may soon become discouraged and give up.

Group items also according to subject matter and to type of item, and always in order of increasing difficulty. This system has real merit because it reduces confusion and helps the student focus more efficiently on the task to be accomplished.

d. Word directions for pupils clearly, specifically, and without ambiguity. The student must know exactly the manner in which he is to select and record his response and also the amount of time allotted for the test.

e. Analyze and classify pupil's responses to tests. They should not just be scored and then forgotten, but can be used by the teacher to gain valuable information regarding student difficulties, teaching techniques, and the test itself.

Observation Used for Evaluation

One of the most useful techniques for evaluating the attainment of many objectives of the science curriculum is teacher observation of student behavior. For example, two objectives of a unit on microbes might be

1. To help students learn simple laboratory techniques with which they can grow and prepare micro-organisms for observation and study, and
2. To help students learn to use a microscope and a microprojector.

Progress toward these objectives can be evaluated best when student behavior is observed in the realistic laboratory situation, but the observation cannot be random or casual. In the first place, the teacher should know exactly what he is looking for. Some indications of a student's ability to use a microscope properly are that he

1. Handles the instrument with great care.
2. Cleans the lenses only with lens tissue or with a soft, clean cloth.
3. Never focuses the microscope downward toward the slides; always moves the objective downward while the eye is away from the eyepiece, and then focuses the microscope upward with the eye looking through the microscope.
4. Arranges the mirror for optimum amount of light.
5. Prepares material for observation, using the techniques most appropriate to whatever is being examined; uses depression slides or bridge arrangements for comparatively large material; uses cover slips to cover smaller items.

1. CHECKLISTS AND RATING SCALES

Having determined the desired behaviors, the teacher can prepare a checklist or a rating scale containing a list of all the actions that relate to student behavior in a particular area. By using a check mark, the teacher can record his observations of a student's performance. The following is an example of such a checklist:

	Always	Sometimes	Never
Is careful in handling microscope			
Cleans lenses properly			
Focuses instrument properly			
Prepares slides correctly			
Arranges mirror for correct amount of light			

The data yield by this checklist can indicate how well students have achieved the objective of using a microscope properly. Such information is usually qualitative and subjective, but when teachers know what they are to observe, the subjective generally can be made more objective.

In the same way, to check whether the children have learned the simple laboratory techniques with which they can grow and prepare micro-organisms, direct observation of the student's behavior in the situation will provide the teacher with more accurate evidence for evaluation than will responses by the children to written questions. Obviously, answers to written questions can give some evidence and should be used too. But what is wanted from the children is not so much the ability to verbalize about what they should do, as actions which show that they can conduct themselves in the desired manner.

2. AREAS WHERE OBSERVATION IS INDICATED

An analysis of many areas of the curriculum reveals long-term goals which depend mainly upon observation for their evaluation. For example, there are goals like assuming responsibility, sharing and communicating with others, practicing proper health habits, developing sound attitudes toward learning, or participating in classroom activities. Attaining such long-term goals is an essential part of the science program. Observation is the most effective way by which to determine how well they are being achieved.

To sum up: Observation as an evaluation technique can be effective if the teacher has a clear understanding of the behavior to be assessed. Furthermore, it is incumbent upon the teacher to provide equal opportunities for all the students to respond in the desired manner; every child must have his chance. This requires a conscious effort on the part of the teacher. Finally, a written record of such observations is not only desirable, it is imperative. How these records are made out—whether they be in anecdotal form, in rating scales, or on check sheets—is not too important. Any of these forms can serve the teacher's purposes. What is essential, however, is that the teacher make a written appraisal of what each child actually has shown himself able to perform in certain areas of behavior according to a set of criteria.

Appraising Children's Projects

Another very significant way of finding out how well children are meeting the objectives of the science program is the teacher's examination of the material which the children produce. After all, what a child does and what he produces can tell much about the way he meets the objectives of the program. For example, we know that third and fourth-graders are collectors. But collections have little worth from a science point of view unless they are organized. One indication of a scientific attitude is the manner in which a person employs a theme for his ideas, and organizes his facts and information in a planned classification. A teacher of the third or fourth grade will want the children to begin to develop the ability to conceive of such themes and such frameworks, and to organize their collections and categorize them accordingly. Thus, the teacher examines a collection of rocks and looks to see how the rocks are grouped.

Are they organized according to the place where the rocks are found? Are they grouped as igneous, sedimentary, and metamorphic? Are they exhibited to show certain interesting phenomena such as weathering, water erosion, or ice scratches? Or are they just a hodge-podge of pretty stones? Neatness, beauty, novelty are all important, but not for science. What is being evaluated as far as science is concerned is the ability to organize and classify materials in a sensible and reasoned way.

Then there are the experiments which children design and the models which they construct to illustrate applications of scientific principles. An analysis of such materials can reveal much more clearly the extent of a student's attainment of the goal of expanded understandings of science than can any paper-and-pencil test. A careful study of such materials is one important way of determining growth toward extended vision and richer insight into the meanings of science and the applications of these meanings to appropriate situations. But such study requires that the teacher be sure about the objectives he is trying to reach. If this evaluation procedure is to have validity, the teacher must appraise a project on the basis of the processes used by the student in reaching his conclusion. Extended vision of one's environment, insight into the scientific concepts derived from facts, and understanding of how such concepts may be applied to specific problems cannot be measured by the quality of the art work involved in lettering the parts of an exhibit. Rather, it is measured by the clarity of thinking that shows in the resultant project. It is measured by the extent to which the exhibit explains a scientific principle through clear and simple examples.

Science reports, too, need this same kind of evaluation. It is not a matter of how many pictures are included in a report. Rather, it is the appropriateness of the pictures as illustrative of the points being made. It is not the length of the report, but the thoughtful organization and clear explanation of the material presented. And, as far as writing goes, a teacher may very well refuse to accept a report from a child because it is not up to the level of neatness or standards of language skill of which he is capable. Misspelled words and poor grammar are not acceptable in science reports any more than they are in English reports. But having to return such a report for rewriting should have no bearing on the science evaluation. In evaluating a science report, the teacher should appraise its worth as science—its accuracy of information, its appropriate explanations, its resultant generalizations, its organization. Science reports must be judged in the light of science objectives.

The teacher must be certain that the objectives upon which the work will be built and upon which it should eventually be appraised are stated in such forms as to indicate the type of resultant behavior desired. If the objective of a weather unit is to have the children understand the water cycle, the exhibit or project which shows, simply and clearly, how water evaporates and then condenses is much more truly an example of sound science thinking than is an elaborate poster of the various kinds of clouds, beautiful as the art work may be. And a simple home-built model of the workings of a gasoline engine—a model made from cardboard, paper fasteners, and crayons—is a much more acceptable project than a plastic cross-sectional, commercial model of a complex Diesel engine, even though the Diesel engine is put together with great care. What is wanted is a demonstration of how children are thinking, of how well they understand the scientific principles which they are studying. The home-built model shows this; the purchased plastic model does not. Only as the teacher knows clearly the kind of behavior he eventually expects from his students, and as he helps his students carry out projects which lead to this kind of behavior, can he develop an adequate basis for evaluating the work which his students produce.

Bibliography

Ahmann, J. Stanley, and Glock, Marvin. *Evaluating Pupil Growth*. Boston: Allyn and Bacon, Inc., 1958.

Ahmann, J. Stanley; Glock, Marvin; and Wardeberg, Helen. *Evaluating Elementary School Pupils*. Boston: Allyn and Bacon, Inc., 1960.

Remmers, H. H., and Gage, N. L. *Educational Measurement and Evaluation*. New York: Harper and Bros., 1955.

Thomas, R. M. *Judging Student Progress*. New York: Longmans, Green and Co., 1954.

Thorndike, Robert and Hager, Elizabeth. *Measurement and Evaluation in Psychology and Education*. New York: John Wiley & Sons, Inc., 1961.

Torgerson, T., and Adams, G. *Measurement and Evaluation*. New York: The Dryden Press, 1954.

Travers, R. *How To Make Achievement Tests*. New York: The Odyssey Press, 1950.

Materials and Facilities for Elementary Science

INTRODUCTION

Of all the areas in the elementary school curriculum, science holds a unique position because it offers countless opportunities for the children to do experiments. When children are able to work with a wide variety of materials, their learning experiences become real rather than vicarious. Not only do the children acquire skill in manipulating the same kind of equipment that scientists use, but they also gain greater insight into the key operations, or processes, of science and the scientist.

The strong interest in science education during the past few years has resulted in the development of comprehensive elementary science programs throughout the country. These programs require adequate amounts of supplies and equipment if they are to be effective. Local, state, and federal authorities recognize this need and have shown their willingness to support elementary science financially. Money is now being allocated in school budgets for the purchase of supplies and equipment, library resources, textbooks, and other printed instructional materials.

It should be kept in mind that the materials should be built around the program, rather than the program built around the materials. The learning activities selected for the program should determine what science materials will be needed. If the science program has a well-developed curriculum guide, then the materials needed will be those necessary to conduct the learning activities described in the guide. This same rationale would apply if the science program were developed around a single or multiple science textbook series.

As a rule, simple supplies and equipment are used in elementary science. This makes it possible to purchase much more materials, and increases the possibility of allowing the children to experiment individually rather than in groups. Also, simple materials can be replaced more easily when they are damaged or broken. Homemade or improvised equipment can be very useful, if the learnings that result are worthwhile and if an inordinate amount of time and effort do not have to be spent in either finding or making the equipment. However, no science program can be maintained by using only homemade equipment. Many commercial materials must be purchased if the program is to be effective.

Very few elementary schools have adequate classroom facilities for teaching science. Each classroom should have a fixed or movable table for conducting experiments and demonstrations. Water should be easily accessible, and there should be electrical outlets in each room. The teacher should be provided with suitable sources of heat, such as a portable gas burner, a hot plate, and an alcohol lamp. Facilities should be provided for classroom storage of supplies and equipment. This can be accomplished by using either commercial or homemade storage cabinets. Another possibility would be the use of wall counters, with storage space and shelves below, installed along one wall of the classroom.

There will also be many items that are used only periodically. These include special pieces of equipment and an assortment of chemicals. All of these materials must be stored. Each school should have its own central storeroom for science materials. If this is not possible under existing conditions, perhaps some space can be allocated in another supply room. If necessary, large storage cabinets could be purchased or constructed and placed in a convenient location.

Science Facilities for Our Schools K-12 *

NATIONAL SCIENCE TEACHERS ASSOCIATION

The teaching of science is concerned with helping students understand the facts, concepts, principles, and generalizations of science. Greater emphasis is now given to helping students think critically, be creative in their approach to problem-solving, and develop skills and techniques in the use of scientific methods of thinking and acting. To accomplish these goals and accommodate changing procedures, time, space, and adequate facilities must be provided for a wide variety of learning activities and experiences. This excerpt, a portion of a larger article that deals with science facilities for elementary, junior high, and high schools, discusses nine current trends in science education and their concomitant effects on materials and facilities. Twenty principles for planning facilities are set forth. Finally specific recommendations are made regarding facilities for elementary school science.

Current Trends in Science Education

Facilities that meet today's needs and yet look to the future must be related to trends, just as the trends themselves relate to the evolving goals of science.

An emerging pattern of changes in the teaching of science, as seen by identifiable trends, points toward the necessity for continuous evaluation of facilities and evaluation on the basis of sound educational specifications. Those who are planning facilities for science education today need to weigh their plans in relation to trends in science teaching. The resulting facilities should meet present needs and, at the same time, remain flexible for an evolving science program for the future.

Today's trends indicate . . .

1. Greater emphasis on inductive development of concepts and principles through the discovery or problem-solving approach in science teaching.

* REPRINTED FROM *The Science Teacher*, Vol. 30, No. 8, December 1963, pp. 48–60. Copyright, 1963, by the National Science Teachers Association, Washington, D.C. Reprinted by permission of the publisher.

Less emphasis is placed on the verification "of basic principles through demonstrations and laboratory exercises." As often as feasible, teachers permit students to discover principles for themselves through experimentation and problem-solving. Thus, the teacher often acts as a director of research rather than as the ultimate source of information. At other times, information is obtained through reading, discussion, lecture demonstrations, and even verification exercises.

The laboratories, then, must provide space and equipment for a wide variety of experiments performed by the students under the direction of the science teacher, as well as demonstration facilities. Space for reference work will also be needed.

2. *A shift away from teacher demonstration as a prime method of teaching and toward pupil experimentation.*

At all grade levels, teaching now attempts to involve the student in inquiry and discovery and uses a variety of methods to help the student learn the basic concepts of science. This trend seems to have special importance at the junior high school level since laboratory teaching at this level is thought to result in continued motivation for science study in the senior high school.

All grade levels need instruments, supplies, and equipment that the students can manipulate. Space should be available both inside and outside the building for pupil activity in all areas of science.

3. *A movement toward more pupil-teacher planned experiments and away from simple manipulation directed by detailed instructions.*

There is a decrease in the lockstep of requiring all pupils to perform the same experiment at the same time. The teacher also introduces students to methods of planning and carrying out activities that will test their own hypotheses.

Arrangement of facilities must be such that the teacher can direct varied activities with a minimum of traffic and confusion and with a maximum of safety and control. The kind and arrangement of furniture, the completeness of mechanical and electric services at work stations, and the adequacy of safety arrangements are important for success with this type of science teaching.

4. *A movement toward science for all students and away from science for only the college-bound students.*

Science for all students means not only serving more students but also serving many different levels of ability and motivation.

More classrooms and laboratories will be required, and it will be necessary to provide facilities suitable for a wide range of learning activities and abilities.

5. *The traditional science sequence of general science, biology, chemistry, and physics giving way to other sequences and patterns.*

New units and new courses in the curriculum, as well as renewed emphasis on earth science and the introduction of study about space, all make specific demands for science facilities in the junior and senior high schools.

Facilities will need to be adaptable to the teaching and learning of broad concepts, to the possible merging of certain subjects, and to the new needs of study of earth and space science. Facilities must also be prepared for the introduction of new subjects as well as rearrangements of the old.

6. *More homegeneous grouping of students in science classes.*

Such grouping facilitates flexibility in, and adaptation of, learning experience on various levels of ability and interest. For example, some educators believe that first-hand experiences may be even more important for the slow or average student than for those of greater intellectual ability.

Facilities and equipment should provide for a wide variety of learning experiences and for ways that these experiences can be appropriate to the learning potential and interest of students of all capabilities.

7. *Activities such as science fairs, science clubs, and out-of-class science projects on the increase.*

Any large-scale program of science project work places a heavy burden on school facilities.

Where participation in outside science activities is important to a school, adequate facilities must be provided if all of the objectives of the science program are to be achieved.

8. *Increased use of audio-visual instructional materials by small groups or by individual students.*

It is recognized that there are times, lessons, and objectives for which audio-visual materials are the most appropriate teaching tools available. In other instances, these materials may supplement laboratory or textbook. Such materials have an important role in the teaching and learning of science.

Provision should be made for use of audio-visual materials both by the whole class and by individuals or small groups. Educational television, programed instruction, and other teaching devices may also need to be considered.

9. *Increasing provision for flexibility in design and construction of science facilities.*

This trend reflects the need for changes in room arrangements required by evolving science curricula and the emerging philosophy which places increasing emphasis on learning science through inquiry and discovery. Flexibility also gives the possibility of adapting physical facilities to new methods and procedures and recognizes that there may be several such new methods during the lifetime of the building.

Flexibility in room arrangement will include furniture and major items of equipment, as well as work surfaces, storage space, and teaching materials.

Principles for Planning Facilities

The importance of principles to be observed in the design of science facilities was recognized by the National Science Teachers Association in the report of its first study devoted to this phase of science teaching. The introductory chapter of this publication contained a list of "General Principles Concerning Facilities for Science Instruction." In the study on which this present bulletin is based, respondents to the questionnaire commented on the principles and ranked them in order of importance for those who are planning science facilities today. At least 88 per cent of the participants in the current study considered each principle to be valid today. The following list is arranged in order of importance, as they were judged by the present respondents.

1. *School facilities for science should include space for proper storage of all materials related to science.*

Adequate storage for the wide variety of materials and equipment needed in science teaching presents an acute problem in many old and new facilities. This is borne out by the number one rank given this principle. Planners must consider the need for generous and proper storage of such essentials as apparatus, equipment, chemicals, consumable materials, models, charts, audio-visual materials, and tools. Laboratory furniture makers have developed excellent cabinets and shelving for many kinds of storage needs. The quality and flexibility of such furniture will pay big dividends over the years in protecting students and teachers and in reducing loss of apparatus caused by improper or unprotected storage.

2. *The planning of science facilities should utilize the ideas of many qualified persons.*

Architects, administrators, school board members, and also science teachers, supervisors, and laymen in the community should all be a part of the planning team. If plans are to result in the best possible facility, each planner should recognize and respect the areas of competence of the others. Care must be exercised that the whimsy and idiosyncrasy of any of the planning team not create unworkable or inflexible facilities. A wise balance between creativity and experience should be sought.

Administrators and teachers, for example, must agree on class sizes, number of classes that will be assigned to each room during a given day, number of periods per week a teacher will have for planning and preparation, and number of teachers using each classroom and laboratory.

The science teacher will often be the team member most able to contribute to the educational specifications area of planning. Such specifications should include the objectives of the science program; the variety of methods, techniques, and procedures that will be used; special requirements of the various courses and units of study; and the projected use of the facility both at the time of its completion and in the future.

3. The unique needs of science teaching should be anticipated in planning such general features as floors, illumination, heating, ventilation, plumbing, and electrical services.

The science area requires special planning for materials and structural details required for the science activities. The use of acids, bases, and a variety of solvents should be considered in selecting materials and finishes for floors as well as for laboratory furniture. Laboratory work requires optimum illumination at all work stations. Electric outlets for 110–120 volt alternating current are also essential at most work stations, and other outlets are needed for audio-visual devices and laboratory equipment. Ventilation will often require fume hoods and rapid venting with resultant adjustment in the heating system in cold climates. Plumbing needs include numerous sinks, especially for the biology and general science laboratories.

4. The amount of space in the science rooms should be adequate for a wide range of essential learning activities.

To accommodate the number and variety of learning activities taking place in modern science classes, more space per pupil will be required than for more formal academic courses; rooms should be wide, rather than long and narrow; and arrangement of laboratory furniture should help to cut down on traffic and confusion. The need for individual work stations in the laboratories has increased, and teachers have found that rooms with a width of 30 or more feet best accommodate such arrangements. Participants in the study agreed almost unanimously that from 35 to 45 square feet per student was essential for efficient classroom-laboratories.

The concept of a science suite or science center has prevailed in the design of many schools. In addition to the classroom laboratories, some of the essential areas of such a suite are preparation and storage rooms, reading areas, project laboratories, shop facilities, darkrooms, plant growing areas, and animal rooms. Of the total space used for science, approximately three-fourths should be used for classroom laboratories and one-fourth for preparation and storage rooms, reading areas, project rooms, shop facilities, or other supplementary areas.

5. Facilities for science instruction should include provisions for students to do individual experimental work.

Recent trends in science curricula and teaching methods have greatly increased the need for individual experimental work stations. The degree of sophistication of experimental work will vary as the interests and abilities of students vary. Stations for experimentation by all students should be provided, but a project room for highly motivated students must also be included if the maximum potential of these students is to be attained.

6. Furniture adaptable to class, small group, and individual work should be provided for science rooms.

This principle is closely associated with the concept of flexibility in science facilities. Recent designs of furniture for science classrooms make possible rapid changes in work areas for a variety of learning activities. The classroom-laboratory in which rapid shifting from class instruction to laboratory work may take place at any appropriate time is an example of such a facility.

Perimeter arrangement of work counters with regularly spaced outlets for utilities allows the use of movable tables and chairs for different arrangement of work spaces. Fixed peninsular work stations also give considerable flexibility for a variety of learning activities.

7. *School facilities for science should include provisions for the science teacher to work on plans, records, orders, tests, and the like.*

Efficient utilization of the science teacher's time and energy should be considered in planning facilities. Effective science teachers must do as much paper work as do teachers in other academic areas. In addition, they must plan and prepare for many kinds of activities in their daily teaching. They must select and set up the materials and apparatus to be used in the classroom for demonstrations and laboratory experiments. They must select and prepare teaching aids and devices and try them out before the class meets.

Most classrooms and laboratories must be used every period during a school day to accommodate the increasing student population. In such cases a convenient and well-equipped preparation room including outlets for utilities should be provided. This room might also serve as an office for the teacher.

8. *Rooms used for science should be so planned and equipped that their flexibility will provide for a variety of uses and for changes and adaptations to meet evolving needs.*

Individual laboratory work, small-group activities, whole-class discussions, and demonstrations may require rearrangement of tables and chairs. As curriculum experiences and teaching methods evolve, school facilities must accommodate changes in furniture arrangement and space usage. Walls and utility services should be planned so that expansion of the science facilities into adjoining sections of the building is possible at reasonable costs if new needs become apparent. Increasingly, the rooms themselves are being grouped into a science suite or wing.

9. *School facilities for science teaching should make provisions for use of an abundance of real materials and forces.*

Developing a functional understanding of science concepts, of cause-and-effect relationships, and of the processes and safeguards of scientific thinking make experiences with real materials and forces essential elements in the methods of science teaching. Facilities must provide space for students to have these first-hand experiences and space for the materials and equipment necessary for a wide variety of such activities.

10. *Schools should provide facilities for using audio-visual and other sensory aids in science teaching.*

Certain kinds of science learnings may best be accomplished through the use of motion pictures, slides, filmstrips, tape recordings, or television. The need for such supplementary devices and material is important for any quality science program. Thus, the facilities must provide for effective and efficient use of audio-visual devices and materials.

11. Science facilities should permit students and teachers to carry on experimental projects without daily moving or dismantling of equipment.

Rooms for research and experimental projects have become an essential part of science facilities. Teachers must continue to grow in their understanding of science and in their skills in the methods of science. If teachers are to motivate pupils toward continuing in science, they must have an opportunity to demonstrate their own competence in carrying on scientific investigations. The able students may partcipate in such activities either with their own investigations or as a team working with the teacher on a broader problem.

Space for these activities must be separate from the classroom-laboratory, and at the same time it must be an integral part of the total facility. A well-planned project room with large work stations is needed.

12. School facilities for science should include provisions for students to use published materials in planning their work, interpreting their observations, and studying the activities and findings of scientists.

Students need a place where they can read, think, and plan if they are to experience the processes of the scientific enterprise. Every science classroom, therefore, should contain shelves and files for the wide range of printed materials needed in the science programs—for example, reference books, a variety of texts at different reading levels, pamphlets, research reports, periodicals, and instruction guides for apparatus. These should be readily available in an organized file in the science area rather than in a library far from the place where they are immediately needed. A reading table and chairs where data can be noted and directions outlined will facilitate use of this resource area of the classroom-laboratory. Some schools are providing carrels, study alcoves, or other arrangements for individual study, either in a classroom or library area.

13. School facilities for science should include provisions for the science teacher to confer with students as individuals or as small groups, and with parents, with the privacy necessary for satisfactory conferences.

The concept of the office-conference room as an integral part of any teaching facility needs no justification in modern schools. Many planners have found that a room which serves both as a preparation room and as a teacher's office is a satisfactory provision for this need. Privacy must be assured, yet easy access to classroom-laboratories and storage areas must be provided. An entrance to the area from the corridor should also be considered to prevent interruption of classes when parents or others come for conferences with the teacher.

14. School facilities for science should reveal that science is a community as well as a school activity.

Many school systems have acquired and developed their own school camps, wooded parks, and nature trails. These areas as well as planetariums installed within the school, become an extension of the science facilities within the community. Learning experiences in earth science, ecology, and conservation are only a few of the science activities carried on in such areas. Supporting areas within the school building would include reference materials as well as space for display of, or work with, specimens brought back from field trips.

Facilities within the school should also offer opportunity for students to hear guest speakers and to be informed—through bulletin board space, for example—of science-related events and programs in the community.

15. Schools should provide facilities where experiments and projects may be carried on for others to observe.

A wider learning experience for all students is made possible through demonstration and exhibit of other students' individual projects. A demonstration table should be available for such student activities. Other areas for exhibiting the results of individual or group experimentation and projects should be provided within the science area.

16. Rooms used for science should be so designed and decorated that they are pleasant and attractive to the students, teachers, and others who use them.

The atmosphere of science as an active process is an important feature of the science classroom-laboratory. Many participants in the study also expressed the belief that students are attracted to science, in part, by the quality and atmosphere of facilities in the school. Both architects and furniture makers have recognized the importance of this principle. Color and form in room decoration and furniture must continue to be used in planning science facilities.

17. School facilities for science should include provision for constructing and repairing science apparatus and equipment.

Science teachers have found that it is often necessary or desirable to improvise equipment for developing an understanding of certain scientific concepts. Students also find the construction of equipment and apparatus for their own individual experiments to be highly effective in developing their understanding of the problem on which they are working. Therefore, an area within the facilities should provide appropriate work surfaces, materials, and tools for the construction of such equipment. This area may also provide for simple repairs on commercially obtained equipment. Safety considerations are important for this area.

18. School facilities for science should include provisions for students and teachers to use mass media in bringing science to the school and community.

Communication between the school and community is important in our democratic society. Moreover, adequate support for the science program in a school may result from the skillful use of mass media in presenting the activities taking place in the classrooms and laboratories. Facilities should provide opportunities for such activities as science assembly programs, science fairs, store window displays, programs for service clubs, television and radio programs, and news-type photographs of science activities in the school.

19. *The selection of the site for a new building should be made, in part, with regard for the potential contributions of the site and its surroundings to the teaching of science.*

In some instances, farsighted school boards have been able to acquire undeveloped land for school sites and to select and preserve the natural resources of the area for use in the school's science program. "School grounds are becoming increasingly valuable and recognized as important outdoor laboratories for school programs of study in science, agriculture, mathematics and other subjects." Ecology and conservation are receiving increasing emphasis in the new biological curricula. Therefore, it seems essential that the potential of school surroundings be explored and developed for maximum use in learning experiences. With the cooperation of the community, such areas as school gardens, wildflower and rock gardens, arboretums, school forests, wildlife sanctuaries, bog gardens, fish ponds, nature trails, weather stations, and outdoor classrooms should be developed.

20. *School facilities for science should include provisions for displaying both improvised and manufactured products and devices.*

Much learning will occur from observing well-planned displays, and students will often be motivated to further learning in science as a result of such vicarious experiences. Nor should the learning that takes place when students themselves plan and make good displays be overlooked. This activity may be a worthwhile learning experience for some students and may lead to further motivation in classroom activities. Therefore, modern science facilities should include display cases and tackboards, with some of these being placed in corridors as well as in the science rooms. Living things and their habitats are well displayed in the open courts of modern school buildings.

Facilities for Elementary School Science

In its earlier years, science in the elementary school was chiefly nature study. Natural objects were collected, identified, displayed, observed, and talked about. Incidental and accidental happenings made up a large part of the learning experiences in science. Little or no curricular design prevailed, and in many schools no science could be found.

Educators are now increasingly recognizing the importance of a K–12 program in science. They are also recognizing that such programs don't just happen—they must be carefully planned, constantly evaluated and strengthened, and energetically supported. Facilities, of course, play a large part in the program, but first must come understanding of what makes a good program, time planned for the program, and teachers competent to carry it out. Since not all elementary school teachers will be competent in science, administrators must provide inservice training programs, an atmosphere in which teachers are not afraid to try new methods of teaching, and continuing leadership for the program.

OBJECTIVES OF SCIENCE PROGRAMS IN THE ELEMENTARY SCHOOL

Programs of learning in science at the elementary school level should:

1. Provide experiences through which boys and girls can arrive at some of the concepts of science through observation, inquiry, problem-solving, and study of cause-and-effect relationships.
2. Provide science experiences planned around activities of significance to boys and girls.
3. Organize the learnings in science so that they will result in certain desirable outcomes by the time the child completes the elementary grades—for example, beginnings of habits of systematic observation, of quantitative thinking and representation; some acquaintance with modes of scientific thought; beginnings of a scientific vocabulary; and a desire for scientific explanation.
4. Help the child, wherever possible, to apply the methods of science to arithmetic, language arts, and other studies.

Space should be arranged and facilities and equipment chosen to support these objectives—not just to demonstrate or to be the center of attention in themselves.

Further guidance in planning for science in the elementary school can be gained from familiarity with apparent trends and recognition of relationship between school organization and facilities for science.

TRENDS IN ELEMENTARY SCHOOL SCIENCE

Analysis of replies from persons queried in this study indicate trends in elementary school science toward:

1. *Planning of experience in science.* Such planning includes both scope and sequence of science experiences. The content of the program has been broadened with much more emphasis being given to concepts in the physical and earth sciences.
2. *More adequate instructional materials in science.* This is especially true of printed material. Space is needed for housing and using these materials.
3. *Problem-solving activities in science.* The problem-solving approach using both materials and equipment from the pupils' own environment and commercial scientific equipment is increasingly central to the ele-

mentary science program. No longer is the cluttered table in the science corner adequate for elementary school science teaching.

4. *More effective teachers and better programs for preparing teachers for elementary school science.* A deeper understanding of science for children also requires a greater competence in the use of science facilities.
5. *Increased specialized personnel with competence in science.* Resource teachers and supervisors for elementary science are increasingly being used, often as team teachers with the classroom teachers. The effective use of such resource persons depends, in part, upon the quality and arrangement of the facilities within the elementary school.

SCIENCE FACILITIES IN THE SELF-CONTAINED CLASSROOM

The organization of a school has a direct relationship to the kinds of facilities needed. Where the self-contained classroom is in the pattern of kindergarten through grade six, at least two alternatives are possible. In one arrangement, work surfaces, storage space, and electric outlets are provided in each classroom. Flexibility within the room is an essential feature, not only for science activities but for learning activities in all areas of the elementary school curriculum. Chalkboards, tackboards, display areas, provisions for projection, workbenches, movable tables, and storage cabinets are necessary for good elementary teaching whether it be in language arts, social studies, mathematics, art, or science. A reading area with a place for a wide range of printed materials should be available with science materials taking their rightful place among these resources.

A dynamic science program creates special needs to be met within the self-contained classroom. The following provisions are essential:

A work counter with one or more sinks provided with hot and cold water.

A convenient electric outlet (110–120 volt AC) for a hotplate at the work counter.

Safe sources of heat for experiments, such as the small liquid petroleum burners.

Dry cells or a low-voltage direct and alternating current power pack for electrical experiments. (These electric substations may either be portable or permanently installed in the work counter; for safety, they should be installed beyond reaching distance of the sink and its hardware.)

Space for work and for storage should be planned together. Beneath the window ledge, counter tops of sufficient depth provide for some important science activities. They provide space for such things as terrariums and growing plants. Space for an aquarium may be provided but not in a position where it will get long hours of sunlight. When heating units allow, space below work counters can be used for excellent storage spaces for a variety of things for science. Adjustable shelves are essential for efficient use of all cabinet spaces.

Furniture within the room should be movable. Flat-top desks may be placed together for larger work areas, or the furniture can be moved to clear the center of the room for certain essential science activities. At least one suitable table in the elementary classroom is a great aid in carrying on science experiments and projects. The table, and other tables used for experiments, should have an acid- and water-resistant surface. The workbench with its tools for construction of simple apparatus is likewise an essential part of the facilities.

Many small and rather inexpensive items of equipment, such as glassware, magnets, dry cells, thermometers, pans, and plastic containers should be a permanent part of the equipment for each room. Adequate storage space must be provided, although the storage of science materials should not crowd out the materials needed for other areas of the elementary school program.

THE ELEMENTARY SCHOOL SCIENCE CENTER

A science center for the elementary school is an excellent provision for the science program and is an alternative to having all facilities in the classroom itself. The center may function both as a place for storing materials and equipment and as a place for preparing these materials for use in the classroom. At times the teacher may send a student or a small group of students to this area to prepare materials for a science project. A room smaller than a classroom but larger than a storage closet will serve for the center.

The science center needs large amounts of storage space in both closed cabinets and open shelves, a work counter with a sink with hot and cold running water, and electric outlets. A workbench or worktable greatly increases the center's value. Wood, hammer, nails, wire, cloth, metal, string, and many other kinds of construction materials should also be available in the science center.

Larger and more expensive pieces of equipment which should be shared by several classes may well be kept in the closed cabinets in this room. A rollable table may be provided to transport equipment and materials to and from the classrooms and as a table for class experimentation. Careful cataloging of equipment and supplies with storage space for each item increases effective use of the science center.

ELEMENTARY SCIENCE LABORATORIES

Another arrangement of facilities for elementary science teaching may be associated with a departmentalized organization of the school at least in grades four, five, and six. Parenthetically, it should be noted here that many educators object seriously to a departmental arrangement. They claim that certain outcomes of the self-contained classroom cannot be achieved by the regimentation of a departmentalized program. However, until all elementary teachers can be brought to a much higher level of competence in science teaching than they now have, some special arrangements will be required. In schools that do have a departmental organization, a science classroom-laboratory with adjoining preparation and storage area should be provided. Classes participating in such a program would be regularly scheduled for this room.

The special science classroom-laboratory has many fascinating possibilities for the elementary school, if imaginatively furnished and arranged for young children. It need not be, in fact must not be, a miniature replica of a traditional high school science laboratory.

The teacher in charge must be especially prepared and highly competent in the teaching of elementary science.

Flexibility is an essential quality of a room for science. Rearrangement of the room must be possible with a minimum of effort and confusion. Tables and chairs should be movable and should come in several appropriate heights for the variety of students who will use this room. Folding tables may be used so that large areas of the floor can be cleared for various activities. Adjustable chairs may also be provided.

As much counter space as possible should be provided around the perimeter of the room. Several sinks with hot and cold running water should be spaced within the counter top. Storage below the counter should include both drawers and shelves. Electric outlets should be provided at various points in the room. Storage cabinets in various parts of the facility should include appropriate space for models, globes, charts, large and small pieces of apparatus, plastic items and glassware, hand tools, kits, and tote-trays. A variety of materials for construction should be available.

Facilities for elementary school science should also provide for living plants and animals. Many schools have inside courts. With careful planning and work, such areas may become excellent extensions of the science facility. Small ponds for fish and frogs, or a variety of living plants and small animals may be maintained in such an area. Trees, shrubs, and bird feeders will increase the interest and value of the school's surroundings for elementary science. The science room should be placed so that it can have an exit leading directly to the out-of-doors.

Elementary School Science Facilities[*]

LOU WALTERS

Lou Walters describes seven current trends in science education which may help in finding the answer to the question as to whether science facilities are really needed in the elementary school in light of a tightening of school expenditures. With these current trends in mind, the author offers a number of guidelines for planning elementary science facilities. Although much that is recommended for elementary school science facilities is best provided when building new schools or through major renovations, the author believes a great deal can also be done with existing facilities.

The changed financial climate in North America has caused some educators and parents to reevaluate their priorities as they relate to school expenditures. For the last ten years the science program has been in a relatively favorable position in terms of financial support. Currently money has become considerably tighter and the question should be asked: Are science facilities really needed in the elementary school? To help find an answer it may be helpful to consider some current trends in science education.

Increasing emphasis on a strong, concrete, experimental foundation as the basis for teaching science. The result of this trend most certainly is an increased need for laboratory workshop space where students can be involved in a variety of activities. Facilities must include areas where students can be physically and mentally involved in manipulating science materials, performing and observing demonstrations, reading, or using other suitable instructional aids.

A shift away from the reading-discussion—demonstration lesson to an experimental approach. At all grade levels, students may be profitably involved in inquiry and discovery methods of learning. As a result, all available space both inside and outside the classroom must be utilized. Science facilities can include almost everything within the physical range of the students—the cloakroom, the school hall, the school grounds, the neighborhood, nearby ponds, woods, and streams.

A trend away from "cookbook" type activities and toward teacher-pupil

* REPRINTED FROM *Science and Children*, Vol. 9, No. 8, May 1972, pp. 8–10. Copyright, 1972, by the National Teachers Association, Washington, D.C. Reprinted by permission of the author and the publisher. Dr. Walters is Associate Professor of Education at the University of British Columbia.

planned experiments at all levels. When effective teacher-pupil planning is in operation, a class will likely have many different activities in progress at one time. Such variety of activity requires facilities planned so that several small groups may function independently yet under the supervision of the classroom teacher. A great deal of flexibility of facilities is necessary to cope with small groups and highly unstructured situations.

A *trend for more science, earlier, for more students.* At one time science was thought to be primarily for college-bound students. It was also thought that science instruction should begin seriously in high school. Later the junior high school became the starting point. Now nearly all educators feel elementary school is the starting point. Some science educators and some psychologists say that the elementary school may be *the* most important area of instruction. They feel that skills, interests, and positive attitudes toward science must be developed in the early grades or they will not be developed at all. There is some consensus that negative attitudes toward science may be due in large measure to the kind of elementary science program found in many schools. Statistical studies of science interests of children tell the sad story that somewhere between kindergarten and junior high school a tremendous curiosity and natural enthusiasm for science brought to school by five and six-year-olds has been ignored or beaten out of them, and has been replaced in twelve and thirteen-year-olds by apathy and unmistakable dislike for anything scientific. If the trend for more science, earlier, for more students persists, schools must provide science facilities at all grade levels.

Better-prepared science teachers and more science specialists in the elementary school. As a result of this trend, we are finding more special science workrooms or science areas being developed. Even small schools can profitably use full-time science facilities. In some cases the science area may have to be used to house other subjects, but that does not really present a problem. The difficulty lies in trying to teach science with inadequate facilities.

A *trend toward more out-of-school science.* The numbers of science clubs, science fairs, and long-term science projects are increasing. Science facilities should be adequate to accommodate and encourage these activities. Science projects sometimes entail a whole year's work, and storage or display space in conventional rooms becomes a limiting factor. In some communities science facilities might be planned on a broader level to include use by community groups, nature clubs, sportsmen's clubs, and adult education classes.

A *trend toward the increased use of audiovisual aids and other educational technology in science instruction.* In many cases teachers think of audiovisual aids in terms of sound motion pictures; but today a wide variety of aids exists to help instruction—slides, filmstrips, overhead projection materials, loop films, auto-tutors, and TV. Huge corporations are spending millions of dollars researching and developing other aids in the field of education. The science facilities in a school should be prepared to accommodate modern technology as it provides more effective ways of teaching science.

With these current trends in mind, consider these guidelines for planning elementary science facilities:

1. *Science facilities in the elementary school should be thoughtfully planned by qualified, involved people.* On the basis of current trends in science teaching and on the advice of professionally qualified experts in facility planning, each school should do its own planning for the science program in its particular situation. Although the idea of planning facilities for maximum use seems obvious, few elementary schools have been designed that way. The administrative offices are planned, the janitor's facilities are planned, and in some cases the cook's facilities are meaningfully planned, but science facilities? Rarely! Members of the planning committee should include the Department of Education, the school board, school architects, and epecially the science teachers. Further, each school should do its own planning, keeping in mind the utilization of any unique features that may be around the school—parks, public aquaria, wildlife areas, a school woods or game area, etc. A properly organized team of planners will almost insure rooms that are both functionally and educationally sound. This first guideline is the all-inclusive Golden Rule; succeding guidelines are merely extensions of it.

2. *Adequate facilities in which the students are able to work must be provided.* To accommodate the kind and variety of learning activities of a modern elementary science program, more per-pupil space is required. Facilities should be planned so both individual and group work are possible.

Furniture to be included should be carefully considered. Science cannot be well taught in rooms where desks are bolted to the floor. Rooms that have "skidfuls" of desks are also inadequate. The furniture provided for a new room should be as flexible and as utilitarian as possible. The furniture should not be bought with the convenience of the janitor as a prime consideration. To insure usability, flat-topped desks are absolutely necessary.*

In terms of flexibility, the furniture must be adaptable to individuals and small groups as well as to large groups. Many science teachers find that tables with two students per unit provide the greatest flexibility, and units with attached seats are not so functional as are those with separate chairs. Granted, the two-piece units are not so easy to keep tidy or to

---

* Some of the more traditionally-minded educators have considered sloping desks necessary for writing instruction, but an example of any place where people actually write on a sloping surface becomes more and more difficult to find. Actually there has been a decrease in the amount of slope on new desks in recent years. Now there seems to be just enough to be unhandy.

clean, and the movement of furniture may result in some noise, but those considerations are minor in the total science program.

3. *The planning of the general features of the room should reflect the particular requirements of science teaching.* When science rooms are being planned, special attention should be directed toward the materials used and the structural details required for science instruction. The use of a variety of chemicals is becoming more common in elementary science programs. Floors, tables, and counter tops with resistant surfaces should be provided. Electrical outlets should be spaced for easy access. Plumbing needs should be anticipated. In many cases, extra ventilation is necessary for the science room. Experience indicates that a minimum of three sinks is necessary, and a refrigerator is handy.

4. *Facilities should include provision for adequate storage space.* Both long-term and day-to-day storage of materials currently being used by students—bits and pieces, projects in progress, experiments unfinished—should be provided.

The problem of long-term storage can probably best be met by some form of centralized arrangement. If too many materials, supplies, and equipment are kept in one room, the room soon becomes overcrowded. Then, too, storage in each room results in some teacher's taking a proprietary view of "my equipment." The net result is unnecessary duplication. To ease the situation, a small room—not a classroom—is valuable. It may be located almost anywhere in the building if carts are provided to move the supplies. Care should be taken to insure adequate safety standards for storage of chemicals. To insure that all teachers know what is available, a list of the equipment and supplies should be given to each teacher involved in teaching science, and a running inventory and reordering system should be developed to maintain the necessary supplies and to provide new items as needed.

Provision for day-to-day storage may be easily made by building counters around two sides of the room, with shelves above and below. These counters should have open, movable shelves rather than the closed, locked variety. Materials currently being used may be stored on the counter tops and lower shelves, while the upper shelves may be used for display areas and book storage. This arrangement would allow students to carry on large, long-term projects without the inconvenience of having to dismantle or move them each day.

5. *Schools should plan their facilities so audiovisual aids may be used easily.* In some schools audio-visual aids are ineffectively used because the physical facilities are just too inadequate. A permanently mounted screen in every room is highly desirable. A teacher may wish to show only one slide or a few frames from a filmstrip, and to requisition and set up a screen for each showing is just too time-consuming. At times a teacher does not know until a situation arises that a screen will be needed. Sliding

panels for the windows to permit darkening of the room are excellent. In the *up*-position, they serve as attractive display areas; in the *down*-position, they darken the room completely.

The inclusion of several new audiovisual facilities may reduce the traditionally acceptable amount of chalkboard space. However, as teaching techniques become less lecture-oriented, the need for chalkboards decreases. Maybe the technique of having the notes for the day hidden under a map on the chalkboard and sprung on the students at the end of the discussion period will die, as it so richly deserves to do!

6. *Facilities should include provision for the construction and repair of equipment.* No one would favor elementary science reverting to "cigarbox" science conducted with a variety of homemade scrap, however, some equipment may be made or repaired in class. This might be facilitated by provision of a workbench, or merely by using about five feet of wall counter surfaced with edge-grained wood rather than with the conventional covering. Such an area could then be used as a place to drive nails, saw boards, drill holes, or to perform other activities that might otherwise not be allowed.

7. *The selection of the site should provide easy access to the outdoors.* If teachers are to make maximum use of their outdoor environment, getting to it should not be a major task. In many cases, absolutely direct access to the outside is possible.

8. *Facilities should include space for the display of reading materials.* Although current elementary science programs tend to emphasize the inquiring aspects of science, it should be remembered that man's scientific heritage is still transmitted primarily by the printed word. Each science room should have an area where reference books, pamphlets, and periodicals—including newspapers—are displayed. A reading table should be provided where students may use these materials.

9. *The room should be pleasant.* In planning any room, attention should be given to the color, design, and atmosphere. Nobody likes to work in an area which is depressing. It may be that more students will be attracted to science if they find attractive surroundings in their school's science facilities.

Much of what has been recommended for elementary school science facilities is best provided when building new schools, or when rooms are in the process of major renovations. A great deal can be done with existing facilities, however. Almost any school that utilizes local talent can modify an existing classroom to be at least adequate. If the science teacher, the industrial education teacher, the school custodian, the administrators, and perhaps other concerned people cooperate, much can be accomplished. Temporary coverings for desks may make them usable work surfaces; movable shelves and drawers on an empty wall may facilitate storage; utilization of an empty basement room may provide centralized storage of science supplies for an entire school; inexpensive and easy-to-build carts may be constructed for the movement of supplies from the long-term storage room to individual classrooms.

Perhaps the most neglected science facility is the immediate environment. Even the most urban schools have materials suitable for science instruction within access of the classroom. Parks, vacant lots, ponds, the school grounds, and anything else that furnishes materials and/or stimulation may be used with some planning.

Planning a Science Facility*

LAWRENCE J. HELDMAN

Appropriate facilities are a necessity if an elementary school science curriculum is to be successful. Dr. Heldman lists alternative ways in which an existing school can obtain a full-time science room. He also lists some necessary criteria for the selection of such a room. Structural changes will have to be made in order to provide for adequate water supply, electrical facilities, storage space, and work areas. Finally, a checklist is included for school personnel as they explore, consider, and plan for their own science facility.

The continued emphasis on science as a part of the elementary school curriculum has caused educators to re-examine the need for appropriate facilities to serve their science program.

The development of a school's science facilities can be realized in a variety of ways and from a variety of possibilities. If the school requires a full-time facility capable of handling a regular class then the educators must look for at least a classroom. If, on the other hand, only a part-time facility is needed primarily for storage and perhaps occasionally used by small groups, then a different type of facility must be sought. The purpose of this article is to explore the range of possible solutions and offer some suggestions for consideration.

There are perhaps three ways an existing school can obtain a full-time science room: (1) By incorporating it in the plans for an addition to the building, (2) Through a decrease in enrollment so that an empty classroom

* REPRINTED FROM *Science and Children*, Vol. 4, No. 5, February 1967, pp. 17–19. Copyright, 1967, by the National Science Teachers Association, Washington, D.C. Reprinted by permission of the author and the publisher. Dr. Heldman is Associate Professor of Education at the State University College, Oneonta, New York.

is available, or (3) Through some administrative re-organization of the school such as departmentalization or team teaching that would permit the existing rooms to be set up for curriculum areas. In this last case, the arrangements can be so structured that the existing rooms continue to serve the same number of children, but each room is shared by several classes. The Dual Progress Plan is one example of this arrangement while other variations can be found among some of the team-teaching programs.

Shared use of the facility does not necessarily mean an increase in staff. Some school organizations, however, parallel the programs in art, music, and physical education, by hiring specialist teachers in addition to the regular staff. What is best for your school system and what you can afford is something you will have to explore.

Assuming that there will be a room available in an existing building, here are some items to consider when deciding which room to choose:

The room should be on the first floor.

It should be as large as other classrooms or larger, if possible.

It should have a door leading to the school grounds or be located close to such a door for easy access to the school grounds.

It should have windows with a southern exposure which will provide a maximum amount of natural light for science experiments and demonstrations.

Facilities such as water and electricity must be available and in sufficient supply. Investigate not only the number of electrical outlets but also the service. How much electrical equipment can operate without blowing a fuse? Can an additional sink be added?

Additional items that merit some consideration concern the proximity to the arts and crafts facility if one exists, and the location of the room in relation to the rooms of the youngsters who will use it most. The professional staff responsible for the total educational program will have to weigh all the advantages and disadvantages before coming to a decision. For once the room is selected and certain structural changes are made, it will be difficult to make alterations.

After the room has been selected the next major step is to effect any structural changes that must take place. Utilities must be considered first.

The room should include at least one large sink with hot and cold water and a second sink if the budget will permit. One of the sinks should be large enough to hold a ten gallon aquarium or a small mammal cage for easy cleaning purposes. One suggestion is to design a sink that sits on the floor, similar in nature to the custodial mop sinks or the base of a shower stall. For example, a unit that is 24 × 36 × 8 inches with a six-inch tile lip would be adequate and especially practical for children of all heights. Remember, that in the elementary school, the science room might be used by children who range in age from five to twelve years. If there is some chance that an exterior greenhouse will be attached to the room at some later date, then one of the sinks should be located along this wall or adjacent to it. Water can then be provided for the greenhouse easily.

Providing additional electrical and plumbing facilities is sometimes difficult and almost always expensive. Devices requiring electricity are becoming more and more common in all schools and particularly in their science facilities. Therefore, it is essential that the services be sufficient for today and for future needs. It is suggested that 100 ampere service be supplied to a circuit-breaker equipped panel in the science room. From this panel, appropriate service could be installed in other parts of the room. This amount of service should provide for all present needs and future expansion. The number of outlets or other surface installations can then be determined by studying the types of equipment in operation at any one time. These will probably range from the more permanently used aquarium devices to occasionally used equipment such as movie and slide projectors.

The next areas of concern should be the storage units and work surfaces. When considering the space to allot for storage, it would be wise to examine the wide range of materials that are found in the science room. For example:

1. Published materials—*textbooks, supplementary books, paperbound or pamphlet materials, charts, maps.*
2. General classroom supplies—*paper, pencils, compasses, protractors, paste.*
3. Free or scavenged materials—*electrical parts, rocks or other collections, commercial samples.*
4. Chemicals—*special requirements for volatile, caustic, or poisonous items.*
5. Demonstration equipment and supplies—*hundreds of items ranging in size, material, and value from a slide cover slip to a 36-inch globe.*
6. Kits—*a variety of sizes, shapes, and frequency of use.*
7. Miscellaneous—*planting mediums, AV equipment, live specimens, materials requiring other than classroom temperature, hand tools.*

Naturally, storage units that provide for this variety of materials must include open shelves for books, cabinets for maps and charts, various size drawers for the smaller materials, and lockable cabinets for chemicals and delicate or expensive equipment. The use of book carts, tip-out bins, and portable storage units might provide some additional flexibility. Every storage unit should have a label-holding device. Built-in units can be floor-mounted and also hung on the wall. Floor units will provide work surfaces. Wall-mounted units should be hung at a convenient height and the space above them used for storage or for the display of student projects.

Work surfaces should have a heat and mar resistant finish. Stainless steel, ceramic tile, and a variety of synthetic materials are available to choose from.

Remember, the arrangements and materials suggested here are only guides to needs and not specifications that set a standard for combined storage capacity in an elementary science room. The storage capacity of the room when completely furnished should meet the needs of your program and be flexible enough to meet future needs. Keep in mind the following when planning:

1. What has to be stored?
2. What combination of storage units will the design of the room permit? What will fit?
3. How much is available to spend?
4. Can the room be added to at a later date?

A woodworking bench is very useful in an elementary science room. Such a unit should be equipped with cabinets and/or drawers for the storage of tools and materials. The top should be hardwood and equipped with at least one vise. In addition, the room should also have a demonstration unit from which the teacher can work or prepare materials. Some of these units are portable while others are built-in. The portable unit has the inconvenience of having to run an extension cord for electricity and carting the water to and from it. The built-in unit should have both electricity and water as an integral part.

A darkroom can be provided in one corner of the room by partitioning it off with drapes. The drapes can be mounted on a track in the ceiling so that they will form a quarter circle when drawn closed. If there are windows in this area, they must be draped and the ceiling light should be separately controlled.

Work areas for the students in addition to the ones provided by storage facilities can include tables or individual desks. Tables are convenient for group work, or the laying out of materials that would extend beyond the top of an individual desk.

The science room, like other classrooms, requires chalkboards and tackboards. Perforated board panels, particularly in the area of the sinks or over the perimeter work surfaces for the display or storage of materials are also useful. In addition, a rod should be hung near the teacher's demonstration area for a fire blanket. Paper-towel dispensers, a first-aid kit, and eye hooks mounted in the ceiling should also be considered. The ceiling hooks should be permanently placed in each corner of the room and in the center and positioned low enough so that wire or string running from one hook to another will not interfere with the lighting fixtures. A larger hook with the ability to hold a block and tackle or other pulley arrangements is an added convenience.

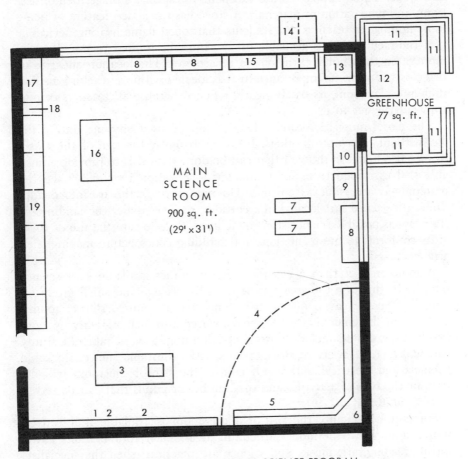

FLOOR PLAN FOR AN ELEMENTARY SCHOOL SCIENCE PROGRAM

LEGEND

1. Chalkboard
2. Book shelves above and below chalkboard
3. Teacher's demonstration area
4. Darkroom curtain
5. Counter top work area with sink and cabinets below, with tack boards against wall
6. Additional storage above tack board units (above sink)
7. Portable books carts
8. Student work tables (movable)
9. Oven and range unit
10. Refrigerator
11. Planting tables with storage below
12. Preparation table
13. Recessed tub
14. Indoor-outdoor cages
15. Storage unit with ceramic tile work surface
16. Shop table
17. Double-door storage cabinet with adjustable shelves
18. Map and chart storage closet
19. Student coat storage with tack board on doors

Consideration should also be given to the installation of a refrigerator and stove. These appliances are excellent for special storage, demonstrations, and preparation of materials. A stove has the added feature of being more familiar to teachers and students than open flame heating devices.

If the facility that is available for use must be limited to storage only, more often than not it turns out to be a closet. The location and size of this closet is of prime importance. If it is located within a teaching facility such as a classroom, its use is greatly reduced because all teachers cannot conveniently get to it.

The closet must be located where it can be used anytime during the day without interrupting others. In all probability, the size of the closet cannot be altered so the best that can be done with it is to provide adjustable shelves, adequate lighting, and an organization that will make the materials as accessible as possible. Do not overlook the use of corridor shelves, a science cart located in a corridor, or areas under the landings of stairways as possible science storage facilities. But, be sure the use of these areas conforms to fire regulations and building codes before making such arrangements.

A room smaller than a classroom is sometimes available as a science facility. In this case the area can be used for storage and small group instruction. Such areas as offices, conference rooms, unused shower rooms, and certain "basement" areas can be converted into such a facility. A room of this type should include water, good lighting, a work table (a sturdy cart will do), a variety of storage units with adjustable shelves, lockable cabinets and electrical outlets. Of course, the size of the room will determine the type of activities and the number of pupils that can be served at any one time.

Sometimes a facility the size of a classroom is available if it can be shared among two or more curriculum areas. Such combinations as remedial reading, art, music, and science are practical when the specialists in these areas serve the building on different days of the week. This arrangement necessitates that all facets of the facility, teaching space, teaching time, tackboards, chalkboards, and storage units are shared.

With any of the "art-time" facilities described (a storage closet, a spare office, or a shared all-purpose room), the major portion of the science program must be taught in the self-contained classroom.

The development of an elementary school science room as an integral part of the total elementary school requires a great deal of planning on the part of the school personnel. As you explore your science facility needs, take these suggestions into consideration and then make plans for your school. Below is a checklist that may be helpful.

Checklist for an Elementary Science Facility

1. Does the location of the room provide for an easy access to the out-of-doors? ☐
2. Does the location of the room provide for maximum natural light? ☐
3. Is the room located near the arts and crafts facility? ☐
4. Is the room designed in such a way that youngsters will not be hidden from the teacher's view? ☐
5. Has consideration been given to the occasional use of other areas in the building for the science program? ☐
6. Will the room be large enough to accommodate the largest class that is expected to use it? (900 square feet for 25 youngsters) ☐
7. Has sufficient space been allowed for the storage of text and supplementary books? (approximately 50 feet of shelving) ☐
8. Is the storage for maps and charts sufficient and of the proper design? ☐
9. Has a locked storage unit been provided for chemicals? ☐
10. Is there a sufficient number of storage units, including cabinets and drawers in a variety of sizes, to accommodate the equipment and supplies planned? ☐
11. If it becomes necessary to use the science room as a homeroom, have plans been made to accommodate clothing and other pupil articles? ☐
12. Have a refrigerator and stove been included in plans? ☐
13. Will a woodworking bench be included among the furnishings? ☐
14. Has a work area or demonstration unit been provided for the teacher? ☐
15. Have sufficient work areas been provided for student use? (tables and countertops) ☐
16. Are there at least two work areas in the science room with hot and cold water taps and large sinks? ☐
17. Has some consideration been given to the inclusion of a greenhouse, darkroom area, and cages? ☐
18. Have the school grounds been developed so that they can serve the science program as outdoor classroom? ☐
19. Have chalkboards, pegboards, and tackboards been included in sufficient quantity? ☐
20. Will the electrical services provide for today's needs and allow for expansion in the future? ☐
21. Have audiovisual blinds been planned for the room? ☐
22. Have other services such as gas, a television antenna, intercom system, and clocks been given consideration? ☐
23. Has an examination been made of the many miscellaneous suggested items that should be built into the room? ☐

24. Has some list of necessary supplies and equipment been drawn up to serve as a guide for teachers and administrators? ☐
25. Has a plan been devised which will provide annual financing that will allow for the continued growth and development of the elementary science program? ☐

Selecting Equipment and Materials for a Science Program *

ALBERT PILTZ

Albert Piltz discusses the role of equipment and materials in the elementary science program and cautions against the use of too complicated materials. The uses of film, filmstrip, opaque, and overhead projectors are presented. Dr. Piltz briefly takes up science kits, and describes the place of both homemade and commercial materials in the science program. The need for adequate storage of equipment is stressed. This article is an excerpt from the U.S. Office of Education Bulletin Science Equipment and Materials for Elementary Schools.

In learning science, children plan, discuss, read, report, and listen, but these alone do not add up to effective science teaching. The vital elements are experimentation and demonstration.

Equipment in Relation to program

What is to be taught in a science program and how it is to be taught should determine the equipment and material needs. It would be untenable to purchase a model of a power dam, a science kit, or some object and then build a program around it. If children are to assemble or construct instruments for a weather station, the purpose of the instruction should determine what will be purchased and what will be constructed. For example, a barometer or thermometer may need to be purchased, but a weather vane may be constructed. In each instance the value to the learner should be considered.

* REPRINTED FROM *Science Equipment and Materials for Elementary Schools,* U.S. Office of Education, Document OE-29029, Bulletin No. 28, 1963, pp. 20–31. Dr. Piltz is Specialist for Elementary Science at the U.S. Office of Education, San Francisco Regional Office.

Complicated materials and apparatus are usually not suitable for elementary school children, since they may confuse the child and sometimes actually interfere with the principle to be taught. Concepts developed with formal, complex laboratory equipment are often isolated thoughts in the mind of the child. Ideally, most demonstrations or experiments should be such that they can be repeated, varied, or extended at home.

The grade level, the geographical location, the textbook or the science guide or manual, availability of utilities in the classroom, and the ingenuity of the teacher are some of the factors which determine the materials and the equipment needs for a given classroom. Also, equipment which might be suitable for individual or small-group experimentation might be too small to be seen easily if used for demonstration purposes. Thus, content and method are factors which bear directly on the needed materials.

Since careful observation is an important aspect of science learning, much valuable experience may be gained by simply viewing the natural environment either in the immediate vicinity of the school or on an extended field trip in which ecological relationships are sought. Often observations which children make of the day and the night sky, of natural habitats of plants and animals, and of land and rock formations require no equipment or materials but result in considerable learning.

The teacher as well as the children can be alert to science materials in the environment. Collections of materials, besides being useful in study, may often lead to careers, hobbies, and leisure-time activities. Children may sometimes be encouraged to bring to school specimens from the out-of-doors or articles from home. It is natural for a youngster to bring a cocoon, a new toy, or a budding twig to school to "show and tell." This becomes a resource for the teacher and a stimulus to learning. A personal contribution helps the child to identify more closely with the project and to develop self-direction and resourcefulness. However, too much dependence by the teacher on the contribution of the children is impractical, since responses are often capricious. The practice of engaging children in participation by having them contribute material or construct apparatus should in no way replace the use of essential equipment and materials provided through the school budget.

Projection Equipment and Materials

Motion picture and filmstrip projectors have become almost standard equipment for most elementary schools and, in general, are accessible to teachers. For easy handling, many projectors are mounted on mobile carts which can be moved to the room where they are to be used. Classrooms are either equipped with projection screens and darkening facilities or special rooms are equipped and designated as projection rooms. With the greater availability of motion picture films on elementary school science and with funds for purchase being greatly increased, the use of films is becoming more widespread. The quality of films is constantly improving and they are geared more and more to the instructional program. Science films for elementary school children deal with subject matter that emphasizes, to some degree, the process and the application of scientific principles, as well as the products of science. Films that emphasize the products of science are oriented to the social studies and center around themes of transportation, communication, and devices which have made life easier in the home.

Filmstrips (or slidefilms) are usually 35mm. in width and often present a sequence of still pictures on a specific area in science. The teacher may use all or a portion of the sequence. Sometimes individual frames from a filmstrip are used for instruction. Synchronized recordings of commentary can be used to create a "sound filmstrip."

There is a great versatility in the use of slides, since the teacher can do his own photography and make or procure a slide for almost any subject. Slides may also be used with sound accompaniment—mainly from record discs or tape recordings. Bird calls and various animal sounds have been effectively used with picture projection. Many teachers make a hobby of taking their own slides in color.

Microscopes have many uses in elementary classrooms. Magnifying a specimen in science often helps the teacher get across an idea which may not be in evidence when the specimen is viewed macroscopically. However, it is important with children not to use so high a power of magnification as to make the part which is enlarged seem totally unrelated to the whole specimen being examined. Even if the teacher helps the pupil properly focus and adjust the microscope for viewing, he is not always certain that he will see what is actually on the slide or even the section of a slide that needs to be observed for study. The problem is even greater with live and moving material. Microprojectors have some advantages in this respect. Although microprojectors are usually limited in magnification compared to some microscopes, the enlargement in projection will generally suffice for most elementary school children. While a microscope can be used by one person at a time, the microprojector projects the object or specimen on the screen so that the entire group can see it. This enables pupils to discuss the material shown on the screen and helps the teacher to clear up certain points for the entire class. In addition, each individual has the same focus on the image at the same time. This may be useful in certain instances.

Since an opaque projector can project on a screen nontransparent pictures, flat specimens, and even shallow containers, its possibilities for elementary science are manifold. Photographic and hand-drawn or handwritten illustrations are commonly used. In addition, botanical and animal specimens of some types can easily be projected. Opaque projectors can be used for children in almost all grades. Some specimens too fragile to be passed around for individual examination can be projected for an entire class. Children also can prepare material for projection.

Overhead transparency projectors have a distinct advantage in elementary science classes because the teacher can face the pupils in front of the class when projecting the material. The teacher can also draw or write on a plastic sheet in the course of his presentation with an overhead projector. The chalkboard may be comparatively limited in this respect, since a greater number of pupils can readily view an overhead projection with ease. Much of the material used can be prepared by teacher and pupil, using various colored wax pencils for color if desired. With successive layers of transparencies or overlays, various stages in a scientific process may be illustrated or changes which occur in a life science sequence shown dramatically.

As projective techniques and materials are developed further, their place in instruction must be constantly evaluated by both teachers and administrators. It is well to keep in mind that projective techniques are used mainly with groups of children, whereas nonprojective techniques are more for individual use. Both types have their place in a good science program.

Kits, Carts, and Package Materials

Science kits and so-called "packaged science" are of particular concern to program builders because of their popularity and their potential misuse. The busy administrator who lacks the time to select and order separate items from the various catalogues looks upon the kit as a solution to his program and equipment problems. Likewise the teacher who is inexperienced in building a science curriculum welcomes the readymade program. Although the cost of some kits may exceed that of the same items purchased separately, the kits do contain useful materials. Some supervisors of science, however, have emphasized that an overdependence on science kits may have a limiting effect on an instructional program. This equipment, like other types of equipment, can be used effectively or ineffectively. Some persons are concerned with the stereotyped use of equipment, leading to the so-called "cookbook" science. To a large extent the kit may determine the program.

The several commercial kits familiar to most teachers and available in elementary schools have quite a range of price depending on the amount and quality of the contents. They contain a variety of physical science items, such as magnets, spring-balance, thermometer, and magnifier. They are usually marketed in specially built boxes with handles, which makes them convenient to carry.

Some schools or school systems make their own kits; they construct the box and obtain the materials for it from many sources. One type of school-built kit is designed to provide materials for the study of concepts in a specific unit or area in elementary science, such as earth science, the night sky, light, heat, sound, magnets and weather. In some school systems these kits are called "shoebox kits"; in other places they are called "science-concept boxes."

Some kits emphasize the assembly of a particular kind of equipment, such as a toy motor, telegraph set, question-and-answer boards, or optical system. The skills developed in putting the component parts together would justify the activity, providing the purpose of the activity is clear at the outset.

To relieve the problem of storing and transporting materials and equipment, a cart or mobile arrangement has been made available to teachers in various school systems. Some carts have been constructed in local mill shops; others have been built by school personnel. The cart usually contains basic science materials, both commercial and improvised, arranged in an orderly fashion. Much of the material is contained in boxes or in compartments, according to topics, and is labeled and inventoried. Some mobile units contain a source of water and a source for heat, and can be moved from classroom to classroom.

There are currently available several commercially designed laboratory units for use in elementary schools. Much like the handmade cart, they are more elaborate in construction and are intended to provide the laboratory facilities which many elementary classrooms lack. They come in a wide range of prices, depending on construction, features, and size. In the opinion of many school people these carts have solved, in part, some of the problems of work space, utilities, availability of demonstration equipment when needed, and mobility of use.

The Place of Commercial and Improvised Equipment

There is clearly a place in the science program for both commercial and improvised equipment. The value of each for its contribution to the educational process must be studied carefully, and the determination to purchase or improvise can then be made in relation to program needs and the purposes to be achieved in the learning activities.

In many areas of science study there are a number of satisfactory ways to demonstrate the same principle. To show the effects of air pressure, for example, the teacher may use either an elaborate vacuum pump or the classical "egg in bottle" demonstration. Each can show the effects of reduced or increased pressure. If resources are plentiful, a variety of experiments may be used. To reinforce learning and stimulate critical thinking, children should be challenged to devise their own methods of illustrating principles and experimenting.

To avoid frustration, all projects for construction should be carefully considered in terms of the children's ability and the availability of tools and materials. Adequate raw materials, tools, and work space are essential. If small-group experimentation is to be encouraged, equipment should be sufficient to allow all children to participate.

In a successful activity in which a model of a solar system was contrived, children used numerous references for information, many aids, creativity in mounting, and arithmetical concepts in measuring distances and making models to scale. They soon learned the limitations of the models but were stimulated to learn more about the night sky and achieved great appreciation of telescopes and optical equipment. If in construction of equipment a child is helped to better understand a science concept or can better apply a principle of science, then the activity is warranted.

In the past, because science and equipment facilities were often inadequate, teacher education emphasized skills designed to develop resourcefulness in borrowing, salvaging, and improvising materials and equipment to provide low-cost aids for teaching science. As a result, valuable teaching time and effort often were spent in the creation of makeshift facilities. As greater amounts of equipment and materials become available, more instruction can be done with commercial scientific equipment. Elementary school pupils may continue to build thermometers so that they may better understand the principles of temperature and measurement, but they will need precision thermometers for exact readings of temperature. Simple materials from the child's environment can provide rich learning experiences, but dry cells, wire, meters, and other apparatus cannot all be improvised. The child who constructs a telegraph set or miniature motor from metal, wood scraps, wire and nails, learns about materials, electromagnets, and principles of rotation. He also exercises manipulative skill in the activity. The commercial motor, however, gives him opportunity to study construction and, further, to explore the operation that makes motors useful.

Organization, Storage, and Distribution of Equipment

To insure adequate classroom control during periods of class activity, the teacher will need to work out a plan for distributing and collecting materials. Frequently used items should have storage facilities close at hand. When a classroom is being designed to include adequate storage, consideration should be given to the characteristics of each item, such as kind, quantity, size, shape, durability, and frequency of use, and, then, the storage facilities planned accordingly. Storage appropriate for chemicals differs from that necessary for telescopes, microscopes, large charts, or demonstration apparatus. Delicate or expensive equipment which requires special handling, such as galvanometers or microscopes, should be kept under lock and key. Chemicals should also be stored some distance from any equipment that will corrode.

Some costly equipment items which are used infrequently might be stored in a central location either in a school building or central warehouse or in a cooperating children's museum, materials center, curriculum laboratory, or audiovisual center. Much will depend on the facilities available in the school system. If items are distributed to classrooms from a central supply room in a building, a system of classification, labeling, and inventory will help in locating and distributing them.

Whether equipment is stored in a school building or at an instruction center, it is important that an easy method be devised of making it available to teachers if frequent use of the item is desired. Some provision also should be made for repair and replacement of materials and equipment.

Improving the Quality of Elementary Science Teaching

INTRODUCTION

A well-structured elementary science program requires the teacher to be cognizant of key concepts from the three broad branches of science: physical, biological, and earth science. This knowledge calls for a more extensive science background than most elementary school teachers now receive in their pre-service training. At the same time, the rapid and continuing increase in knowledge in science makes it difficult for the teacher in the classroom to keep abreast of new developments. It is a well-known fact that when teachers have a limited science background, they become extremely reluctant to teach science. Consequently, if the elementary science program is to be effective, consideration must be given to the preparation and professional growth in science of the elementary teacher.

The elementary teacher should be provided with a broad general education which includes preparation in the humanities, the arts, and the sciences. This is necessary because the teacher must teach not only science but also language arts, social studies, and mathematics. Very often the teacher is also responsible for the teaching of music, art, and physical education. A broad education, then, should enable the teacher to coordinate all the learning experiences of the children during the day. Because the teacher is working with children, the education of the teacher should also include an insight into the growth and development, learning, and behavior of the child.

The preparation of the elementary teacher in science should include the learning of as many key concepts in the biological, physical, and earth sciences as time and effort will permit. The teacher should also learn something about the relationship of these branches of science to each other and about the relationship of science to other areas of knowledge. Since teachers tend to teach in the same manner as they have been taught, it is important that the science courses for elementary teachers stress scientific inquiry and the opportunity to work with the materials of science. Finally, the elementary teacher should be given the opportunity to acquire depth in science, as well as breadth, if the teacher so desires.

In-service education is needed for the elementary teacher to grow professionally and to acquire increased competency in the teaching of science. Typical in-service activities include workshops, seminars, study groups, college courses, and special programs by state and national agencies.

The growth of elementary science and in-service education in science has created a strong need for supervision. Many school systems are now beginning to employ science supervisors. These persons, also called science coordinators or consultants, are experienced and competent teachers who have leadership qualities and a strong science background. Science supervisors can do much to make the science program more effective. They can help teachers by demonstrating special teaching procedures, preparing and distributing materials, and showing how to organize and plan for teaching science. They can help develop in-service programs and, when necessary, conduct the programs. They can inform teachers, administrators, and the public about new developments in science education and research. They can assist in the selection of supplies, equipment, facilities, books, films, and other instructional materials. They can work with elementary, junior high, and high school teachers to develop a continuous K–12 science program for the school system. Finally, they can maintain a liaison with college, university, and state department personnel in science.

The improvement of science education in our elementary schools has become a matter of local, state, and national concern. On the local level the principal and superintendent are beginning to take a leadership role in fostering and instituting curriculum developments and innovations in the teaching of science. State departments of education are strengthening their position and efforts in improving science education in the schools. On the national level the U.S. Office of Education, through its specialists, continues to make excellent contributions to science education. The National Science Foundation, in existence only since 1950, has extended its broad program to include institutes for improving the science teaching of elementary teachers.

Preservice Science Education of Elementary School Teachers[*]

AMERICAN ASSOCIATION for the ADVANCEMENT of SCIENCE

The following article presents pertinent sections from a report which was the product of a project sponsored by the American Association for the Advancement of Science (AAAS) Commission on Science Education, and was sponsored by the National Science Foundation. The report, taking into consideration the new elementary science programs that have been developed, offers comprehensive guidelines, standards, and recommendations for the preservice science education of elementary school teachers. It attempts to suggest how the teachers should be prepared, both to teach these new programs and to continue their study after graduation in order to adjust to a changing curriculum.

The success of the new programs in science for high schools pointed up the urgency of, and possibilities for, improving science teaching in elementary schools and colleges. Now new science programs for elementary schools are available and are being introduced into schools. At the same time important changes are taking place in college science teaching and preservice teacher education programs are under constant study. Many innovations are being introduced. The support by the U.S. Office of Education of the development of Model Projects for the preservice education of elementary teachers may result in changes on a wide scale.[1] Furthermore the more realistic and flexible standards of the National Council for Accreditation of Teacher Education not only make change more possible, but actually place a premium on carefully conceived innovations. The time could scarcely be more propitious for a re-constitution of the preparation of elementary teachers to teach science.

New materials have become available within the past eight years which

---

[*] REPRINTED FROM *Preservice Science Education of Elementary School Teachers*, American Association for the Advancement of Science, Washington, D.C., Misc. Publ. No. 70-5, 1966, pp. 5, 6, 11, 12, 14–21, 23–32, 44–47, by permission of the publisher.

[1] Here and throughout the report, "Model Project" refers to one of the nine models for elementary teacher education developed under contracts with the U.S. Office of Education, Bureau of Research. Models were submitted to the Bureau on October 31, 1968. Further information about the projects can be obtained from Elementary Teacher Education Project, Division of Elementary and Secondary Education Research, Bureau of Research, U.S. Office of Education, 400 Maryland Avenue, S.W., Washington, D.C. 20202.

make possible a dramatic revolution in the teaching of science in elementary schools. The standards, guidelines, and recommendations in this report have been prepared for all of those responsible for assisting prospective elementary teachers to acquire the competencies necessary to teach the new science programs. Each of the new science programs is unique in its own way but all possess certain commonalities which should become the principal focus of the teacher preparation program.

Some of these are:

1. an emphasis upon the investigative nature of science (inquiry and discovery).
2. a conviction that children need to be actively involved with materials that are conceptually rich for the learning of science.
3. an emphasis upon independent learning with opportunities to explore, "try out," "play with" and in other ways initiate their own learning.
4. an attempt to establish a sequence of instruction to help assure the child's acquisition of skills in the processes of sciences as an important part of their intellectual growth.
5. a valid presentation of science materials so that concepts will not need to be corrected later.

Although the primary concern is with science teaching, it is impossible to look at the preparation needed for elementary teachers to teach science without considering other aspects of preservice teacher education. Considerations have ranged from elementary science to liberal education in college, from attitudes to manipulative skills, from performance objectives and individualized instruction to the spirit of inquiry and being human. It is clear that the problem involves more than the revision of college science courses or reordering the professional education sequence.

How Should Science Be Taught?

In this section an attempt is made to outline the competencies in science that elementary school teachers should have. These competencies can and must be acquired in a reasonable amount of time. Time is also needed to study literature, the arts, and social sciences. The focus is on the kinds of science experiences that elementary teachers should have in order to teach as well as to live in contemporary (or ever changing) society.

The teaching functions required of a teacher of elementary school science are likely to vary from region to region and from year to year. For this reason a teacher's preparation through college programs must provide a base which is sufficiently broad and flexible to permit continued study and adaptation to new findings in science and to new teaching methods.

It is well to remember that the general approach of a teacher to his teaching functions usually reflects the pattern of instruction which he himself received in college. That is, a teacher who fails to acquire excitement and the spirit of inquiry and relatedness from his own preparation in science is not likely to convey these qualities to his own students.

The adage that "we teach as we are taught" is not without foundation. If elementary teachers are to present science as an exciting exploration of the natural world where pupils have ample opportunity to interact with that world, to ask questions of nature as well as of people, and to discover that even young people can find order there, teachers, too, must have such opportunities. What is done in college science courses will materially affect the way that elementary teachers teach science.

SCIENTIFIC INQUIRY

Guideline I. Science for elementary teachers should be taught in the same style of open inquiry that is encouraged in elementary science programs. The student's science experiences should develop his ability to actively investigate natural phenomena and should result in his enthusiasm for and confidence in teaching science through inquiry to children.

Objectives

A *Ability to investigate.* The teacher will demonstrate his ability to carry out an investigation when presented data or a question about a natural phenomena.

B. *Science as inquiry.* The teacher will demonstrate his enthusiasm for teaching science as inquiry to children by emphasizing investigation over memorization of facts.

C. *Teaching science as inquiry.* The teacher will demonstrate confidence in his ability to teach science as inquiry by selecting the inquiry approach rather than the show and tell approach.

ATTITUDES TOWARD SCIENCE

Guideline II. Science experiences of elementary teachers should develop in teachers an appreciation for the historical, philosophical, and current significance of science to society, and positive attitudes about science which result in a more objective approach to everyday problems, in improved teaching of science in their classroom as well as in increased interest in science-related activities.

Some Objectives

A. *Demand for data.* The teacher will demonstrate confidence in scientific measurements, empirical data and accepted principles, and to question unsupported pronouncements.

B. *Nature of concepts and theories.* The teacher will recognize that the established concepts and theories of science are valid only insofar as they are constant with the observed phenomena of nature and that they must be modified if this is necessary to accommodate new findings.
  1. Given experimental results in which the mass of the identifiable products is not the same as the mass of known reactants, search for some explanation for the apparent disagreement with the law of mass conservation.

C. *Interest in science.* The teacher will demonstrate his interest in science by activities such as reading and conducting experiments.
  1. Read science-related articles and books which are not required as part of a course.
  2. Plan and conduct experiments on his own volition or manipulate science equipment provided by the professor when he is invited (but not required) to do so.

D. *Encouraging science activities in pupils.* The teacher will encourage pupils to show curiosity and inventiveness in science by helping pupils design experiments that will answer their questions.

E. *Relevance of science.* The teacher will state how the lives of some members of a community have been affected by science and technology resulting from science.
  1. Suggest investigations of the development and use of forms of energy such as electricity and nuclear energy.
  2. Plan and conduct a visit to an installation which processes the wastes of society.
  3. Suggest investigations that will illustrate the effects of waste products from engines upon plant and animal life.

THE PROCESSES OF SCIENCE

Guideline III. The science experiences for elementary teachers should develop competence in inquiry skills or processes of scientific inquiry.

A. *Observation and inference.* The teachers will distinguish observations and evidence from inferences and conclusions, and will demonstrate his ability to make reasonable inferences when presented with empirical data. For example:

1. Given data concerning the fossil records of a region, voluntarily construct inferences concerning its geologic history.
2. Construct testable inferences to explain the unusual growth rate of a plant without being asked to do so.

B. *Variables.* Through the observation of a phenomenon the teacher will be able to state a problem to be investigated, identify the variables which affect the results of the investigation and how and why they are or are not controlled.

C. *Definitions.* The teacher will distinguish between operational and conceptual definitions.

D. *Measurement.* The teacher will demonstrate the measurement of variables such as length, mass, force, time, temperature, and volume in standard and arbitrary units and estimate the error of measurement. The following areas should be included:
Determination of Magnitudes
Finding rate of change, given measurements that change with time
Probability and uncertainty

E. *Classification.* The teacher will construct a classification scheme for a set of objects, given objects which differ in more than one way. Use a given classification scheme to identify living and nonliving materials. Objects from the biological, physical and earth sciences should be used for classification.

F. *Organization of data.* The teacher will collect and organize data and describe the rationale for the organization.
1. Present data obtained in a science experiment by describing, drawing a diagram, graphing, or tabulating.

G. *Constructing hypotheses and generalizations.* The teacher will construct a hypothesis, or generalization based on data or a question.
1. Construct a hypothesis to explain an unfamiliar phenomenon demonstrated by the professor or shown in a film clip.

H. *Testing hypotheses.* The teacher will construct an experimental test of a hypothesis, inference, generalization, or question.

1. Test the validity of the hypothesis made to explain an unfamiliar phenomenon by performing an appropriate experiment.

I. *Modifying hypotheses and generalizations.* The teacher will accept, reject, or modify hypotheses and generalizations based on new data and describe the basis of the decision.
1. Modify a generalization and justify the modification on the basis of empirical data or of assumptions of a theory.

J. *Verifications.* The teacher will demonstrate a recognition of the need for additional information in some situation by searching out the information or designing an experiment.

1. When confronted with alternative interpretations of data which are obtained, check the results by returning to the laboratory or referring to a reference work to obtain additional data.

K. *Communication.* The teacher will describe an experiment orally or in writing with sufficient clarity that another person could replicate the experiment.

L. *Model Building.* The teacher will devise and use a mathematical or physical model of the system being studied which contains the essential variables and their relationship.

SCIENTIFIC KNOWLEDGE

The elementary teacher should possess a background of science information. It is unreasonable and unnecessary to expect elementary teachers to learn all of their science while they are teaching it to children. Yet elementary teachers frequently complain that this is precisely what they are required to do because they see no relationship between the content and mode of instruction of their college courses and science they are expected to teach. Efforts should be made to relate the science topics that are taught to teachers to the science topics that are taught to children. The college professor must constantly remind himself that the teachers will not become research scientists. They may benefit more from qualitative and semi-quantitative treatments which are correct but incomplete than from rigorous arguments which depend on mathematical sophistication or logical subtleties that they are unprepared to follow.

To accomplish the objective of providing appropriate science education for teachers, professors of education and professors of science must cooperate in planning and implementing these science programs.

Guideline IV. The content of college science experiences for elementary teachers should be selected so that the topics studied by teachers provide, as a minimum, an adequate background for the topics taught in elementary schools.

Suggested Topics

A. *Composition, characteristics, and structure of matter.* The teacher will describe observations of living and nonliving objects in terms of their physical, chemical, and biological composition, characteristics, and structure. He will demonstrate the use of the particle nature of matter—molecules, atoms, atomic nuclei—and kinetic theory to explain the observations he describes. The following areas should be included:

Physical properties such as density, viscosity, pressure, solubility, elasticity, surface tension

Physical changes in physical, biological and geological systems

Morphology of living things

Atomic theory

Kinetic theory

B. *Interactions of matter*. The teacher will describe observed interactions of living and nonliving matter using concepts such as forces, electrical charge, magnetic fields, biological tropisms, and food webs. He will construct hypotheses and tests of hypotheses concerning the observed interactions.

C. *Conversion and conservation of energy*. The teacher will demonstrate the conversion of energy from one to another, will measure the amounts of energy transformed, and will search for sources of energy loss when observations appear to contradict the generalization that energy is conserved. The following areas should be included:

Transfer of energy

Transformation of energy in living and nonliving systems

Conservation of energy

Energy carried by waves

D. *Growth and reproduction*. The teacher will describe the processes of growth and reproduction in plants and animals including man.

E. *Evolution and genetics*. The teacher will construct inferences about the long range effects of selective mating and genetic mutation on plant and animal communities and sometimes including human communities and societies. Topics should include the following:

Variation

Adaptation

Mutation

Principles of Evolution and Genetics

Structure and Function

F. *Ecology*. The teacher will describe the interactions which exist among living organisms in ecosystems.

G. *Human perception, learning, and behavior*. The teacher will describe the neurological basis of perception, learning, and behavior.

H. *Conceptual structure and world view*. The teacher will describe the nature of the earth, the universe and the biotic world and construct physical and mental models that can be used to explain natural phenomena they encounter. The following areas should be considered:

Observational astronomy
Historical geology

I. *The development of scientific ideas.* The teacher will describe the relationship of the progress of science to the development of modern thought.

The unknowns of science as well as the knowns
The failures as well as the successes of scientific endeavors
The relationships of scientific disciplines to each other

J. *Social implications of science.* The teacher will state evidence of changes in society and culture that have resulted from the products of scientific work, and of the influence of social conditions on scientific activities.

Relationship of science to the progress of civilization
The cybernetics aspects of scientific thought and social phenomena

CONTINUOUS LEARNING

Science experiences should develop in teachers habits of continually seeking new information, of testing old concepts against new ideas, and of modifying their instructional procedures if new information about science or learning suggest modification. The way in which science is taught can have a significant effect on developing these habits in teachers. Developing the habit of continuous learning in teachers is probably the single most important outcome of preservice education. Without the habit, a teacher will quickly become obsolete and ineffective; with it, he can continually improve his teaching skill and effectiveness. Without the habit he will have difficulty coping with future changes in elementary science education; with it he will welcome the challenge of change.

Guideline V. Science experiences should be selected so as to develop a capacity and disposition for continuous learning which the teacher should demonstrate by engaging in science activities which will provide new information and experiences capable of affecting existing attitudes, ideas, and teaching.

Objectives

A. *Capacity and disposition for continuous learning.* The teacher will demonstrate his capacity and disposition for continuous learning by habitually engaging in activities which will provide new information capable of affecting existing attitudes and ideas.

    1. Identify and describe view points on contemporary scientific issues and on the learning process as presented in current literature, or

through personal contacts.

2. Demonstrate the ability to obtain relevant information on scientific and educational issues.
3. Identify possible interrelationships between events in different fields of knowledge.
4. Identify weaknesses in his educational background and correct them accordingly.

SPECIALIST SCIENCE TEACHERS

In the above list of competencies no distinction is made between the person who will teach in a self-contained classroom and the special science teacher. The question of whether science should be taught by a special teacher or the teacher responsible for all other subjects was discussed at all seven conferences and good arguments were heard for both sides.

The nature of the science programs for pupils will determine the competencies their teachers should possess. Thus, it is the nature of the science that is to be taught in elementary schools rather than the instructional organization that dictates the requirements of the preservice program. The important question is what any teacher who teaches science should be qualified to do. At the same time the desirability of having some teachers who can do more is fully recognized.

The science specialist may be defined as a person who assumes a leadership role in the development of curriculum materials and the inservice education of other teachers. The specialized part of the education of this kind of science specialist is commonly postservice rather than preservice, and a description of the unique set of behaviors required is beyond the scope of this report.

Children, Teaching, and Schools

Everyone would agree that to teach science a teacher must know something about science; he must understand the attitudes, the principles, and the procedures from which the scientist operates; and he must be able to operate within this same framework, though at a different level of sophistication. Even if the science experiences produce the attitudes, the knowledge, and the process skills described previously, there is no assurance that the teacher will be able to communicate science to children. It is one thing to believe in conservation of substance; it is another to select activities which will convince children that such a generalization is plausible. It is one thing to be able to observe, classify, define operationally, or to make and test a hypothesis; it is another to lead children to do the same.

Much of what prospective teachers must learn about teaching will develop out of carefully planned experiences with children and schools. Early experiences of the teacher with children in schools should occur during the first or second undergraduate year when the prospective teacher is enrolled in science and other courses which provide background for his future career. These early experiences may involve in-class observations and part-time work as a teaching aide but many of them could be simulation experiences presented by film or video-tape and designed to focus attention on particular science teaching strategies. Provision should be made for the teacher to suggest possible strategies that he might use at critical points in the lesson.

The observations and simulated classroom episodes should be followed by opportunities for students to teach science lessons; first with one child in a tutorial, later to a small group in a microteaching format, and finally in a self-contained classroom or as a member of an instructional team. Many opportunities should be provided for the student and professional staff to evaluate the student's teaching performance. Only when the student shows proficiency in teaching science in a small group teaching situation should he proceed to work with larger groups with all of the complex interactions which characterize the science classroom.

INSTRUCTION

Guideline VI. The institution, working cooperatively with schools, should provide experiences with children and schools so designed that the teacher develops the skills required for effective instruction in the science program.

Objectives

A. *Objectives of instruction.* Upon being asked the purpose of an activity in the classroom, the teacher will be able to describe the objectives of the science instruction in precise terms and support his choice of objectives.

1. Identify objectives appropriate to developing (a) intellectual or process skills, and (b) concepts in science.
2. Identify examples of objectives which relate to systematic thinking.
3. Identify examples of objectives which relate to creative thinking.
4. Select objectives for his class in terms of the unique needs and characteristics of his group and individual children in the group.
5. Identify or construct instructional modules or units which contribute to specific goals of science teaching.

B. *The learning environment.* The teacher will demonstrate the organization and maintenance during instruction of a classroom environment which fosters inquiry.

1. Schedule class time to allow for both group and individual activities designed to accomplish specific objectives.

2. Demonstrate the introduction of a science activity in such a way that pupils are motivated to conduct investigations.
3. Create an atmosphere in which children participate freely in planning, carrying out, and interpreting results of investigations.
4. Use questions to assist children in conducting an investigation without telling them what to do or giving away the expected results.
5. Arrange instructional resources in the classroom to maximize pupil interaction with the materials.
6. Locate and use instructional resources available in the school and community.
7. List sources of science materials.

C. *Instructional strategies.* The teacher will demonstrate the ability to select and use a variety of learning strategies appropriate to various learning requirements.
1. Given an objective for science instruction, select materials, media, and activities in terms of the needs and characteristics of his group and the individual children in the group.
2. Identify instructional materials and learning activities for different learner interests and capabilities.
3. Encourage and enable the children to plan, carry out, and interpret the results of class or individual investigations.
4. Modify planned strategies as a result of unexpected pupil performance.
5. State the basis for his selection of learning strategies.
6. Demonstrate the ability to use effectively both the hardware and software of instructional technology and the willingness to learn how to use new technology.

D. *Constructing a sequence of learning activities.* The teacher will construct a sequence of learning activities on the basis of long-range objectives and knowledge of prior pupil performance.
1. Select, or construct, alternative learning activities when pupils demonstrate that they have achieved the objective of a science activity prior to its being carried out.
2. Select, or construct, alternative science activities when the prior instruction has been unsuccessful.
3. Construct appropriate and significant science activities for pupils whose lack of achievement indicates that they are not ready to continue with the rest of the class.
4. Identify a learning sequence appropriate to the development of skills and attitudes which may emerge over a long (at least two-month) time interval.
5. Identify the experiences, information, and conceptual knowledge prerequisite to specific science principles, laws, and theories.

6. Relate curriculum and methodology to the development of logical processes in children.

E. *Evaluation of pupil progress.* The teacher will demonstrate the use of various individual and group assessment devices to determine whether specified objectives have been met and other desirable outcomes have been achieved.
1. Select, or construct, and administer science assessment items which require pupils to use concepts in new contexts and inquiry skills in new problem situations.
2. Distinguish between acceptable and unacceptable responses to assessment items in science.
3. Use various assessment devices to determine the degree to which pupils possess necessary prerequisites for a learning task in science.
4. Use the results of evaluation in planning subsequent science learning activities.
5. Describe the results of evaluation to pupils and parents so that it is clear whether the pupil is or is not making reasonable progress in science.

RELATIONS WITH CHILDREN

Guideline VII. The institution should insure that the teacher possesses skills required for effective human relations with children in the classroom by carefully and continually screening candidates for the teacher education program and providing experiences in which students develop the desired behaviors.

Objectives

A. *Recognition of the importance of individual children.* The teacher will demonstrate the ability to accept pupils as individuals by responding to manifestations of individual differences in a controlled manner.
1. Demonstrate ability to guide pupils who are creative, who ask probing questions and who present challenging ideas in science.
2. Exhibit competence in working with the pupil who has poor manipulative skills in handling equipment or who is slow in acquiring process skills by providing experiences in which the child can succeed, by giving words of encouragement, and by deferring required performance when the child shows evidence of extreme frustration.
3. Demonstrate empathy, appreciation, and ability to work with children of divergent backgrounds and interests that affect their motivation for participation in science experiences.
4. Demonstrate empathy toward pupils with personal problems by

modifying requirements for the individual and obtaining professional outside help where necessary.

5. Encourage the child to express himself in those ways which are most familiar and understandable to the child, in speech patterns other than the conventional, allowing the child to express himself in a variety of ways, such as through pictures, demonstrations, models, and role playing activities.

6. Demonstrate faith in the ability of each child to make a valid contribution to the solution of the group's problems by listening to and accepting the ideas and suggestions of each pupil.

7. Demonstrate the ability to assist pupils in becoming more sensitive to the needs and capacities of other pupils, by encouraging them to ask questions of each other, to respond to the questions posed by other pupils, and to plan together to solve problems.

B. *Showing confidence and flexibility in relations with children.* The teacher will demonstrate confidence and flexibility by making reasonable alterations in teaching procedures in the face of unexpected events.

1. Demonstrate self-control over attitudes, feelings, and emotional reactions as shown by voice quality or facial and body gestures when responding to children, and ability to listen to children with interest and involvement.

2. Demonstrate confidence in his knowledge of science by failure to display frustration or embarrassment in the face of questions that he cannot answer.

3. Demonstrate the ability to turn ambiguity and unpredictable events which occur during the course of a science investigation into learning experiences.

4. Foster an atmosphere in which individual children and small groups can work independently in science.

5. Demonstrate the ability to guide children in making plans for a science activity without making the decisions for them.

6. Demonstrate the ability to assist pupils in carrying out and in interpreting the results without telling them what must be done or what conclusions are reasonable.

RELATIONS WITH OTHER TEACHERS
AND THE ADMINISTRATION

In his preservice years the teacher must learn about relationships among members of the school staff. He must be able to work effectively with parents, administrators, and other teachers. The development of these abilities is the concern of Guideline VII. Guidelines of the USOE Model Projects also provide needed guidance on the development of these important competencies.

When he assumes a teaching position the teacher may be asked to participate in any one of a variety of organizational patterns for instruction. He may be a self-contained classroom teacher with much or little assistance from helping teachers, principals, or other supervisory or administrative personnel. He may work as a member of an instructional team, a practice that can be effectively used in teaching science. It will be important that he understand the role of the teacher, assistant teacher, teacher aide, educational clerk, media aide, science consultant and other members of the instructional staff or team. He should be able to work effectively with all of these people in planning and executing science instruction.

In this section and the one which follows, Relations with the Community, the competencies identified apply to all teachers and, in general, are not unique for teachers of science. Nevertheless the importance now placed on science, and the concerns about science felt by many, make these abilities of special importance for the science teacher.

Guideline VIII. The institution should provide experiences which will enable the teacher to develop cooperative working relationships with other teachers and administrators of the school faculty which he joins and to work effectively in a variety of organizational patterns for science instruction.

A. *Relations with other teachers.* The teacher will demonstrate his sensitivity toward, and respect for, other teachers as persons and as professional colleagues. He will show appreciation for the contributions of other teachers to the total school program, to the science program, to each other, and to him.

1. Demonstrate respect for the opinions of others. Listen to what others have to say about science and science instruction. Seek rational bases for the views of others when they are different from his own.
2. Seek assistance and counsel from more experienced colleagues, including secondary school science teachers, and take appropriate action.
3. Demonstrate the ability to tolerate differences in values, language, and behavior patterns of other teachers.
4. Demonstrate self-control by not showing frustration or anger in the face of probing questions or ideas which challenge his own position.
5. Exhibit courage and confidence in his ability by taking considered action that may be criticized by others. Agree or disagree with policy set by teacher groups and give reasons for his position.
6. Demonstrate the ability to show appreciation for the achievement of his colleagues, and recognition given this achievement.

B. *Relations with the administration.* The teacher will demonstrate the same sensitivity toward, and respect for, the administration of the school, as he shows for his fellow teachers. The behaviors described under A are applicable to administrators as well as teachers, and there are, in addition, some special relationships which he needs to be prepared to carry out with emotional maturity.

1. Demonstrate respect for the authority that the school system has placed in the office of the administrator.
2. Where differences of opinion arise concerning the science program, present evidence in support of the teacher's point of view.

C. *Relations as a member of an instructional team.* The teacher will demonstrate the ability to contribute to cooperative team planning of science instruction, and to work in a team without alienating others or becoming alienated.

1. Demonstrate the ability to cooperate in team planning by negotiating and accepting compromises while developing or prescribing science activities to be carried out by the cooperating team.
2. Modify teaching behaviors consistent with cooperative teaching.
3. Direct a teacher aide in a task supporting the team effort without alienating the aide.
4. Modify the directions given to supporting personnel on the basis of their suggestions.
5. Accept directions or help from another member of an instructional team in science without demonstrating personal disaffection.

RELATIONS WITH THE COMMUNITY

In his preservice years the teacher must learn about schools and their relationship to the community. He must be able to work effectively with parents. He will be called upon to meet with community groups interested in the schools, and he should be prepared to listen to their ideas and present his own in a straightforward and confident manner. The importance now placed on science by many in the community will provide the science teacher special opportunities to discuss his school's science program. As a part of his preparation to work cooperatively with the community, he must learn about the school as a part of the community and the school as an essential part of a democratic society.

Guideline IX. Experiences in schools and in a community should be provided to develop a sensitivity toward, and an appreciation for, the school as a part of the community and as a democratic institution, and for individuals in the community.

A. *Relations with parents.* The teacher will demonstrate his understanding that good relations with parents can be an important asset in the development of an effective science program.

1. Describe the results of evaluation to parents so that it is clear whether the pupil is making reasonable progress in science.
2. Recognize the personal concern of a parent for his child, and show respect and appreciation for this concern.
3. Show patience when a parent values his child's welfare above that of the class as a whole.
4. Demonstrate respect for the opinion of parents.
5. Encourage parents to relate out-of-school science experiences in which their children are involved.

B. *Relations with the community.* The teacher will take into account the local community values and institutions as he works with his class and in his school, and will demonstrate an active interest in local community values and institutions.

1. Demonstrate a knowledge of the science resources of a community and the ability to capitalize on these resources to create a more effective teaching situation in science.
2. Present science experiences which allow pupils to reexamine prejudged values and stereotypes.
3. Become aware of local values, including attitudes toward science and science education.
4. Demonstrate an active interest through participation in local community affairs.
5. Indicate through his actions an acceptance of the people of the community though he may disagree with some of their values and mores.

C. *The School as a democratic institution.* The teacher will demonstrate his knowledge of the school as a part of a community, and as an essential democratic institution in society.

1. Demonstrate pride in his school and his profession, and in the kinds of science experiences that children in his class are having.
2. Recognize the role of the school in community life.
3. Take an active interest in local, state, and national affairs that affect education and its support.

Institutional Standards

The purpose and primary force of this Report is to describe competencies that will enable elementary teachers to provide exciting and profitable science experiences for children. The competencies have been derived from nine guidelines stating what the elementary teacher should be able to do when he has completed a preservice program. The guidelines are applicable to planning, executing, and evaluating preservice science education programs for elementary teachers.

This section states five institutional standards that seem essential if the institution is to be able to achieve the broad goals set forth in the guidelines. These standards are guidelines to institutions in establishing a framework in which effective teacher education programs can function.

A COOPERATIVE ENTERPRISE

Responsibility for teacher education programs is properly placed on many individuals and groups associated with institutions of higher education; the schools, state departments of education, professional organizations, and the public served. Greater involvement of all of these individuals and groups is extremely important in all phases of teacher education from initial planning through evaluation, teacher placement, and follow-up after graduation. This broad involvement is also important for special parts of the teacher education program, including preservice science teacher education to which the standards are directed.

Standard 1. The institution should make certain that science and elementary education departments share the responsibility for the preservice science education of elementary teachers and that in meeting this responsibility these departments cooperate fully with each other and with schools, state departments of education, and interested persons and agencies.

STAFF

The most critical factor in good teaching is the staff. In no segment of higher education is excellence of teaching more important than that in the teacher education program. The quality of planning for teacher education, counseling future teachers, leadership in both class and out-of-class science experiences of prospective teachers, and the search for knowledge through research and development also depend upon staff competence. Some members of the staff should have had experience in teaching elementary school science; and all of them should be knowledgeable about recent research and development projects related to elementary school science. Participation in such projects is an exceedingly valuable experience for one who teaches courses for preservice elementary school teachers.

Standard 2. The institution should insure that the science preparation of elementary teachers is under the direction of a professional staff which (a) exhibits competencies in science; (b) is knowledgeable about elementary school methods and programs; and (c) works cooperatively with colleagues in other departments.

CURRICULUM

Next in importance to staff is the curriculum for the preservice science education of elementary teachers. The nine guidelines provide the framework upon which the curriculum of science and science teaching experiences can be based. Curriculum as used here refers to all experiences that the institution provides to assist the prospective teacher in acquiring competencies needed for teaching science to children.

Standard 3. The institution should structure a curriculum designed to: (a) provide a full liberal education for the future teacher, including a strong science component; (b) prepare the student for life as a useful citizen and responsible leader in a society whose every aspect is conditioned by science; (c) enable the student to become a proficient and knowledgeable teacher of science and other subjects that he will be called upon to teach; and (d) enable the student to be confident of his professional role as a science teacher, and of the importance of what he does for society.

INDIVIDUALIZING INSTRUCTION

In this report, individualizing instruction means that the past experience and the learning rate of each student are considered when instruction is planned. It means that experiences are assigned on an individual basis. It does not mean that a single person is the learning audience; some instruction may be done better in groups and some may be done better with individuals. The most efficient organization for a particular type of learning is still a matter for research. It is the belief that instruction can be made more efficient and meaningful when students are considered individually that led to Standard 4.

Standard 4. Institutions which prepare teachers should make every effort to allow for individual differences among students by planning instruction so that students may progress at different rates and by giving credit in completing program requirements for learning that is acquired before entering college or that is acquired through informal experiences during college.

FACILITIES AND MATERIALS

Throughout this report the emphasis is on the competencies that elementary teachers should exhibit. There is no intent to describe the equipment, the written materials, or the laboratory facilities that colleges and universities should have to conduct a teacher education program. Still, it is not uncommon for elementary teachers to take all of their science courses without laboratory experience. Many elementary teachers are graduated without an opportunity to see equipment and materials designed for teaching science to elementary school children. Libraries that they use have few books that may, be used for reference when planning science experiences for children.

Standard 5 makes explicit the desire for proper facilities for the teaching of science to teachers. It pertains to conditions that should be provided by the teacher preparation institution.

Standard 5. The institution should (a) provide laboratory facilities which will accommodate student activities that range from predetermined exercises proposed by the professor to student-constructed experiments, (b) furnish science equipment and materials similar to those in elementary schools; and (c) provide reference books suitable for use in a school setting.

Model Programs for the Education of Teachers in Science*

STEPHEN S. WINTER

This article is a portion of a progress report from the Eastern Section of the Association for the Education of Teachers in Science. Four groups presented recommendations for the preparation of elementary, junior high, and high school teachers in science. The individual reports of the four groups were edited into one comprehensive report by Stephen S. Winter. This portion of the report is concerned only with the professional education (reported by Harold E. Tannenbaum of Herbert Lehman College) and with the pre-service science education (reported by Paul S. Hiack of Trenton State College) of elementary teachers.

I. Recommendations for Professional Education—Non-Science

Group I considered the desired behavioral characteristics of beginning teachers in the professional, non-science areas. The group generally agreed upon three areas of concern:

A. Philosophic foundations.
B. Social foundations.
C. Psychological foundations.

The major portion of the group's time was spent considering the first two of these areas. It was agreed that the third area should receive further consideration at the next conference of the group.

* REPRINTED FROM *Journal of Research in Science Teaching,* Vol. 3, Issue 2, 1965, pp. 102–104, by permission of the author and the editor. Dr. Winter is Professor of Education at Tufts University.

A. PHILOSOPHIC FOUNDATIONS

A prospective teacher of science (K–12) should through his actions, even more than through his oral and written statements, indicate the beginnings of a mature personal and social philosophy consistent with the characteristics of American society. He should demonstrate a consistent value system through the ways he behaves, not only professionally but personally. It was the consensus of the group that one important aspect of the personal behavior of the beginning professional should be determined by his attitudes towards the scientific enterprise of the contemporary world. Included in the desired behavior patterns should be an active understanding of the roles of science in modern society: what science can do *for* us, what science can do *to* us. Furthermore, the beginning teacher should demonstrate his appreciation not only of the rational aspects of science processes but also of the creative and intuitive aspects of these processes.

Finally, the group agreed that an essential behavior of the beginning teacher would be found in his philosophic approach to his teaching assignment. The purposes of education to which he adheres as well as his own views on the role of the teacher in the general framework of the educational enterprise should be clearly evident from his written and oral statements. Even more important, his views and positions on matters of educational philosophy should be evident from his professional behavior.

It seemed to the group that the curricular work related to developing a personal philosophy needed to come early in the pre-service education of the teacher, while those aspects of the curriculum related to the development of a consistent and functional educational philosophy might well come toward the close of the pre-service program, concurrent with or following an internship experience.

B. SOCIAL FOUNDATIONS

The group generally agreed that the social behavior of the young professional would be a very significant indicator of his education. Does the young teacher indicate concern for the social issues of the day both through his own out-of-school activities and through the kinds of activities he fosters and encourages in his classroom? Does the young teacher, through his own behavior, indicate an awareness of the significant contributions of the behavioral sciences to the understanding of contemporary society? Does the young teacher, through professional behavior, indicate a consistency in the philosophy he espouses and the personal and professional activities in which he participates?

The group recognized that social foundations had been included in most curricular designs for at least the past thirty years. It was noted with considerable emphasis, however, that a curriculum was being advocated which included not mere courses in sociology, anthropology, social psychology, and the like, but opportunities for active social participation by students during their pre-service education.

C. PSYCHOLOGICAL FOUNDATIONS

As was pointed out earlier, the psychological foundations for teacher preparation did not receive the needed attention from the group. However, the group was in agreement that the young teacher needs to demonstrate his awareness of the characteristics of children and youth of all ages and to be particularly cognizant of the psychological characteristics and needs of the age group with which he is working. A further discussion of this aspect of teacher preparation is contemplated for the next meeting of the group.

D. OTHER CONSIDERATIONS AND SUMMARY

Running through the entire discussion was a constant emphasis on the importance of personal experience in the education of the prospective teacher. We want our pre-service personnel to have experiences in various parts of the nation, to know our cities, our rural areas, our various geographic sectors, our many ethnic groups, and our neighbors, near and far. These should be provided, in so far as possible, through personal activities; where such personal involvement cannot be achieved, the best available vicarious experiences that modern educational media can provide should be substituted. We want our young teachers to have worked with children and youth from many social, economic, and ethnic backgrounds during their pre-service preparation. We are convinced that a well planned internship, jointly sponsored by the preparing institution and the employing school system, offers great promise (if it is not, indeed, the *sine qua non*) for sound professional preparation. We want our future science teachers to have personal experiences in the science centers and workshops of the nation, under the supervision of practicing scientists.

In short, we see the education of a future teacher as something much broader and deeper than a mere series of college courses, either in the liberal studies or in professional education. We propose during our further deliberations to turn to a consideration of the kinds of activities we would advocate for the preparation of such teachers.

II. Recommendations for Pre-Service Education of Elementary Teachers

Group II considered that the science education of the individual teacher will depend in part on the extent of his responsibility for teaching science. Various organizational patterns based on this assumption were discussed. It was recognized that additional research is needed to resolve the question of which pattern will best support the teaching of science in the elementary school. Therefore, at present the general classroom teacher should be trained to assume responsibility for the teaching of science and should have available adequate consultant help in this area. Adequate help in this context was defined as a science consultant for each building and, in addition, a teaching staff of which 20–25 per cent has a science emphasis pre-service preparation. A staff so prepared would seem to offer good flexibility should it become apparent that some other administrative pattern is more desirable.

The group then identified the needs of the personnel in this organization for scientific instruction. The needs of all teachers were identified and recommendations were made for the pre-service education programs of the three types of teachers: the general classroom teacher, the teacher with a pre-service emphasis in science, and the science consultant. However, the group also recognized that additional research is needed in all areas of elementary school science, especially in the area of teacher preparation.

A. GENERAL COMPETENCIES FOR ELEMENTARY SCIENCE

Among the competencies necessary for effective teaching of elementary science which are directly related to pre-service education in science are the following:

1. Awareness of content and structure of science, of the relationship among the branches of science, and the relationship of science to other areas of knowledge.
2. Skill in working with the materials of science.
3. A knowledge of and skill in the use of methods which have been shown to be useful in achieving the objectives of elementary school science.
4. The ability to work with children who have special interest or ability in science and to assist further in the development of that interest and ability.

B. THE GENERAL CLASSROOM TEACHER

This preparation would include training in each of the broad course areas of science, *i.e.*, physical, biological, and space science. Twelve to twenty hours of such science courses should be completed. These are to be courses in which the major ideas of these areas are used as unifying concepts. Laboratory and field work are considered essential. In addition, a methods course specifically directed toward teaching of science in the elementary school must be included.

C. THE TEACHER WITH PRE-SERVICE EMPHASIS IN SCIENCE

Preparation here includes all the requirements for the general teacher plus additional courses in formal science comprising about one fourth of the total pre-service preparation. Student teaching in science is assumed to be an integral part of the pre-service preparation and is not included in the formal science course preparation.

D. THE SCIENCE CONSULTANT

This area requires the above preparation plus teaching experience on the elementary level and at least one year of courses on the graduate level.

Science Methods Courses for Elementary Teachers*

MILDRED T. BALLOU

Mildred Ballou recognizes that there are a great number of skills and competencies an elementary teacher must acquire to do a qualitative job when working with children at a significant time in their social and intellectual development. She hypothesizes regarding some of the characteristics of a good elementary science teacher. The author lists seven such characteristics and makes some suggestions as to ways that teachers of methods courses can contribute to the development of these characteristics. She also lists nine prerequisites of a good science methods teacher.

The task of training an elementary teacher is not an easy one. The skills and competencies he or she must acquire to do a qualitative job are overwhelming. An elementary teacher must know a good deal about children, how they grow, how they interact, how they learn. A teacher must teach them the expressive and receptive language arts: speaking, writing, reading, spelling, and listening. She must teach children social studies, science, mathematics, and often art, music, and physical education. She must orchestrate the various educational experiences of children in such a way that each pupil becomes an active, aggressive learner, with an adequate foundation in all of the basic disciplines. Much excellent teaching is going on in elementary schools, in spite of the magnitude of the task.

However, there are too many cases where elementary teachers are not doing an adequate job of teaching science, and educators who work in teacher training and supervision must turn their attention to what can be done to increase the odds that the people who come through their pro-

* REPRINTED FROM *Science and Children*, Vol. 7, No. 1, September 1969, pp. 7–9. Copyright, 1969, by the National Science Teachers Association, Washington, D.C. Reprinted by permission of the author and the publisher. Dr. Ballou is Head of the Department of Elementary Education at Ball State University.

grams can and will do a better job with the children whose lives they touch at such a significant time in the social and intellectual development of those children.

First, let us admit that no one *knows*, with fool-proof certainty, how to train a good elementary science teacher. In the absence of such information, I would like to hypothesize regarding some of the characteristics of these teachers and suggest some ways teachers of methods courses can contribute to the development of those characteristics.

1. *A Good Elementary Science Teacher Likes Science.* Ask a college student what, of all the things she has done in science, was most satisfying to her. (And it is likely to be *her*. Eighty-five percent of our elementary teachers are women.) Then ask her to plan a single twenty-minute experience for one child, based on that pleasurable memory. Next, the college student could do the activity with a child. Having direct experience with children early in the course is crucial, and why complicate matters by having her work with five or thirty children before she has learned to focus on individuals? One way to handle the logistics problem is to invite thirty children from a nearby school into your class for the period. The thirty tutorial situations, going on simultaneously, would provide an exciting learning laboratory. Some of the children could report what they did. Children's enthusiasm is contagious. One would expect the range of processes and content included to be wide, which might help the college students widen their own interests in science. Self-evaluation on the part of college students might help them find out what skills and information they need to acquire during the course. Additional experiences with a single child or groups of children should be planned. Educators talk about the importance of laboratory experience, when the most important thing is real, live children.

The course instructor should also provide college students with some adult level science experiences which are pleasurable, using techniques he would deem acceptable in an elementary classroom.

2. *A Good Elementary Science Teacher Has a Multiple Offense.* When educators confine an elementary teacher to one *best* program or approach to science teaching, they make it difficult for the teacher to change when new programs are developed. Methods teachers should turn the students loose to investigate three or four approaches, with all the books, kits, and materials available in the room. They should be unobtrusive guides in helping students teach themselves how to teach AAAS, ESS, a text program, COPES, etc. Every elementary supervisor and science coordinator knows there are some teachers who can, on their own, read the how-to-teach-it materials that come with new programs and do a good job of implementing that program, with a minimum of help. Part of their success is based upon an attitude, a willingness to try, and acceptance of their responsibility to continuously be their own teachers of teaching.

Knowing several approaches to science teaching can help a teacher find techniques that work with individual children or groups of children. It will also help her take qualitative aspects of several programs and use them to develop a rich and varied curriculum.

3. *A Good Elementary Science Teacher Has Some Ideas about What Science Experiences Are Appropriate at Various Stages in a Child's Development.* Reasonable, flexible levels of expectations based on children's interests, age, stage of development, intelligence, and environmental conditions should be investigated in the methods class. A beginning teacher needs to have some notion as to where to aim. "Keyholing" in teaching is as important as it is in the space shots. Overshooting or undershooting can have disastrous results. The work of psychologists, science educators, scientists, sociologists, and classroom teachers gives us some indications of levels of children's cognitive and manipulative skills. The teacher should have some idea of where she's going. Teaching experience helps, but does not guarantee, selection of appropriate activities. Pre-service courses must provide enough information so that beginning teachers will not experience gross failure nor the frustration that goes with it.

4. *A Good Elementary Science Teacher Is a Constant Evaluator.* Pacing is an essential ingredient in good teaching. Prospective teachers need opportunity to develop an awareness of the pacing clues they can pick up by observing children's behaviors as they teach. Observing behaviors of children, and modifying one's teaching minute by minute as a result can be systematically studied in a methods course. Simulated materials are often helpful, as are classroom observations and the teaching experiences suggested earlier in point one. The teacher becomes a human seismograph and re-programs her output constantly as she observes and predicts child behavior.

5. *A Good Elementary Science Teacher Knows and Uses Processes and Content of Science.* A prospective elementary teacher must observe, classify, measure, record, compare, experiment, infer, etc., as part of a methods class. The emphasis on process is clear in recent literature, even if it is not universally true in practice. If teachers are concerned with ends as well as means, they will not define process too narrowly. Processes should refine techniques which should increase one's knowledge about science. A good methods course helps prospective teachers to understand the importance of learning ahead of the children as well as with them and to recognize that there will be times when children will ask questions teachers cannot (and sometimes should not) answer. Trade books, textbooks, newspapers, magazines, other teachers, films, and television programs can all be very helpful in upgrading an elementary teacher's content background. *Most important, the teacher must realize that keeping up with science content is continuous—and her responsibility.* She must become an autonomous student.

6. *A Good Elementary Science Teacher Relates Science to the Rest of the Curriculum.* Science is a part of one's life style. It is not a 10 o'clock to 10:20 class activity. It is a way of thinking, a way of behaving, a dimension of self. Elementary teachers have a unique opportunity to break away the artificial boundaries of "science" and follow the threads of science through meaningful pathways in literature, arts, mathematics, everywhere. Consider Kipling's *Rikki Tikki Tavi*; Menaboni's *Menaboni's Birds*; the see-saw on the playground; a study of urban problems in social studies; a visit to an airport; a tasting party with turnips, apples, and butter. A space songs record can provide a delightful tie-up of music with science experiences. A science methods teacher must understand the unified curriculum concept and help teachers put the parts together into a meaningful whole.

7. *A Good Elementary Science Teacher Is a "Center of Infection" for Science Teaching in a School.* The pupils from this classroom spread the word, with gusto, about the neat things they're doing in Miss Jones's room. Their enthusiasm is catching, and their schoolmates may begin begging their teachers to let them grow molds, build an air tunnel, or investigate ways to keep their bicycles from rusting. The methods instructor's responsibility is to help the prospective teacher realize that she can truly be an agent for change in a school, and that the success of her efforts must be measured, largely, by what children do, and how they think on their own, in and outside of the classroom. I also like to think that this excellent elementary science teacher has a deep concern for all children; this teacher will serve as a valuable resource person in the school, and to the colleges to help train teachers for the elementary school of the future.

A massive study might show us many more things about these excellent elementary science teachers, such as that they like to garden or fish or bird watch or fix things; that they are avid readers; that they have a greater-than-usual tolerance for smelly things, gadgets, boys, ambivalence. They probably are not awed by equipment, for they are, themselves, curious and will be eager to see how they can make that equipment in the closet help them with the teaching-learning task.

Good Methods Teachers Should:

1. Have successfully taught science on a sustained day-to-day basis for several years to elementary children.
2. Make prospective elementary teachers confident about teaching science.
3. Demonstrate his genuine interest in elementary science and children by spending a good bit of time in elementary classrooms.
4. Be willing to help college students after they have begun teaching.
5. Teach as he would have his students teach.

6. Keep up. Too many future teachers are learning 1949 teaching techniques in 1969.
7. Work as a team member with elementary methods teachers in other curricular areas. College students complain (and rightly so) about repetition and lack of coordination.
8. Work closely with science content professors. If a large part of the methods course has to be content, perhaps the students are not having adequate instruction in biology, chemistry, physical science, etc. It is not what is thrown at students, it is what students take away that counts.
9. Be an eternal optimist. Believe that girls wearing mini skirts and sorority hats and boys leading fraternity dogs and wearing Ben Franklin glasses just might do a top-notch job of teaching science to children, given a sense of responsibility, concern for a better world, and a chance to do their own thing.

In-Service Science Activities for the Elementary School Teacher*

MARJORIE S. LERNER

Marjorie Lerner describes how elementary school teachers can continue their professional growth through varied in-service activities. In-service education in elementary school science can be derived from three basic sources: (1) programs occurring within the local school system, (2) opportunities provided by colleges and universities, and (3) activities that can be self-initiated by the teacher. Dr. Lerner also discusses briefly the role of the school administrator in promoting effective in-service education.

The professional growth of the elementary school teacher is a necessity as long as the teacher continues to teach. In order to develop and maintain a high level of competence, the teacher must be provided with continued opportunities for in-service education in all areas of the elementary school curriculum.

Today there is a vital need for in-service education in the area of elemen-

* REPRINTED FROM a presentation made on July 13, 1966, at the Summer Conference on Science Education sponsored by the Northwestern University School of Education in Evanston, Illinois, by permission of the author. Dr. Lerner is principal of the Donoghue Elementary School in Chicago.

tary school science. There are several factors responsible for creating this need. A number of new programs have been developed based on an approach to the teaching of science in the elementary school which stresses the development of the skills or processes of science, and which also aims for the inculcation of scientific attitudes and critical thinking. Programs such as these require elementary school teachers to review and extend further their understanding of the different ways of teaching science.

The recent explosion of science knowledge has produced an impact all the way down to the elementary school, making it imperative for teachers who are already in service to upgrade their science knowledge and background. Money is now being allocated in school budgets for the purchase of materials and facilities for elementary science, making it possible for the elementary schools to acquire a large quantity and variety of much-needed scientific equipment. As a result, teachers must now become familiar with many different kinds of equipment, learn the purposes for which the equipment can be used, and develop proficiency in manipulating the equipment.

Three Basic Sources for In-Service Education

In-service education in science for the elementary school teacher can be derived from three basic sources. First, there are programs that can operate within the local school system. Second, there are opportunities provided by colleges and universities. Third, there are in-service activities that can be initiated and sustained by the teacher alone.

WITHIN THE LOCAL SYSTEM

WORKSHOPS. Science workshops can be helpful to teachers in a number of ways. They can be used to evaluate and revise an existing science program, to organize and develop a new science program with scope and sequence, to coordinate a science program so that it becomes part of an overall K–12 science program, to construct teaching units, to investigate and determine ways of obtaining and using materials and equipment, to select textbooks and reference books, to provide the teachers with a series of lecture-demonstrations by science specialists, and to help the teachers become more proficient in methods of teaching science to children.

Science workshops are usually conducted under the leadership of a science supervisor, if the school has one, or by a special committee appointed for that purpose. In some workshops academically and professionally trained persons are asked to serve as consultants and as resource specialists to provide either science information or methodology or both. Some workshops make use of their high school and junior high school science teachers as well.

What characteristics are necessary for a successful workshop? To begin with, workshops cannot be artificial situations with manufactured problems. The problems must be of real concern to the teachers who are participating in the workshop.

In order to ensure that teachers have profitable experiences, workshops should be cooperatively planned with carefully designated objectives. These objectives may be immediate objectives or long-range objectives. For example, a workshop for elementary teachers to acquaint them with the use of several new pieces of equipment has an immediate objective of developing teacher competency in using this new equipment. This new equipment is then scrutinized in perspective with other science equipment, and decisions are made as to where and how this new equipment will best be used. An example of a workshop with long-range objectives would be one where all the science equipment is evaluated, for the purpose of determining specific needs for the future rather than ordering new materials on a "guess" basis.

Some workshops should be specifically designed for the teacher new to the local system. New teachers need orientation to the guiding philosophy in the science program. New teachers also have to see the entire scope and sequence of the science program in order to understand their specific role in the program. Workshops designed to help new teachers learn what resources are available to them and where they may obtain assistance in their science teaching can be of tremendous assistance.

The experienced teacher usually has problems that are different and more sophisticated than those of the new teacher, and therefore needs a workshop with different objectives: How do I apply new approaches to teaching science at my grade level? How do I recognize changed scientific behavior? How do I evaluate my teaching in terms of desired changed behavior? How do I construct valid tests for the objectives set forth in the science program? How do I individualize science instruction? What textbooks are best suited to the program?

COMMITTEE WORK. Teachers can further their professional growth by serving on both small and large committees. Committees provide a wide range of opportunity for in-service education because they permit teachers to engage in many types of activities. Teachers may be encouraged to try out new science programs and report on the progress of such programs. Perhaps the teacher will design new activities to be incorporated into new programs. The teacher can become involved in writing curriculum materials. The study of current research and literature is an important facet of science curriculum development. There are opportunities for the exchange of ideas with other teachers and with various science supervisors and consultants. In evaluating programs and materials, the goals for teaching science in the elementary school become clarified.

THE SCIENCE SUPERVISOR. Quite often elementary teachers fail to realize that their most immediate source for a wide range of in-service activities lies within their grasp by making proper use of their science supervisor. The following is only a partial list of the various ways teachers can obtain help from the science supervisor.

1. Request the observation and evaluation of the teaching-learning situation.
2. Have the science supervisor teach a science session, perhaps one that involves the use of science equipment.
3. Discuss new ideas or approaches to the teaching of science, and request aid in carrying them through.
4. Request assistance in locating needed equipment or in constructing simple equipment.
5. Seek aid in locating or evaluating instructional material.
6. Ask for a specific type of workshop to help solve special problems.
7. Seek advice on local resources.
8. Request aid in planning profitable field trips that will enrich the science program.
9. Ask for help on how to use new equipment or materials.
10. Request the recommendation of certain teachers to be visited and observed for competence in teaching science.
11. Ask for recommendations for professional literature that will assist the teacher in teaching science.
12. Request aid in the construction of tests that will best suit the goals and objectives of the science program.
13. Seek aid in the selection of appropriate films, filmstrips, and other audio-visual materials.
14. Seek advice on summer offerings at local colleges and universities.

Even though this is a partial list of the ways the science supervisor can help the elementary school teacher, it clearly shows how the science supervisor can be a valuable resource person for assisting teachers to continue their professional growth while teaching.

THE ROLE OF TELEVISION. Television possesses tremendous opportunities for use in in-service education of teachers. Television has the advantage of being able to reach large numbers of teachers through a single telecast or series of telecasts. Teachers can learn much by observing a skillful classroom teacher work in her classroom. By using television, this one skillful teacher can be observed by a great many teachers.

The science supervisor often needs to serve large numbers of teachers. His time and efforts can be conserved through the use of television. New advances in science can be brought to the immediate attention of teachers through the use of science consultants. Entire college courses are now being taught on television. Perhaps here is the opportunity for the elementary teacher to obtain needed knowledge and background in physics, chemistry, geology or astronomy. Some instructional courses are presented during the pre-school hours, others during the school day.

COLLEGES AND UNIVERSITIES

An examination of the backgrounds of most new elementary school teachers reveals in most cases a woeful lack of science background. Our colleges and universities often allow the science requirements for graduation to be fulfilled by the election of just one year of a science in an area which the college student chooses. It is, therefore, not uncommon for the elementary school teacher to arrive on the job with a one-year sequence in biology and, perhaps, the professional science methods course. In many instances, it is possible for the new teacher to have had absolutely no laboratory experience in fulfilling the college science requirement. Even the elementary school science methods may be part of a multiple methods course involving other elementary curricular areas such as social studies and/or mathematics. Yet a cursory examination of elementary science textbooks reveals that only about one third of the science content is in the area of the biological sciences. Approximately another third is devoted to the area of physics. The remaining third is concerned with the areas of astronomy, geology, meteorology, and chemistry.

It is quite evident that a four-year college program cannot produce elementary teachers with the proper science background to teach elementary school science effectively. After a year or two of teaching, therefore, elementary teachers should begin to become aware of the gaps in their science background and should begin to fill these needs. Summer study at colleges and universities can fill these gaps.

The teachers must be careful, however, to select courses that truly fill their needs. An introductory course in geology can be more immediately fruitful to the elementary school teacher than an advanced course in educational psychology. The teacher should select science courses that will provide laboratory experience. Teachers without such experiences are generally fearful of science equipment. As a result, experiments and/or demonstrations will rarely occur when such teachers are teaching science.

Many school systems base salary increments only upon graduate study and additional degrees. As a result, teachers cannot gain recognition or credit by taking the introductory course, even though such a course meets a definite need for the professional growth of the teacher. Consequently, teachers are discouraged from taking beginning courses in a science area. There is a great need for school systems to re-evaluate their attitudes toward such introductory courses. In the long run, it is the child in the classroom who benefits by the teacher who seeks and attains competence in subject matter. This, then, should be the criterion used by school systems rather than the level of the college course taken by the teacher.

NATIONAL SCIENCE FOUNDATION

The Cooperative College-School Science Program (CCSS)[1] of the National Science Foundation provides opportunities for colleges and universities to work with schools and school systems in improving elementary and secondary school science and mathematics programs. Many of the projects in CCSS have as their purpose the introduction into the classroom of one of the new science or mathematics curriculum programs which have been developed. These projects are scheduled during the summer or the academic year or both. Projects which include intensive summer work on the campus of the sponsoring college or university usually have a coordinated academic year phase as well. The academic year phase frequently involves study and laboratory investigations or demonstrations in the participants' own schools, or Saturday or weekday meetings on the college campus, or both.

SELF-INITIATING ACTIVITIES

Elementary teachers can and should afford themselves the opportunity for professional growth through reading current professional literature. *Science and Children* is an excellent publication of the National Science Teachers Association, devoted exclusively to science for grades K–6. Frequently, this publication presents outstanding talks from the association's annual convention or from regional conferences. *The Grade Teacher* and *The Instructor* have devoted entire issues to science for the elementary grades. *School Science and Mathematics* (the publication of the Central Association of Science and Mathematics Teachers[2]) and *The Science Teacher* (another publication of the National Science Teachers Association) occasionally feature articles pertinent to elementary school science. The same holds true for the *National Education Association Journal*. If these publications do not appear in your professional school library, consult your school librarian. She is usually eager to obtain professional publications that will be helpful to the teacher.

Membership in a professional science education organization on a local, state, or national level will afford many opportunities for professional growth through bulletins, newsletters, publication announcements, or attendance at meetings, regional conferences, and conventions. Many publishers of elementary science textbooks issue curricular bulletins and charts, and are always interested in communicating with teachers. In school systems where in-service education is entirely an individual matter, self-initiating activities make it possible for elementary teachers to continue their professional growth.

[1] Now called Instructional Improvement Implementation Program. (*Ed.*)
[2] Now called School Science and Mathematics Association. (*Ed.*)

The Role of the School Administrator

The school administrator plays a crucial role in the effectiveness of any in-service education program. He must be aware of the strengths and weaknesses of his teachers, be able to identify their widely divergent problems and needs, and provide a variety of opportunities to help the teachers according to their specific needs.

He should encourage teachers to seek new approaches to the teaching of science. Provisions must be made for teachers to observe good teaching practices and to attend workshops, conferences, and conventions. He must provide necessary materials, establish effective schedules, and coordinate the activities of teachers, supervisors, and consultants. Unless the administrator plans for school in-service activities, they will not take place, and professional growth will be held to a minimum.

Science in the Elementary School: An NSTA Approach*

GLENN O. BLOUGH

Dr. Blough describes the contributions which the National Science Teachers Association, since its inception in 1944, has made to elementary science teaching. He also lists the various services available to elementary school teachers through NSTA membership: a magazine, a variety of publications, and national and regional meetings and conferences. He looks to the future and speculates about the direction elementary school science learning will take in the next ten years.

Since its inception in 1944, the National Science Teachers Association has emphasized that science teaching begins at the Kindergarten level (or earlier) and ends—well, ends wherever science teaching and learning end. The Association has stressed this point of view and each year has widened its influence through its increasing membership and services to all teachers of science.

NSTA has made significant contributions to the growth of science

* REPRINTED FROM *Science and Children,* Vol. 6, No. 3, November 1968, pp. 24–26. Copyright, 1968, by the National Science Teachers Association, Washington, D.C. Reprinted by permission of the author and the publisher. Dr. Blough is Professor of Education Emeritus at the University of Maryland.

teaching in the elementary school. In fact, the field of elementary science has itself sprinted, indeed raced, ahead and can scarcely be recognized as the one that the executive secretary was thinking of years ago when he said, "We ought to do more to help all those elementary teachers who wish they were doing better science teaching."

In considering the vast number of elementary teachers, the Association has realized from the beginning that they vary greatly in their science background, interest in science, and ability to teach it. The great gap continues—all the way from a teacher who is almost afraid of a dry cell to one who will build his whole curriculum around science activities. The amount of assistance available to teachers varies almost as much. Some teachers must rely on their own initiative to improve, while others work in an environment teeming with help for the asking.

What kinds of help can an association offer under these conditions? It can produce reading material, hoping that it will reach those who need it and that it will be appropriate and helpful. It can provide speakers, panels, symposia, and so on, at its many meetings that will attract and assist elementary teachers. It can sponsor conferences designed especially to explore problems and solutions in science at the elementary level. At these meetings participants have personal contact with leaders in the field, discuss and compare guidelines, review teaching standards, peruse new materials, and generally grow professionally. Each year the Association has continued to expand its efforts along these avenues, always revising its offerings on the basis of what it can learn about their effectiveness from teachers and others.

In recognition of the special needs of teachers in elementary schools, the Association has designed special membership services. At present the elementary teachers who join the Association as Elementary Members receive a year's subscription to *Science and Children*, are kept informed of national and regional meetings (which they are urged to attend and participate in), learn about new publications appropriate for them, and enjoy full rights and privileges in the Association. Elementary Membership in NSTA is available to all persons engaged in or interested in elementary education.

Magazines

At the outset of the Association, *The Science Teacher* included in each issue material helpful to elementary teachers. But soon the Association faced the fact that this publication could not spread itself enough to do justice to all levels of science teaching—secondary, collegiate, and elementary. To continue help to elementary school teachers, the first issue of the *Elementary School Science Bulletin* was published in May 1952. This four-page publication contained articles about science subject matter and methods of teaching, notations about books and materials, and meeting announcements. *ESSB* caught on at once and grew to 12 pages and a circulation of 40,000.

Although the *ESSB* was a success to its readers, it wobbled along chiefly with the help of a volunteer crew scattered in teaching institutions around the country and the "spare" time of NSTA office personnel. Eventually, the increased emphasis on teaching science in the elementary school pointed to the need for a more substantial publication, and in September 1963, *Science and Children* came into being—an over 40-page magazine with editors, other assistance from the NSTA office, an advisory board, a group of scientists to act as technical consultants, and a budget. Here at last was a publication devoted specifically to the teaching of science in the elementary school. Now in its sixth year, it reaches over 30,000 teachers with articles, book reviews, important announcements, special features such as reviews of materials, and short descriptions of successful science teaching practices of and by its readers. Commercial advertisers in *Science and Children* inform teachers of the materials available for science teaching. Scientists, teachers, supervisors, college and university personnel, photographers, and others regularly contribute to *Science and Children*.

Examine the various issues of *Science and Children*, and you will see that many of the innovative practices reported have come when scientists, psychologists, and educators have worked together—each contributing his special talent. In many instances NSTA led in sponsoring such coalition, and it will continue to do so.

Meetings and Conferences

The amount of time devoted at the annual and regional meetings of NSTA to science in the elementary school has increased with the interest and need. Here elementary teachers have been able to meet and hear the outstanding educators in elementary school science, participate in panels and symposia, attend seminars, see the latest in books and materials at vast exhibits, and get acquainted with others with similar interests and problems. Each year the number of elementary school teachers attending these meetings has increased. As an example of the opportunities afforded elementary teachers, a recent annual meeting provided opportunities to hear and participate in programs on educational TV in science; the new science curriculum programs; effective inservice programs; physics, chemistry, earth science, and biology seminars; theory of learning; teaching techniques; and communication and transportation workshops.

The Association also sponsors ten or more regional conferences each year throughout the United States. Each of these meetings provides a portion of the program especially for elementary teachers. NSTA's Saturday Science Seminars also offer elementary teachers of science access to resources, information opportunities, and services during one-day workshop programs.

In addition to the annual and regional meetings, the Association has long sponsored special conferences. A particularly productive one, in 1958, was supported by funds from the National Science Foundation. About thirty-five of the most knowledgeable educators—school superintendents, science supervisors, principals, science consultants, teachers, and others—participated in that conference to develop promising recommendations and actions for extending and strengthening programs of science in the elementary school. As a result of these deliberations a publication, *It's Time for Better Elementary School Science* (1),† was prepared. Its recommendations have had wide influence on plans and practices in such areas as elementary school science programs, improving the curriculum and teaching methods, inservice education, preservice programs, and materials.

Further contributions to the field have been made by the Association through its interest in curriculum building and evaluation. *Theory Into Action* (6), a publication which resulted from the work of an NSTA curriculum committee, has had a strong influence in establishing criteria for sound curriculum development.

In 1961, NSTA added the position of a specialist in elementary science to the headquarters staff. This individual fulfills the role of consultant to special projects and programs, and acts as a liaison between other education organizations—in particular, the growing number of elementary school science associations around the country. Presently, there are three of these groups that are affiliates of NSTA (the Elementary School Science Associations of Northern and Southern California and the Elementary School Science Association of New York). These associations hold their own annual conferences and seasonal workshops.

Other Publications and Services

In response to requests for more specific teaching suggestions, the Association planned and has published several items in a continuing series of instructional aids, the "How-to-do-it" publications. Titles include *How to Care for Living Things in the Classroom, How to Evaluate Science Learning, How to Record and Use Data* (4), and others. These are mainly aimed at elementary school teachers who want to improve their teaching and need a clear, concise treatment of a specific problem.

To help meet the needs of teachers who lack a good background in science subject matter, along with hints for teaching it, the Association has produced a series of six books titled *Investigating Science with Children*

† See Bibliography.

(5). Thousands of teachers have learned to teach more effectively through using these publications. They meet the needs of the beginning as well as the experienced teacher.

In 1950–51, NSTA produced a series of seven booklets by Guy V. Bruce called Science Teaching Today, which included demonstrations and projects on air, water, heat, sound, etc. The series was one of NSTA's early bestsellers with five editions printed.

As a service to elementary teachers who "can't find the issue that had that article about . . .," the Association decided to select some of the most significant articles from the first three years of publication of *Science and Children* and combine the collection into a single volume, *Helping Children Learn Science* (3)—a compact source of information describing objectives for elementary school science, background information, resources for teaching and learning, classroom ideas, and strategies for now and the future.

Council on Elementary Science International

In 1920, the National Council of Garden Teachers was organized. In 1930, this group was renamed the National Council of Supervisors of Elementary Science, and eventually in 1963 became the Council on Elementary Science International (CESI). CESI was supported by many of the same educators who were also involved in activities of the National Science Teachers Association. Its chief contributions were sponsoring meetings in conjunction with other organizations concerned with elementary education, particularly the Association for Childhood Education International (ACEI) and the Association for Supervision and Curriculum Development (ASCD). The officers and members of CESI felt that its objectives could best be realized through affiliation with an organization with an executive secretary and other staff members to carry on this work, and, so, in July 1964, CESI voted to affiliate with NSTA as a section, thus combining the offerings of both associations. Among its activities, the section sponsors a luncheon program at the annual NSTA meeting. These sessions attract large numbers of teachers, administrators, and others interested in science at the elementary level.

The Future

NSTA looks to the future from a well-established interest in science teaching in the elementary school. Even if NSTA continues only as it is now operating, its contributions to the field of elementary school science would be of great importance. But science in the elementary school will not continue as it is now. Hopefully, new methods, new materials, more research, and certainly new science subject matter will appear, both from inside and outside NSTA. The Association will act to disseminate them. And hopefully NSTA, composed as it is of the most creative minds in the field, will take the lead in sponsoring promising practices, and publish and in other ways make known these practices.

Who can guess the directions elementary school science learning will take in the next ten years? Consider, for example:

1. *The use of special science teachers in various capacities.*
   Is this desirable? How can these special teachers be used to best advantage? What should be their preparation?
2. *Changes in the nature of the self-contained classrooms.*
   What changes will take place? What will be the role of science in a changed organization? What problems will be involved?
3. *The integrated package deals that supply books, apparatus, visual aids, and other learning materials.*
   How will the publication of such materials change the present methods of instruction? How can their effectiveness be evaluated?
4. *The plans for individualized instruction.*
   What changes are necessary before individualized instruction can really take place? How important is individual instruction? How can it best be accomplished?
5. *The establishment of laboratories or more individualized laboratory experiences.*
   What kinds of laboratory experiences are important in the elementary school? How can these laboratories be set up and used most effectively? Are they really important?
6. *Increased use of TV and other media of communication.*
   What new skills will teachers need in order to participate in and make use of communication media?
7. *The advent of ungraded primary schools.*
   How will an ungraded plan affect science instruction? What preparations are essential for teachers in such situations?
8. *The establishment of outdoor laboratories for both urban and suburban student populations.*
   Are such laboratories important? What effect will they have on the inner-city dweller?

All of these problems and others will receive attention in the years to come. The Association will assume leadership in assisting its members in evaluating new practices through reports at conferences and meetings. With the growth in number and quality of regional meetings, the work of the Association will come within reach of more and more teachers and other educators.

Bibliography

1. Blough, Glenn O., Ed. *It's Time for Better Elementary School Science*. National Science Teachers Association, Washington, D.C. 1958.
2. Blough, Glenn O. *You & Your Child & Science*. Department of Elementary-School Principals and the National Science Teachers Association, Washington, D.C. 1963.
3. Hopman, Anne B., Compiler. *Helping Children Learn Science*. National Science Teachers Association, Washington, D.C. 1966.
4. "How-To-Do-It" Series. *How to Utilize the Services of a Science Consultant*, 1965; *How To Care for Living Things in the Classroom*, 1965; *How To Teach Science Through Field Studies*, 1965; *How To Record and Use Data in Elementary School Science*, 1965; *How To Individualize Science Instruction in the Elementary School*, 1965; *How To Evaluate Science Learning in the Elementary School*, 1968; *How To Use Photography as a Science Teaching Aid*, 1968. National Science Teachers Association, Washington, D.C.
5. *Investigating Science with Children*. Vol. 1, *Living Things*; Vol. 2, *The Earth*; Vol. 3, *Atoms and Molecules*; Vol. 4, *Motion*; Vol. 5, *Energy in Waves*; Vol. 6, *Space*. NSTA. Published by Teachers Publishing Corporation, Darien, Connecticut.
6. NSTA Curriculum Committee and the Conference on Science Concepts. *Theory into Action in Science Curriculum Development*. National Science Teachers Association, Washington, D.C. 1964.

The Supervision of the Science Program*

NATIONAL SOCIETY for the STUDY of EDUCATION

Supervision plays an extremely important role in any school organization. As the school system grows, specialists in science education are needed to provide for the constant growth and improvement in the science curriculum and instruction. This comprehensive discussion considers the various roles of the supervisor on the state, county, and local levels. The special problems that arise at each of these levels are presented, and suggestions are made as to how to meet these problems. This discussion is an excerpt from Chapter 12, "The Supervision of the Science Programs," of the Fifty-

* REPRINTED FROM *Rethinking Science Education*, Fifty-ninth Yearbook of the National Society for the Study of Education, Part I (Chicago: University of Chicago Press, 1960), pp. 213–224, 226–228, by permission of the publisher.

ninth NSSE Yearbook, Part I, Rethinking Science Education. Members of the committee who wrote this chapter include Donald Stotler, Lorenzo Lisonbee, Elra Palmer, Samuel Schenburg, and Henry Shannon.

The Nature and Importance of Supervision

Operational problems of one kind or another will quite certainly confront any established organization. If an organizational group is to remain dynamic, it must struggle toward equilibrium in structure at the very time that it is seeking ways to unbalance the equilibrium in order to improve the structure. This conflict between stability and change is blended most successfully in organizations where the expectancy is one of "structural mobility" or "organized change." In such situations the energy typically spent in resisting change is channeled into seeking and fostering types of change designed for the improvement of the whole organization.

THE NEED FOR SUPERVISION
Supervisors are needed to help an organization live successfully as a "family" within its structural plan while at the same time helping to rebuild the structure. Doing this is difficult enough, but doing it with methods which permit acceptance of the supervisor as a member of the "family" is the acid test of modern supervision.

For this difficult role effective supervisors are in constant demand, for the part they play in an organization is somewhat like the role of the catalyst in an organism. Membership in smaller educational organizations is often limited to planners (administrators) and teachers. Such an organization may be very successful; or it may result in the development of an arbitrary plan of action with little provision for reorganization and growth. More flexibility often results if the administrator provides some time for supervisory work or arranges to have a teacher released on a part-time basis for this type of service

As a school system grows in size, both advantages and disadvantages emerge. One advantage arises from the fact that, between the administrative and the implemental levels, specialists in subject matter and methodology can be provided to play the catalytic role.

THE SUPERVISOR AS A CONSULTANT
When a supervisory program becomes more inhibiting than catalytic, the reasons are usually less obvious than those indicated in the preceding paragraphs. The latter may be only contributing influences. In an honest attempt to reduce friction and increase the effectiveness of a program,

especially in larger systems, a stifling accumulation of rules, procedures, clearances, and general protocol may accrue. Out of this complexity may arise an atmosphere known in popular jargon as "bureaucratic." In this type of organization, the supervisor tends to become so preoccupied with procedure that proceedings grind to a snail's pace. It becomes so difficult or irritating to bring about change that initiative and creativity are stifled.

A new concept is arising in the field of supervision. In some systems the title of supervisor has actually been replaced by the title of consultant. Even where the title has been retained, the supervisor has become a consultant. The word itself denotes the change. A consultant is a person who is sought for suggestions and assistance in planning. The emphasis upon being sought is an invitation to initiative in others. It also means that to be successful a consultant must have something to offer in the way of knowledge and method.

SUPERVISION: A COOPERATIVE ENDEAVOR

The modern concept of supervision is one of helping people help themselves. This is also the modern concept of classroom instruction. The supervisor is wise, therefore, to make all details of his approach consistent with the approach he advocates for teachers. If he believes teachers should set a wholesome emotional tone in the classroom, then he should seek a similar tone in the educational system. If he believes teachers should develop experimental-mindedness, curiosity, leadership, and self-analysis, he should seek to bring out these qualities in the adults with whom he works. If he believes that the teacher should use multiple approaches, employ diverse materials, encourage problem-exploration, and emphasize individual differences, this belief should be reflected in his own activities.

All of this calls for that healthy give-and-take called cooperative planning. The supervisor by no means abdicates the role of leadership, nor does the classroom teacher who organizes the classroom in such a manner that she is freed to be a consultant. People seek the consultant in order to become oriented and to discuss new pursuits. The consultant, in approaching problems cooperatively, helps draw a larger circle with new problems. This may be an extension of a new interest or an enlargement of an old one, but it leads to a desire for leadership in opening up new frontiers.

Teachers may use the consultant approach with students, and consultants may use a similar approach with adult personnel within the educational system—and still the education of youth could be jeopardized if the community does not understand the modern approach. The supervisor uses the same approach with the community which he uses with the adult personnel in the school system and which he encourages teachers to use in the classroom. The attitude is not one of salesmanship of a finished program but cooperative problem-exploration in improving the program.

The State Consultant for Science

A typical state school system might have one thousand secondary schools in operation in one hundred fifty local school units. Each of these schools is an integral part of a complex machine devoted to the job of educating youth. If one were to evaluate the science programs in these schools, a normal distribution would probably be the result. The schools would vary in the effectiveness of their programs from very poor to very good, in much the same manner that members of a heterogeneous biology class would vary in their achievements. However, there would be many schools which failed to realize their potential and operated below their capacity, thus providing sufficient reason for initiating plans for improvement.

THE NEED FOR A CONSULTANT

The state consultant for science occupies a unique and challenging position in programs for improvement. He works with all schools and with groups within the schools including administrators, teachers, pupils, and school boards. He endeavors to direct their energies into appropriate channels and to help them formulate plans of action for long-range improvement. He performs a motivating function, an analysis function, and a synthesizing function. The schools with weaker programs are encouraged to analyze their resources with the view of preparing a program which will raise the instruction to a higher level. Schools with strong science programs are guided into well-planned experiments to discover more effective ways of handling the various aspects of the curriculum, and these are translated into procedures which can be used later by all schools.

THE ROLE OF THE CONSULTANT

The science consultant representing a state department of education will find himself involved in the thinking and other activities of many groups. He must work with all groups which are genuinely interested in providing the best scientific education for youth. With these groups his role will be that of a listener, an originator of ideas, a co-ordinator of activities, a procurer of help, and an encourager. In short, he will serve as the director of a team composed of many members, each of whom must be placed in the type of work which will assure the best results.

All of this means that the state consultant in science must know and understand the spectrum of science education in his state, which will include bases of the curriculum; relation of administration, teachers, and students to the program; physical facilities; experimentation; and new curriculum materials. When he finds there are gaps in this spectrum, he must work in such a manner that these voids are gradually filled. Unfortunately, this is an unending task for, as one gap is filled, another appears. Therefore, review of the spectrum and efforts to keep it unbroken must be continuous.

RESPONSIBILITIES OF THE CONSULTANT

As indicated in the preceding paragraph, the consultant, to be effective, must contribute to the achievement of the general goals by assisting in the solution of a variety of problems as they arise or become acute. A number of serious gaps have appeared in the science-education spectrum in recent years. One of these is the inadequacy of teaching personnel with respect to both numbers and training. This problem has arisen because of the upsurge in school enrollments, low salaries, poor working conditions, and the rapid change from an agricultural to a technological society. To make this situation more serious, the subject matter in the various science courses has necessarily undergone rapid change. Perhaps an answer is needed to the question, "What kind of program should be established to provide science teachers who will be able to channel the energies of youth into more productive efforts?"

The solution to this problem must be a co-operative affair, involving the science consultant, the state department of education, the colleges, the science teachers, administrators, and resource persons such as industrial chemists and conservationists. With the consultant as a co-ordinator these groups can participate in science-teacher work conferences in local school systems and in programs on sectional and state levels. The work of these conferences might be centered on such topics as the cell, the atom, photosynthesis, metabolism, chromatographic analysis, materials, and professional organizations. However, such conferences affect directly only those persons already teaching. Paralleling these activities must be others which deal with pre-service teacher education. With vitalized programs at the pre-service level, progress should be noticeable within a few years.

A second gap in the spectrum has occurred in the area of curriculum. The large volume of scientific information collected cannot be covered in the courses, and, as a result, important questions have been asked: What should be eliminated? What should be added? What sequence should be followed? What should be provided for the rapid learner? What background in science is needed by all citizens? These are only a few of many questions, most of which are difficult to resolve. Again, the science consultant is in a position to provide leadership in the development of good curriculum bulletins and in the planning of workshops and work conferences to attack these problems. But placing a bulletin in the hands of administrators and teachers will not insure beneficial changes. To accomplish needed changes, the science consultant must organize groups of teachers and selected consultants to develop the bulletin and then hold work conferences to study the finished product.

A third gap has occurred in the spectrum in regard to physical facilities for teaching science. The filling of this gap involves more than the provision of funds. A prerequisite is a clear understanding of the activities in which modern-day science students should engage and the type of facilities and equipment which will encourage the many aspects of problem-solving. In helping to fill this gap, the role of the consultant is obvious. He must present ideas to school personnel and architects and lend assistance in designing programs and facilities which reflect the best of available ideas.

Another responsibility of the science consultant is to provide the public with accurate information regarding the status of the science programs in the state. To do this effectively, he will find it necessary to collect and summarize pertinent data each year, and to make his findings available through the press, the radio, and television.

Supervision at the County Level

Harold Spears is quoted as authority for the statement that "The improvement of instruction for about half of the nation's school children is largely dependent upon the supervision that comes out of the office of the county superintendent." [1] He also reports that half of the counties do not employ supervisors, the superintendent carrying all supervisory responsibility. [2]

In a survey of the 49 states made for this study, [3] it was revealed that science supervision is, to the extent that it exists, provided by general supervisors or by the county superintendent. In some counties, certain county staff members with some competence in science education are employed. A few state departments reported that excellent work in science education was being done by these specialists. Leaders in a number of state departments reported a need for specialized supervisors at the county level, while others indicated a preference for general supervisors who would concentrate their efforts on teaching methods rather than on subject matter.

SPECIAL PROBLEMS

AT THE ELEMENTARY LEVEL. Replies to the questionnaire from the state departments can be summarized thus: (a) Elementary teachers, in the main, lack sufficient training in science and tend to shy away from science. (b) The combination of not having specially trained supervisors at the county level and not having classroom teachers trained in science renders unlikely any attempt on the part of the two groups to co-operate in the improvement of science education. (c) The lack of training indicated in (a) and (b) above is responsible, in large measure, for the lack of minimum physical facilities for a minimum program in science.

[1] Harold Spears, *Improving the Supervision of Instruction* (New York: Prentice-Hall, Inc., 1953), p. 235.
[2] *Ibid.*, p. 236.
[3] In June 1958, an inquiry concerning the status of science supervision at the county level was mailed to all the state departments of education. There were 45 replies.

The consensus indicated that the first step in upgrading science-teaching in schools of the county is to obtain competent supervisors who have an interest in science and who would encourage the schools to employ science teachers who are competent and are interested in teaching science. This appears to be essential if children of high ability in science and mathematics are to be identified early and started on their way to science careers.

THE ROLE OF THE COUNTY CONSULTANT

Responses to the questionnaire from state departments gave general support to the idea that county consultants should be specialists in (a) supervision and curriculum, (b) the basic sciences, (c) methods of teaching science, and (d) human relations. The consultant is a resource person, ready to serve where and when needed. His association with teachers in the county should make them more confident of their ability to teach science. He is a leader in the broadest sense.

The science consultant provides liaison between teachers and administrators. He advises the superintendents and principals and reports to them on the progress and needs of the schools. He attempts to develop a unity of purpose among the schools of the county and co-ordinates the over-all effort from Kindergarten through Grade XII. He recognizes weaknesses in the programs of the schools and, in a democratic way, helps teachers and administrators correct them. He places proper emphasis on science instruction and assists in integrating science into the curriculum.

RESPONSIBILITIES OF THE COUNTY CONSULTANT

All of the science consultant's efforts are pointed toward upgrading science education in the county. He works constantly with teachers and administrators to improve instruction and to expand the opportunities afforded children for the study of science. He develops or assists in the development of a science program from the elementary grades through high school; helps develop programs of in-service training; trains teachers in methods of instruction, giving classroom assistance where needed and wanted. The consultant coordinates the county program as a whole and evaluates the curriculum in individual schools annually. He assists teachers and administrators in the reorganization of the curriculum and makes arrangements for institutes and workshops for the improvement of instruction.

Supervision in Large City Systems

The attributes of good supervision are the same regardless of the size of the school system; the problems involved, however, are of a different order of magnitude. The number and nature of opportunities for supervision differ from level to level and even at the same level. Although ideas do not easily flow among a large number of teachers, the existence of a large staff makes possible the addition of consultants, specialists, and supervisors with only a small percentage increase in the school budget.

SPECIAL PROBLEMS

AT THE ELEMENTARY LEVEL. The increase of dependence of our way of life upon scientific achievements has convinced educators that science must become an essential part of the elementary school curriculum. Elementary science is being increasingly introduced in many parts of the country, and the preparation of the elementary teachers to teach with confidence in that field is one of the primary aims of elementary education today. Since many school principals are not science specialists and many elementary teachers have little or no background in science, the problem of adequate supervision becomes a formidable one. A supervisor at the elementary level is called upon to perform many important functions. Among these the following are suggestive:

1. He must participate in the formulation of a science program which will explore scientific concepts and provide experiences for children from the Kindergarten through Grade XII.
2. He must participate in the preparation of resource publications which describe a variety of appropriate activities for implementing the science program.
3. He must engage in a broad teacher-training program designed to provide background and engage in workshop courses which will enable teachers to secure first-hand experiences with science subject matter, materials, and techniques.
4. He must recommend selections of supplies and equipment and proper procedures for obtaining them.
5. He must participate in the formulation of programs for talented students.
6. He must participate in the formulation of continuous in-service science programs which will supplement the initial background courses and workshops and will insure the professional growth of teachers throughout their teaching lifetime.
7. He must evaluate instruction through such methods as direct classroom visitations and follow-up conferences.

There are some elementary-science supervisors who are performing only part of the foregoing functions. In some cities some of these functions are being performed by science specialists. They are usually highly successful teachers with good backgrounds in science, who are freed from teaching to operate from a field superintendent's office. The specialists visit elementary school teachers in accordance with an arranged schedule or upon specific request of principals and teachers. The specialists can usually assist only in the performance of a few of the functions. They work with the teachers individually and in small groups. One consultant to every 120 to 150 elementary teachers is recommended.

The evaluation function, together with one or more of the other functions, is usually performed by the principal or assistant principal of the school. Either operates under a disadvantage when he attempts classroom supervision because his background in science may be too meager. Also, principals and assistant principals are so occupied with administrative duties and the entire program of elementary education that they are often unable to provide the leadership needed for science work at the elementary school level.

In this period of transition, when in-service science training of the present corps of elementary teachers is paramount, effective elementary supervision should remain the joint responsibility of the science specialist and the principal of the school.

To assure the proper supervision of classroom instruction and the professional growth of the elementary-school teachers, it is recommended by some that at least one person who possesses an adequate science background and supervisory training should be assigned to each elementary school. He would be responsible for the supervision of science instruction in addition to other duties.

Supervisors should not disregard the fact that the elementary and secondary schools are operating upon the *same* child at different stages of his development. Supervision on one level cannot, therefore, ignore the fields of science as they are explored on other levels if it is to assure the proper ordering of scientific concepts and activities for the maturing child. Thus vertical articulation, so obviously needed in our school systems, should be a prime responsibility of the science supervisor.

Supervision in Smaller City and Suburban Systems

The large number of relatively small school systems in the country makes it necessary to study problems of supervision in such systems. Statistics indicate that 75 per cent of American high schools have enrollments of less than three hundred pupils, while 90 per cent have fewer than a thousand.

THE ROLE OF THE CONSULTANT

Supervision is an expert professional service which is primarily concerned with the improvement of learning. Thus, supervision deals with the improvement of the total teacher-learning process; orients learning and its improvement within the general aim of education; and co-ordinates, stimulates, and directs the growth of teachers through co-operative leadership. It is deeply concerned with the long-range improvement of science education.

To accomplish these aims and those stated in the first part of this chapter, the supervisor or consultant offers such services as:

1. Developing in-service educational programs.
2. Developing a science curriculum.
3. Visiting classrooms.
4. Establishing and implementing educational goals.
5. Planning demonstration lessons.
6. Coordinating services.
7. Suggesting and supplying resource materials.
8. Helping in the selection and purchase of textbooks and equipment.

The supervisor or consultant also has obligations to raise professional standards, build teacher morale, serve as a resource person, encourage advanced study and research, and interpret the science program to the staff and the community.

One of the major advantages that the science consultant in smaller cities has is the opportunity to know his teachers well and to recognize their strengths and weaknesses. The possibility of developing an exceptional *esprit de corps* is greater than in the larger cities.

PROVIDING FOR ADEQUATE SUPERVISION

In this period of increasing emphasis upon science education, it is imperative that small city and suburban systems provide adequate science supervisory service. It is a prime factor in the improvement of science instruction.

Wherever feasible, a full-time science consultant should be employed to assist with the program in Grades I through XII. In those cities of approximately 200,000 an assistant may be employed who is a specialist in the field of elementary science. In small districts science leadership can be provided by the head of the school science department. This individual should be given adequate time and compensation for performing the services needed to facilitate an on-going science program.

Within the framework of the American philosophy of education, the schools belong to the people. The schools reflect this concept, and, therefore, will generally be only as good as the citizenry demands.

GENERAL QUALIFICATIONS OF THE SCIENCE CONSULTANT

The science consultant should have a thorough subject-matter background, a basic knowledge in the major branches of science and their interrelationship. In addition to the subject-matter qualifications, the consultant should have professional training in supervision and administration. It is important that the supervisor be familiar with recent developments in the fields of science and education. The consultant certainly must qualify as a superior teacher and should have at least five years of successful teaching experience in the grade levels concerned. It is unrealistic to require previous experience in science supervision since such a small percentage of the school systems, up to the present time, have employed science consultants. A lack of experience in supervision may well be offset by experience within a school system. One of the most important competencies lies in the field of personality. The consultant must be able to work well with his peer group and possess a deep insight into the problems of human relations. He must establish rapport with his teachers in order to carry on free and frank discussions. He must have the ability to assume a leadership role. He should bring to the position a high degree of imagination and creativity. He should be able to recognize the need for specific kinds of help—corrective, preventive, constructive, and creative. He should possess a sense of humor and the maturity to accept decisions adverse to those he has made or would make. These traits and abilities may well serve as guideposts for the selection of a consultant, and it is hoped that they will develop more fully with experience on the job.

Improving the Education of the Science Superivisor*

J. DARRELL BARNARD

J. Darrell Barnard defines the qualities that make a good science supervisor. He groups these qualities into two categories: (1) there are attributes, which refer to those qualities that one innately possesses or comes to possess by processes not clearly revealed; (2) there are competencies, which refer to those qualities that one learns or may learn as a part of his professional education or experiences. Dr. Barnard lists ten attributes and sixteen competencies that should become the goals of a graduate program for the education of science supervisors.

It seems reasonable to begin an exploration of this topic by asking the question: What is a science supervisor? The question can be asked but there is no simple answer. Based upon the findings of his survey of the science supervisor, Ploutz concludes, "Due to differing conditions within school systems throughout the United States, there is probably no such thing as *the model supervisor*." [1] Among the 100 supervisors of science

* REPRINTED FROM a paper presented on March 30, 1965, at the Thirteenth Annual Convention of the National Science Teachers Association in Denver, Colorado, by permission of the author and the National Science Teachers Association. Dr. Barnard is Professor of Science Education at New York University.
[1] Ploutz, Paul F. "Survey of the Science Supervisor," *The Science Teacher* 28: p. 411 (October 1961).

included in his study, he found four different models. There was the K–8 or elementary school model; the 9–12 or secondary school model; the K–12 or total curriculum model; and finally the state department model. He also found a variety of titles given to persons who assumed a science supervisory role in schools: science-helping teacher, science-resource person, science consultant, and science coordinator. We could add others such as departmental chairman and director of science.

It is my understanding that NSSA has had a commission working upon the problem of defining a science supervisor model based upon the duties he should properly perform. Until such a time as the NSSA model has been developed, we shall have to resort to our own definitions. For purposes of this paper a science supervisor is any one in a school system who has been trained in science education and who, because of this training, has been given official responsibility for the management of all or some part of the science program, beyond the specific science courses that he teaches. He may assume this responsibility on a full or part-time work schedule. I realize that this is a broad definition, but so is the present status of science supervision in the schools. A part of this might be accounted for by the fact that little distinction has been made between the education of the science teacher and the science supervisor. I am hopeful that this paper may help to clarify some of the confusion—not compound it further.

Working within this rather nebulous concept of the science supervisor, I have attempted to define qualities that go to make a good one. In part this has been done by making case studies of some science supervisors as I have come to know them and their work. The remaining qualities have been identified by analyzing duty lists for supervisors prepared by school administrators, teachers (both the beginning teacher and the experienced one), and by supervisors themselves. I have divided my items of quality into two categories. For want of a better term, I refer to my first category as *attributes* and to my second category as *competencies*. As you can predict, the distinction between these two categories is a relatively tenuous one. *Attributes* refer to those qualities that one innately possesses or comes to possess by processes not clearly revealed. *Competencies* are those qualities that one learns or may learn as a part of his professional education or experience.

None of the persons included in my case studies arrived at his position as a supervisor by satisfactorily completing a collegiate program specifically designed to educate him for his position as a supervisor. Excluding school systems where qualifying or licensing examinations are required, there are probably as many ways to become a science supervisor as there are science supervisors. Be that as it may, I have found what appears to be certain common prerequisite qualities possessed by my subjects.

Some time prior to being made a supervisor, they had demonstrated that they were "good" science teachers. (I have put good in quotes because this may mean slightly different things to different evaluators.) Second, they had identified themselves as "leaders" among their peers. (Again I have put leaders in quotes for much the same reason.) Third, they were not satisfied with models of science teaching as they had observed them. Fourth, they had "ideas." These included ideas about improved models of science teaching. Fifth, they were "aggressive." I do not mean aggressive in a derogatory sense, but in the sense they moved out to get things done.

The above are five attributes generally shared by my subjects. However, there are five other attributes that are possessed in varying degrees by different subjects. And yet they appear to be qualities of a high order of importance in becoming a good supervisor. They include modesty, adaptability, critical mindedness, a well developed system of values, and respect for the worth and dignity of each teacher with whom he works.

For the most part these qualities are beyond the purview of formal education. Or to put it another way, if the prospective candidate for a supervisory position does not possess a good proportion of these qualities, not much more can be done to help him become a supervisor. It would seem that these attributes represent a basic list of qualities which one should possess before he is admitted into a graduate program for science supervisors. How to determine their possession becomes a perplexing admissions problem.

As I mentioned before, the second list of qualities represents competencies, or "abilities to do," which to a large extent can be developed, in fact, they should become the goals of a graduate program to educate science supervisors. I hold no brief for the completeness of this list, however, I do consider the 16 listed here to be important ones based upon analyses of the various lists of duties:

1. He should be able to envision the essential features of an articulated K–12 science sequence. This does not mean that he should have a neat little K–12 package worked out on paper or in the head. But he should be able to tell what the principal features of a good one would be, and therefore to provide leadership in developing one or in evaluating "ready-made" packages that may be available to schools.

2. He should be able to innovate and objectively to evaluate the innovations of others as they relate to methods, content, equipment and sequences. This would mean that he has developed a rational frame of reference, philosophically and psychologically, which he consistently applies in evaluating "new" ideas.

3. He should be able to distinguish clearly between effective and ineffective teaching practices and to rationalize the bases for the distinctions he makes. He must be more than an intuitive evaluator of teaching.

4. He should be able to motivate teachers to seek means of improving their practices and to counsel them regarding effective ways of going about it.

5. He should be able to use effective procedures for evaluating the progress of students, as well as the effectiveness of teachers in directing the learning experiences of students.

6. He should be able to design and conduct investigations that will yield reliable evidence regarding the effectiveness of instructional programs.

7. He should be able to interpret science education, in general, and his school's science program, in particular, to other educators and to laymen in the school community.

8. He should be able to design and administer inventory systems and prepare defensible budgets for the procurement and proper maintenance of science materials and equipment.

9. He should be able to initiate and direct in-service science curriculum studies and workshops or institutes for upgrading and updating science teachers.

10. He should be able to keep teachers informed regarding current developments in science education and promising innovations in science teaching.

11. He should be able to demonstrate effective ways of teaching for the various outcomes, especially the less tangible ones such as critical thinking.

12. He should be able to adapt his method of working with teachers to the idiosyncrasies of teachers. Teaching is basically a personal accomplishment. He should not only accept it as such, but strive to get teachers to do so.

13. He should be able to *listen* to teachers and to gain insights regarding their points of view, their aspirations, their frustrations, their fears and their needs. Just as a good teacher listens more than he talks, so should a supervisor.

14. He should be able to identify the strengths and weaknesses of individual teachers and to help each teacher overcome his weakness without depreciating the teacher's self-image.

15. He should be able to conduct group conferences and work sessions in ways that maximize the contributions of participants.

16. He should be able to help teachers understand the objectives of science teaching in terms of their consequent behaviors. He should be able to operationalize objectives.

The above list of 16 competencies, supplemented by the 10 attributes mentioned earlier, should provide a basis for thinking about ways in which the education of supervisors might be improved.

It would seem that we begin with the assumption that one who would become a supervisor must first have been a teacher. Next, we assume that all science teachers will not or should not become supervisors; that the prerequisites for becoming a supervisor involve something more than being a teacher. Finally, we assume that the education of science supervisors is a joint responsibility of public school systems and collegiate institutions.

Just what the relative roles of each should be have not been clearly delineated. In fact, I am hopeful that the remainder of this paper might throw some light upon the subject.

There is a pre-service and an in-service phase to the education of science supervisors. The in-service phase has to do with those who are practicing the profession of supervision. The pre-service phase has to do with those who seek to prepare themselves to be supervisors.

What has been the pre-service education of supervisors? Most of those in supervisory positions began their careers as secondary school science teachers. Their academic preparation was basically that required to be certified as secondary school science teachers. Their science content courses were those that were assumed to prepare them to be either chemistry, physics, earth science, or biology teachers. Outside of the foundations courses in philosophy of education, history of education and/or educational sociology, their professional courses were geared to the secondary level: principles of secondary education, general methods of teaching at the secondary level, methods of teaching secondary school science, and adolescent psychology. Pre-student teaching observation and student teaching were limited to secondary schools. In other words, their orientation was almost exclusively secondary, which represents only the upper half of the K–12 science sequence. I do not believe that this pattern is adequate either for the secondary school science teacher or for the prospective science supervisor.

How should the pre-service education of prospective science supervisors be improved? The content background required to be competent science supervisors, precludes prospective candidates coming to such positions through the elementary school. Most will continue to enter supervision by way of the secondary-school-science-teacher route. Secondary school science teachers know relatively little about elementary education, and more specifically about elementary school science. In part, this accounts for some of the difficulties which schools encounter in their efforts to develop K–12 articulated programs in science. Why shouldn't secondary school science teachers be more knowledgeable in elementary education? I believe they should and propose the following changes in the professional courses which they are required to take in preparation for teaching at the secondary school level.

Instead of a course in principles of secondary education, I would propose a course in principles of education. In this course the principles would be applied to both elementary and secondary education. Instead of a course in adolescent psychology, they should have one or more courses that deal with growth and development from 5 years to 17 years of age. The concepts of growth and development as they relate to learning should be high-lighted. The general methods of teaching at the secondary school level would become a general methods course for teaching at both the elementary and secondary school level. The science methods courses would deal with methods of teaching science at the various grade levels. Pre-student teaching observation would include observation in both elementary and secondary schools. Student teaching would be done at both levels.

The implementation of such a proposal calls for some radical changes in our colleges of education where specialization in elementary and secondary education has become unreasonably entrenched. In spite of the tenability of assumptions underlying such a proposal, the specialists in elementary education and the specialists in secondary education will probably contend that such courses cannot be taught within the conventional limitation of credits allocated for professional courses. After some radical surgery of present courses, I believe they could.

With this broad-based background in elementary and secondary education, secondary school science teachers should be much better equipped to perform their duties within a K–12 science sequence. Furthermore, the potential pool of candidates for supervisory positions in science at the various levels will become enlarged.

It would seem to me that science teachers who aspire to prepare themselves for supervisory positions should have taught a minimum of five years. They should have had experience at the elementary, junior high school and senior high school levels. They should take at least one year of graduate study beyond the masters. Whether the advanced work is recognized academically by a sixth-year certificate or applied toward a doctorate, it should be designed to accomplish the following:

1. Bring the candidate's science background up to a minimum of 18 points in graduate courses. (6)
2. Provide an internship in supervision for at least one semester. (6)
3. Include a full-year practicum to deal with such topics as: (6)
   a. The K–12 science sequence.
   b. Innovations in science teaching.
   c. Evaluation of teaching practices.
   d. Objectives as behavioral goals.
   e. Demonstration teaching.
   f. Adapting methods of supervision to the idiosyncrasies of schools and teachers.
   g. How to listen to teachers.
4. Include these courses:
   a. Research design and statistics. (6)
   b. Tests and measurements. (3)
   c. Group dynamics. (3)

Let's look next at the in-service phase of the supervisor's education. Except in large school systems, the science supervisor finds few professional associates within the system who share his specific interests and problems. In various ways he may become associated with supervisors of other subject fields when general problems of supervision are considered, and this can make an important contribution to his education as a science supervisor. Through membership in NSSA, he may become involved in conferences and clinics dealing with problems of the science supervisor. He may read the professional literature and even contribute articles. He may have the good fortune of working with a group of science teachers who stimulate him to push out beyond the fringes of established routines. From time to time he may even seek assistance with certain problems from the professors in nearby collegiate institutions. He may spend all or part of several summers at institutes and work conferences for supervisors. He may have the privilege of working on one of the course improvement projects. Along the way he may even complete his doctorate in science education and thereby earn his union card. Through these and other self-initiated activities, he provides for his in-service education as a science supervisor. My guess is that the above is representative of the logs of many of the supervisors attending this conference. Does the procedure need to be improved? If so, should collegiate institutions become more actively involved?

Collegiate institutions have three major responsibilities: 1) Inquiry; 2) Instruction; and 3) Service. There are two of these that have particular implications for improving the in-service education of science supervisors.

Some institutions have distinguished themselves for the consultant services which their professors have provided to schools. In fact, the demands from schools for such services have often diverted professors from their more fundamental responsibility, inquiry. Professors have rationalized their neglect of research by citing their busy consultation schedules and contending that the feed-back from this effort is helping to advance knowledge in science education. Except in those institutions, such as Florida State University, where the service to the schools is one of conducting formal inquiry into teaching problems on a cooperative basis, such contentions of productive feed-back are largely wishful thinking.

If institutions were to limit their school services to cooperative research projects, both schools and institutions would profit. Schools would profit through the involvement of its supervisory staff and its teachers in research, as well as getting more definitive answers to many of their questions. The collegiate institution would profit through the redirection of its energy into channels that are more traditionally the responsibility of the university, a fundamental responsibility not generally assumed by any other institution in our society.

In terms of their professional performance, supervisors share with many college professors a critical deficiency. Few, if any of them, are actively involved in research designed to advance our understanding of problems related to science teaching. It is toward the correction of this situation that collegiate institutions could contribute most to the improvement of the in-service education of science supervisors and to the upgrading of its own contributions to the profession.

If the research is to be cooperative it should deal with unresolved problems faced by the schools in their efforts to advance science teaching. The processes involved in the identification of these problems and in asking the questions that should, and can, be researched not only represents a real challenge to the schools but will also require the best research talents that collegiate institutions can provide.

It is unreasonable to assume that sustained cooperative research efforts of any significance will be accomplished by forcing supervisors and/or professors to become involved. The consequences of such "forced feeding" is that as soon as the pressure is removed, the research effort terminates. For example, how many of those who were "forced" to do research in fulfilling their requirements for the doctorate have continued to be active in research? It would seem that the one-shot deal immunizes against further research rather than spreads the infection.

Somehow we need to develop a climate in which we habitually turn to research for answers to the many unresolved and critical questions that face us in science education. Many of the persistent problems in science education result from practices based upon *superstitious* beliefs and pedagogical *folklore.*

In our efforts to change the intellectual climate of science education we should begin with the research that has been done. I cannot agree with those who contend that most, if not all, of the research in science education is worthless. For 25 years prior to the recent efforts to improve science curriculums we had evidence that something was wrong. Furthermore, there was abundant evidence from the research that the teaching methods so commonly practiced were not only ineffective, but actually deleterious. But it was not until the scientists intuitively arrived at this conclusion that it was given effective visibility. And they have had their problems in convincing some teachers whose behavior has been guided by superstitious beliefs and the folklore of science teaching.

In professional courses for science teachers and supervisors, research findings should be used in dealing with the basic questions of what, how, and why. Where the findings from research are not adequate, it should be clearly indicated that we tentatively rely upon best judgments. Teachers supervisors, and professors should become conditioned to distinguish between fact and opinion in dealing with curriculum problems in science. We should adopt the attitude of Dr. Anton J. Carlson, the distinguished physiologist, who became a thorn in the side of many a glib physiologist by repeatedly asking the question: What is your evidence? But Dr. Carlson did not merely ask the question. Where there was no evidence, he set about to find it. This led to many of his classical experiments on the physiology of hunger and digestion. Furthermore, his book *The Machinery of the Body*, is an exemplary physiology text in which the concepts of physiology are largely taught by reviewing the research that led to them.

Why, in the community of science educators, is there not a greater professional interest with opinions lacking the support of evidence? Is it because we have become enamored with the doctrine of expediency? Is it because we are unwilling to subject ourselves to the discipline required of him who would search for evidence? Is it because the profession and the public put higher premiums upon other kinds of performance, such as attending conferences, conducting institutes, developing "new" curriculums, making speeches, and writing textbooks? Is it because our "busy" schedules allow no time for the reflective thinking, reading and probing that is required to get started?

Money buys time and increasing amounts of money are becoming available to buy a part of the time of those qualified persons who would commit themselves to do research. In our own institution, released time from one or more classes is now given to professors who wish time to design investigations. Funds are also available for travel and consultant assistance. I imagine that our institution is not unique in this respect; that other institutions are also developing climates that are conducive to the spawning of a greater research effort in science education. As this becomes more of a way of academic life at institutions where supervisors and potential supervisors obtain their training, there will be more research infections and fewer research immunizations.

If I seem to have overemphasized involvement in cooperative research as an approach to the improvement of the in-service education of science supervisors, it is because I strongly believe that it is the most neglected aspect of our efforts to advance professionally. If more of it were being done, conventions such as this one might become disturbing, enlightening, dynamic forums rather than polite gatherings for purposes of listening to rehashes of ideas such as those presented in this paper.

An Analysis of Research on Elementary Teacher Education Related to the Teaching of Science*

PATRICIA E. BLOSSER and ROBERT W. HOWE

The Educational Resources Information Center (ERIC) comprises a network of decentralized clearing houses in various locations throughout the United States. The ERIC clearinghouse for science education, located at Ohio State University, is designed to help teachers keep informed of new instructional techniques and materials. The purpose of this article is to report recent research related to the preparation of elementary school teachers to teach science. The following six categories, together with an extensive bibliography, are included: (1) Certification and Requirements for Elementary Teachers, (2) Status of Elementary School Science Teaching, (3) Preservice Preparation in Science for Elementary Teachers, (4) Teacher Competence Research, (5) Teacher Behaviors and Characteristics, and (6) Use of New Media and Techniques in Teacher Education.

The purpose of this article is to report to the profession an analysis of recent research related to the preparation of elementary school teachers to teach science. When a comparison is made with the number of studies of the education in science of elementary teachers with those studies dealing with the preparation of secondary school science teachers, it would appear that science educators have tended to concentrate more of their research efforts on the preparation of teachers for the secondary schools rather than attempting to identify and define problems involved in preparing elementary teachers to do a competent job of teaching science. This situation persists despite the continuing criticisms that many elementary teachers do an inadequate job of teaching science, and also that many are reluctant to teach science. If this situation is to be changed, attention should be given to such problems as finding methods for improving the science competencies of teachers, determining the optimal content background and types of experiences in science for elementary teachers, building more positive attitudes toward science on the part of elementary teachers,

* REPRINTED FROM *Science and Children*, Vol. 6, No. 5, January-February 1969, pp. 50–60. Copyright, 1969, by the National Science Teachers Association, Washington, D.C. Reprinted by permission of the authors and the publisher. Ms. Blosser is Assistant Professor of Education at Ohio State University. Dr. Howe is Director of ERIC and Chairman of the Faculty of Science and Mathematics Education at Ohio State University.

as well as continuing the investigations into the area of science content and experiences that should be part of the elementary school curriculum.

Certification and Requirements for Elementary Teachers

The problem of providing an adequate preservice preparation program in science for elementary teachers has been one of continuing concern to science educators. The recommendation that elementary teachers have at least 20 hours in science was made in the 46th Yearbook of the National Society for the Study of Education, *Science Education in American Schools*, published in 1947. In 1963, the National Association of State Directors of Teacher Education and Certification (NASDTEC) and the American Association for the Advancement of Science (1)† published a set of guide-lines for science and mathematics in the preparation program of elementary school teachers. This joint committee recommended that every elementary teacher be educated in the fundamental concepts of the biological sciences, the physical sciences, the earth sciences, and mathematics. The development, by colleges, of interdisciplinary courses to illustrate these fundamental concepts was also recommended.

If these recommendations have been acted upon, this action is not yet apparent in state certification requirements as reported by Woellner and Wood (49). There is wide variation among the states in so far as the amount of science which an elementary teacher must have for certification. According to their publication, some states do not specify the amount of credit hours in science needed for certification. Requirements which are specified range from 6 to 15 semester hours, on the average. (California requires a major or graduate work in a single subject, amounting to 24–28 semester hours.) In some states, the amount of science required for certification varies with that required as a part of the general education component of the teacher's under-graduate program. There is very little uniformity to be found. The number of hours required for certification serves to set the minimum standard for preparation, not the optimum.

Status of Elementary School Science Teaching

The publication and dissemination of these recommendations and guidelines appear to have had little effect on science teaching as evidenced by research studies in which the status of elementary science teaching has been investigated: Blackwood (5), Smith and Cooper (38), Piltz (31), Moorehead (29), Verrill (44).

† See References.

Blackwood (5) conducted a survey, under the auspices of the U.S. Office of Education, of science teaching in the elementary schools as it was reflected in teaching practices. As a result of the information gained from the questionnaire sent to elementary schools during 1961–62, Blackwood found that a great variety of purposes, methods, and resources for teaching science existed. He also found that science in the elementary schools is not a subject required by law in most states.

However, science was taught in most of the elementary schools responding to Blackwood's survey. The most common pattern in the early grades was that of science integrated with other subjects. The frequency with which science was taught as a separate subject increased by grade in all school enrollment groups up through grade 5. This tendency toward separation increased in grades 7 and 8. Science taught as (A) a separate subject and (B) as a separate and incidental subject were the most common patterns in the upper grades.

Historically, science in the elementary schools has been taught by the classroom teacher. This was still the situation in the majority of the schools responding to the questionnaire. The frequency of this pattern decreased with increasing grade level. In a large percentage of schools with enrollments of 400 to 800 students, special teachers teach science to seventh- and eighth-grade students. Some schools, especially those with larger enrollments, had special science teachers from fourth through eighth grades. Regardless of whether a specialist or the classroom teacher taught science, some type of consultant help was available in most schools. A variety of personnel served as consultants, ranging from general elementary supervisors to high school science teachers.

Schools were asked to rank 13 items considered as barriers to effective science teaching. "Lack of adequate consultant service" was ranked first. Blackwood found that science was taught by a classroom teacher without the help of an elementary *science* specialist in over 80 per cent of the schools in grades 1 through 5 and in over 70 per cent of the schools in grades 6 through 8.

"Lack of supplies and equipment," "inadequate room facilities," and "insufficient funds for purchasing needed supplies, equipment, and appropriate science reading materials" were ranked second, third, and fourth in importance. "Teachers do not have sufficient science knowledge" was ranked fifth as a barrier to effective science teaching.

Blackwood concluded that if the inadequacies, revealed through this survey, are to be corrected and the present programs of elementary science are to be improved, reassessment is necessary. Attention should be given to such factors as (A) class size, (B) number of minutes per week that science is taught, (C) developing a systematically planned curriculum in science, (D) the acquisition of adequate supplies and equipment, including library books and other supplementary books and materials, and (E) provision for consultant services, among others.

Smith and Cooper (38) conducted an investigation to determine the frequency of use of eight science teaching techniques by elementary teachers. They attempted to determine the significance of the relationship between the frequency of use of each technique and certain professional and personal characteristics of teachers. They found that teachers with the most formal study in science, in addition to the undergraduate degree, used all the techniques, except reading and discussion of the textbook, with significantly greater frequency than teachers with little or no additional formal study in science. Teachers with the most college training generally used techniques other than reading and discussion of the textbook with greater frequency than those with lesser amounts of college training. However, there was little difference in the frequency with which the two groups of teachers used pupil recording and reporting observations. The researchers concluded that more variety in techniques for teaching science may be expected with better preparation programs and more knowledgeable teachers in the field of science.

Piltz (31) conducted a study to determine what factors, in the opinion of classroom teachers, handicap the teaching of science in the elementary school. He also wished to determine what relationship, if any, existed between the aspirations of teachers and the difficulties they thought they faced. He found the teachers surveyed to be in general agreement concerning the factors limiting science teaching in the elementary school. The difficulties were of two types: (A) those which could be remedied if the teachers were to attain a better understanding of science and how to teach it, and (B) other difficulties over which the teachers had little or no control. Piltz found conflict concerning content emphasis. He speculated that this conflict arose from the variety of factors that determine the focus of what is taught: the teacher's individual interest and competency, pressure from administrators, pupil achievement, environmental conditions, and the teacher's perception of what is important in the curriculum and in the lives of boys and girls.

Piltz found that a majority of teachers participating in his study considered inadequate physical facilities to be the greatest of all obstacles to effective science teaching. Another obstacle was that of lack of proper materials, equipment, and resources. He also found that some teachers lacked confidence in teaching science and that the majority were weak in the methodology of science teaching. The principals surveyed expressed the opinion that lack of training, of teacher interest, and of time and materials limited science teaching. Few, however, appeared to be doing anything to improve the situation.

Preservice Preparation in Science for Elementary Teachers

Apparently elementary teachers are frequently handicapped in teaching science effectively by conditions existing in many public schools. They may also be handicapped by the preservice preparation they receive. A number of studies related directly or primarily to the problem of preservice preparation in science for grade teachers are: Gant (19), Banks (3), Moorehead (29), Hardin (22), Eaton (15), Service (35), Kisner (24), Chamberlain (10), Esget (17), Bryant (7), Weaver (46), Lerner (26), Gaides (18), Gega (20), Michals (28), Eccles (16), Victor (45), Verrill (44), Cheney (11), Hines (23), Soy (39), Oshima (32).

Banks (3) conducted a study to determine what curriculum arrangements and classroom practices were employed at various teacher education institutions to meet the needs of elementary science teachers. He inferred that science educators may be instilling an "isolationist posture" in preservice elementary teachers by not preparing them to utilize the services of science supervisors and consultants, and also by not emphasizing the possibilities inherent in such cooperative ventures as team teaching. Banks found inadequacies in the present organization of the teacher education program. The fact that science in the elementary school should be an integral part of the curriculum is not stressed. The pre-service program for elementary teachers, according to Bank's data, also appeared to isolate practical experience, the study of educational psychology, and child growth from science teaching methodology. Another apparent weakness of many science education courses for elementary teachers was that preservice teachers were not involved in a sufficient variety of meaningful situations. Many courses did not appear to be designed to develop, in the preservice teacher, any depth of understanding of why science should be included in the elementary curriculum. Banks theorized that this aspect might have been neglected because the science educators were preoccupied with attempting to convince the perservice teachers that science is not so abstract and incomprehensible as they might have thought.

Gant (19), in a study made from 1957 to 1959, attempted to determine the experiences that elementary student teachers had in science programs in off-campus centers in New York. He concluded that too few elementary student teachers appeared to have problem-solving experiences in science teaching in off-campus cooperating schools, that there was insufficient use of community resources in the science program, that few science consultants were available to help elementary teachers, and that there was a definite lack of experience with such evaluation techniques as achievement and standardized test results, individual interviews with students, and pupil self-evaluation.

Gant suggested that a thorough appraisal of several possible approaches to science instruction be an integral part of the methods and materials course in elementary school science. Responses from the student teachers involved in this study seemed to indicate that the teaching experience would have been more satisfactory if they had had more instructional materials, more guidance in science teaching experiences, and more opportunity for participation in classroom science activities.

Verrill (44), as a part of a study designed to survey the preparation of general elementary teachers to teach science from 1870 to 1961, studied the teacher preparation programs in colleges and universities in a six-state area. He found that few schools had science subject-matter courses especially designed for elementary teachers. Only 19 of the 133 schools surveyed offered survey courses. The number of preservice elementary teachers who obtained their science subject-matter background as a part of the general education requirement was more than double that of any other one particular arrangement.

Chamberlain (10) also investigated the preservice education of elementary school science teachers. As a part of his research, he obtained information from in-service elementary teachers. When these individuals evaluated their college science courses, they found the basic courses in all sciences to be of value as well as courses in science education. They felt that, in pre-service programs, there was a lack of qualified faculty to handle courses in elementary school science. Their replies seem to support the assumption that if teachers are adequately prepared in science, their problems related to actual teaching are fewer. Many respondents felt that additional training in science would be desirable, but more teachers were concerned with physical problems in the schools, such as lack of space and equipment, which they considered handicaps to effective teaching.

Hardin (22) surveyed the science preparation of preservice elementary teachers at The University of Miami. After analyzing the results of the students' scores on a test designed to reveal competency in science, Hardin concluded that preservice teachers are inadequately prepared. Women students showed greater inadequacy than men students; prospective primary teachers indicated more inadequacy than prospective intermediate teachers. The degree of inadequacy of preparation was revealed to be substantially the same for all five major areas of science. Hardin also concluded that laboratory experiences in addition to the completion of a course in science content and methods were significantly related to competency in science, as evaluated by the instrument used in the investigation.

Service (35) investigated the preservice education in science of elementary teachers at selected California teacher education institutions. He attempted to develop a proposed program of science preparation for elementary teachers. Service suggested that the science preparation program for preservice elementary school teachers should consist of (A) broad, survey-type courses in the biological, physical, and earth-space sciences with emphasis on concept formation, scientific principles, demonstrations and opportunities for practice in science inquiry and (B) courses affording opportunities for study in depth in specific areas, designed for the elementary school teacher.

Gega (20) asked 104 elementary teacher education students to list the things they liked most and disliked most about science courses in an attempt to determine if such information could be useful in improving preservice preparation for elementary teachers. He found that students objected to attempts to cover too much material, emphasis on memorization of unrelated details, tests on trivial objectives, and little or no application of material studied to every-day life, among other things. Gega concluded that, if the comments from the students were acted upon, the preservice courses would have objectives based on student performance, subject matter organized about relatively few generalizations, an emphasis on important social and practical applications of material studied, and would involve laboratory experiences. He suggested that these courses be taught by instructors with interests and training suitable for teaching an interdisciplinary course in science for non-majors.

Gega noted that a professional education course in elementary science should introduce students to basic knowledge and methods in several areas of science. Such a course should also include information on how science is organized in elementary schools, the strategies and tactics of science teaching, methods of evaluation, and methods to plan lessons that incorporate all these considerations.

Lerner (26) conducted a study to determine the status, trends, objectives, content, instructional procedures, and problems related to the methods course in elementary school science in selected four-year institutions of higher education. She found that 78 percent of the 291 institutions she surveyed provided training in methods for elementary school science, although some institutions apparently had a multiple methods course for elementary teachers rather than one devoted solely to the teaching of science in the elementary school. The instructors surveyed reported three major problems: the poor science background of their students, lack of favorable facilities for laboratory work, and class enrollments which they considered too large for effective teaching conditions. One of the primary problems in the multiple methods course was the lack of time to teach methods for more than one content area in a single course.

Victor (45), operating on the premise that the assumption that elementary teachers were reluctant to teach science was a valid one, surveyed 106 teachers in one school system to determine why they were reluctant to teach science. He found that a lack of familiarity with science content and materials, due to an inadequate science background, was a major factor. Eleven of the teachers responding to Victor's questionnaire had had no science beyond general science in high school. However, 75 per cent of those surveyed had two full years of college science. Victor found that those teachers with a background in college science spent more time teaching science and used demonstrations and experiments more often than did those teachers having fewer courses in science.

Hines (23) also conducted a study related to the assumed reluctance of elementary teachers to teach science. She attempted to determine possible relationships existing between this reluctance and nine different factors. She found that teachers were providing more time for science teaching, demonstration, and experimentation than one would expect from a review of the research. She also found that an inadequate science background is a definite factor influencing science teaching at the elementary school level. Hines concluded that the number of years of teaching experience, the grade level being taught, and the experience of having had a science methods course appeared to have little effect on the teaching performance of the population involved in her study. The differences that occurred among groups appeared to be due primarily to the types of classroom teaching situations.

Eaton (15) surveyed elementary education students enrolled at the University of Texas to determine why few of them elected science as an area of subject-matter concentration. He found that the students received little guidance from the faculty although they received considerable discouragement from their peers in selecting an area of science. After observing teacher behavior and surveying prospective teacher attitudes, he concluded that students lacked insight into the application of a concentration in subject matter to the teaching act. Apparently they need help in perceiving the relationship between content and instruction.

Soy (39) also investigated the attitudes of prospective elementary teachers toward science as a field of specialty. She found that interest was a most important reason for choosing a subject field. She discovered that science received the fewest votes as a high school subject in which students had felt most successful. Science ranked fifth of the seven subject areas in which students felt prepared to teach, although it was ranked first among the subjects which the student teachers felt elementary students would like to study. Soy concluded that something must be done to give preservice elementary teachers more satisfying experiences in science.

Oshima (32) compared two methods of teaching a science methods course for prospective elementary teachers. He found that the two different methods used in the study, lecture-demonstration and individual investigation, produced no significant changes in attitudes toward science. However, the experimental group which had been conducting individual investigations did make significant gains in their confidence toward teaching science.

Cheney (11), in a study designed to increase the commitment of preservice elementary teachers to teaching science, found that the students involved had little inclination to become specialists in elementary science either before or after the teaching-learning experience. He found that the tendency of the students to deplore their weaknesses in science knowledge was not matched by efforts to remove deficiencies through self-study or extended laboratory investigations. The students did appear, however, to gain confidence in their ability to teach science.

The breadth and depth of science content background acquired by an elementary teacher appears dependent on a number of factors. One of these relates to the graduation requirements of the particular institution in which the preservice teacher is enrolled. The amount of science required in the general education component of a preservice teacher's preparation is limited. Often no provision is made for attaining a balance in the various fields of science. Another determining factor is that of the teacher's interest in and attitude toward science. Attitude development is, apparently, a long term process. Attitudes, once established, are not likely to be changed as a result of the experiences which the preservice teachers have in one course of only one quarter or one semester's duration. The preservice teachers frequently take only one methods course which is a general one related to the various disciplines involved in the elementary curriculum. Again, time is too limited for provision of adequate experiences in science teaching methodology. A third factor is that of the guidance, or lack of it, which the individual receives in planning his program. The majority of the researchers whose studies are cited in this part of the paper appear to conclude that the present preparation programs are inadequate for teaching science, in an effective manner, in the elementary school.

Teacher Competence Research

Perhaps the teaching of science in the elementary school could be improved if science educators were to concentrate upon developing a set of competencies which elementary teachers should possess relative to the teaching of science rather than assuming that the completion of a certain number of credit hours of course work will produce teaching effectiveness in a classroom situation. A current interest in teaching education appears to be concerned with this approach to preservice education. A number of investigations were concentrated upon the determination and development of competencies in science that elementary school teachers should possess: Uselton (43), Uselton, Bledsoe, and Koelsche (42), Sharefkin (36, 37), Reed (33), Michals (28), Butts (8), Mattheis (27), Moyer (30a), Cunningham (13), Weigand (47), Senter (34), DiLorenzo and Halliwell (14), Bryant (7).

Michals (28) conducted an investigation relevant to the topic of teacher competence. He attempted to determine the desired objectives for the preparation of teachers for teaching elementary science, the kinds of experiences that would produce competent elementary teachers, and the kind of science education programs needed. He selected as desired competencies three of the six roles of the teacher formulated in a study by the California Teachers Association: the director of learning, the mediator of the culture, and a member of the profession. Course activities were considered for selection in terms of three criteria: (A) is the experience practical preparation for elementary science teaching? (B) is the experience related to the operational definition of objectives? and (C) can the experience be evaluated? Three courses were set up at two different institutions and evaluated on the basis of a rating scale and the results of an Elementary Science Education Test. Michals found that there was a higher level of student achievement in the general discussion and group activities class than in the lecture-demonstration class. The schedules of the two institutions were not identical. This resulted in one class, at one institution, meeting 40 times as compared with the 24 times that each of the other two classes met. Michals found, upon analyzing the data, that approximately the same per cent of students in the two experimental courses, at the two different institutions, achieved the objectives when an equal amount of time was available for each topic and the same method of presentation was used. However, when additional time was available, a higher per cent of students achieved the objectives. It would appear that the amount of time needed to achieve the desired objectives needs to be investigated. The level of achievement of these objectives also needs to be assessed.

Sharefkin (36) investigated the science knowledge and competencies of students enrolled in a liberal arts college. She attempted to identify the relationship between the college science training of student teachers and the student teachers' appraisal of their need for, as well as the extent to which they believe they possess, science abilities. She considered such abilities as those related to (A) identifying and defining problems, (B) suggesting or screening hypotheses, (C) selecting validating procedures, including the design of experiments, (D) interpreting data and drawing conclusions, (E) evaluating critically claims and statements of others, and (F) reasoning quantitatively and symbolically. The majority of the students participating in the study were aware of their need for science abilities. They appeared to feel that they were strongest in the areas of identifying and defining problems and in interpreting data and drawing conclusions. Only 34.8 per cent of those investigated thought they needed to be able to reason quantitatively. Sharefkin suggested that criteria are needed to help student teachers clarify their own conceptions of, as well as identification of, children's behaviors which exhibit the science abilities emphasized in the study. She inferred that the student teachers' major difficulties were related to evaluating their science teaching and implementing science objectives. She concluded that elementary school student teachers need to develop awareness of their limitations so that they can critically examine their approach to teaching science and can function constructively in professional growth and teaching competence.

Problem-solving is another skill which it is assumed that teachers should possess. Butts (8) conducted a study with 21 college seniors in an elementary science teaching methods course in order to measure their problem solving behavior. He wanted to determine the possible relationship between the knowledge of scientific facts and principles and the problem-solving behavior of the students. He found that problem-solving behavior was not characterized by patterned thought in this study. He hypothesized that teachers need to be trained to (A) focus on their ability to use knowledge rather than on the accumulation of knowledge, (B) search for basic principles rather than to memorize facts, (C) critically analyze data rather than to accept scientific facts without qualification, and (D) generalize from basic principles and scientific applications.

Mattheis (27) investigated the effect on the competence of preservice teachers for teaching science produced by two different types of laboratory experiences. He was interested in competence as it was reflected in subject-matter achievement and interest in science. He tested the assumption that laboratory experiences in science are necessary if the pre-service education of elementary school teachers is to be successfully accomplished. The experimental group used a science-project approach to laboratory work while the control group was taught by the conventional replication-verification method. Mattheis found that, with respect to knowledge of science, the project approach to laboratory experiences was more efficient for students who exhibited strong interest and a proficient knowledge of science. However, students who were not interested in and who did not know very much about science learned more science when they were in the control group. Students were divided in their preferences for the two approaches to laboratory work. Some suggested that the good points of both types of laboratory work be utilized to develop a suitable laboratory course for preservice elementary teachers.

Two studies, Moyer (30a) and Cunningham (13), were concerned with development of competence in question asking. Moyer observed and tape recorded 14 science lessons, in five different elementary schools, involving 12 teachers. He compiled a total of 2,500 questions. Moyer found that over 50 per cent of the questions were initiated with WHAT, HOW, WHY, WHO, WHERE, WHICH, and WHEN. He did not, however, find any evidence of a question that required students to evaluate. Moyer found that teachers with undergraduate majors in a field other than education tended to ask more questions requiring the children to explain than did those who had majored in education. He inferred that teachers are not prepared to develop and use questions effectively, and that teachers tend to frame questions in such a way that their pupils are not truly stimulated to think about and develop adequate concepts.

Although many teacher educators emphasize the use of sound questions to encourage children to think and caution their students to avoid telling children everything, this advice does not appear to be followed. However, Moyer found that the teachers he interviewed reported they received almost no instruction or suggestion relative to the methods of developing and utilizing questions as a part of their preparation for teaching.

Cunningham (13) conducted a study to determine the effects of a method of instruction designed to improve the question-phrasing practices of prospective elementary teachers. Forty elementary education majors participated in the study. He found that the ability of the prospective elementary teachers to construct a greater proportion of effectively phrased questions could be improved by the techniques which he used. The students who participated in the study also learned to construct a greater proportion of divergent questions for their science teaching.

Weigand (47) investigated another facet of the questioning process. He wished to determine if the ability of prospective elementary school teachers to ascertain the relevancy or irrelevancy of children's questions in elementary school science could be improved. He also investigated the effects, if any, of the preservice teacher's content background and academic grade-point average on this ability. He found that prospective teachers could determine the degree of relevancy of children's science questions and that this ability could be improved. Academic ability did not prove to be a factor affecting the ability to analyze questions. On the basis of the data he collected, Weigand inferred that factors other than subject-matter content were important in analyzing the relevancy or irrelevancy of science questions of children.

Two research studies were concerned with the use of specialists to teach science in the elementary schools, Senter (3) and DiLorenzo and Halliwell (14). Senter investigated the level of science achievement of sixth-grade students as it was related to teacher factors such as age, teaching experience, concentration in science courses, and styles of teaching. Analysis of the data relative to certain science knowledge, understanding, and concepts held by the students did not reveal any significant differences in the test results between students from self-contained classrooms and those in departmentalized classroom situations.

DiLorenzo and Halliwell (14) investigated the science achievement of 258 sixth-grade children to compare the scores of those taught by regular classroom teachers with the scores of children taught by special science teachers. They found no true difference in achievement of the two groups for either boys or girls. They did, however, hypothesize that different results might have been obtained if their investigation had lasted longer than seven months. They also questioned the use of available standardized tests in science as being valid appraisals of the objectives of the newer science programs.

It might be assumed that the competencies needed by teachers in the primary grades would be different from those needed by upper elementary school teachers. Bryant (7) considered this possibility as a part of his investigation designed to determine the amount of attention given, in required science courses, to the science understandings considered important for children. He found no substantial evidence of any difference in training in the institutions studied. Only 3.7 per cent of these institutions reported any differentiation in requirements. In general, the science training programs for elementary school teachers were the same for all grade levels. There was no evidence to indicate that those who plan the programs think that it should be otherwise. Bryant found discrepancies between what children are expected to learn in science and the science education of preservice teachers to prepare them to facilitate this learning. This would suggest that elementary science curricula of institutions preparing teachers should be critically examined.

The question of teacher competence requires further investigation. Definite objectives need to be defined and assessed. The degree of competence a preservice teacher can be expected to achieve as a result of courses and experiences gained during a period of undergraduate education needs to be ascertained. Research should be done to determine if primary teachers need a set of competencies different from those needed by upper-grade teachers. If a set of desired competencies can be formulated, further research will need to be done to determine the sequence of courses and experiences to be included in the preparation program in order to achieve these competencies.

Teacher Behaviors, Characteristics

A number of researchers were interested in investigating the variables of teacher behavior and characteristics as these related to effective science teaching in the elementary school: Reed (33), Wishart (48), Beringer (6), Taylor (40), Hardin (21), Uhlhorn (41), Coffey (12).

Wishart (48) conducted research to determine the relationship of selected teacher factors to the character and scope of the science teaching program in self-contained elementary school classrooms as evidenced in 48 elementary classrooms. He found a number of significant differences among teachers relative to their backgrounds and understandings of science. Considerable differences were revealed relative to science teaching practices. Teacher understanding of science and understanding of child development appeared to be significantly related to each other. Understanding in those areas appeared to be greatest for teachers with the least authoritarian tendencies.

Reed (33) conducted a study of the influence of teacher variables on student learning. He chose to investigate teacher warmth, teacher demand, and the teacher's utilization of intrinsic motivation. His learning criterion was the pupils' interest in science as measured by the Reed Science Interest Inventory. There appeared to be a positive correlation between the teacher's use of intrinsic motivation and pupil interest in science. There was also a positive and moderately strong correlation between teacher warmth and pupil science interest.

Reed found a strong tendency for teacher demand or the degree of expectations concerning the students' maintenance of high standards of performance on school tasks and the utilization of intrinsic motivation to exist in the same teacher. He found the variables of teacher demand and warmth to be independent. Reed inferred, from an analysis of his data, that moderate demand does not necessarily sacrifice such goals as science interest. He postulated that preservice teachers could learn to become skillful in the use of intrinsic motivation as a part of their preparation programs in science education. Warmth, however, is a characteristic less amenable to development through teacher education experiences.

Beringer (6) was interested in determining whether the recency of a teacher's preservice education was related to the teacher's ability to understand scientific facts. She was also interested in discovering if the grade level at which the teacher worked and the amount of physical and biological science background the teacher possessed were relevant to this ability. After analyzing the 290 returns from the *Scientific Fact Test for Elementary Teachers*, Beringer concluded that teachers who were trained 1 to 4 years ago had a better understanding of scientific fact than teachers who have been out of college for 25 years. She found that teachers in the upper-elementary grades have a better understanding of scientific fact than teachers in the lower-elementary grades. Teachers appeared to have a better understanding of the biological sciences than of the physical sciences. However, in every category there were great variations in the percentages of correct answers. Apparently there are gaps in teachers' understandings of scientific fact in all areas of science.

Taylor (40) analyzed the teachers' attitudes toward instructional materials in a programed learning situation in science and the relationship of these attitudes to pupil achievement. He worked with 16 fourth-grade teachers and 89 randomly selected pupils for a four and a half month period. He concluded that while teacher attitudes toward programed science materials do not contribute significantly to measured pupil attitudes toward these materials, there was evidence that teacher attitudes influenced potential pupil achievement. Teacher attitudes appeared to contribute 18 per cent of the variance in pupil final achievement. The teachers' attitudes were significantly correlated with their responses to the instrument *How I Teach: Analysis of Teaching Practices*.

Hardin (21), in a study designed to investigate dimensions of pupils' science interest and of their involvement in classroom science experiences in selected fifth- and sixth-grade classes, found that pupils could distinguish various aspects of their classroom experiences. The pupils appeared to be keenly aware of the teacher-pupil relationships. These relationships were highly significant to pupils, with warm teacher-pupil relationships being an important component of an effective teaching-learning situation.

Uhlhorn, Boener, and Shimer (41) found the ability to establish rapport with children to be an important teacher characteristic. They conducted an investigation in conjunction with a pre-student teaching experience in science for elementary education students at Indiana State University. Two other characteristics that appeared to be important in determining the success of the lesson were the ability to use teaching aids and the depth and breadth of knowledge of the subject included in the lesson. The researchers felt that further investigation needs to be done before it can be concluded that these characteristics are vital to successful science teaching.

Coffey (12) investigated the verbal behavior of teachers of the lower-elementary grades. He found significant differences between the pre- and post-tests of the experimental group, based on an analysis of interaction analysis data, relevant to their understanding of science and their attitudes toward science. He inferred that the procedures used in this study facilitated the teachers' perceptions of learner needs and strategies of teaching which enhance learner needs.

Use of New Media and Techniques in Teacher Education

Two investigations were reviewed which involved the use of some of the newer procedures in the education of elementary school teachers: Ashlock (2) and Kriebs (25). Ashlock (2) used micro-teaching in an off-campus methods course for elementary school teachers. Micro-teaching involves teaching a lesson of 5 to 20 minutes length to a class of 4 to 8 students. The students taught a 5-minute lesson, which included a demonstration, to four of their peers who served as pupils for the microclass. Ashlock and his students found that if the lesson objectives were not stated in terms of the desired pupil behavior, the teacher had difficulty in achieving instructional closure.

Kriebs (25) conducted a study to compare the effectiveness of two types of videotaped instruction for preparing elementary school teachers to teach science. She was interested in determining if preservice teachers who observed videotapes of elementary school children using scientific methods performed significantly better as science teachers than did those preservice teachers who observed videotapes of a traditional lecture-demonstration class not involving children. The students involved in the study were videotaped in a teaching situation before the experimental treatment began and were again videotaped at the end of the experimental treatment. Kriebs based her comparison on the results of a paper and pencil test as well as on direct observation of teaching performance. She found there was no significant change in the pre-service teachers' classroom performances as a result of the experimental treatment. However, those students who had viewed the videotapes involving children tended to receive higher ratings on their classroom performance than those who had viewed the control videotapes. The preservice teachers who had viewed the control videotapes gained significantly more science knowledge over the same content than did those who had viewed the experimental videotapes involving children. It would appear that there is no one easy method to provide both science content and teaching methodology.

Summary and Recommendations

Research studies concerned with the preparation of teachers to teach science to elementary school children have been reviewed, as have guidelines for preparation programs. Studies which focused on the status of elementary school science teaching were also included in the review. Research related to inservice education programs in science for elementary school teachers was not included in this article.

It might be inferred, from an analysis of these research reports, that elementary school science teaching is handicapped by deficiencies in both course content and teaching methodology in so far as teachers' backgrounds are concerned as well as by inadequate teaching conditions in the schools. Individuals desiring to teach at the elementary school level cannot be prepared as specialists in all of the subject-matter areas which they are called upon to teach in a self-contained classroom, at least within the present four-year preparation period. If the length of the preservice program is not to be extended, preparation in depth and breadth within a particular subject-matter area is limited. Students preparing to teach elementary school frequently take one general course in teaching methodology. Again, due to time limitations, they do not receive training and experiences in sufficient depth in all of the subject-matter areas. Frequently, students do not have the opportunity during their student teaching experience to teach all of the subjects included at that particular grade level. Elementary school teachers, because they lack familiarity with science content and materials, express reluctance to teach science. Research needs to be done to determine how the preservice program for elementary school teachers can be structured to provide as wide a range of experiences and instructional content in science as possible.

Current certification patterns appear to be based on courses completed rather than upon classroom performance. Are the concepts of *legally qualified* and *competent* teachers equivalent ones? More research should be conducted relevant to the problems of teacher competence. A publication entitled *Six Areas of Teacher Competence* (9) details six roles of the teacher: director of learning, counselor and guidance worker, mediator of the culture, link with the community, member of the school staff, and member of the profession. Are all of these of equal importance in the preparation of elementary teachers? The authors of this publication expect beginning teachers to possess minimum competence in each role. Is it possible that not all beginning teachers are aware of the fact that they are expected to function in these roles? Are preparation programs perpetuating the stereotype role of the teacher as a purveyor of information? Does current emphasis upon learning by discovery hold implications for the modification of any of these roles? Does an individual who thinks of himself as a *director* of instruction function in a manner calculated to develop students who are independent learners? More research needs to be done in science education at the elementary school level to show the relationship between preparatory programs and product outcomes.

Teaching involves interaction between the teacher and students. Research studies based on the investigation of teacher-pupil interaction in science need to be extended downward into the elementary school. Those studies which have been done have been limited to observations of situations involving the teacher and the majority of the class. Elementary teachers work with individual students and with small groups to an even greater extent than do secondary school teachers. Research should be done to determine how science activities taking place during such sessions differ, if they do, from those times in which the teacher is involved in working with the entire group.

Few research studies have been done to lead to the development of any theory of instruction relative to science teaching, at either the elementary or the secondary school level. Would adequate research result in the development of a theory of teaching science that would differ from theories for teaching other subjects? Would it differ for different levels of maturity of the students? Would it differ if science were to be taught to elementary school children by a teacher specializing in science as opposed to the present classroom teacher who has been trained to function as a generalist?

Research needs to be done relevant to the ways in which elementary teachers handle the problem of individualization of science instruction and the ways in which they accommodate for individual differences of their students.

Within the last five to eight years new programs have been appearing in elementary school science. Are preservice teachers being prepared to do an effective job with these new courses and materials? Teachers have to implement programs which they did not help to originate. Both beginning and experienced teachers need to know what to do in terms of both content and instructional strategies, how to implement the strategies involved, and they also need to understand the underlying rationale of the program. Research should be done to determine the degree to which prospective elementary teachers are being prepared to make effective use of the new elementary science projects.

In addition to the development of new programs in elementary school science, elementary education is being affected by such developments as team teaching, the ungraded elementary school, programed instruction, and new materials and media. Are prospective teachers being prepared to function in such a changing environment?

Barnard (4), in discussing Bruner's *The Process of Education*, says that Bruner's ideas imply ". . . all children should be able to find the cognitive aspect of science an intellectually stimulating experience." This implies that elementary school teachers need to help children learn how to learn and to structure the experiences so that the students can be led to discover concepts on their own. To accomplish this, the teachers should be individuals who have found the study of science to be a personally satisfying experience. Can the preservice program be restructured to accomplish this goal?

Science education is faced with unresolved issues in the different areas described in this paper. Exact knowledge of these issues is essential for continued development of the education of science teachers, at both the elementary and secondary school levels. Basic questions need to be asked and researchable problems identified. Areas for study should include those concerning the content and experiences to be provided in the preparatory programs, the relationship of the content and experiences to teacher behavior, and the relationship of resulting teacher behavior to the behavior of students in the classroom situation.

References

1. American Association for the Advancement of Science. "Guidelines for Science and Mathematics in the Preparation Program of Elementary School Teachers." Washington, D.C. 1963.
2. Ashlock, Robert B. "Micro-Teaching in an Elementary Science Methods Course." *School Science and Mathematics*, January 1966.
3. Banks, William Henry. "Practices in the Preparation of Elementary Teachers for the Teaching of Science." University Microfilms, Ann Arbor, Michigan. 1965.
4. Barnard, J. Darrell. "What Can Science Contribute to the Liberal Education of All Children?" *The Science Teacher*, November 1965.
5. Blackwood, Paul E. "Science Teaching in the Elementary Schools." U.S. Office of Education, Washington, D.C. 1965.
6. Beringer, Marjorie L. "A Critical Analysis of Teacher Understanding of Scientific Fact." University Microfilms, Ann Arbor, Michigan. 1965.
7. Bryant, Paul P. "Science Understandings Considered Important for Children and the Science Required of Elementary School Teachers." University Microfilms, Ann Arbor, Michigan. 1959.
8. Butts, David P. "The Relationship of Problem-Solving Ability and Science Knowledge." *Science Education*, March 1965.
9. California Teachers Association. "Six Areas of Teacher Competence." Burlingame, California. 1964.
10. Chamberlain, William D. "Development and Status of Teacher Education in the Field of Science for the Elementary School." University Microfilms, Ann Arbor, Michigan. 1955.
11. Cheney, Bruce D. "Commitment of Science Teaching Among Prospective Elementary School Teachers: An Exploratory Study." Unpublished doctoral dissertation. University of Illinois, Urbana, Illinois. 1966.
12. Coffey, Warren C. "Change in Teachers' Verbal Classroom Behavior in Science Education." Unpublished doctoral dissertation. University of California, Berkeley, California. 1967.

13. Cunningham. Roger T. "A Descriptive Study Determining the Effects of a Method of Instruction Designed to Improve the Question-Phrasing Practices of Prospective Elementary Teachers." Unpublished doctoral dissertation. Indiana University, Bloomington, Indiana.

14. DiLorenzo, Louis T. and Joseph W. Halliwell. "A Comparison of the Science Achievement of Sixth-Grade Pupils Instructed by Regular Classroom and Special Science Teachers." *Science Education*, March 1963.

15. Eaton, Edward J. "An Examination of the Development of Science Concentrations for the Prospective Elementary School Teacher at the University of Texas." *Journal of Research in Science Teaching*, September 1966.

16. Eccles, P. J. "A Comparison of the Science Background of Elementary Teachers-in-training at the University of Alberta, Calgary, and the University of Illinois." *Alberta Journal of Educational Research*, March 1962.

17. Esget, Miles H. "Developing and Using an Objective Instrument To Measure Student Growth in College Elementary School Science Courses." University Microfilms, Ann Arbor, Michigan. 1958.

18. Gaides, Glen E. "A Comparison of Learnings by Elementary Education Majors in Selected Physical Science Courses." University Microfilms, Ann Arbor, Michigan. 1962.

19. Gant, Kenneth A. "A Survey of the Curricular Experiences Available to Elementary Student Teachers in Science Programs in Northern Zone (New York State) Schools During the 1957-59 Period as Evidenced by Reactions of Elementary Teachers, Elementary Supervisors, and Elementary Student Teachers and Compared with 'Best Practices' as Indicated by Selected Jurors." University Microfilms, Ann Arbor, Michigan. 1962.

20. Gega, Peter C. "The Preservice Education of Elementary Teachers in Science and the Teaching of Science." *School Science and Mathematics*, January 1968.

21. Hardin, Elizabeth H. "Dimensions of Pupils' Interest in Science and of Their Involvement in Classroom Science Experiences in Selected Fifth- and Sixth-Grade Classes." University Microfilms, Ann Arbor, Michigan, 1964.

22. Hardin, Henry N. "An Analysis of Selected Aspects of the Science Preparation of Prospective Elementary Teachers at the University of Miami." University Microfilms, Ann Arbor, Michigan. 1965.

23. Hines, Sallylee H. "A Study of Certain Factors Which Affect the Opinions of Elementary School Teachers in the Teaching of Science." Unpublished doctoral dissertation. Oklahoma State University, Stillwater, Oklahoma. 1966.

24. Kisner, Andrew J. "Science Content Preparation of Prospective Elementary School Teachers in Eight Oklahoma Institutions of Higher Education." University Microfilms, Ann Arbor, Michigan. 1963.

25. Kriebs, Jean O. "The Effect of Videotaped Elementary School Science Classroom Demonstrations on Science Teaching Performance of Preservice Teachers." Unpublished doctoral dissertation. Temple University, Philadelphia, Pennsylvania. 1967.

26. Lerner, Marjorie S. "An Investigation of the Status of the Methods Course in Elementary School Science in Selected Teacher-Training Institutions." University Microfilms, Ann Arbor, Michigan. 1964.

27. Mattheis, Floyd E. "A Study of the Effects of Two Different Approaches to Laboratory Experiences in College Science Courses for Prospective Elementary School Teachers." University Microfilms, Ann Arbor, Michigan. 1962.
28. Michals, Bernard E. "The Preparation of Teachers to Teach Elementary School Science." *Science Education*, March 1963.
29. Moorehead, William D. "The Status of Elementary School Science and How It Is Taught." University Microfilms, Ann Arbor, Michigan. 1965.
30a. Moyer, John R. "An Exploratory Study of Questioning in the Instructional Process in Elementary Schools." Unpublished doctoral dissertation. Teachers College, Columbia University, New York City. 1965.
30b. Obourn, E. S.; Blackwood, P. E.; *et al.* "Research in the Teaching of Science," July 1957–1959. U.S. Office of Education, Washington, D. C., 1962.
31. Piltz, Albert. "An Investigation of Teacher-Recognized Difficulties Encountered in the Teaching of Science in the Elementary Schools of Florida." University Microfilms, Ann Arbor, Michigan. 1954.
32. Oshima, Eugene A. "Changes in Attitudes Toward Science and Confidence in Teaching Science of Prospective Elementary Teachers." University Microfilms, Ann Arbor, Michigan. 1966.
33. Reed, Horace B. "Implications for Science Education of a Teacher Competence Reesarch." *Science Education*, December 1962.
34. Senter, Donald S. "An Appraisal of an Elementary School Science Program." Unpublished doctoral dissertation. Wayne State University, Detroit, Michigan, 1966.
35. Service, Randolph G. "A Proposed Program of Science Preparation for Elementary Teachers." University Microfilms, Ann Arbor, Michigan. 1964.
36. Sharefkin, Belle D. "A Possession of Science Abilities and Its Relationship to Student Teacher Training in a Liberal Arts College." *Science Education*, December 1962.
37. Sharefkin, Belle D. "The Relationship Between Elementary School Student Teachers' Science Abilities and Their Self Appraisals." *Science Education*, October 1963.
38. Smith, Doyne M., and Bernice Cooper. "A Study of the Use of Various Techniques in Teaching Science in the Elementary Schools." *School Science and Mathematics*, June 1967.
39. Soy, Elois M. "Attitudes of Prospective Elementary Teachers Toward Science as a Field of Specialty." *School Science and Mathematics*, June 1967.
40. Taylor, Alton L. "Teacher Attitudes, Pupil Behavior, and Content Attributes in Relation to the Use of Programmed Science Materials at the Fourth Grade Level." University Microfilms, Ann Arbor, Michigan. 1965.
41. Uhlhorn, K. W., C. M. Boener, and S. S. Shimer. "An Evaluation of the Science Pre-Student Teaching Experience for Students Enrolled in the Elementary Education Curriculum at Indiana State University." Paper presented at NARST meeting. 1967.
42. Uselton, Horace W., *et al.* "Factors Related to Competence in Science of Prospective Elementary Teachers." *Science Education*, December 1963.

43. Uselton, Horace W. "Factors Related to Competence in Science of Prospective Elementary Teachers." University Microfilms, Ann Arbor, Michigan. 1962.
44. Verrill, John E. "The Preparation of General Elementary Teachers To Teach Science, 1870 to the Present." University Microfilms, Ann Arbor, Michigan. 1961.
45. Victor, Edward. "Why Are Our Elementary School Teachers Reluctant To Teach Science?" *Science Education*, March 1962.
46. Weaver, Allan D. "A Determination of Criteria for Selection of Laboratory Experiences Suitable for an Integrated Course in Physical Science Designed for the Education of Elementary School Teachers." University Microfilms, Ann Arbor, Michigan. 1954.
47. Weigand, James E. "The Relative Merits of Two Methodologies for Teaching the Analysis of Children's Questions in Elementary School Science." University Microfilms, Ann Arbor, Michigan. 1965.
48. Wishart, Allington P. "The Relationship of Selected Teacher Factors to the Character and the Scope of Science Teaching Programs in Self-Contained Elementary School Classrooms." University Microfilms, Ann Arbor, Michigan. 1961.
49. Woellner, Elizabeth H., and M. A. Wood. *Requirements for Certification*, Third Edition. University of Chicago Press, Chicago, Illinois. 1968.

Teacher Education and Elementary School Science—1980 *

WILLARD J. JACOBSON

Willard J. Jacobson describes what the elementary school teacher of tomorrow must be in order to fulfill the demands of elementary science education for the future. The author believes that the future teacher should develop an understanding of the scientific view of man and his world, the conceptual structure of science, the process of science, and the inter-relationship of science, technology, and society. A teacher should also devote a significant portion of his education to the study of man. The future teacher will spend his time planning individual programs of study, considering laboratory investigations, analyzing his teaching experiences. and discussing thought-provoking ideas in education and science.

* REPRINTED FROM *Journal of Research in Science Teaching*, Vol. 5, Issue 1, 1968, pp. 73–80. Reprinted by permission of the author and the publisher. Dr. Jacobson is Chairman of the Department of Science Education at Teachers College, Columbia University.

How can we prepare the elementary school teachers of tomorrow? How can we educate the teachers who will help our children to have rewarding and significant experiences in science? Before we consider some of our approaches to teacher education, let us try to picture the teacher of the future. What will this teacher look like? What should he† be able to do? Let us try to describe what this teacher for tomorrow may be like and some of the ways in which he will operate.

Obviously, our teacher of the future should have a pleasant, warm personality, love for children, and a curiosity about the world in which we live. Perhaps, there is very little that we can do through education to develop these personality traits, but some of them may be acquired in elementary schools through association with fine teachers. In the tomorrow, we shall be more selective as we choose candidates for our teacher preparation programs. Since it will be recognized that teaching is our most important social undertaking, some of our best young people will be attracted to careers in teaching.

Our teachers of the future should have a general understanding of the nature of the physical and mental growth of children. They will understand the stages of growth and be able to use this understanding in planning educational programs. Of perhaps greater importance, they will be able to use this understanding to interpret the behavior of children. For these teachers, this interpretation will not take the form of a protracted analysis. Instead, it will be an almost intuitive operational analysis used during the process of teaching. They will know children and use the knowledge to know the child.

Our teacher of the future will have mastered a wide range of approaches to teaching. He will know how to ask questions that lead children into inquiry. And he will listen to the responses of children and build educational experiences in terms of these responses. He will work with children as individuals, in small groups, and as an entire class and know how to help them initiate projects and how to support them when they meet frustration. He will know how to organize laboratory experimentation, but he will also work with groups in cooperative investigations. Field studies, whether they be in the community or in the school system's outdoor laboratory, are a part of his program. His children learn to use the library and the many learning resources available there. Our future teacher will deliberately use a variety of approaches to teaching during the course of a day. Since he will be sensitive to the moods and attention of the children, the changes in teaching style will seem to be naturally coordinated with the changing moods and interests of the children.

We are developing a wider range of possible approaches to elementary science. Resources, materials, and equipment of many different kinds are available. Our future teacher will keep informed of these new developments, and will know how to use the new materials. Hopefully, his school will make them readily available for his use.

---

† One of the characteristics of our future elementary school teacher population should be that it contains both men and women. It is suggested that each child should have the experience of having a male teacher at least once during the years that he is in the elementary school. In this paper the masculine pronoun represents both male and female teachers.

This teacher of the future will also know how to use the many technological devices that are available to teachers. The teacher can bring the outside world into the classroom via television, radio, and conference telephones. The conference telephone brings a variety of experts into the classroom; the communications satellites bring the world onto the screen. Projectors of a variety of kinds are used to illustrate ideas. Technological devices for which suitable programs have finally become available are used by the children as they study and learn. These are all technological devices that can be used to improve instruction. Very sophisticated information retrieval systems to obtain information that is needed will also be available, as the children explore in science. The teacher and his class have the resources of the Library of Congress readily available to them. The children can "be there" as recent events in the history of science are recapitulated via the video tape recorder.

The children in this classroom of the future are widely traveled. None of them began his education in this school; many of them have attended three or four other schools. This is now considered to be an advantage rather than a handicap. Our teacher of the future knows how to use the battery of diagnostic instruments available to him to prescribe the "ideal" education for each child. The variety of experiences that the children have had lead to rich and informative discussions. For example, when a group becomes engaged in the study of fossils, one child recalls his visits to the LaBrea Tar Pits, while another has taken part in the excavation of a dinosaur footprint in the Connecticut River Valley.

Our teacher of the future will have a fine operational understanding of the broad generalizations of science. True, he will not have studied the details of anatomical structures (that drove some of his predecessors away from science when they took the biology course designed for pre-medical students), nor will he work some of the time-consuming problems at the end of the chapters in the book used in a physics class that once served as a screening device for a graduate department of physics; but, he will know science. He will have a mental picture of man and the world that is generally consistent with that developed in the various sciences. He also will have an understanding of the conceptual structure of science. Perhaps, this teacher will have a particular interest in the relationships between science, technology, and society.

This understanding of science includes an understanding of the methods of inquiry in various sciences. Some of our future teachers, for example, may be especially interested in the methods of collecting, handling, and evaluating of data. As they collect evidence of physical growth or of the developing understanding of scientific concepts and try to relate the data to phases of the instructional program, they will encounter some of the same problems that scientists meet.

As a result of the liberating education that they will have had, many of these teachers will have developed a special interest in one area of science. One of these teachers may be interested in the breeding of a rather rare species of tropical fish. Each year several children become interested enough in this study to work with him on certain aspects of it. He subscribes to journals in this field and has attended national conventions when they have met in his area. Other teachers in his school have similar interests related to other areas of science.

Our teachers of the future will have to work well together. At times, they may develop a team-teaching arrangement in which all children can benefit from the unique competencies of each teacher. However, the arrangement will be very flexible; they will move in and out of the team teaching arrangement as they decide which is the best way to develop their programs of education.

Our future teachers will work to help each child achieve optimum growth. About two-thirds of the children in our elementary classroom of the future will have considerable aptitude for science. They will be encouraged to "stretch" as they study. The youngsters in the other third of the class, at this time, seem to have interests and aptitudes in other directions. They will be helped to develop a broad view of science. Our future elementary teachers will consider their primary function to be to help each child achieve his optimum intellectual, social, and physical growth, and they will know how to work with children to achieve this.

These teachers will teach in communities that care deeply for the education of their children. The members of the communities have become convinced that an individual's potentialities are profoundly affected by the kinds of educational experiences he receives early in life. The parents will be determined that their children shall receive the best possible education. As a result they will invest heavily in their schools, which are better than those in many other communities. Fortunately, there will be loud voices in other communities who will ask, "Why shouldn't our children have as good a chance in life as those in other school systems? Why should our children be cheated?" The school systems that develop exemplary programs contribute to the variety that is essential for the evolution of social institutions.

Every four or five years, our teachers of the future will devote a year to further study. The study often will not be done in colleges and universities; many aspects of their programs began to ossify beyond recall in the 1960's. While the university priesthood remains engaged in its rituals of meaningless research and time-wasting regurgitation, enterprising educators in government, industry, school systems, and in universities will organize institutes that actually consider problems that teachers and administrators face. Forward-looking school systems will have contracts with such institutes which make it possible for its teachers to engage periodically in further studies.

This brief description of teachers and teaching in the future has implications for our teacher-education programs. Most of the suggestions that follow are within our grasp, if we have the imagination and the will to strive for them.

Education in Science for the Future Teachers

Hopefully, in the near future we will achieve a synthesis out of the many efforts that are underway in elementary-school science. The nature of this synthesis is already becoming apparent, with its implications for the kinds of education that future elementary school teachers should have in science. The future elementary school teacher should have fourteen years of science before undertaking the professional work in teacher education. In this work in science such matters as the following should be stressed:

(1) Future teachers should develop an understanding of the scientific view of man and his world. For example, these teachers should have a conceptual understanding of the conservation laws, and how they operate in the various sciences. Understandings from such sciences as cosmological astronomy, evolutionary biology, human physiology, and historical geology will be of special importance in developing this scientific view. The work in these areas of science should be planned to help students develop a modern, scientific view of the world. The needs of future professionals in these fields should be of secondary importance in these courses. However, these understandings in science are probably of importance to most people. A start has already been made in the development of such courses.

(2) The conceptual structure of science should be emphasized. Teachers will have firsthand experiences in developing operational definitions in science and in studying the interrelationships between definitions. They will study a variety of physical and biological systems and will develop operational concepts of the broad generalizations of science. In addition they should have experiences with a variety of interactions, become aware of the role of the observer in the study of phenomena, and gain some comprehension of the nature of evolution and revolution in scientific thought. The conceptual structure of science is of central importance in at least one science curriculum study, and teachers with some understanding of the nature and structure of science will be better prepared to work with children in such a program.

(3) There should be considerable emphasis upon the processes of science. The processes of science dealt with in teacher education will be somewhat different from those now being delineated for elementary-school science. Many of the processes dealt with in teacher education are related to scientific enterprise as contrasted to those of the individual scientists. These experiences will provide the intellectual foundations that will make it possible for teachers to achieve some of the potentials inherent in elementary science programs that emphasize process.

(4) A significant portion of the program of teacher education in science is devoted to the study of man. For some reason, there has been very little attention to the study of man in our science-curriculum improvement projects. A project, somewhat like the Illinois Elementary School Science Project, focussing on the study of the human body, could make an important contribution. Certainly, teachers need some understanding of the area.

(5) Some systematic attention should be given to the interrelationships of science, technology, and society. Since science and technology may be among the greatest shapers of the future, it is essential that teachers have some understanding of these interrelationships.

The science courses which the future teacher takes will probably be developed cooperatively by scientists and science educators. Some such courses are already in a development stage.

However, much more emphasis will be given to individualized study, cooperatively planned with small committees of teacher educators. Development in this area has been slow because the books, programs, and other instructional materials have not been available in sufficient variety. By 1980 we should have them, and our instruction in science should become more efficient and effective.

It may be that considerable emphasis will be placed on science investigations that have relevance to elementary-school science. Laboratory and field investigations can be set up in which teachers have experiences in investigating science questions and problems to which answers are not known. For example, there are many questions related to the ecology of the local region that can be studied, such as the seasonal changes that take place in a small bog or the changes that take place over a period of time in an abandoned field or garden. In a sense, teachers would be carrying out original studies in which the answers are not known.

Such science investigations give teachers some firsthand experience in tackling problems in science. One of the possible disadvantages of a science program that stresses discrete processes of science is that the student may not recognize how these processes are interrelated. As they carry out science investigations, teachers have experiences in using various processes as they need them to deal with a question or problem. By 1980 it is to be hoped that we shall know much more about how to engage future teachers in such investigations.

Elementary Science Methods

In their professional work in elementary school science, future teachers should learn how to work effectively with children in science. It is becoming more and more apparent that teaching style is of critical importance in science. Approaches to teaching that may conceivably be effective in some other areas of the curriculum are singularly inappropriate for science. Teaching style in science must be consistent with the nature of science as a human activity. Or, to put it negatively, science cannot be taught effectively in an unscientific way.

Science, for example, has an "endless frontier." Accomplishments great and small lead to new questions and more challenging problems. In fact, it has been suggested that the worth of scientific work be judged by the nature and quality of the questions that are uncovered. The discovery that "inert" gases could be made to combine with other chemical elements was important, but the questions that were uncovered by this discovery were, perhaps, of greater importance. Future teachers should gain an appreciation for the questions uncovered by investigations in science. If science is characterized by an "endless frontier," how can it be taught in neat, tidy lessons which end in conclusions that tend to stifle further inquiry, rather than to encourage and stimulate it?

Science as an enterprise is a cumulative undertaking. We do know more now about certain aspects of our universe than did previous generations. In some science programs an almost completely heuristic approach is attempted; if the students did not already know better, they might be led to believe that nothing is known, and everything must be "discovered." In other programs almost total attention to the written word tends to inhibit inquiry rather than to support it. An important aspect of teaching style is to help students learn how to use the cumulative dimension of science as a resource, rather than as an inhibition of inquiry.

The nature of the teaching styles that are most effective for science instruction is being studied. By 1980, we shall know much more about them, as well as how to develop the teachers who will be able to use effective teaching styles.

More use will be made of diagnostic tools throughout education. With great mobility in population and inevitable loss of some school days because of sickness or travel, it will become more important to make periodic appraisals and prescriptions to overcome educational lacks. Diagnostic instruments are already under construction; more will be needed if we are to help teachers educate themselves.

The new tools becoming available for teacher education will aid the teacher in analyzing his own teaching. The video tape recorder has the potential of being used by teachers to analyze and improve their teaching styles. Films and tapes have long been used by football coaches to improve the performance of their teams; in a somewhat similar way they can be used to improve teaching.

We need to develop teaching simulators. This can conceivably be done with film, video tape, computer, and student response systems. The student will be presented with a teaching problem. He will be asked to respond to this problem as if he were the teacher of the class. He will then be shown the consequences when a teacher actually reacted in this way to such a problem. This will lead to further problems, and other reactions will be asked for. Highly sophisticated simulators have been used for a long time in flight instruction. Student response systems are already commercially available for use in schools. Teaching simulators with carefully prepared programs can be used to give students experiences with teaching problems before they move into the actual classroom.

Future teachers will give considerable time to preparation for the use of new elementary science programs and materials. Naturally, this will involve examining the materials, "doing some of the experiments," and observing in schools where the programs are being used. However, this will not be enough. It is becoming apparent that the new programs depend very greatly upon the imagination and resourcefulness of the classroom teacher. Effective science teaching is not a step-by-step procedure; instead, it is an interaction between children, teacher, materials, equipment, and facilities. The teacher nurtures, stimulates, and guides these interactions. In order to do this effectively, the teacher needs foundational understanding of the new programs. In order to develop these understandings, specially designed teacher education programs will have to be prepared for use in conjunction with the new programs. The Science Curriculum Improvement Study (SCIS) is in the process of developing such a specially designed teacher education program. Our future teachers will have participated in one of these teacher-education programs. These experiences will provide them with the intellectual resources to recognize and develop some of the educational opportunities that arise in the use of the new programs.

Teachers will have some experience in using new teaching tools. Tele-conference and tele-consultation procedures will be used extensively in the teacher education programs. With them, future teachers can have direct contact with scientists and educators working at the frontiers of inquiry. The potentialities of these procedures have hardly been tapped. As they are used in teacher education, students will learn how to adapt them for use in elementary schools. Of course, the future teacher will be skilled in the use of radio, television, and all the various kinds of projectors. All of these devices are seen as ways of bringing the world of science into the classroom.

Students will also learn how to use efficient referral and retrieval systems. Information in the major libraries of the nation will be quickly available to teachers in school. Elementary-school teachers will also be able to get quick print-outs of procedures that can be used in their classrooms. Lack of information will no longer be a serious limiting factor. For example, the teacher who wishes to engage in studies of the instinctive behavior of sticklebacks will quickly be able to get the information necessary to launch the study. The programming of the elementary-science information that might be useful to classroom teachers will have absorbed a considerable fraction of the energies of the entire work force of science educators available in the late 1960's and early 1970's.

A great variety of educational procedures and materials will be available for teacher education, and a rigorous analysis will be made to choose those that will be most effective to achieve the ends that are desired. Much teacher education will be in the form of guided individual study. Very little teacher time will be used for the transmission of information. Instead, precious teacher time will be used for the planning of individual programs of study, the consideration of laboratory investigations, analyses of teacher experiences, and discussions of thought-provoking ideas in education and science.

Theoretical Foundations of Education

By 1980, a rigorous reappraisal will have been made of the goals of education. The enrichment and enhancement of the life of each individual will be considered the central goal of education. The concern for the various academic disciplines will have declined. They will be viewed as being important only as they contribute to the lives of people. Similarly, societal demands will be appraised in terms of their contributions to individual development. Each individual human organism will be seen as having possibilities that formerly were not even imagined. The central function of the school, including the child's experiences in science, will be to stimulate and help the child to reach for his potentialities. As in science, course-content improvement programs in these areas will involve the cooperation of thoughtful teachers, professional educators, and academicians who have an insight into education.

It will have been shown beyond any reasonable doubt that children's early experiences during the pre-operational and concrete operational stages of intellectual development are of critical importance. It will be seen that if the child's early years are intellectually sterile, his total development will be stunted. Experiences in science, with the emphasis upon multi-sensory experience with the concrete objects of the physical and biological environment, will be viewed as being of special importance in the education of young children. The recognition of the importance of early childhood education will lead some of our ablest young people to choose this area as their field of work.

The spirit of science will suffuse most areas of education. The publication of *Education and the Spirit of Science*[1] will be viewed as a landmark in the field. The characteristics of a rational person (longing to know and understand, questioning of all things, search for data and their meaning, demand for verification, respect for logic, consideration of premises, and consideration of consequences) suggested in this monograph give direction to the work in all areas of the curriculum.

Leadership in Elementary School Science

A major dimension in future teacher education in science will be the development of outstanding leaders who can give direction to developments in the field. These leaders in science education will be involved in the following five kinds of leadership functions:

(1) *Teacher education in science.* Most of these science educators will be involved in some way in educating teachers in science.

(2) *Research in science education.* Many science educators will be doing and directing research into some facets of science education.

(3) *Explainers and interpreters of science.* We are becoming more and more aware of the need for people who can explain and interpret science and scientists to children, teachers, and laymen. Many science educators will be involved in these endeavors.

(4) *Leaders in science curriculum development.* Since they have some understanding of science, schools, children, and the educative process, science educators will continue to give leadership in the never-ending task of perfecting our science curricula.

(5) *Consultants in science education.* The growing involvement of school systems, governmental agencies, and industry in science education will call for science educators to provide leadership in the areas of their expertise.

It may be recognized that these five functions serve to define the field of science education. By 1980, perhaps some of our leading institutions will have learned how better to prepare future science educators for these functions of leadership.

Research in Elementary School Science

Research will be accorded a more important role in elementary-school science education than it was in the 1960's; but it will be, to a large extent, a different kind of research. Too often, our research has been inconsequential; some almost appears to have been designed to make it possible to use complicated techniques. Rather than being masters of problems, we have been mastered by techniques. It is little wonder that very few pay much attention to science education research. In the 1960's, such research had very little influence and made few contributions to the improvement of the education of children. In the 1980's, it will be the most important avenue for the improvement of elementary science education.

One of the developments that will lead to greater significance of research will be the increased attention given to problem definition. It has been said that, "a problem well stated is half solved." There are no clear-cut steps toward problem definition; the most effective approach has been to become steeped in the problem situation. In elementary school science, this means gaining a profound understanding of issues in elementary school science, a thorough acquaintance with the literature, practical experience in working with children, and an awareness of some of the approaches that have been attempted in the past. The increased emphasis on problem definition will lead to research on more significant problems and to a growth in the public stature and teacher acceptance of science education research.

Some fascinating questions will be systematically studied:

"How do early firsthand experiences with science materials and objects affect the consequent intellectual development of the child?"

"How do new ideas in science education diffuse throughout the nation? What are obstacles to diffusion? How do various promising approaches to diffusion work?"

"Under what conditions will various ways of organizing elementary school science instruction be most effective?"

"Are there early science experiences that have a positive relationship with creativity in science? If so, what is the nature of these experiences?"

"What are effective ways of helping experienced teachers to make fundamental changes in their teaching styles?"

From a careful study of such questions we can expect improvement in elementary school science and in teacher education in science.

The increased emphasis on problem definition will make the research experience a much more important one for future learners in science education. There will be no more handing out of research problems by professors who want a job done. This action deprives the fledgling researcher of the most difficult and significant experience in educational research—the definition of the problem out of the confusion of the problem situation. The steeping of one's self in a problem situation in order to reach problem definition is probably one of the most important experiences for future leaders in science education.

Greater emphasis will be placed on cumulative research. It is recognized that every research study cannot begin at the beginning. Although they may not have 100 per cent acceptance in the science education fraternity, the results of some prior research will be accepted and further studies will be based upon them. For example, it will be agreed that there are a variety of effective approaches to working with children, and a series of studies will be conducted to discover the conditions and goals for which various approaches are most effective. This willingness to build research studies upon the results of prior studies will finally lead science education research into the natural history stage of development.

The results of research will be easily and quickly available to the researcher and to the practicing teacher. Printouts of all research results related to a specific question or problem may be obtained on short notice at centers throughout the nation, and hopefully, may help the teacher choose among various approaches to teaching.

Tomorrow

Our visions of tomorrow are limited by the blinders we wear today. Though our vision is limited, we try to see. Tomorrow will be shaped by many influences. As variety is important in evolution, it appears also to be important in the evolution of human enterprises. We can make a plea for variety, because it will be through the interplay of a variety of influences that progress is made.

But, hopefully, we can give direction to the winds of change and try to shape a better tomorrow. As we peer ahead to 1980, we see pitfalls that can be avoided and opportunities that must not be missed. It is one of the functions of leaders in elementary science education to look ahead. Our look to the future provides a theoretical framework for our research and a base for our attempts to build a better education for future teachers and much more rewarding experiences in science for our children.

Reference

1. Educational Policies Commission, *Education and the Spirit of Science*, National Education Association, Washington, D.C., 1966.